BRAIN MECHANISMS IN MEMORY AND LEARNING:
From the Single Neuron to Man

International Brain Research Organization
Monograph Series
Volume 4

INTERNATIONAL BRAIN RESEARCH ORGANIZATION MONOGRAPH SERIES

SERIES EDITOR: MARY A. B. BRAZIER

INTERNATIONAL BRAIN RESEARCH
ORGANIZATION MONOGRAPH SERIES
Volume 4

Brain Mechanisms in Memory and Learning:
From the Single Neuron to Man

Edited by

Mary A. B. Brazier
Department of Anatomy
and
Brain Research Institute
University of California Los Angeles
Los Angeles, California

Raven Press ▪ New York

Raven Press, 1140 Avenue of the Americas, New York, New York 10036

Made in the United States of America

Library of Congress Cataloging in Publication Data

Main entry under title:

Brain mechanisms in memory and learning.

    (International Brain Research Organization monograph series; v. 4)
    Includes bibliographical references and indexes.
    1. Memory--Physiological aspects--Congresses.
2. Brain--Congresses. 3. Learning--Physiological aspects--Congresses. I. Brazier, Mary Agnes Burniston, 1904-   II. Series: International Brain Research Organization; v. 4. [DNLM: 1. Memory--Congresses. 2. Learning--Congresses. 3. Brain--Physiology--Congresses. W1 IN71S v. 4 / WL300.3 B814 1977]
QP406.B73   153.1   78-67019
ISBN 0-89004-160-1

The IBRO Monograph Series

The International Brain Research Organization (IBRO) was founded in 1960 and chartered in Ottawa, Canada, in 1961, with the goal of fostering, in all countries, fundamental research leading to knowledge of the brain, both normal and abnormal. IBRO is represented by more than 1,400 members drawn from 47 countries. Membership carries no individual dues and is focused essentially on the contribution that the individual is making to brain science.

Financial support comes from the dues and donations of 14 national committees for IBRO: Austria, Canada, Chile, Finland, Germany DDR, Germany FDR, Hungary, India, Israel, Japan, Switzerland, the USA, the USSR, Italy, and one multinational society: the Society for Neuroscience (USA, Mexico, and Canada).

Nine categories of membership (the panels) subdivide the membership according to major interests, namely, neuroanatomy; neurochemistry; neuroendocrinology; neuropharmacology; neurophysiology; behavioral sciences; neurocommunications and biophysics; brain pathology; and clinical and health-related brain science.

In order to effect its major goal, IBRO, among its several activities, designs and runs, with major support from UNESCO, educational workshops in brain science in less scientifically developed countries; sponsors fellowships; and organizes major symposia, as evidenced by this volume, usually one a year on some special topic, to which members gather from many countries.

The first volume of the series, published in 1975, contains the proceedings of a symposium held in New Delhi as a satellite to the XXVIth International Congress of Physiology in 1974: The subject was *Growth and Development of the Brain: Nutritional, Genetic, and Environmental Factors.*

The next volume was an invited symposium, held in Toronto in October 1975, ancillary to the 1st International Congress of Child Neurology. The subject was *Brain Dysfunction in Infantile Febrile Convulsions* and forms the second in the IBRO Monograph Series, and was published in 1976.

The third volume, *Architectonics of the Cerebral Cortex,* contains the proceedings of a symposium held under the auspices of the University of Vienna and the Austrian Academy of Sciences to mark the centenary of Von Economo in 1976, and was published in 1978.

This volume, the fourth in the IBRO Monograph Series, contains the papers contributed to a symposium at the Royal Society, London, in 1977 on *Brain Mechanisms in Memory and Learning: From the Single Neuron to Man.* This was an official satellite to the XXVIIth International Congress of the Physiological Sciences in Paris.

Mary A. B. Brazier

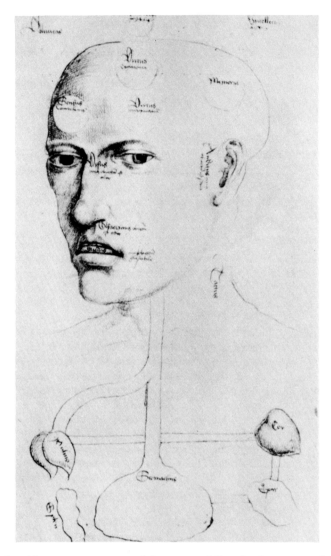

From the 4th century A.D., and for several hundred years to follow, the faculties of the mind were thought to be housed in the ventricles of the brain. Many crude drawings, mapping these as cells on the surface of the head, are to be found in medieval manuscripts variably depicting mental functions such as sensation, reasoning, imagination, intellect, but invariably including memory. These diagrams persisted into the 17th century, all, with one exception, drawn with crudity. The exception, reproduced here, was produced in 1494 to illustrate a 15th century Latin translation of Aristotle's *de Anima*.

The four regions on the skull are labelled "sensus communis," "virtus cogitativa," "virtus imaginativa," and, most posteriorly, "memoria."

(Courtesy of the Incunabula collection at the National Library of Medicine, Bethesda, Maryland.)

Preface

This volume, the fourth in the IBRO Monograph Series, contains the proceedings of a symposium held at the Royal Society, London, in July 1977, as a satellite to the International Congress of Physiological Sciences, held the preceding week in Paris.

To this symposium on *Brain Mechanisms in Memory and Learning,* speakers came from 14 countries, including scientists from as far away as Israel, Australia, and Iran. The program was designed to follow the experimental search for an understanding of brain mechanisms in memory and learning from the single neuron to man. The material presented represents many experimental strategies including anatomical, biochemical, and electrophysiological approaches to the behavioral expression of memory. As pointed out by Richard Mark in the thoughtful last chapter, in all animal studies the behavioral change is an indirect clue to memory storage and the challenge remains to design an approach more directly mirroring the central element in the triad: acquisition of information, storage in memory, recovery from storage. Behavioral change reflects recovery of the acquired information, and many of our electrical and biochemical manipulations may be acting not on storage but on the mechanisms for this readout, the third of the triad. Discussion among those present revealed a recognition of this crucial problem and the urge to progress to a closer analysis. Those who contributed to the final session on memory in man have access to methods of interaction with the subject denied to the worker with animals and, consequently, follow an additional approach to the study of learning.

This volume should be of interest to all scientists interested in brain mechanisms.

Mary A. B. Brazier
Organizer and Director
IBRO Symposia

Acknowledgments

It was a pleasure to welcome attendance at the symposium of five young scientists invited from different countries, Drs. Stefano Allegra (Italy), Holger Bienholt (Germany, FDR), Jellemer Jolles (The Netherlands), Jean-Pierre Lecanuet (France), and Michel Maitre (France). The presence was greatly appreciated of Dr. A. Karamanlidis from the University of Thessaloniki, Greece, Dr. Leonard Libber, Director of Physiology, Office of Naval Research USA, Dr. Jacques Richardson, representative for UNESCO, Dr. David Cohen, representative for the Society for Neuroscience, Dr. Elizabeth Warrington from the National Hospital, Queen Square, and Dr. E. Meisami from the University of Tehran who contributed to the program.

The symposium received generous funding from UNESCO, the Office of Naval Research USA, the Physiological Society UK, and from IBRO's own funds. The additional grant given by the European Training Program in Brain and Behaviour Research provided the travel expenses for the five young scientists from different European countries to attend as auditors. This opportunity is taken to express gratitude on behalf of IBRO for this generous support, to the Royal Society for its hospitality, and outstandingly to Dr. Derek Richter for his help both with the program and the local arrangements.

Finally, the excellence of the preparation of the manuscripts for publication is owed by the Editor to her assistant, Melody Horner.

Mary A. B. Brazier

Contents

Contributors

Natalia P. Bechtereva
Institute for Experimental Medicine
Academy of Medical Science of the
USSR
Leningrad, USSR

*Vincent Bloch
Université de Paris-Sud, and
Département de Psychophysiologie
Laboratoire de Physiologie Nerveuse
Centre National de la Recherche
Scientifique
91190 Gif-sur-Yvette, France

B. Bohus
Rudolf Magnus Institute for Pharma-
cology
Medical Faculty
University of Utrecht
Vondellaan 6
Utrecht, The Netherlands

*Nathaniel A. Buchwald
Mental Retardation Research Center
University of California Los Angeles
Los Angeles, California 90024

*Jan Bureš
Institute of Physiology
Czechoslovak Academy of Sciences
Budejovicka 1083
142 20 Prague 4-KRC, Czechoslova-
kia

O. Burešová
Institute of Physiology
Czechoslovak Academy of Sciences
Budejovicka 1083
142 20 Prague 4-KRC, Czechoslova-
kia

*Timothy J. Crow
Division of Psychiatry
Clinical Research Centre

Northwick Park Hospital
Watford Road
Harrow, London HA1 3JU, England

*T. Desiraju
Neurophysiology Research Unit of the
Indian Council of Medical Re-
search and the Department of
Neurophysiology
National Institutes of Mental Health
and Neurosciences
Bangalore 560 029, India

*Robert W. Doty
The University of Rochester
School of Medicine and Dentistry
Center for Brain Research
260 Crittenden Boulevard
Rochester, New York 14642

Elaine Elisabetsky
Disciplina de Neurofisiologia
Departamento de Biofísica e Fisiologia
Escola Paulista de Medicine
Rua Botucatu 862
04023 São Paulo, SP, Brasil

*Reuven Feuerstein
Hadassah-Wizo-Canada Research In-
stitute
6 Karmon Street, Beit Hakerem
96308 Jerusalem, Israel

*H. Flohr
University of Bremen
Achterstrasse NW2
2800 Bremen 33, Germany FDR

Paul E. Gold
Department of Psychology
University of Virginia
Charlottesville, Virginia 22901

Mark J. Handwerker
Laboratory of Neurobiology
San Juan, Puerto Rico 00901

_____

* Present at the symposium.

Elizabeth Hennevin
*Université de Paris-Sud, and
Département de Psychophysiologie
Laboratoire de Physiologie Nerveuse
Centre National de la Recherche
    Scientifique
91190 Gif-sur-Yvette, France*

C. D. Hull
*Mental Retardation Research Center
University of California Los Angeles
Los Angeles, California 90024*

*Ivan Izquierdo
*Departamento de Bioquímica
Instituto de Biociencias
Federal University of Rio Grande do
    Sul
90,000 Porto Alegre, RS, Brasil*

Robert A. Jensen
*Department of Psychobiology
University of California
Irvine, California 92717*

*Eric R. Kandel
*Division of Neurobiology and Be-
    havior
Departments of Physiology and Psy-
    chiatry
College of Physicians and Surgeons
Columbia University
New York, New York 10032*

*A. Kitsikis
*Laboratoire de Neurophysiologie
Département de Physiologie
Faculté de Médecine
Université Laval
Quebec G1K 7P4, Canada*

Gabor L. Kovacs
*Institute of Pathophysiology
University Medical School
Szeged, Hungary*

P. Leconte
*Université de Paris-Sud, and
Département de Psychophysiologie
Laboratoire de Physiologie Nerveuse
Centre National de la Recherche
    Scientifique
91190 Gif-sur-Yvette, France*

M. S. Levine
*Mental Retardation Research Center
University of California Los Angeles
Los Angeles, California 90024*

Rudolfo Llinás
*Department of Physiology and Bio-
    physics
New York University Medical Center
550 First Avenue
New York, New York 10016*

A. V. Loud
*Department of Physiology and Pathol-
    ogy
New York Medical College
Valhalla, New York 10595*

*Paul Mandel
*Centre National de la Recherche
    Scientifique
Faculté de Médecine
67 Strasbourg, France 67085*

*Richard Mark
*Department of Behavioural Biology
Research School of Biological
    Sciences
Australian National University
Canberra, Australia*

Joe L. Martinez
*Department of Psychobiology
University of California
Irvine, California 92717*

*Housjünge Matthies
*Institut für Pharmakologie und
    Toxicologie
Medizinische Akademia Magdeburg
Leipziger Strasse 44
301 Magdeburg, Germany DDR*

*James L. McGaugh
*Department of Psychobiology
University of California
Irvine, California 92717*

*Henry McIlwain
*Department of Biochemistry
Institute of Psychiatry
(British Postgraduate Medical Federa-
    tion University of London)
De Crespigny Park
London SE5 8AF, England*

*Esmail Meisami
Institute of Biochemistry and Bio-
physics
University of Tehran
Tehran, Iran

John A. Meligeni
Department of Psychobiology
University of California
Irvine, California 92717

G. Oakson
Laboratoire de Neurophysiologie
Département de Physiologie
Faculté de Médecine
Université Laval
Quebec G1K 7P4, Canada

*Neil O'Connor
Medical Research Council
Developmental Psychology Unit
Drayton House, Gordon Street
London WC1H OAN, England

*Alberto Oliverio
Laboratorio di Psicobiologie e
Psicofarmacologie
Via Reno 1, Rome, and
Istituto di Psicologie
Università Roma
Rome 00198, Italy

*Steven P. R. Rose
Brain Research Group
Department of Biology
The Open University
Milton Keynes MK7 6AA, England

*Allen M. Schneider
Department of Psychology
Swarthmore College
Swarthmore, Pennsylvania 19081

*Manik Shahani
Everest Chemical Industries Institute
of Electrophysiology for Fundamental and Applied Research
Parel, Bombay-400 012, India

*Mercia Steriade
Laboratoire de Neurophysiologie
Département de Physiologie
Faculté de Médecine
Université Laval
Quebec G1K 7P4, Canada

*Gyula Telegdy
Institute of Pathophysiology
University Medical School
Szeged, Hungary

*Kihumbu Thairu
Department of Medical Physiology
University of Nairobi
P.O. Box 30197
Chiromo, Nairobi, Kenya

*Janett Trubatch
Neurobiology Program
National Science Foundation
Washington, D.C. 20550

*Nakaakira Tsukahara
Department of Biophysical Engineer-
ing
Faculty of Engineering Science
Osaka University
Toyonaka, Osaka, Japan

A. Van Harreveld
Departments of Physiology and Pathol-
ogy
New York Medical College
Valhalla, New York 10595

Beatriz J. Vasquez
Department of Psychobiology
University of California
Irvine, California 92717

K. Walton
Department of Physiology and Bio-
physics
New York University Medical Center
550 First Avenue
New York, New York 10016

*David de Wied
Rudolf Magnus Institute for Pharma-
cology
Medical Faculty
University of Utrecht
Vondellaan 6
Utrecht, The Netherlands

*Boguslaw Zernicki
Department of Neurophysiology
Nencki Institute of Experimental Bi-
ology
Pasteura 3
02–093 Warsaw, Poland

STUDIES AT THE NEURONAL LEVEL

Brain Mechanisms in Memory and Learning:
From the Single Neuron to Man,
edited by M. A. B. Brazier.
Raven Press, New York © 1979.

Cellular Aspects of Learning

Eric R. Kandel

Division of Neurobiology and Behavior, Departments of Physiology and Psychiatry,
College of Physicians and Surgeons, Columbia University, New York, New York 10032

It has recently become possible to begin to explore the cellular mechanisms underlying behavior and learning. This opportunity follows from the realization that to study the biological basis of learning one must first develop systems in which the neural circuit controlling the behavior of interest can be completely specified. Only after the wiring diagram of a behavior is known does the analysis of its modification by learning become feasible. Thus a key prerequisite for studying learning is the selection of a behavior that can be fully analyzed on the cellular level.

At first thought, the idea of specifying a behavior on the cellular level seems awesome. Most behavior in higher animals involves thousands of nerve cells. Fortunately this task can be experimentally simplified in two ways. One simplification is the use of the nervous system of *higher invertebrate animals* such as snails, lobsters, leeches, and crayfish, which contains only 10,-000 to 100,000 cells. Indeed, certain ganglia contain only 1 to 2,000 neurons yet mediate several different behavioral responses. Furthermore, in some of these ganglia, the cells are large and distinctive in position, appearance, and physiological properties so that they can be repeatedly identified in every member of the species. A second simplification is the selection for study of simple forms of behavior that are mediated by less than 100 cells. In a number of these cases, the neuronal circuit underlying the complete behavioral act has been described (see for example refs. 14,15, and 17).

Once the neuronal circuit of a behavior is known, it becomes possible to examine the changes produced in that circuit by learning. With this goal in mind Castellucci, Carew, Byrne, and I have developed a system in the opisthobranch mollusc *Aplysia californica* in which the mechanisms of several different types of learning can be studied, first on the cellular level and then, in the long run, on the subcellular and molecular levels.

In this discussion I outline briefly three aspects of our work. First, I describe the system that we have studied and review earlier work on the capabilities for learning that this system exhibits. Second, I consider studies on the cellular mechanisms of habituation, a simple form of learning that we have used to explore the mechanistic interrelationship between short- and long-term memory. In particular I describe experiments designed to investigate whether short- and long-term habituation involve two separate and distinct memory traces with different loci and different mechanisms or both involve a single memory trace that changes in character. Third, I discuss studies of sensitization, a second and slightly more complex type of learning, and describe our attempts to relate biochemical changes in the presynaptic terminals to the synaptic plasticity underlying short-term behavioral modification.

The nervous system of *A. californica* is attractive for combining these behavioral and cellular approaches for two reasons. First, it contains relatively few cells. The whole nervous system contains only about 15,000 neurons that are grouped into about 10 clusters called ganglia. Each ganglion contains only 1,000 or 2,000 neurons, and individual ganglia arc capable of generating specific behaviors. Second, the cells of this nervous system are exceptionally large. The smallest cells in *Aplysia* are usually larger than the largest cells in man's brain, and the largest cells are gigantic, reaching 1 mm in diameter, and can be seen with the naked eye. As a result of their enormous size, these cells are advantageous for electrophysiological, biochemical, and pharmacological studies. In addition, many of these neurons are recognizable individuals whose unique cellular properties make it possible to identify them in all members of the species.

Because of these two features, the nervous system of *Aplysia* is free of many of the methodological restrictions that have traditionally handicapped the cellular study of behavior. For example, it is possible to map the connections between cells and between a given cell and an effector or sensory structure on a cell-to-cell basis. From electroanatomical mapping on the cell-to-cell level, one can learn three features about synaptic interconnections that could not emerge from the use of morphological mapping techniques alone: (a) the existence of a functional connection, (b) the sign of the connection (excitatory or inhibitory), and (c) the effectiveness of the connection.

The behavior we have studied with this approach is a defensive-withdrawal reflex of the external organs of the mantle cavity. The mantle cavity of molluscs is a respiratory chamber that houses the respiratory organ, the gill. In *Aplysia* this chamber is covered by a protective sheet, the mantle shelf, which terminates in a fleshy spout, the siphon. When a weak- or moderate-intensity stimulus is applied to the siphon, the gill contracts and withdraws into the mantle cavity (Fig. 1).

This reflex is analogous to defensive escape and withdrawal responses found in almost all higher invertebrates as well as in vertebrates. A nice feature of this reflex is that it can readily be modified to undergo two *elementary forms* of learning—habituation and sensitization. I first focus on *habituation.*

Habituation is probably the most ubiquitous behavioral modification found in animals, including man. It refers to a decrease in behavioral response that

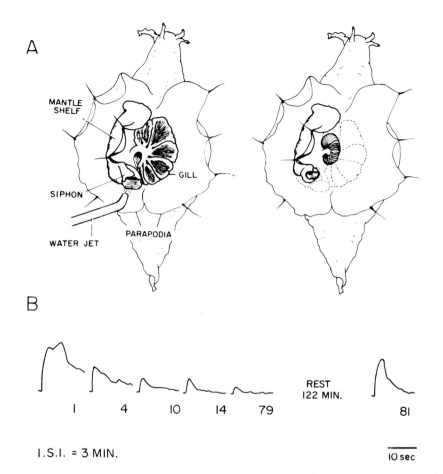

FIG. 1. A: The defensive-withdrawal reflex of the siphon and gill in *Aplysia* (*dorsal view of an intact animal*). Since the parapodia and mantle shelf ordinarily obscure the view of the gill, they must be retracted to allow direct observation. The tactile receptive field for the gill-withdrawal reflex consists of the siphon and the edge of the mantle shelf. A1: Relaxed position. A2: Defensive-withdrawal reflex in response to a weak tactile stimulus to the siphon (a jet of seawater delivering an effective pressure of 250 g/cm²). The relaxed position of the gill is indicated by the dotted lines. (From Kandel et al., ref. 13.) B: Habituation and spontaneous recovery of the gill-withdrawal reflex. Habituation of the response with 80 repetitions of the stimulus at 3-min intervals. The major decrease occurs within the first 10 stimuli. Following a 122-min rest, the response recovered partially. (From Pinsker et al., ref. 18.)

occurs when an initially novel stimulus is repeatedly presented. Habituation is the means by which animals and man learn to ignore stimuli that have lost novelty or meaning.

The gill-withdrawal reflex of *Aplysia* undergoes both short- and long-term habituation. Recovery in this type of learning is equivalent to the forgetting of a learned response, and the time course of recovery is a measure of retention. In response to a single training session of 10 to 100 trials, recovery from habituation usually takes 15 min or at most a few hours (Fig. 1; see also ref. 18). However, habituation can readily be prolonged with repeated training sessions. Thus, four repeated training sessions of 10 stimuli each produce long-term habituation that lasts several weeks (Fig. 2, and ref. 4).

We have worked out almost the complete wiring diagram of the gill component of the reflex to weak- and moderate-intensity stimuli applied to the siphon (Fig. 3, and refs. 8,13, and 15). The neural circuit proved to be remarkably simple. There are six motor cells to the gill. These motor cells receive information from the skin by means of 24 sensory neurons and three interneurons—two excitatory and one inhibitory. The sensory neurons make direct connections to the interneurons and to the motor cells, and the motor cells connect directly to muscle.

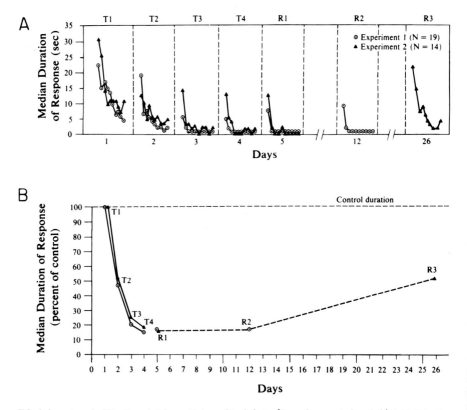

FIG. 2. Long-term habituation of siphon withdrawal in *Aplysia*. (From Carew et al., ref. 4.) A: Habituation during four daily sessions of training (T1 to T4), and retention 1 day (R1), 1 week (R2), and 3 weeks (R3) after training. Each session consisted of 10 trials (10 stimuli). Data from two experiments are compared. In experiment 1, retention was tested one day (R1) and 1 week (R2) after training. In experiment 2, retention was tested 1 day (R1) and 3 weeks (R3) after training. Each data point is the median response of the population in a single trial. B: Time course of habituation, based on the experiments illustrated in A. The score for each daily session is the median of the sum of 10 trials. Control duration (100%) is the response time during the first day of training.

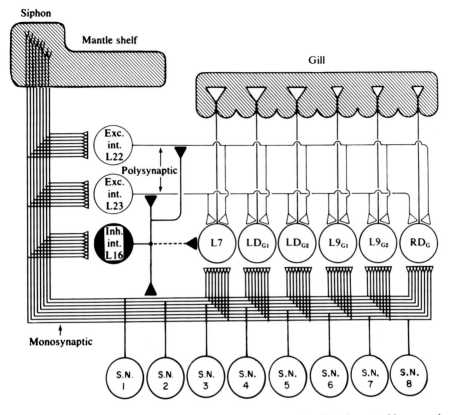

FIG. 3. Wiring diagram of the defensive gill-withdrawal reflex. The siphon skin is innervated by approximately 24 mechanoreceptor sensory neurons. The diagram has been simplified to illustrate that a tactile stimulus to a point on the skin only excites approximately eight sensory neurons. The sensory neurons make direct (monosynaptic) connections to six identified gill motor neurons and to at least one inhibitory (L16) and two excitatory (L22, L23) interneurons. (Adapted from Kandel et al., ref. 13.)

Because there are so few cells, one can begin to relate specific cells to behavior in a causal and quantitative way. For example, one can remove a motor or a sensory cell from a behavior by hyperpolarizing the cell and determine thereby what the cell contributes. By these means we have been able to determine that some motor cells (such as L7, LDG$_1$, and LDG$_2$) make substantial contributions to the withdrawal reflex, whereas other cells make minor contributions.

By examining the various sites within the circuit during habituation *in the intact animal,* Castellucci and I found that the critical change underlying habituation occurs at the various synapses made by the sensory neurons on their central target cells, the interneurons and the motor neurons (Fig. 3). The changes in the effectiveness of these connections, as measured by recording the changes in the amplitude of the unitary excitatory postsynaptic potentials (EPSPs) produced in the motor cells by stimulation of a single sensory neuron, parallel the habituation (Fig. 4, and refs. 5 and 8).

With repeated stimulation at rates that produce habituation, the EPSP undergoes depression. After a single training session of 10 to 15 stimuli, the EPSP recovers slowly, usually over a period of minutes but sometimes requiring 1 or more hr. A second training session produces even more profound depression (Fig. 4). With the third and fourth training sessions, the EPSP is often completely eliminated by depression (3).

Are these changes in synaptic effectiveness presynaptic, reflecting a reduction in transmitter release, or postsynaptic, reflecting a change in receptor responsiveness? This question can best be answered with a quantal analysis. This analysis provides a means for assaying, electrophysiologically, the num-

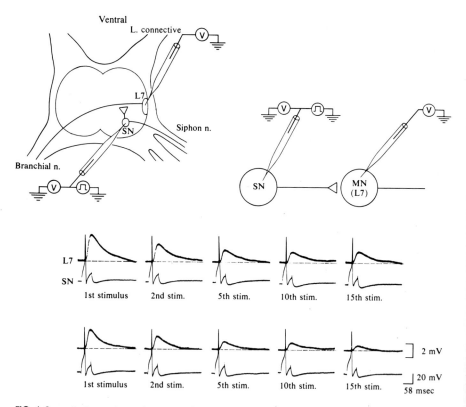

FIG. 4. Synaptic depression at the synapse between mechanoreceptor neurons and motor neurons. Above: Diagram of the abdominal ganglion of *Aplysia* showing schematic innervation of gill and siphon and illustrating simultaneous recording from gill motor neuron (L7) and a mechanoreceptor sensory neuron. Below: Synaptic depression of the monosynaptic EPSP produced in motor cell L7 by stimulation of a single sensory neuron in high divalent cation solution (138 mM Mg²⁺, 62 mM Ca²⁺). Interstimulus interval (ISI) 10 sec. Two series of 15 stimuli each were presented with a rest of 15 min in between. The rest led to partial recovery, but a slight build-up of the depression is evident in the second run. (Adapted from Castellucci and Kandel, ref. 5.)

ber of quanta released by an action potential in the presynaptic terminals. According to the quantal analysis (11), the average amplitude of a synaptic potential, the synaptic efficacy ($\bar{E}$), produced by a presynaptic impulse is given by:

$$\bar{E} = m \times \bar{q}$$

where $\bar{q}$ is the average amplitude of the unit synaptic potential or the potential produced by a single quantum and m is the average quantal content or the average number of quanta released in a series of stimuli.

The reason an analysis of synaptic effectiveness by means of quantal transmission is powerful is that the quantal content m is a measure of the amount of transmitter released, and changes in this parameter reflect alterations of quantal release associated with changes in synaptic efficacy. On the other hand, a stable quantal size ($\bar{q}$) indicates that the sensitivity of the postsynaptic receptor to the transmitter substance is unaltered.

Figure 5 summarizes the results of a quantal analysis on synaptic depression using the method of failure (5). Eight experiments were normalized to the first region where failures were encountered. Note that the quantal output (m) parallels the average amplitude of the EPSP ($\bar{E}$). As the average amplitude of the EPSP decreases, m, the quantal output, decreases by 50%, whereas $\bar{q}$ does not change significantly.

Thus these studies indicate that habituation involves a homosynaptic depression at a specific but distributed locus, the various synapses made by the sensory neurons on their central target cells. The depression results from a progressive decrease in the amount of transmitter released. This finding is therefore consistant with the idea that genetic and developmental processes

$$\bar{E} = m \times \bar{q}$$

FIG. 5. Comparison of the average EPSP during depression with quantal size and quantal output estimated by the failure method. Five experiments on synaptic depression were normalized to the first region, where failures were encountered. During depression, the estimated value of $\bar{q}$ did not change significantly between successive regions, whereas $\bar{E}$, the average EPSP amplitude, and m, the quantal output, decreased by 50%. (Adapted from Kandel et al., ref. 13.)

determine the connections between neurons; what they leave unspecified is the strength of the connections. It is this factor—the efficacy of synaptic connections—that is played on by environmental factors such as learning.

But what are the limits of this plasticity? How much can the effectiveness of a given synapse change, and how long can such changes endure? With these questions in mind, we began to explore the mechanisms by which the long-term process is generated. We first looked at the whole sensory input, both the monosynaptic and the polysynaptic contribution to the EPSP in the motor cell, during acquisition. Second, we examined individual sensory connections to the motor neuron during retention.

Our experiments on the acquisition of long-term habituation showed a profound depression of synaptic transmission at the synapses made on the motor neurons by the sensory neurons and interneurons (2). Is this depression retained? If so, will retention be evident even at the level of the elementary synaptic connections made by the sensory neurons on the motor cells?

To carry out this analysis, Castellucci, et al. (7) compared the connections between the sensory neurons and motor cell L7 in three groups of animals—control, 1 day after the acquisition of long-term habituation, and 1 week after acquisition of long-term habituation. We found that in the control animals 90% of sensory neurons connect to L7. By contrast, in both groups of long-term habituation animals, the percentage of connections was reduced to 30%. Thus 70% of the previously functional connections had been inactivated as a result of long-term habituation (Fig. 6). This inactivation paralleled the behavior. It persisted for a week and was only partially recovered 3 weeks later.

From these studies it is clear that short- and long-term habituation share a common neural locus—the synapses that the sensory neurons make on the motor neurons and interneurons. Both forms of habituation also involve

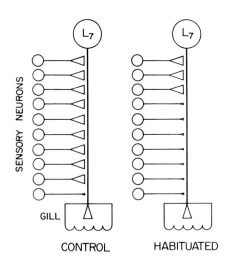

FIG. 6. Diagram of functional inactivation of some of the connections between sensory neurons and motor neurons of the gill-withdrawal reflex following long-term habituation. (From V. Castellucci, T. J. Carew, and E. R. Kandel, *unpublished observations.*)

aspects of the same cellular mechanism—depression of excitatory transmission. We now need to do a quantal analysis, however, to see whether the synaptic depression is pre- or postsynaptic. If long- term depression proves also to be presynaptic, it would support, on a more fundamental level, the behavioral notion of a *single trace*.

I have so far described a very elementary form of learning by which reflex activity is depressed. To what degree can one now apply this strategy to a slightly more complex form? The next step in complexity is a form called *sensitization*.

Sensitization is the mirror image process of habituation. It is the process— somewhat akin to arousal—by which a strong or noxious stimulus enhances an animal's preexisting reflex response. Sensitization is more complex than habituation and resembles classic conditioning in that activity in one pathway facilitates reflex activity in another. Unlike classic conditioning, however, the reflex facilitation does not require specific temporal association of the two stimuli. In addition to being of interest in its own right, sensitization is also a means for enhancing habituated responses. Studies by Spencer and his colleagues (20) on the flexion reflex in the cat spinal cord and our studies on *Aplysia* have shown what is called dishabituation—the enhancement of a habituated response by a strong stimulus—is only a special case of sensitization.

A noxious stimulus to the head produces sensitization of the gill-withdrawal reflex (Fig. 7, and ref. 18). At the cellular level, Castellucci and I found that sensitization involves an enhancement of synaptic transmission at the same locus that is involved in habituation. But now transmitter release, rather than being depressed, is enhanced (Fig. 8, and ref. 6). Our analysis of sensitization suggests that it is mediated by neurons that synapse on the presynaptic terminals of the sensory neurons and regulate its transmitter release (6,13). Thus the same synaptic locus is modulated in two ways: habituation depresses release and facilitation enhances it.

The interesting thing about the facilitation is that we have some clues to its molecular mechanism. Castellucci and I first approached this problem in a

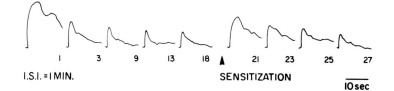

I.S.I. = I MIN.   SENSITIZATION

10 sec

FIG. 7. Sensitization of the gill-withdrawal reflex. Same experiment as in Fig. 1, but showing a later training session after the animal had fully recovered. The response was habituated a second time at 1-min intervals. A sensitizing stimulus, consisting of a strong and prolonged tactile stimulus to the neck region, was presented. Following the sensitizing stimulus, responses were facilitated for several minutes. (Adapted from Pinsker et al., ref. 18.)

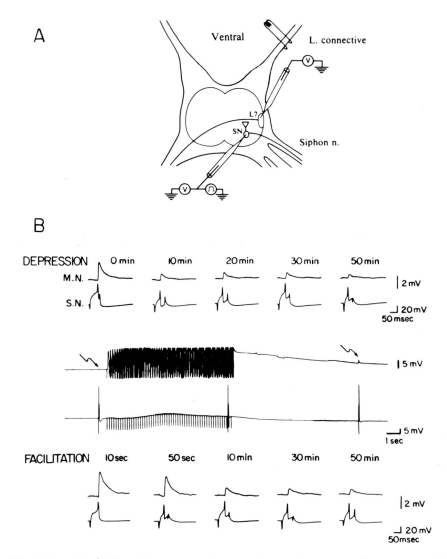

FIG. 8. Synaptic facilitation at the synapse between mechanoreceptor neurons and motor neurons. A: Ventral aspect of the abdominal ganglion of *Aplysia* illustrating simultaneous recording from gill motor neuron L7 and a mechanoreceptor sensory neuron. B: Depression and subsequent facilitation of a monosynaptic EPSP after a strong stimulus. Arrows in middle set of traces indicate the last EPSP before the facilitating stimulus (see also "50 min" in top set of traces) and the first EPSP after the stimulus (see also "10 sec" in bottom set of traces). S.N., sensory neuron; M.N., motor neuron. (Adapted from Castellucci and Kandel, ref. 6.)

series of collaborative experiments with Schwartz (19) in which we examined the consequences on sensitization of inhibiting protein synthesis and found that short-term sensitization did not require the synthesis of new proteins. This suggested that sensitization may depend on a small molecule, perhaps an intracellular messenger like cyclic AMP, that could regulate distribution of transmitter quanta within the presynaptic terminals. With this in mind, Cedar et al. (10) examined the effects of stimulation of the pathways that mediate sensitization on the level of cyclic AMP. We found that strong and prolonged stimulation produced a synaptically mediated increase in cyclic AMP in the whole ganglion.

Subsequent studies by Cedar and Schwartz (9) and by Levitan and Barondes (16) showed that this type of increase could be produced by three biogenic amines—dopamine, octopamine, and serotonin. The interesting aspect of this increase is that it is maintained for almost an hour and thus parallels, at least superficially, the time course of presynaptic facilitation.

The prolonged increase in cyclic AMP elevation following connective stimulation suggested to us the specific hypothesis that presynaptic facilitation is due to the action of one of the three biogenic amines—octopamine, dopamine, or serotonin—and that the amine mediates its effect on transmitter release by increasing the level of cyclic AMP in the presynaptic terminals of the sensory neuron.

We therefore examined the actions of the three amines on the monosynaptic connection between the sensory neurons and the motor cell L7 and found that one of them—serotonin—in a concentration as low as 1×10^{-6} M enhanced synaptic transmission. In addition, the enhancement produced physiologically by a sensitizing stimulus is blocked by the serotonin-blocking agent cinanserin (1).

To determine whether serotonin might act by means of cyclic AMP, we applied dibuteryl cyclic AMP in the bathing solution and found that it enhanced synaptic transmission at this synapse, but not at two other excitatory synapses that we examined. To obtain a more direct test, we injected cyclic AMP intracellularly into the cell body of the sensory neuron with hyperpolarizing current pulses through electrodes filled with 1.5 M cyclic AMP and tested the monosynaptic connections 2 min later. Intracellular cyclic AMP produced no alteration in the presynaptic spike, but did produce facilitation that simulated the action produced by the behavioral sensitization (1).

Figure 9 summarizes our speculations about how cyclic AMP might produce its actions and specifies some requirements for the neuron that lead to the cyclic AMP increase.

Our data suggest that repeated activity in the sensory neurons that accompanies habituation leads to synaptic depression by causing a depletion of a readily releasable pool of transmitter; this can be conceived of as the vesicles that are already in release sites or about to be loaded into them. Short-term habituation probably does not lead to depletion of the storage pool of transmitter in the terminal as is evident by the speed with which sensitization can restore transmission. It seems rather more likely that even at low levels of release repeated action potentials in the presynaptic terminals of these synapses do not lead to the effective mobilization of transmitter that

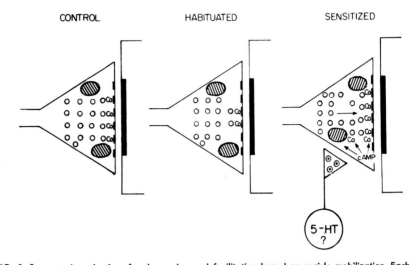

FIG. 9. Suggested mechanisms for depression and facilitation based on vesicle mobilization. Each consecutive action potential in the terminal of a sensory neuron may lead to a progressively smaller increase in free Ca^{2+} either because of a high density of mitochondria that take up free Ca^{2+} as it comes in with the action potential or because of a progressive decrease in the Ca^{2+}-permeability of the terminal membrane. As a result, repeated stimulation does not lead to effective mobilization of vesicles to the release sites at the terminal, and a partial depletion of vesicles is achieved after five to 15 impulses. This could account for habituation. Dishabituation is mediated by serotonergic interneurons and produces two complementary actions: (a) a synaptic action, which increases the Ca^{2+} concentration and briefly enhances mobilization, and (b) a prolonged increase in cyclic AMP, which increases Ca^{2+} levels by inhibiting Ca^{2+}-uptake by the mitochondria or increasing Ca^{2+} influx, thereby enhancing mobilization of transmitter vesicles. (Adapted from Kandel et al., ref. 13.)

occurs in most other chemical synapses examined. Why mobilization in the sensory neurons is ineffective we do not know; perhaps it is ineffective because the action potential leads to an inactivation of the membrane conductance to Ca^{2+} or to an enhanced Ca^{2+} uptake by mitochondria or endoplasmic reticulum.

Sensitization is a form of behavioral arousal. Unlike habituation, which is restricted to the stimulated pathways, sensitization affects a variety of related reflexes. It is therefore perhaps not astonishing that it represents a type of hormonal regulation by which a first messenger—a biogenic amine, serotonin —produces its action to enhance transmitter release by increasing the level of cyclic AMP, a second messenger, in the terminals. The increase in cyclic AMP may operate by enhancing mobilization, perhaps by acting on external membrane Ca^{2+} conductance or on the mitochondria or endoplasmic reticulum to increase free Ca^{2+}. *One conclusion of this model is that neurons can use common cellular regulating mechanisms—in this case a common type of modulation—in novel ways to achieve storage of information necessary for the readout of memory.*

Moreover, this model may be quite general. Analysis of sensitization of feeding by Weiss et al. (21,22) and of heart rate by Dieringer et al. (12)

indicates that in each case a serotonergic action is involved and produces its effect by means of cyclic AMP (23).

I would emphasize that two aspects of this model are based on pharmacological data and are therefore indirect. We need to determine more directly whether the neurons mediating facilitation are serotonergic and whether the action of these neurons can increase the endogenous level of cyclic AMP. Although we have not yet obtained compelling evidence for either of these points, we are making some progress on each of them. Thus, the availability of simple systems for the study of learning has allowed us to develop specific hypotheses about the subcellular mechanisms of habituation and sensitization. In the long run these systems should also allow us to test these hypotheses in a fairly direct way.

REFERENCES

1. Brunelli, M., Castellucci, V., and Kandel, E. R. (1976): Synaptic facilitation and behavioral sensitization in *Aplysia:* Possible role of serotonin and cyclic AMP. *Science,* 194:1178–1181.
2. Carew, T. J., and Kandel, E. R. (1973): Acquisition and retention of long-term habituation in *Aplysia:* Correlation of behavioral and cellular processes. *Science,* 182:1158–1160.
3. Carew, T. J., Castellucci, V. C., and Kandel, E. R. (1973): On the relationship of dishabituation and sensitization in *Aplysia.* In: *Neurobiology of Invertebrates,* edited by J. Salanki, pp. 381–389. Akademiai Kiado, Budapest.
4. Carew, T. J., Pinsker, H. M., and Kandel, E. R. (1972): Long term habituation of a defensive withdrawal reflex in *Aplysia. Science,* 175:451–454.
5. Castellucci, V., and Kandel, E. R. (1974): A quantal analysis of the synaptic depression underlying habituation of the gill withdrawal reflex in *Aplysia. Proc. Natl. Acad. Sci., USA,* 71:5004–5008.
6. Castellucci, V., and Kandel, E. R. (1976): Presynaptic facilitation as a mechanism for behavioral sensitization in *Aplysia. Science,* 194:1176–1178.
7. Castellucci, V., Carew, T. J., and Kandel, E. R. (1977): Cellular studies of long term habituation in *Aplysia.* In: *Proceedings of the International Union of Physiological Sciences XXVIIe Congress des Sciences Physiologiques, Paris,* 13:123.
8. Castellucci, V., Pinsker, H., Kupfermann, I., and Kandel, E. R. (1970): Neuronal mechanisms of habituation and dishabituation of the gill-withdrawal reflex in *Aplysia. Science,* 167:1745–1748.
9. Cedar, H., and Schwartz, J. H. (1972): Cyclic AMP in the nervous system of *Aplysia californica.* II: Effect of serotonin and dopamine. *J. Gen. Physiol.,* 60:570–587.
10. Cedar, H., Kandel, E. R., and Schwartz, J. H. (1972): Cyclic AMP in the nervous system of *Aplysia californica.* I: Increased synthesis in response to synaptic stimulation. *J. Gen. Physiol.,* 60:558–569.
11. del Castillo, J., and Katz, B. (1954): The effect of magnesium on the activity of motor nerve endings. *J. Physiol. (Lond.),* 124:553–559.
12. Dieringer, N., Koester, J., and Weiss, K. R. (1978): Adaptive changes in heart rate of *Aplysia californica. J. Comp. Physiol. (In press.)*
13. Kandel, E. R., Brunelli, M., Byrne, J., and Castellucci, V. (1976): A common presynaptic locus for the synaptic changes underlying short-term habituation and sensitization of gill-withdrawal reflex in *Aplysia.* In: *Cold Spring Harbor Laboratory Symposium on Quantitative Biology LX: The Synapse,* pp. 465–482. Cold Spring Harbor Laboratory, Cold Spring Harbor, N.Y.

14. Kennedy, D., and Davis, W. J. (1977): The organization of invertebrate motor systems. In: *Cellular Biology of Neurons, Vol. 1, Sec. 1 Handbook of Physiology. The Nervous System,* edited by E. R. Kandel, pp. 1023–1087. Williams & Wilkins, Baltimore.
15. Kupfermann, I., and Kandel, E. R. (1969): Plasticity in *Aplysia* neurons and some simple neuronal models of learning. In: *Reinforcement and Behavior,* edited by J. Tapp, pp. 356–386. Academic Press, New York.
16. Levitan, I. B., and Barondes, S. H. (1974): Octopamine and serotonin stimulated phosphorylation of specific proteins in the abdominal ganglion of *Aplysia californica. Proc. Nat'l. Acad. Sci. USA,* 71:1145–1148.
17. Nicholls, J. G., and Purves, D. (1970): Monosynaptic chemical and electrical connexions between sensory and motor cells in the central nervous system of the leech. *J. Physiol. (Lond.),* 209:647–667.
18. Pinsker, H., Kupfermann, I., Castellucci, V., and Kandel, E. R. (1970): Habituation and dishabituation of gill-withdrawal reflex in *Aplysia. Science,* 167:1740–1742.
19. Schwartz, J. H., Castellucci, V. F., and Kandel, E. R. (1971): Functioning of identified neurons and synapses in the abdominal ganglion of *Aplysia* in absence of protein synthesis. *J. Neurophysiol.,* 34:939–953.
20. Spencer, W. A., Thompson, R. F., and Neilson, D. R., Jr. (1966): Response decrement of the flexion reflex in the acute spinal cat and transient restoration by strong stimuli. *J. Neurophysiol.,* 29:221–239.
21. Weiss, K. R., Cohen, J., and Kupfermann, I. (1975): Potentiation of muscle contraction: A possible modulatory function of an identified serotonergic cell in *Aplysia. Brain Res.,* 99:381–386.
22. Weiss, K. R., Cohen, J. L., and Kupfermann, I. (1978): Modulatory control of buccal musculature by a serotonergic neuron (metacerebral cell) in *Aplysia. J. Neurophysiol. (In press.)*
23. Weiss, K. R., Schoenberg, M., Cohen, J., Mandelbaum, D., and Kupfermann, I. (1976): Modulation of muscle contraction by a serotenergic neuron: Possible role of cyclic AMP. *Abstr. Soc. Neurosci.,* 2:338.

Brain Mechanisms in Memory and Learning:
From the Single Neuron to Man,
edited by M. A. B. Brazier.
Raven Press, New York © 1979.

Place of the Cerebellum in Motor Learning

R. Llinás and K. Walton

Department of Physiology and Biophysics, New York University Medical Center,
New York, New York 10016

Among the clearest examples of the learning properties of the central nervous system is that of the acquisition of new motor skills. It is agreed that vertebrates and many of the invertebrate forms are capable of modifying their motor performance with experience (29,34). Furthermore, it is clear that the acquisition of new motor skills requires time and involves a minimum number of successive attempts. In general terms, the more difficult the motor task (i.e., the more it departs from the usual movement pattern), the more laborious and time consuming its acquisition. This has rightly been assumed to indicate that motor learning, and indeed learning in general, requires a gradual modification of the functional properties in the brain.

Regarding the acquisition of motor skills, one of the obvious places to search for such modifications is the cerebellum since its role in the coordination of movement has long been known. Nevertheless, the rule of thumb in clinical neurology has been that although the cerebellum is of central importance in the organization of movement, its absence can be easily compensated for by the rest of the nervous system (cf. 19). This has been taken to indicate that this organ is primarily concerned with control rather than with plasticity *per se.*

In recent years, however, detailed understanding of the circuits in the cerebellar cortex raised the theoretical possibility that heterosynaptic interaction leading to functional plasticity is operant in this cortex. In fact, Brindley (8) initially suggested that the two basic afferents to the cerebellum—the climbing fiber and the mossy fiber–parallel fiber–Purkinje cell systems—interact in a manner such that the climbing fibers are capable of modifying the efficiency of the parallel fiber–Purkinje cell synapse. Basically, new experience would then slowly modify the parallel fiber–Purkinje cell system through the activation of the climbing fibers in order to allow the cerebellum to store the functional modifications underlying the newly acquired motor skill. This hypothesis was formalized by Marr (41). A variation of it was then published by Albus (1), who suggested the opposite arrangement, i.e., that the climbing fiber input, rather than reinforcing the parallel fiber–Purkinje cell synapse, exercises a negative action such that parallel fiber–Purkinje cell synapses become less

17

effective when their activation is paired at short intervals with the climbing fiber response.

An altogether different view was reached in our own work, based on the same empirical findings as the above. We assumed the cerebellum to be a rather stable neuronal system whose main *modus operandi* is based on the constancy of its neuronal circuits (35) rather than on its long-term potential modifiability. From this point of view, new motor sequences would not reside in the cerebellum but rather at other levels in the neuraxis, leaving the cerebellum free of extensive "plastic" modifications and thus allowing it to be an almost invariant "reference line" by which modifications of motor patterns could overlap with preexisting motor functions.

These two distinct positions regarding the role of the cerebellum in motor learning are still a subject of controversy, and the matter is far from being clarified. Since our own experimental evidence seems to point in the direction of a passive cerebellum in the acquisition of new motor abilities, we pursue here the reasons why we believe this to be so. (Opposing views may be found in refs. 41 and 53.)

COMPENSATION FROM VESTIBULAR LESION AS A PARADIGM FOR MOTOR LEARNING

The possibility that the cerebellum is implicated directly in motor learning and furthermore is the *seat* of such learning has been suggested by Robinson (53) and Ito (26), following the theoretical work of Marr and Albus and based chiefly on the discovery by Gonshor and Melvill Jones (21) that humans wearing inverted prisms for protracted periods show a change in direction of vestibuloocular reflex.

Our own approach was developed following that of the classic neurological school starting with Bechterew (6). The basic concept, as expressed by Magnus (40), is that the compensation of the deep motor disturbance that follows peripheral vestibular lesion must involve a significant reorganization of activity of the brainstem. This rather robust reorganization is one that can be easily studied and that has the potential to become a basic paradigm in the study of the neuronal basis for motor learning. In our particular case the animal of choice was the rat, because of (a) the ease with which vestibular lesions can be generated in this animal, (b) the rat's rapid compensation from such lesion, and no less importantly (c) the possibility of modifying in the rat, by pharmacological and physical means, the basic cerebellar circuit and thus providing a direct test of the above hypotheses.

Specifically, the cerebellar circuitry may be experimentally modified in three major ways. First, the inferior olive (now agreed to be the main, if not the sole, source for the climbing fiber system) can be destroyed by the injection of 3-acetylpyridine (3-AP), as first demonstrated by Desclin and Escubi

(16). This procedure, which has been modified in our laboratory (38), allows a determination, through the distinction of the inferior olive, of the alleged role of the climbing fiber system in the acquisition and retention of vestibular compensation. In addition, we have recently further modified this technique in order to generate partial olivary lesion. Second, the use of animals subjected to localized cerebellar X-irradiation during development allows a study of vestibular compensation in the absence of parallel fiber–Purkinje cell synapses (at least in the vermis) in the presence of the climbing fiber–Purkinje cell synapse. Finally, surgical decortication, in principle, permits removal of the entire cortex as a contributing parameter in vestibular compensation and clarifies the extent to which the presence of cerebellar cortex is required for such modification to occur.

In a previous publication (38), it was reported that, in the normal rat, overall compensation for vestibular lesion, as indicated by the return of normal somatomotor patterns, took an average of 24 hr. It was further shown, at that time, that in the absence of the inferior olive, vestibular compensation failed to occur. Moreover, following compensation, damage of the olivocerebellar system resulted in an immediate abolition of the compensation, indicating that this input is *necessary for acquisition and retention of vestibular compensation* in this animal. The latter point addresses the question directly of whether motor learning occurs as a modification of the parallel fiber–Purkinje cell synapse via the action of the climbing fiber–Purkinje cell system. In this particular case the compensation was already present, and, therefore, according to the cerebellar learning theorists, the engram should have been encoded in the parallel fiber–Purkinje cell at the time the olive was lesioned. Since our results failed to confirm this view, we consider that, at least for short-term experiments, the acquisition and retention of this particular motor compensation requires the presence of the olivocerebellar system. In order to study this problem further, two sets of experiments were designed—one on long-term plasticity and the other on partial olivary lesions. The results from these experiments are reported here for the first time in full detail.

EXPERIMENTS ON LONG-TERM PLASTICITY

The basic experimental paradigm consisted of making central or peripheral lesions in young rats and allowing them to recuperate for 1 to 1½ years in order to test the long-term modifiability of the circuits under scrutiny. Three basic experiments were attempted with these animals: (a) lesion to the vestibular nerve in young animals followed by inferior olivary lesion a year or so later, (b) lesion of the inferior olive shortly after birth (15 to 22 days) followed by vestibular nerve lesion more than a year later, and (c) damage of the neonate cerebellar cortex followed by vestibular lesion 3 months to a year later.

Normal Development of Vestibular Compensation

In order to appreciate the variation in time course and extent of compensation in these animals, a brief description of vestibular compensation in normal adult rats is necessary.

Although there is some variability among animals in the time course of somatomotor signs of compensation following vestibular lesion, a pattern can be detected. Immediately following lesion, there is a vigorous rolling of the whole body toward the ipsilateral side, and the eyes take an extreme position with the ipsilateral eye fully down and the opposite eye fully upward. During periods of quiet the head is tilted ipsilaterally by nearly 180°. The next activity pattern—a rapid, forced, turning in tight circles toward the lesioned side—begins at about 30 min and can continue, with decreasing frequency of occurrence, for as long as 10 to 24 hr. This second period can be divided into two parts. At first the animals lie on the ipsilateral side as they turn; then they are able to support themselves on their feet, but stay close to the ground and lean to the ipsilateral side as they continue to turn in place. The circumference of the inscribed circle increases until, at about 6 hr, the animal begins to make open circles that are interspersed with periods of normal movement patterns. These phases, of course, overlap and are punctuated with periods of inactivity, especially during the first 2 to 4 hr.

Head position compensation begins 10 to 20 min after the lesion, reaches close to 20° within 1 hr, and asymptotically approaches an equilibrium near 10°. Eye position compensation begins within the first 30 to 60 min (37). At this time a spontaneous nystagmus of about 160 beats/min begins. The nystagmic frequency decreases logarithmically during the next 24 to 48 hr and stops entirely by 60 hr. There is, therefore, a definite sequence of steps in compensation. First, the correction of the head posture (which generates the initial side rolling) begins, followed by reorganization of limb and spine posture allowing the animal to stand. As the tonal asymmetry is further corrected, the animal walks in ever increasing circles. The posture reorganization is then followed by compensation of the dynamic aspects of execution (normal locomotion and eye movements). These different steps occur, as stated above, in a period of about 24 to 48 hr after vestibular lesion.

Compensation Following Long-term Vestibular, Inferior Olive, and Cerebellar Cortex Lesion

Vestibular Lesion

In the first set of experiments an early lesion of the vestibular system, followed up to 1 year later by damage to the inferior olive, produced immediately an irreversible return of the animal to the precompensated state (37). The results in this set of experiments were unambiguous and completely re-

TABLE 1. *Partial vestibular compensation in animals treated with 3-AP when young*

Animal no.	Age at 3-AP injection (days)	Age at hemilabyrinthectomy (mo.)	Initiation of compensation	Period observed (wk.)	Stable state
BR5	15	20	Few minutes after lesion	4	Head angle 10–20°. Eyes: stable, position normal. Somatomotor behavior normal.
BR6	22	20	2 Days after lesion	7	Head angle 40–90°. Eyes: some slow spont. nystagmus if stressed. Behavior: lies or leans to left; inactive.
BR7	22	20	2 Days after lesion	7	Head angle 30–50°. Eyes: some slow nystagmus when stressed. Behavior: leans to left; occasionally falls to left.
BR9	16	20	Few minutes after lesion	7	Head angle 30–40°. Eyes: slight vertical deviation. Motor behavior normal except few circles in place if stressed.

peatable from one animal to the next. This control we consider essential since the alleged modification of the parallel fiber–Purkinje cell synapse could theoretically occur only very slowly. It is clear, therefore, that even after more than 1 year no "transfer" of information, in Marr's sense, actually occurred.

Inferior Olive Lesion

In the second paradigm an attempt was made to lesion[1] the inferior olive of young animals (15 to 22 days) with the 3-AP, harmaline, and niacinamide treatment. The animals were allowed a full 1½ year recovery from this early lesion before the vestibular damage ensued. The results obtained were unexpected. Some degree of vestibular compensation occurred in all the lesioned animals. However, the time course for this reduced degree of compensation was not normal (Table 1). The progress of four of the animals was followed

[1] Preliminary findings suggest that the effects on compensation of bilateral inferior peduncle lesions resemble closely those of the chemical lesion.

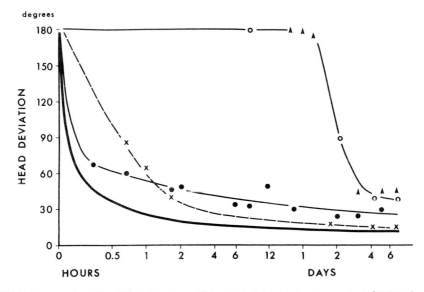

FIG. 1. Compensation of head deviation after unilateral labyrinthine lesion in normal rats (*thick line*) and those treated with 3-AP and harmaline 2 to 3 weeks after birth: animals BR5 (*Xs*), BR6 (*arrowheads*), BR7 (*open circles*), and BR9 (*closed circles*).

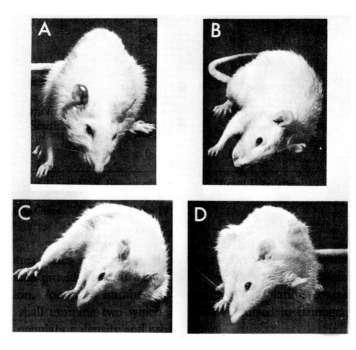

FIG. 2. Stable posture 1 month following unilateral labyrinthine lesion in rats treated with 3-AP and harmaline 2 to 3 weeks after birth. A: BR5, head deviation 15°; B: BR6, head deviation 60°; C: BR7, head deviation 45°; D: BR9, head deviation 40°.

closely. Although the onset of compensation was normal for two animals (BR5 and BR9), it was delayed by 24 hr in two others (BR6 and BR7). Further, the compensation progressed slowly. For example, compensation of head angle is normally almost completed (from 180° to 20°) in 60 min (33). Only one animal reached 20° (BR5) and then after 8 hr (Fig. 1). In the other animals, stable head positions ranged from 30 to 90° (see Fig. 2). The most likely explanation for the finding of compensation in these animals is that the olivary lesions were incomplete. (Indeed, preliminary findings indicate that the time course and degree of compensation in these animals can be correlated with the number and location of remaining olivary cells.) This view is supported by the observation that the administration of harmaline, known to produce tremor only in the presence of the inferior olive (58), elicited different degrees of tremor in each of these animals.

The above set of experiments is in agreement with the suggestion that the olivocerebellar system is necessary for the acquisition and retention of vestibular compensation (37). Further, they indicate that this system is necessary for the long-term maintenance of compensation and that if the olive is damaged a long time prior to the vestibular lesion, the injury to this system markedly interferes with normal compensatory progress. Thus, one cerebellar

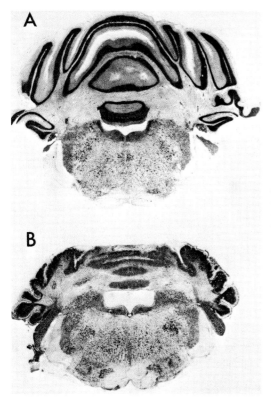

FIG. 3. Transverse section through the brainstem and cerebellum of a normal (A) and X-irradiated rat (B). Note that the brainstem is unaffected by the irradiation, but that the cerebellar cortex is both distorted and severely shrunken and gray matter is also reduced. At higher magnification it is apparent that the change in the vermal cortex is due to an absence of granule cells.

TABLE 2. *Vestibular compensation in X-irradiated animals*

Animal no.	Age at time of hemi- labyrinthectomy (mo.)	Time required to reach stable state (days)	Stable state	Period observed
AG 1	12	Did not compensate	On side; rolling.	4 mo.
AG 2	12	Did not compensate	On side; rolling.	4.5 mo.
AG 6	11	24–32	Head angle 16°. Eye position de- viated. Circles if stressed; otherwise inactive.	4.5 mo.
AG 9	11	3[a]	Head level 10°. Eyes level & stable. No abnormal motor patterns.	13 days
AG 10	3	6–11	Head level. Eyes level & stable. No abnormal motor patterns.	5 mo.
AG 16	3	5	Head angle 10°. Behavior: on belly; falls to lesioned more than intact side.	8 days
AG 17	3	7	Head angle about 20°. Behavior: keeps low but not on belly; falls to lesioned more than intact side.	8 days
AG 18	3	7	Head level. Behavior: keeps center of gravity low. More inform. needed.	12 mo.
AG 19	3	4	Head level. Eyes: stable; posi- tion sl. deviated. Behavior: falls to lesioned more than intact side.	14 mo.
AG 22	3	10	Head angle about 10°. Eyes: stable with normal position. Behavior: seldom falls.	12 mo.

[a] Does not indicate that final equilibrium was reached in this time, only that the major indication of vestibular lesion (e.g., head tilt, eye position and nystagmus, rolling, circling) had disappeared. Animals often continued to improve, but asymptotically.

afferent system—the olivocerebellar pathway—is implicated in this learning paradigm. However, these experiments do not speak to the question of the role of mossy fiber input or, for that matter, the role of the cortex itself.

Cerebellar Cortex Lesion

In order to address the above questions, extensive damage of the parallel fiber–Purkinje cell system was generated by X-irradiation (3) of the vermis of neonate rats (provided through the generosity of J. Altman). Although there was almost complete absence of the granule cell–parallel fiber systems in both the anterior and posterior vermis and although the structure of the remaining cerebellar cortex was abnormal as illustrated in Fig. 3B (cf. 3 for a detailed discussion), eight of 10 animals[2] were able to compensate, many as fully as normal animals (see Table 2). This compensation, it must be noted, often took longer than in the normal controls.

The observation that compensation takes several days to occur in these cases indicates that the proper function of the cerebellar cortex itself expedites and supports the correction, but is not necessary for its occurrence. Since the animals were quite ataxic, it is possible that this, among other effects, tends to mark the normal process. It is unquestionable, nevertheless, that long-term cerebellocortical damage does not prevent vestibular compensation (which is in agreement with results following short-term cerebellar decortication; ref. 38), in contrast to the total absence of compensation in the rat following complete cerebellar nuclear or inferior olive damage.

VESTIBULAR COMPENSATION FOLLOWING PARTIAL INFERIOR OLIVARY LESIONS

Functional Findings

In order to pursue the question whether a particular portion of the olivocerebellar system is necessary for compensation, we took advantage of an early observation that if 3-AP is given in the absence of harmaline, parts of the inferior olive are spared—notably the caudal medial accessory olive (MAO). The reasons for this special distribution of the inferior olivary lesion are still obscure. It is interesting to point out, nevertheless, that this portion of the inferior olive is most sensitive to the tremorigenous action (47) of harmaline (4,36) and that gap junctions are most frequent there (23,30, 31,59).

Under these conditions of partial inferior olivary lesion, compensation occurred, but had a slower time course than normal (see Table 3) with the

---

[2] We suspect that the two animals incapable of compensation had an extensive lesion of the fastigial nuclei.

TABLE 3. *Vestibular compensation in animals treated with 3-AP but not harmaline*

Animal no.	Initiation of compensation (days)	Period observed (mo.)	Extent of compensation	Effect of harmaline	Histology
3AP 2	9–11	4	Head angle 25–30°. Eyes: vertical deviation; spont. nystagmus if stressed. Behavior: sometimes moves in circles.	Head angle increases. Nystagmic rate increases.	Caudal MAO remains.
3AP 3	9	4	Head angle 40–47°. Eyes: small deviation of position; eyes steady. Behavior: leans left; inactive.	Jerky head movements. Spontaneous nystagmus.	Caudal MAO remains (fewer cells than 3AP 2).
3AP 4	—	4	Head angle 90–180°. Eyes: vertical deviation. Behavior: lies on side; some rolling; usually inactive.	Hyperactive. Some rolling. No definite incr. in vestibular signs.	No olivary cells remain.

animals clearly compensated in a period of 9 to 11 days.[3] Given this finding, it seems likely that if the continuing function of the MAO is important in maintaining compensation, altering its functional state by, for instance, the administration of harmaline should affect compensation. This is in fact the case. In addition to the tremor, several signs of vestibular imbalance are evident in these rats following harmaline administration. For example, abnormal motor sequences, such as circling in place (toward the side of the lesion) and frequent turns toward the lesioned side, are always seen. The most marked sign of vestibular decompensation, however, is the return of spontaneous nystagmus. The frequency of these eye movements ranges from 100 to 40 beats/min. The nystagmus, as the tremor, is not continuous. It occurs apparently spontaneously and also following even slight head movements. In the latter case the frequency of the eye movements is damped and over a period of about 2 min can slow to 8 beats/min before the head moves again and the frequency increases. There are also periods of calm during which there is neither tremor, head, or eye movement.

One would expect these signs of decompensation to disappear as the tremor wanes, and, in fact, the tremor and decompensation came to an end simul-

---

[3] One animal in this particular group never compensated and was found to have no olivary cells, in agreement with previous findings (36).

taneously. Thus, the maintenance of vestibular compensation can be related directly to the activity of the remaining MAO. It is interesting, nevertheless, that in animals with intact olives, harmaline does not produce a regression of vestibular compensation, implying that in the normal animal the inferior olive's role in compensation includes subnuclei other than the MAO.

Anatomical Findings

The effect of 3-AP on the inferior olive when administered in the absence or presence of harmaline is illustrated in Fig. 4. Histological sections through the caudal inferior olive are shown for a normal (Fig. 4A) and for the 3-AP-treated (Fig. 4C and E) animals. Note that in the absence of harmaline, the surviving cells are found only in the medial and lateral-most portions of the subnucleus (subdivisions of the inferior olive as in ref. 44). In contrast, when harmaline is given following 3-AP, a complete lesion results at this level. It is immediately evident that in the absence of harmaline, only parts of the caudal MAO, including the beta subnucleus, are spared (Fig. 4D). Very few cells remain in the 3-AP- and harmaline-treated animal (Fig. 4F).

When considering these results, two interpretations for the role of MAO in vestibular compensation come to mind: (a) This is a *specific* phenomenon, i.e., the integrity of the caudal MAO is essential for compensation and although the remaining subnuclei may contribute to recovery, these structures are not essential. (b) This is a *nonspecific* phenomenon. A minimum number of inferior olivary cells are necessary for compensation, but the location of the cells is not relevant.

There are several reasons why we favor the first interpretation. The inferior olive is somatotopically organized, and thus each subnucleus has a specific function that cannot readily be served by the others. Also the afferent and efferent connections of the caudal MAO overlap significantly with those systems thought to be involved in vestibular compensation (e.g., the vestibular nuclei and spinal cord). Furthermore, there is convergence of these various systems within the caudal MAO as well as in the cerebellum and vestibular nuclei (see Fig. 5).

Thus, the major input to the caudal MAO arises from the spinal cord (4,42,48; cf. 10), the input being bilateral from the cervical (7) and lumbar (7,42) segments. Specifically, the spinoolivocerebellar tracts from the hindlimb (dorsal and ventral) and the forelimb (dorsal and dorsolateral) converge on this subnucleus. Spinal fibers also converge with input from the dorsal column nuclei (gracilis) (7,22,42,63) and the lateral cervical nuclei (63; see also 7).

In addition, fibers from the motor cortex (60,61) converge with those from several spinoolivary tracts—dorsolateral and ventral spinoolivocerebellar (46). Furthermore, the caudal MAO is the major recipient of fibers from the contralateral reticular formation (42,62).

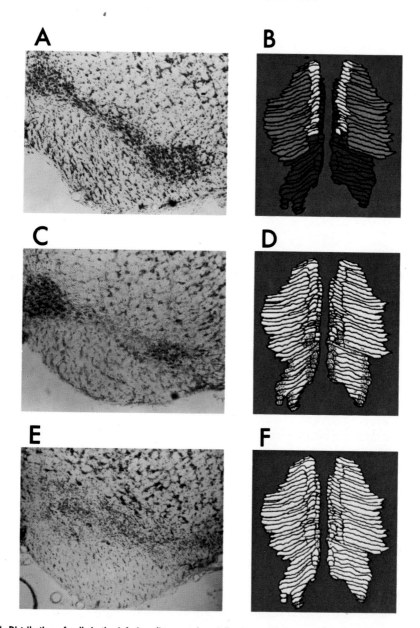

FIG. 4. Distribution of cells in the inferior olivary nucleus following partial complete chemical lesions. Left-hand column: Histological sections through the caudal inferior olive. A: Normal animal. C: Animal treated with 3-AP without harmaline. Note lack of cells in subgroup "b" of the MAO. E: Animal treated with 3-AP and harmaline. Note that there are no cells at this level. Right hand column: A computer reconstruction of the inferior olive, utilizing method of Hillman et al. (25), illustrates the distribution of cells within the nucleus in the 3-AP-treated animals. B: Normal inferior olive. The three major divisions are indicated: principal olive (*white*), dorsal accessory subnucleus (*green*), and medial accessory subnucleus (*red*). D: Distribution of cells following partial chemical lesion. Note that the remaining cells are grouped in the MAO only. F: Distribution of cells following "complete" olivary lesion. For the sake of clarity and to ease comparison, the surviving cells in the 3-AP-treated animals are marked (*red dots*) within an outline of the normal olive.

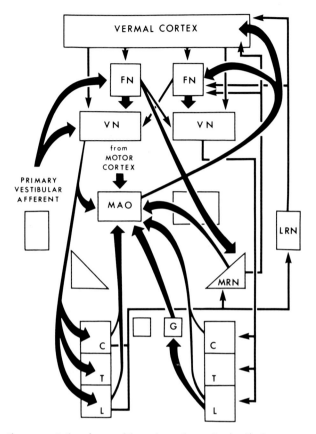

FIG. 5. A schematic representation of some of the major pathways involved in the compensation of postural asymmetry following unilateral (*right*) labyrinthine lesion in rat. For the sake of clarity, many bilateral pathways are shown only on one side. FN, fastigial nucleus; VN, vestibular nucleus (especially those parts concerned with primary vestibular and spinal systems); MAO, medial accessory olivary nucleus (the caudal portion); MRN, main reticular nucleus; LRN, lateral reticular nucleus; C, cervical spinal cord; T, thoracic spinal cord; L, lumbar spinal cord; G, gracilis nucleus.

The caudal MAO in turn projects to the fastigial nuclei (14,22,54), midline anterior cerebellar cortex (lobes I to V), and the posterior cerebellar cortex (lobes IV to IX) (9,22,24). In the cerebellum these fibers converge with vestibular, spinal, and reticular inputs. Although there is probably a direct olivary input to Deiters' nucleus (2,15,22,39), this has not been firmly established. This superficial coverage of the most salient connectivity in the MAO gives a general idea of the great degree of functional specificity present in this subnucleus.

DISCUSSION

Contrary to the views of Robinson (53) and Ito et al. (27) (cf. 20), the data presented here strongly support the thesis that the cerebellum cannot be regarded as the main site of motor learning. In addition, the statement that the cerebellum is a motor repair shop (53) must be seriously questioned.[4] What then would be the role of the cerebellum in this type of motor "learning," and how would vestibular compensation actually take place? The present results tend to support the classic neurological stand that the cerebellum is mainly concerned with the *regulation* rather than the *acquisition* of movement. As far as vestibular compensation is concerned, our initial conclusion that the basic modification must take place in the brainstem is confirmed here and shared by other investigators. For instance, Melvill Jones and Davies (45) have proposed that the compensation produced by inverting prisms most probably resides at the vestibular level itself.

A Locus for Vestibular Compensation?

Although vestibular compensation probably occurs in the brainstem, no precise "anatomical site" may be ultimately responsible. In fact, several functional levels have been considered to play a role in this process. For instance, inputs signalling body posture (such as the proprioceptive input from limbs and neck) and the visual system are known to be significant. Indeed, transection of the spinal cord prolongs head position deviation (56) and produces decompensation in hemilabyrinthectomized animals as does bilateral section of the dorsal roots (5). Further, it has been shown that proprioceptive input from lumbar joint afferents is important in attaining compensation (33).

The role of visual input, however, is variable and depends on the species studied (32). For example, visual deprivation has been found to have little effect on postural compensation in frogs (32) and in rats (*unpublished observations*). However, in cats visual input has been reported to be necessary for compensation of both vestibuloocular reflex (13) and postural deficits (52). Vision is also necessary for the maintenance of stable head posture in cats. In man, darkness may induce the return of spontaneous nystagmus as long as 1½ years after the injury (49).

Central to adjustment to vestibular injury is the vestibular complex. Changes in the activity of the vestibular nuclei have been shown to follow hemilabyrinthectomy as well as to accompany compensation. A bilateral decrease or abolition of activity in the vestibular nuclei (43,57) has been found immediately following vestibular lesion. The decrease of activity in the con-

---

[4] In a recent paper, which appeared after this chapter was written (23a), Robinson acknowledges having been wrong about motor repair in the sense that what he calls balance compensation can occur after vestibular cerebellectomy. However, he states that since the gain control is absent in these animals, "the possibility that gain control might be mediated by modifiable synapses on the Purkinje cells of the vestibulocerebellum remains an open question." A better statement might have been, "It is yet to be demonstrated," since the lack of gain control may refer (as stated below in this chapter) not to the inability of the cerebellum to learn but rather to the lack of cerebellar control.

tralateral nucleus has been attributed by McCabe and Ryu (43) to cerebellar inhibition and by Precht et al. (51) to crossvestibular inhibition. A subsequent increase of activity in some cells of the deafferented vestibular nuclei has been found in compensated cats (43,51). A similar increase has been reported in frog vestibular nucleus and is accompanied by an increase in synaptic efficacy of the excitatory commissural system (17). Also, the spontaneous activity in the descending vestibular nuclei of the hemilabyrinthectomized side has been seen to decrease below normal levels following "spinal decompensation" in guinea pig (28).

The possible involvement of the cerebellum in vestibular compensation has also been widely investigated (cf. 56). Azzena (5) found that cooling the "vermal cortex" by about 20° C produced the reappearance of vestibular symptoms in compensated guinea pigs. The role of the cortex itself in the decompensation is difficult to assess, however, as the fastigial nuclei were also cooled by about 7° C. In decerebellate guinea pigs, the symptoms following vestibular lesion were more pronounced, and compensation of head position was significantly delayed without effect on oculomotor compensation (55). In cats, removing the cerebellum immediately following vestibular lesion eliminated the inhibition of the contralateral vestibular nucleus. However, removal of the cerebellum after compensation had no effect on the increased activity of the ipsilateral medial vestibular nucleus (43), indicating that the cerebellum plays an inhibitory role immediately following injury, but is not responsible for the recovered activity in the deafferented medial vestibular nucleus. More recently it has been suggested that in cats olivocerebellar damage does not prevent vestibular compensation. These experiments, while confirmatory of previous data, are too "anecdotal" to be seriously considered. Carpenter et al. (11) found that bilateral destruction of the fastigial nuclei in previously labyrinthectomized cats eliminated all compensatory adaptation. Our own work in the rat (38) has shown that surgical decortication delays, but, in contrast to cerebellectomy, does not prevent compensation. Finally, ablation of nodulus and uvula in labyrinthectomized primates (18) produced no additional deficits. In short, it seems clearly demonstrated that vestibular compensation requires a complex modification of many aspects of brainstem and spinal function and may be different for different species.

Role of the Olivocerebellar Pathway in Compensation

The rather wide range of anatomical and functional work briefly reviewed above indicates that spinal afferents, the vestibular nuclei, and the cerebellar nuclei (especially the fastigial nucleus), as well as the visual input are involved in compensation for vestibular lesions. Our results suggest that the inferior olive plays a central role in restoring balance to the vestibular system by contributing to increasing the activity of the deafferented vestibular nucleus.

At the level of the vestibular nuclei (Deiters' in particular), input arriving throughout the olivary system would be integrated with that arriving bilaterally from the neck afferents and from the contralateral labyrinth (12,50) to increase the activity of the vestibular nuclei. These inputs, acting through the vestibulospinal pathways (especially vestibulocollar) would bring about bilateral balance of excitability of neck and other motoneurons (see Fig. 5).

The inferior olive does seem ideally situated (as proposed by Oscarsson, ref. 48) to compare inputs from the higher motor centers with information from the spinal cord (especially neck afferents) regarding the state of the musculature; however, its role is most probably one of an important relay station rather than a site of learning!

Implications of Vestibular Compensation Regarding the Question of "Cerebellar Learning"

It is clear that to compensate for vestibular damage, the activity of the deafferented nucleus must be raised to attain equilibrium with its contralateral counterpart. However, there is more to this compensation than the simple symmetry of activity between vestibular nuclei. In fact, in order for the animal to have a normal motricity, the deafferented nucleus must receive information *dynamically equivalent* to that previously subserved by the vestibular nerve.

As indicated previously, this dynamic equivalence is probably subserved by a concerted input to the vestibular system from the sensory system (proprioception, exteroception, vision) as well as from the motor generators, such as the basal ganglia and sensorimotor cortex. It is also clear that the cerebellar cortex must play a role in the generation of this dynamic equivalence. However, rather than generating the correction itself, the cortex probably modulates the subtleties required for a complete compensation, not unlike its role in motor coordination in general (35), which brings us back to the initial question of the role of the cerebellum in motor learning. The answer seems to be, once again, that the cerebellum is primarily an organ of regulation rather than one directly involved, via plastic modifiability, in the acquisition of new motor skills. It is probably unnecessary to argue the rather dead question of localized versus distributed properties in the central nervous system. It is obviously unwise to suppose that learning occurs *at one specific site or at one specific synapse.*

Furthermore, the analysis of such a simple and stereotyped motor reorganization as vestibular compensation indicates that the postural modifications do not occur in a single step but, rather, in a piece-meal fashion, that is, a new motor stance must often be developed before the finer details can be acquired. In this respect then even if plasticity had been found in the cerebellum, to imagine it as the "seat of motor learning" would be, at best, an oversimplification. The functional properties, modified at the neuronal level in order to display new behavioral responses, are probably distributed along the circuitry necessary to perform the given skill. Thus, rather than thinking in terms of "seats" or "loci" for learning, one should consider the changes in the properties of the system as a product of a series of modifications not necessarily very significant at any particular synaptic linkage.

Although it is apparent that the olivofastigial input is of great importance, it is equally true that any information concerning the perception of space and body posture would ultimately be of significance in attaining the final compensation. The importance of this point cannot be overemphasized. The rather prevalent view that reduces learning, especially in higher vertebrates, to modifications at single sites must be vigorously questioned. Although there is no disagreement with the fact that *basic cellular mechanisms, amenable to analysis, must underlie circuit modification,* it seems unwarranted to assume that such mechanisms are unique or uniquely localized. The cellular properties that could, in theory, subserve learning range widely from changes in presynaptic release properties to modification of postsynaptic morphology and excitability. The central question, then, is whether learning in these highly complex nervous systems is localized, in the Marr sense, or is rather a distributed property within the system. It is our feeling that the nervous system modifies itself by using all available resources rather than by limiting itself to a few mechanisms at specialized sites.

ACKNOWLEDGMENTS

Research was supported by USPHS Grant NS-13742 from the National Institute of Neurological and Communicative Disorders and Stroke.

REFERENCES

1. Albus, J. S. (1971): A theory of cerebellar function. *Math. Biosci.,* 10:25–61.
2. Allen, G. I., Sabah, N. H., and Toyama, K. (1972): Synaptic actions of peripheral nerve impulses upon Deiters' neurones via the climbing fibre afferents. *J. Physiol. (Lond.),* 226:311–333.
3. Altman, J., and Anderson, W. J. (1972): Experimental reorganization of the cerebellar cortex. I. Morphological effects of elimination of all microneurons with prolonged x-irradiation started at birth. *J. Comp. Neurol.,* 146:355–406.
4. Armstrong, D. M. (1974): Functional significance of connections of inferior olive. *Physiol. Rev.,* 54:358–417.
5. Azzena, G. B. (1969): Role of the spinal cord in compensating the effects of hemilabyrinthectomy. *Arch. Ital. Biol.,* 107:43–53.
6. Bechterew, W. (1883): Ergebnisse der Durchaschneidung des N. acusticus, nebst Eroerterung der Bedeutung der semicirculaeren Canaele fuer das Koerpergleichgewicht. *Pflueg. Arch. Ges. Physiol.,* 30:312–347.
7. Boesten, A. J. P., and Voogd, J. (1975): Projections of the dorsal column nuclei and the spinal cord on the inferior olive in the cat. *J. Comp. Neurol.,* 161:215–237.
8. Brindley, G. S. (1964): The use made by the cerebellum of the information that it receives from sense organs. *Int. Brain Res. Org. Bull.,* 3:30.
9. Brodal, A. (1976): The olivocerebellar projection in the cat as studied with the method of retrograde axonal transport of horseradish peroxidase. II. The projection to the uvula. *J. Comp. Neurol.,* 166:417–426.

10. Brodal, A., and Walberg, F. (1977): The olivocerebellar projection in the cat studied with the method of retrograde axonal transport of horseradish peroxidase. *J. Comp. Neurol.,* 172:85–108.
11. Carpenter, M. B., Fabrega, H., and Glinsmann, W. (1959): Physiological deficits occurring with lesions of labyrinth and fastigial nuclei. *J. Neurophysiol.,* 22: 222–234.
12. Coulter, J. D., Mergner, T., and Pompeiano, O. (1976): Effects of static tilt on cervical spinoreticular tract neurons. *J. Neurophysiol.,* 39:45–62.
13. Courjon, J. H., Jeannerod, M., Ossuzio, I., and Schmid, R. (1977): Role of vision in compensation of vestibulo-ocular reflex after hemilabyrinthectomy in the cat. *Exp. Brain Res.,* 28:235–248.
14. Courville, J., Augustine, J. R., and Martel, P. (1977): Projections from the inferior olive to the cerebellar nuclei in the cat demonstrated by retrograde transport of horseradish peroxidase. *Brain Res.,* 130:405–419.
15. Desclin, J. (1974): Démonstration en microscopie optique de la dégénérescence terminale d'afférences d'origine olivaire inférieure dans le noyau vestibulaire latéral (Deiters) chez le rat. *CR Acad. Sci. Paris, Serie D,* 278:2931–2934.
16. Desclin, J. C., and Escubi, J. (1974): Effects of 3-acetylpyridine on the central nervous system of the rat, as demonstrated by silver methods. *Brain Res.,* 77: 349–364.
17. Dieringer, N., and Precht, W. (1977): Modification of synaptic input following unilateral labyrinthectomy. *Nature,* 269:431–433.
18. Dow, R. S. (1938): Effect of lesions in the vestibular part of the cerebellum in primates. *Arch. Neurol. Psych. (Chicago),* 40:500–520.
19. Dow, R. S., and Moruzzi, G. (1958): *The Physiology and Pathology of the Cerebellum.* Univ. of Minnesota Press, Minneapolis.
20. Eccles, J. C. (1977): An instruction-selection theory of learning in the cerebellar cortex. *Brain Res.,* 127:327–352.
21. Gonshor, A., and Melvill Jones, G. (1973): Changes of human vestibuloocular response induced by vision-reversal during head rotation. *J. Physiol. (Lond.),* 234: 102–103P.
22. Groenewegen, H. J., and Voogd, J. (1977): The parasagittal zonation within the olivocerebellar projection. 1. Climbing fiber distribution in the vermis of cat cerebellum. *J. Comp. Neurol.,* 174:417–488.
23. Gwyn, D. G., Nicholson, G. P., and Flumerfelt, B. A. (1977): The inferior olivary nucleus of the rat: A light and electron microscopic study. *J. Comp. Neurol.,* 174:489–520.
23a. Haddad, G. M., Friendlich, A. R., and Robinson, D. A. (1977): Compensation of nystagmus after VIII nerve lesion in vestibulo-cerebellectomized cats. *Brain Res.,* 135:192–196.
24. Hoddevik, G. H., Brodal, A., and Walberg, F. (1976): The olivocerebellar projection in the cat studied with the method of retrograde axonal transport of horseradish peroxidase. *J. Comp. Neurol.,* 169:155–170.
25. Hillman, D. E., Llinás, R., and Chujo, M. (1977): Automatic and semiautomatic analysis of nervous system structure. In: *Computer Analysis of Neuronal Structures,* edited by R. D. Lindsay, pp. 73–90. Plenum, New York and London.
26. Ito, M. (1972): Neural design of the cerebellar motor control system. *Brain Res.,* 40:81–84.
27. Ito, M., Shiida, T., Yagi, N., and Yamamoto, M. (1974): Cerebellar modification of rabbit's horizontal vestibulo-ocular reflex induced by sustained head rotation combined with visual stimulation. *Proc. Jpn. Acad.,* 50:85–89.
28. Jensen, D. W. (1977): Vestibular compensation: Influence of spinal cord on spontaneous activity of vestibular nuclei. *Soc. Neurosci. Abstr.,* 3:543.
29. Kandel, E. R. (1976): *Cellular Basis of Behavior.* Freeman, San Francisco.
30. King, J. S. (1976): The synaptic cluster (glomerulus) in the inferior olivary nucleus. *J. Comp. Neurol.,* 165:387–400.

31. King, J. S., Martin, G. F., and Bowman, M. H. (1975): The direct spinal area of the inferior olivary nucleus: An electron microscopic study. *Exp. Brain Res.,* 22:13–24.
32. Kolb, G. (1955): Untersuchungen ueber zentrale Kempensation und Kempensationsbewegungen einseitig entstateter Froesche. *Z. Vergl. Physiol.,* 37:136–160.
33. Lacour, M., Roll, J. P., and Appaix, M. (1976): Modifications and development of spinal reflexes in the alert baboon (*Papio papio*) following an unilateral vestibular neurotomy. *Brain Res.,* 113:255–269.
34. Livingston, R. B. (1966): Brain mechanisms in conditioning and learning. *Neurosci. Res. Program Bull.,* 4, No. 3:235–347.
35. Llinás, R. (1974): Eighteenth Bowditch Lecture: Motor aspects of cerebellar control. *Physiologist,* 17:19–46.
36. Llinás, R., and Volkind, R. A. (1973): The olivo-cerebellar system: Functional properties as revealed by harmaline-induced tremor. *Exp. Brain Res.,* 18:69–87.
37. Llinás, R., and Walton, K. (1978): Significance of the olivo-cerebellar system in compensation of ocular position following unilateral labyrinthectomy. In: *Control of Gaze,* edited by A. Berthoz and R. Baker. Elsevier, Amsterdam. (*In press.*)
38. Llinás, R., Walton, K., Hillman, D. E., and Sotelo, C. (1975): Inferior olive: Its role in motor learning. *Science,* 190:1230–1231.
39. Lorente de Nó, R. (1924): Études sur le cerveau postérieur. III. Sur les connexions extracerebelleuses des fascicules afferents au cerveau, et sur la fonction de cet organ. *Trav. Lab. Rech. Biol. Univ. Madrid,* 22:51–65.
40. Magnus, R. (1924): *Koerperstellung.* Springer, Berlin.
41. Marr, D. (1969): A theory of cerebellar cortex. *J. Physiol. (Lond.),* 202:437–470.
42. Martin, G. F., Dom, R., King, J. S., Robards, M., and Watson, C. R. R. (1975): The inferior olivary nucleus of the opossum (*Didelphis marsupialis virginiana*), its organization and connections. *J. Comp. Neurol.,* 160:507–534.
43. McCabe, B. F., and Ryu, J. H. (1969): Experiments on vestibular compensation. *Laryngoscope,* 79:1728–1736.
44. McGrane, M. K., Woodward, D. J., Eriksson, M. A., Burne, R. A., and Saint-Cyr, J. A. (1977): The inferior olivary complex in the rat: Gross nuclear organization and topography of olivocerebellar projections. *Soc. Neurosci. Abstr.,* 3:59.
45. Melvill Jones, G., and Davies, P. (1976): Adaptation of cat vestibulo-ocular reflex to 200 days of optically reversed vision. *Brain Res.,* 103:551–554.
46. Miller, S., Nezlina, N., and Oscarsson, O. (1969): Projection and convergence patterns in climbing fibre paths to cerebellar anterior lobe activated from cerebral and spinal cord. *Brain Res.,* 14:230–233.
47. Montigny, C. de, and Lamarre, Y. (1973): Rhythmic activity induced by harmaline in the olivo-cerebello-bulbar system of the cat. *Brain Res.,* 53:81–95.
48. Oscarsson, O. (1973): Functional organization of spinocerebellar paths. In: *Handbook of Sensory Physiology,* Vol. II, edited by A. Iggo, pp. 339–380. Springer-Verlag, Berlin-Heidelberg-New York.
49. Pfaltz, C. R., and Kamath, R. (1970): Central compensation of vestibular dysfunction. I. Peripheral lesions. *Pract. Oto-rhino-laryng.,* 32:335–349.
50. Pompeiano, O., and Hoshino, K. (1977): Responses to static tilts of lateral reticular neurons mediated by contralateral labyrinthine receptors. *Arch. Ital. Biol.,* 115:211–236.
51. Precht, W., Shimazu, H., and Markham, C. H. (1966): A mechanism of central compensation of vestibular function following hemilabyrinthectomy. *J. Neurophysiol.,* 29:996–1010.
52. Putkonen, P. T. S., Courjon, J. H., and Jeannerod, M. (1977): Compensation of postural effects of hemilabyrinthectomy in the cat. A sensory substitution process? *Exp. Brain Res.,* 28:249–257.
53. Robinson, D. A. (1975): How the oculomotor system repairs itself. *Invest. Ophthalmol.,* 14:413–415.
54. Ruggiero, D., Batton, R. R. III, Jayaraman, A., and Carpenter, M. B. (1977): Brain stem afferents to the fastigial nucleus in the cat demonstrated by transport of horseradish peroxidase. *J. Comp. Neurol.,* 172:189–210.

55. Schaefer, K.-P., and Meyer, D. L. (1973): Compensatory mechanisms following labyrinthine lesions in the guinea-pig. A simple model of learning. In: *Memory and Transfer of Information,* edited by H. P. Zippel, pp. 203–232. Plenum, New York.

56. Schaefer, K.-P., and Meyer, D. L. (1974): Compensation of vestibular lesions. In: *Handbook of Sensory Physiology, Vol. 1/2 (Vestibular System, Pt. 2),* edited by H. H. Kornhuber, pp. 463–490. Springer-Verlag, Berlin-Heidelberg-New York.

57. Shimazu, H., and Precht, W. (1966): Inhibition of central vestibular neurons from the contralateral labyrinth and its mediating pathway. *J. Neurophysiol.,* 29:467–492.

58. Simantov, R., Snyder, S. H., and Oster-Granite, M.-L. (1976): Harmaline-induced tremor in the rat: Abolition by 3-acetylpyridine destruction of cerebellar climbing fibers. *Brain Res.,* 114:144–151.

59. Sotelo, C., Llinás, R., and Baker, R. (1974): Structural study of the inferior olivary nucleus of the cat. Morphological correlates of electrotonic coupling. *J. Neurophysiol.,* 37:541–559.

60. Sousa-Pinto, A., and Brodal, A. (1969): Demonstration of a somatotopical pattern in the cortico-olivary projection in the cat. An experimental anatomical study. *Exp. Brain Res.,* 8:364–386.

61. Walberg, F. (1956): Descending connections to the inferior olive: An experimental study in the cat. *J. Comp. Neurol.,* 104:77–174.

62. Walberg, F. (1975): The vestibular nuclei and their connections with the eighth nerve and the cerebellum. In: *The Vestibular System,* edited by R. F. Nauton, pp. 31–53. Academic Press, New York.

63. Worden, I. G., and Berkley, K. J. (1975): Input to the inferior olive of the cat. A comparison of spino-olivary projections with those from the dorsal column nuclei, lateral cervical nucleus and cerebellum. *Neurosci. Abstr.,* 1:200.

Brain Mechanisms in Memory and Learning: From the Single Neuron to Man, edited by M. A. B. Brazier. Raven Press, New York © 1979.

Change in Shape of Dendritic Spines Resulting from KCl and 4-Aminopyridine Stimulation of Frog Brain

Janett Trubatch,* A. Van Harreveld, and A. V. Loud

Departments of Physiology and Pathology, New York Medical College, Valhalla, New York 10595

Brain mechanisms underlying memory and learning may be examined at many levels, from the holistic study of behavior in complicated (or simple) organisms to the biochemical analysis of macromolecules. Since information both enters and leaves the central nervous system in the form of electrical signals (action potentials) at the cellular level, changes in the nervous system accompanying learning must result from synaptic activation and may be correlated with changes in neural circuits or with functional or structural alterations in the synapses or the dendritic circuits on which they terminate.

In this chapter we report that stimuli that can produce or enhance synaptic transmission cause an uptake of extracellular fluid by the postsynaptic structures that are often dendritic spines. Our results were obtained by applying stereological methods to electronmicrographs of freeze-fixed tissue to calculate the three-dimensional volume changes caused by stimulation. Fixation by rapid freezing followed by freeze substitution more accurately preserves these changes because it avoids the shift in fluids caused by ordinary chemical fixation procedures (14,15). The change in shape of the dendritic spines following synaptic activation can change synaptic potency (8) and thus provides a possible anatomical correlate of neuronal plasticity.

METHODS AND OBSERVATIONS

In our laboratories, fixation for electron microscopy is carried out utilizing a technique (11,17) in which the tissue is rapidly frozen by bringing it into contact with a polished metal surface (either silver or copper) cooled to about $-200°$ C with liquid nitrogen at reduced pressure. After freezing, the tissue is bathed overnight at $-85°$ C in ethanol or acetone containing 2% OsO_4. The preparation is then slowly warmed to room temperature, and blocks are cut and processed for electron microscopy by washing in ethanol,

---

* *Present address:* Neurobiology Program, National Science Foundation, Washington, D. C. 20550.

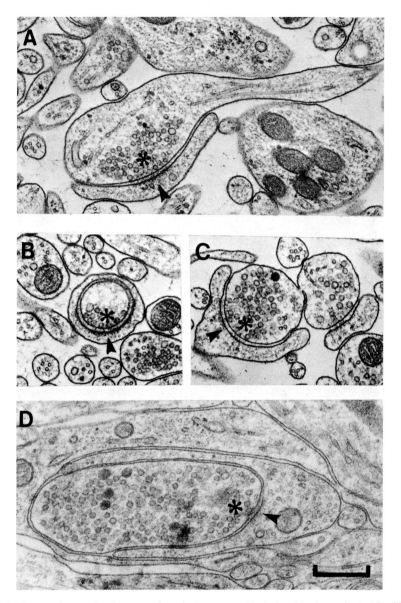

FIG. 1. Electron micrographs of synapses from the frog cortex. The isolated brain was bathed for 15 min in physiological salt solution at room temperature before freezing and freeze substitution. The preparation shows a considerable amount of extracellular space. Presynaptic structures *(asterisks)* show an accumulation of vesicles, and postsynaptic regions are identified by the presence of a synaptic junction *(arrows)*. The calibration line indicates 0.5 μm.

passing through propylene oxide, and embedding in Epon. This rapid freezing technique has been demonstrated to yield a better preservation of the natural fluid distribution in the tissue (14,15) and enables the observation of changes that would be obscured by conventional fixation techniques.

In vitro preparations of frog brain provided the experimental material for two main reasons. It has been demonstrated (16) that the *in vitro* preparation remains viable for several hours after its removal from the animal, potentials can be evoked by gross stimulation, and EEGs may be led off the brain even during exposure to low (5 to 10° C) temperatures. Furthermore, the surface 10 to 15 μm of cerebral cortex, containing a dense population of synaptic junctions, can be preserved with sufficiently small ice crystal artifacts so that quantitative electron microscopic studies can be done.

Forebrains were stimulated by spraying them with an isotonic solution of KCl 5 to 20 sec before they were rapidly frozen or by bathing them in a physiological solution containing 4 mM of 4-aminopyridine (4-AP) for 5 to 20 min before freezing.

The cortical surface of the frog brain consists entirely of neuropil—axons, dendrites, and the synaptic contacts between cell as well as glial elements. Control preparations of brains bathed in physiological solution (100 mM NaCl, 2 mM KCl, 7.5 mM $CaCl_2$, 2 mM $NaHCO_3$, 10 mM glucose) for 15 to 20 min at room temperature contain an appreciable extracellular space and a rather uniform electron density of the tissue elements (Fig. 1). Shortly after stimulation with KCl or 4-AP, there is a rapid loss of extracellular space and a marked swelling of many of the tissue elements (Fig. 2). The majority of these swollen, electron-lucent structures could be identified as postsynaptic regions by the presence of synaptic junctions and their adjacent presynaptic regions. In many cases, these swollen elements could be identified as dendrites or dendritic spines. Presynaptic elements could readily be identified by the presence of a dense pool of synaptic vesicles.

Morphometric measurements have been made of the volume and membrane surface area of presynaptic and postsynaptic structures as well as the volume of extracellular space. For morphometric analysis, 18 micrographs from three stimulated preparations were enlarged to the same final magnification of ×24,200. A grid of 500 sampling points and lines was superimposed on all the prints. For each micrograph the pre- and postsynaptic structures were identified and counted. The percent of the tissue volume occupied by these structures and by the extracellular space was determined by counting the fraction of points overlying these areas. The boundary membrane surface area of the pre- and postsynaptic structures was determined by counting the number of intersections that their membrane profiles made with the sampling lines.

Table 1 shows the comparison of the results obtained from control and stimulated preparations. The data from all the animals in each group have been combined since no significant variation was found among animals in

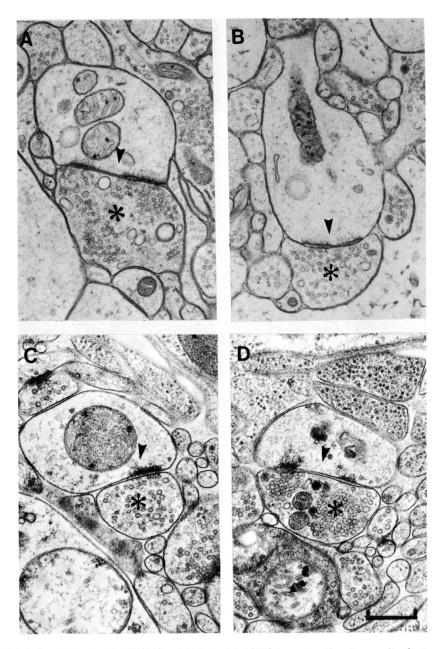

FIG. 2. Synaptic junctions in KCl-(A,B) and 4-AP-stimulated (C,D) frog cortex. There is a paucity of extracellular space. Swollen, electron-lucent tissue elements that can be identified as postsynaptic structures are
indicated by arrows. The subsynaptic webs are considerably larger and darker than in the control preparations. The calibration line indicates 0.5 μm.

TABLE 1. Comparison of stereological data from control and stimulated frog cortices

Tissue elements		Control	KCl	p	4-AP	p
Presynaptic	V%	14.7 ± 0.4	15.7 ± 0.6	0.1	13.3 ± 0.8	0.1
	$S_v \times 10^{-3}$	1.27 ± 0.03	1.21 ± 0.03	0.1	1.30 ± 0.002	0.3
	n	42.2 ± 1.0	39.1 ± 1.0	0.025	42.1 ± 0.5	0.2
Postsynaptic	V%	4.8 ± 0.2	14.2 ± 0.9	0.0005*	7.6 ± 0.4	0.0005*
	$S_v \times 10^{-3}$	0.66 ± 0.04	0.77 ± 0.06	0.1	0.60 ± 0.03	0.2
	n	14.5 ± 0.7	14.4 ± 0.5	0.4	14.4 ± 0.3	0.5
Extracellular space	V%	4.3 ± 0.2	0.6 ± 0.1	0.0005*	2.6 ± 0.04	0.0005*
Other	V%	76.1 ± 0.7	69.5 ± 1.5	0.0005*	77.0 ± 0.9	0.3
Cell membrane	$S_v \times 10^{-3}$	9.2 ± 0.5	8.4 ± 0.3	0.11	9.0 ± 0.3	0.4

For the pre- and postsynaptic structures, the percent of the tissue volume they occupy (V%), their membrane surface per unit volume of tissue $\left[S_v, \left(\dfrac{nm}{nm}\right)_3^2 \right]$, and the number (n) of these regions in each micrograph are tabulated. The percent of the volume occupied by the extracellular space and the "other" or nonidentified cellular elements is listed as well as the total surface area per unit volume of tissue of all the cellular elements. Each number is the average and standard error of 18 micrographs, each micrograph representing a tissue area of 81.7 μm^2. The p values were computed using the Student's t-test, and asterisks indicate significant differences between the control and each of the stimulated preparations.

either group. The most significant quantitative changes coincide with the qualitative observations, namely that in the KCl-stimulated tissue the postsynaptic structures increase from 4.8% in the control to 14.2% in the stimulated tissue, whereas the apparent extracellular space decreased from 4.3 to 0.6%. Neither the number of postsynaptic areas nor their membrane surface area showed any significant change from the control to the stimulated preparations. The number of presynaptic elements in each micrograph showed a small decrease from the control to the stimulated preparations; however, if only those presynaptic structures associated with recognizable synaptic junctions were counted, there was no significant change in the numbers of these elements (14.8 ± 0.7; 14.4 ± 0.5p < 0.2) between the control and stimulated preparations.

A similar uptake of extracellular fluid and concomitant swelling of postsynaptic structures can be demonstrated in frog brains bathed for 5 to 20 min in physiological solutions containing 4 mM of 4-AP. After freezing and freeze substitution these preparations also show, although less dramatically than the KCl-stimulated preparations, a decrease in the extracellular space and a swelling of postsynaptic structures (Table 1).

Although there was no change in the fraction of tissue volume occupied by the presynaptic structures in the stimulated preparations, it is evident that the increase in the volume fraction of the postsynaptic elements from 4.8 to 14.2% is much greater than the apparent loss of extracellular space from 4.3% in the control to 0.6% in the KCl-stimulated preparations. It has been shown (7), however, that the extracellular space, which consists of narrow passages between cell membranes, is systematically underestimated in morpho-metric measurements. This underestimation results from the random oblique orientation of the boundary cell membranes that, when the entire thickness of the section is projected onto the image plane of the micrograph, partially obscures the clear extracellular space. In the control micrographs the apparent volume of extracellular space is 4.8%, whereas other procedures, including extracellular markers and impedance measurements (10), yield values between 15 and 25% for the extracellular space in the central nervous system of various species. This morphometric underestimation of extracellular space may be corrected (7,9), leading to a true value of 19.6% in the control preparations, 6.9% in the KCl-stimulated preparations, and 14.7% in brains bathed in 4-AP.

The underestimation of extracellular space implies a corresponding over-estimation of cellular compartments. Only the regions with small cross-sectional areas will be significantly affected, however, and these are found mostly among the unidentified elements of the neuropil. Subtracting the underestimated volume fraction of extracellular space from the volume frac-tion of unidentified elements (other) yields the corrected volume distributions.

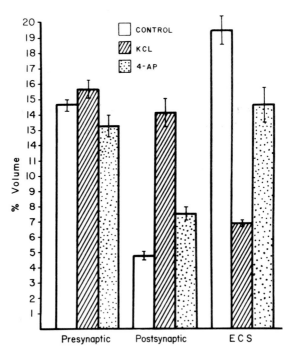

FIG. 3. Bar graph indicating the percent of the tissue occupied by the pre- and postsynaptic elements and by the extracellular space, where the correction for the underestimation of the extracellular space has been included. The white areas represent the average values for the 18 control micrographs; the lined areas, those for the 18 micrographs from KCl-stimulated animals, and the dotted areas, those for the 4-AP-stimulated animals. Standard errors are indicated by the vertical lines.

Figure 3 demonstrates the effects of KCl and 4-AP stimulation graphically. Whereas the percent of tissue volume occupied by the presynaptic elements does not change significantly, the postsynaptic elements increase threefold in the KCl-stimulated, and just under twofold in the 4-AP, preparations. When the corrected figures for the extracellular volumes are used, the extracellular space decreases to about one-third of its control value in the KCl-stimulated brains and to three-fourths of its control value in the 4-AP-stimulated brains.

The major change resulting from stimulation is, therefore, an uptake of extracellular fluid by postsynaptic elements. Since this increase in volume occurs with no change in the number of postsynaptic structures, the volume occupied by individual elements significantly increases in the stimulated

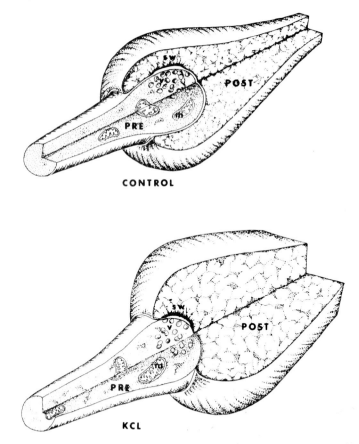

FIG. 4. Diagrammatic representation of the changes in the synapses of the frog cortex induced by KCl stimulation. In the control preparation, the postsynaptic region (dendritic spine) envelops the presynaptic terminal. In the stimulated preparations, the postsynaptic structures show an increased volume but no change in their membrane surface area achieved by assuming an altered shape with a decreased length and an increased cross-sectional area. (From Trubatch et al., ref. 9. Reprinted with permission from Pergamon Press.)

preparations. Furthermore, the increase in the volume of the postsynaptic regions without an accompanying increase in their bounding membrane surface area implies that these regions increased in their volume by changing their shape, i.e., their surrounding membranes did not become enlarged either by stretching or by taking up additional membrane material. The three-dimensional nature of this change can be inferred from an examination of the profiles of the synaptic regions as observed in the micrographs. Figures 1 and 2 show synaptic junctions from control and stimulated preparations. These show how the shape of a postsynaptic region, which is usually a spine, changes after stimulation. In the control preparations (Fig. 1) the region of the postsynaptic ending in contact with the presynaptic terminal is long and narrow and may appear partially or even completely (Fig. 1B) wrapped around the presynaptic region. In the preparations stimulated with KCl (Fig. 2A and B) and 4-AP (Fig. 2C and D), however, the postsynaptic areas do not enclose the presynaptic terminals, and their narrow concave shape has become nearly completely convex.

Figure 4 is a diagrammatic representation of this change of shape of the postsynaptic elements. In the control preparation the spine is long and slim and envelops the presynaptic ending. In the stimulated preparation the spine rounds up, pulls back from the presynaptic terminal, and decreases its length while increasing its cross-sectional area. In this way the volume is increased while the membrane surface area remains unchanged.

DISCUSSION

Stimulation of neuronal tissue with KCl causes depolarization of the neurons and may provide a mechanism for evoking synaptic activation. 4-AP has been shown to increase the end-plate potential at the frog neuromuscular junction and to increase the amplitude and quantal content of both excitatory postsynaptic potential and inhibitory postsynaptic potential in the cockroach ganglion (5) and thus enhances synaptic transmission. The change in shape of the postsynaptic structures after these stimuli may be attributable to a general increase in the membrane permeability of these elements or to a specific increase in sodium conductance. In either case, this would result in an inward movement of sodium ions accompanied by chloride to maintain electrical equilibrium and by water to maintain osmotic equilibrium. The postsynaptic elements would thereby increase their volumes, and to do this without an increase in their boundary membrane surface areas, they must change their shapes by rounding up.

The observed changes in the shape and dimensions of the postsynaptic elements may, under more normal conditions, provide an anatomical basis for facilitation in a neuronal pathway. Van Harreveld and Fifkova (13) observed a similar swelling of dendritic spines in the fascia dentata of mice after stimulation of the perforant fibers, an effect correlated with a long-lasting potentiation of the electrical stimulation (1,2,4,6). The swelling of the post-synaptic structures, which in many instances can be identified as dendritic spines, will decrease their length and increase their cross-sectional area. Since the resistance of an element is directly proportional to its length and inversely proportional to its cross-sectional area, the resistance of the spine will decrease and the effectiveness of synaptic activation (both excitatory and inhibitory) at the junction will be increased (8). Repetitive activation of a pathway may therefore cause the uptake of fluid and electrolytes into post-synaptic structures that in turn would result in an increased synaptic potency. This provides a possible mechanism for plasticity in the central nervous system. Such changes may underlie formation of short-term memory and on stabilization utilizing protein synthesis may serve as a basis for long-term memory as well (3,12).

ACKNOWLEDGMENT

The authors appreciate the expert technical assistance provided by Maria Demeri, Judith Pino, Alfred E. Revzin, and Julie Rotta. Special thanks to Julie Rotta for the beautiful art work.

This investigation was supported by grants from the National Science Foundation (BMS 75–01611), the Whitehall Foundation, and NIH (HI 14713–05).

REFERENCES

1. Bliss, T. V. P., and Gardner-Medwin, A. R. (1973): Long-lasting potentiation of synaptic transmission in the dentate area of the unanaesthetized rabbit, following stimulation of the perforant path. *J. Physiol. (Lond.)*, 232:357–374.
2. Bliss, T. V. P., and Lomø, T. (1973): Long-lasting potentiation of synaptic transmission in the dentate area of the anaesthetized rabbit following stimulation of the perforant path. *J. Physiol. (Lond.)*, 232:331–356.
3. Cherkin, A., Eckardt, M. J., and Gerbrandt, L. K. (1976): Memory: Froline induces retrograde amnesia in chicks. *Science*, 193:242–244.
4. Douglas, R. M., and Goddard, G. V. (1975): Long-term potentiation of the perforant path-granule cell synapse in the rat hippocampus. *Brain Res.*, 86:205–215.
5. Hue, B., Pelhate, M., Callec, J. J., and Chanelet, J. (1976): Action of 4-amino-pyridine. *J. Exp. Biol.*, 65:517–527.
6. Lomø, T. (1970): Some properties of a cortical excitatory synapse. In: *Excitatory Mechanisms, Proceedings of the Fifth International Meeting of Neurobiologists*, edited by P. Andersén and J. K. S. Jansen, pp. 207–211. Universitets Forlaget, Oslo.
7. Loud, A. V., and Trubatch, J. (1976): Morphometric underestimation of narrow interstitial spaces. In: *Proceedings 34th Annual Meeting Electron Microscopy Society of America*, edited by G. W. Baileg, pp. 116–117. Claitor's, Baton Rouge, La.
8. Rall, W. (1974): Dendritic spines, synaptic potency and neuronal activity. In: *Cellular Mechanisms Subserving Changes in Neuronal Activity*, edited by C. D. Woody, K. A. Brown, T. J. Crow, Jr., and J. D. Knispel, pp. 13–21. Brain Information Service. Report No. 3. Univ. of California, Los Angeles.
9. Trubatch, J., Van Harreveld, A., and Loud, A. V. (1977): Quantitative stereological evaluation of KCL induced ultrastructural changes in frog brain. *Neuroscience* 2:963–974.

10. Van Harreveld, A. (1972): The extracellular space in the vertebrate central nervous system. In: *The Structure and Function of Nervous Tissue, Vol. IV,* edited by G. H. Bourne, pp. 447–511. Academic Press, New York.
11. Van Harreveld, A., and Crowell, J. (1964): Electron microscopy after rapid freezing on a metal surface and substitution fixation. *Anat. Rec.,* 149:381–386.
12. Van Harreveld, A., and Fifkova, E. (1974): Involvement of glutamate in memory formation. *Brain Res.,* 81:455–467.
13. Van Harreveld, A., and Fifkova, E. (1975): Swelling of dendritic spines in the fascia dentata after stimulation of the perforant fibers as a mechanism of post-tetanic potentiation. *Exp. Neurol.,* 49:736–749.
14. Van Harreveld, A., and Khattab, F. I. (1967): Changes in cortical extracellular space during spreading depression investigated in the electron microscope. *J. Neurophysiol.,* 30:911–929.
15. Van Harreveld, A., and Steiner, J. (1970): The magnitude of the extracellular space in electron micrography of superficial and deep regions of the cerebral cortex. *J. Cell Sci.,* 6:793–805.
16. Van Harreveld, A., and Trubatch, J. (1974): Conditions affecting the extracellular space in the frog's forebrain. *Anat. Rec.,* 178:587–597.
17. Van Harreveld, A., Trubatch, J., and Steiner, J. (1974): Rapid freezing and electron microscopy for the arrest of physiological processes. *J. Microsc. (Oxf.),* 100: 189–198.

Brain Mechanisms in Memory and Learning:
From the Single Neuron to Man,
edited by M. A. B. Brazier.
Raven Press, New York © 1979.

Selectively REM-Related Increased Firing Rates of Cortical Association Interneurons During Sleep: Possible Implications for Learning

M. Steriade, A. Kitsikis, and G. Oakson

Laboratoire de Neurophysiologie, Département de Physiologie, Faculté de Médecine,
Université Laval, Québec G1K 7P4, Canada

The presence of this chapter on the behavior of cortical cells during the sleep cycle would hardly be justified within a volume on memory and learning if it were not for the discovery that parietal association interneurons dramatically increase their firing rate during rapid eye movements (REMs) of desynchronized (D) sleep. This intense activity of cortical interneurons may account for the consolidation of memory trace that has recently been hypothesized to occur during D sleep.

Previous work in our laboratory on precentral motor cortex of monkeys revealed that the spontaneous discharge of identified pyramidal tract cells increased and their antidromic responsiveness was enhanced during waking (W) compared to synchronized sleep (S), whereas nonoutput, putative short-axoned cells stopped firing on arousal and remained less active during steady W than during S (6). Admittedly, these results do not support the hypothesis (5) that the function of sleep is to permit interneurons to recover from their participation in highly complex processes during W. We decided to extend these initial findings on the sleep-waking behavior of output cells and interneurons to the parietal association cortex of cat and to the D state of sleep, which was not studied in our work on monkey. The association areas, where lesions may lead to a deficit in acquisition or retention of complex learning tasks, or both, appear to be fields of choice to explore the sleep-waking behavior of cells involved in cortical integrative processes. Since interneurons are related to higher nervous activity, as suggested by their late development and their role in the formation of new neural circuits (1,4), the supposition arose, in view of their increased firing rates from W to S (6), that cortical nonoutput cells are most active during D sleep, a state hypothesized in recent years to have a role in the retention of information acquired during W (2,3). We actually revealed that, in contrast with identified corticothalamic and corticopontine cells of areas 5 and 7, which tonically increase their discharge frequencies during W and the whole state of D over rates in S, interneurons in the same association areas have lowest firing rates in W and highest rates in D, selectively occurring during phasic ocular events.

METHODS

Experiments were carried out on nine behaving cats with chronically implanted electrodes. The animals were not deprived of sleep between the recording sessions. During experiments, they reposed comfortably on a pad and could move their limbs freely, only the head being restrained by the cylindric chamber through which recordings were made. Single units were extracellularly recorded in anterior parts of marginal and suprasylvian gyri corresponding to cytoarchitectonic areas 5 and 7. Stimulating electrodes were inserted in the lateralis intermedius-lateralis posterior (LI-LP), ventralis anterior (VA), and centre median (CM) thalamic nuclei and pontine nuclei (PN) for identification of target structures and synaptic drives of neurons. We refer here to two cellular classes—output cells and interneurons. Output cells were identified by antidromic invasion (Fig. 1) from one of the subcortical nuclei (LI, LP, CM, or PN) and, in cases of neurons with branching

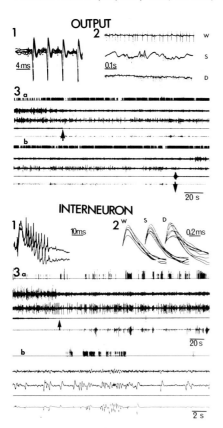

FIG. 1. Identification, discharge patterns, and firing rates during D sleep of output cells and interneurons recorded from the parietal association cortex of cat. In both cases, 1: response patterns, 2: spontaneous discharge patterns, and 3: rate changes in D sleep. The five ink-written traces in 3 represent from top to bottom: unit spikes, slow waves simultaneously recorded by the microelectrode ("focal" EEG), EEG recorded from the depth of the visual cortex, EMG, and eye movements. An output cell was antidromically activated from the centre median thalamic nucleus (1); note sustained spontaneous firing in W and D (2); 3a is separated from 3b by a nondepicted period of 140 sec; onset of D sleep in 3a and awakening in 3b are indicated by arrows; note increased firing rate during the whole D period. An interneuron was synaptically driven from the LP thalamic nucleus with a high-frequency barrage (1); note stereotyped spike bursts during W, S, and D (2); note closely REM-related firing in D sleep beginning at the arrow (3).

axons, from two stimulated sites. Nonoutput cells, putative interneurons, were differentiated from long-axoned neurons by their thalamically evoked responses consisting of high-frequency spike barrages at 200 to 800/sec (Fig. 1), similar spontaneously occurring bursts interspersed with long periods of silence, and lack of antidromic invasion from target structures of the investigated area. Differentiation of the various stages in the sleep-waking cycle was possible by monitoring surface electroencephalographic (EEG) rhythms, focal waves recorded by the microelectrode simultaneously with unit spikes in the depth of anterior suprasylvian and marginal gyri (focal EEG), pontogeniculooccipital waves recorded from the depth of the primary visual cortex, ocular movements [electrooculogram (EOG)], potentials of the neck muscles [electromyogram (EMG)], and animal behavior through a unidirectional screen. Since phasic events make D sleep a heterogenous state, we measured the mean rates of discharge not only during the whole D state, but also during REM (D+) and non-REM or poor-REM (D−) periods separately. REM epochs were determined for each analyzed unit and were considered as those periods comprising sequences of EOG deflections exceeding 0.15 mV. All D+ and D− selected epochs were longer than 5 sec. For data processing, interspike intervals were stored in an Intertechnique DIDAC 800 Analyzer and transferred by a high-speed link to an IBM 370 central computer operating in an APL/SV time-shared environment.

RESULTS AND DISCUSSION

Interneurons discharged at a significantly lower rate in all states than output cells ($p \leqslant 0.0001$, Wilcoxon unpaired signed-rank test). Rate distributions for output cells were mainly situated between 8 and 32/sec, whereas the interneuronal sample exhibited modes of 0 to 0.5/sec for all states.

The striking differences in rate were associated with very dissimilar firing patterns in output and nonoutput cells. The most distinguishing feature between these two cellular classes was the sustained discharge of output cells, especially during states with EEG activation (W and D; Fig. 1), contrasting with long silent periods of interneurons in all states of the sleep-waking cycle. The other characteristic feature differentiating these neuronal types concerned the appearance of high-frequency bursts (at least three spikes above 400/sec). The occurrence probability of such bursts was much higher in interneurons in all states ($p \leqslant 0.005$ to 0.03) (Fig. 1).

We computed mean and median rates for eight output cells and 23 interneurons that could be analyzed throughout all states and substates of the sleep-waking cycle. Output cells exhibited sample mean rates of 11.09/sec in W, 9.27/sec in S, 20.24/sec in D taken as a whole, 17.19/sec in D−, and 21.88/sec in D+. Interneurons had sample mean rates of 0.33/sec in W, 0.66/sec in S, 1.12/sec in D, 0.61/sec in D−, and 1.69/sec in D+. Data therefore showed: (a) *a decrease in rate for output cells and an increase in*

TABLE 1. *Rate change and percent rate change data for eight output cells and 23 interneurons*

State pairs	Output cells			Interneurons			$P_{MED} \leqslant$
	N	$P_R \leqslant$	MED %	N	$P_R \leqslant$	MED %	
W→S	6/8 ↓	0.15^a	−14	20/23 ↑	0.001^b	81	0.002^b
D− →D+	8/8 ↑	0.02^b	17	21/23 ↑	0.001^b	153	0.005^b
W→D−	7/8 ↑	0.03^b	48	16/23 ↓	0.15	74	>0.5
S→D−	8/8 ↑	0.02^b	97	15/23 ↓	0.15	−22	0.004^b
W→D+	8/8 ↑	0.02^b	85	20/23 ↑	0.001^b	364	0.09
S→D+	8/8 ↑	0.02^b	143	18/23 ↑	0.005^b	75	0.2
W→D	8/8 ↑	0.02^b	63	19/23 ↑	0.005^b	225	0.2
S→D	8/8 ↑	0.02^b	129	14/23 ↑	0.12	21	0.05^b

Rate changes in various state-pairs. N, fraction of cells changing rate when comparing first with second state in state-pair; P_R, significance level (Wilcoxon paired signed-rank test) of changes between states; MED, median of percent rate changes calculated for all cells (negative sign denotes decreasing rate in second state of pair); P_{MED}, significance level for comparison of percent rate changes between the two cellular classes (Wilcoxon two-sample rank test, ref. 7).
[a] For all 12 output cells available in W and S, N = 10/12 ↓, p ⩽ 0.05, MED = −14%.
[b] Significance level ⩽0.05.

rate for interneurons in S compared to W; (b) *a large increase in rate for output cells and a decrease for interneurons in D− compared to S;* (c) *a much larger percent increase in rate in D+ compared to D− for interneurons than for output cells* (Table 1).

We then calculated the percent rate change for each cell in a given state-pair, the median of these changes, and we tested for significant differences in percentage rate change between the two cellular types for the same state-pairs (Wilcoxon unpaired rank test, ref. 7). The results, also given in Table 1, show that the percentage changes in rates are significantly different between output and nonoutput cells in W→S ($p \leqslant 0.002$), S→D ($p \leqslant 0.05$), S→D− ($p \leqslant 0.004$) and D− →D+ ($p \leqslant 0.005$). Besides the opposite alterations in firing rate in W and S, which are beyond the scope of this chapter, the other striking difference between output cells and interneurons concerns the contribution of REM-related firing to the increased firing rates in D sleep, which is shown in the statistical data of Table 1 and is also illustrated in Fig. 1. It is obvious from this figure that the output cell increased firing rate in the transition from S to D and exhibited a tonically increased firing rate throughout the D state without apparent relation to REMs, whereas the interneuron discharged during D in spectacularly closed temporal relation with REM epochs and was almost silent in non-REM epochs.

To sum up, corticothalamic and corticopontine output neurons increased significantly their discharge frequencies not only from S to D+, but also from S to D−, the differences in behavior from S to D− in the two cellular samples being highly significant. This implies that output cells undergo tonic excitatory influences during D sleep taken as a whole and that REM-related firing only contributes to a further increase in rate. In contrast, the selectively REM-related discharge of interneurons makes them highly different from output cells when D— and D+ substates are compared. The possibility that such spectacularly increased unit firing during REMs, as seen in Fig. 1, is simply a consequence of eye movements, like some proprioceptive drive preferentially affecting nonoutput cells, seems precluded in view of absence of such events during eye movements occurring in W, when interneurons exhibit the lowest discharge rates. Besides, in some interneurons, increased firing preceded REMs (Fig. 1).

The above findings suggest an active role for interneurons during specific functions of D sleep. There is increasing experimental evidence supporting the idea of the beneficial effect of sleep on the retention of information acquired during W: selective deprivation of D produces a long-term memory impairment without affecting subsequent relearning, and the total duration of D is augmented following learning, due to an increase in the number of D epochs but not in the average duration of each phase (reviews 2,3). It is possible that the increased firing rates of cortical association interneurons during REM epochs of D sleep are related to the maintenance of the soundness of a memory trace. This is in line with the role in memory ascribed to interneurons, on the basis of morphological and developmental arguments (1,4). As interneurons are selectively active during REMs, we would expect that the retention of information particularly increased the duration of REM periods. Some studies indicate positive correlations between intellectual functions and the amount of REMs during D in humans (2), but the experimental studies on animals that report increased duration of D following learning were as yet not directed to dissociate REM from non-REM periods (V. Bloch and P. Leconte, *personal communication*). The next step is to test whether a conditioning paradigm is effective in increasing REM epochs during D sleep and to relate the development of a learning task to activities in cortical output cells and interneurons.

ACKNOWLEDGMENTS

This work was supported by the Medical Research Council of Canada (MT-3689) and the Ministère de l'Education du Québec.

REFERENCES

1. Altman, J. (1967): Postnatal growth and differentiation of the mammalian brain, with implications for a morphological theory of memory. In: *The Neurosciences: A Study Program,* edited by G. C. Quarton, Th. Melnechuk, and F. O. Schmitt, pp. 723–743. Rockefeller Univ. Press, New York.
2. Bloch, V., and Fischbein, W. (1975): Sleep and psychological functions: Memory. In: *Experimental Study of Human Sleep: Methodological Problems,* edited by G. C. Lairy and P. Salzarulo, pp. 157–173. Elsevier, Amsterdam.

3. Fischbein, W., and Gutwein, B. M. (1977): Paradoxical sleep and memory storage processes. *Behav. Biol.,* 19:425–464.
4. Jacobsen, M. (1969): Development of specific neuronal connections. *Science,* 163: 543–547.
5. Moruzzi, G. (1966): The functional significance of sleep with particular regard to the brain mechanisms underlying consciousness. In: *Brain and Conscious Experience,* edited by J. C. Eccles, pp. 345–379. Springer-Verlag, New York.
6. Steriade, M., Deschênes, M., and Oakson, G. (1974): Inhibitory processes and interneuronal apparatus in motor cortex during sleep and waking. I. Background and responsiveness of pyramidal tract neurons and interneurons. *J. Neurophysiol.,* 37: 1065–1092.
7. Wilcoxon, F. (1945): Individual comparisons by ranking methods. *Biometrics,* 1:80–83.

Brain Mechanisms in Memory and Learning:
From the Single Neuron to Man,
edited by M. A. B. Brazier.
Raven Press, New York © 1979.

Neurons and Memory: Some Clues

Robert W. Doty

Center for Brain Research, University of Rochester, Rochester, New York 14642

Although the shuffling of genetic codons assures that each human being is to some degree chemically unique, it is the phenomenon of memory within the brain that imparts the profound individuality of mental life. Bent to the purposes of education, whether at the breast or in the hunt or at the laboratory bench, memory provides the essential substrate for civilization. Yet the true nature of the mnemonic process remains almost as mysterious as it was for Lucretius (ca 99 to 55 B.C.). He attributed it to the mind's capture of free-floating, insubstantial traces surviving from those let loose on the world by existing or preexisting objects ("Dead men whose bones earth bosomed long ago," ref. 40)—perhaps the first wave-holographic theory of memory.

Today it is surmised that mental access to the past demands activation of neurons (although some, in apparent frustration, look to neuroglia) that have somehow altered their excitabilities or connectivity consequent to preceding events. There are actually four "mysteries": (a) the precise nature of the neuronal alteration, (b) the fact that the mnemonic storage capacity in man (65) and, perhaps, macaques (54) is effectively infinite, especially for the visual modality, (c) the speed and accuracy with which this vast store of traces is available, and (d) the degree to which the accuracy of the memory recalled can be estimated (i.e., what serves as the basis for comparison about accuracy if not the memory itself!?). Essentially nothing can be said concerning the nature of neural activity in relation to items (c) and (d). Item (a) is critical to all the others, and it is the primary focus of the present volume. I do not pretend to offer here any solution to this exceedingly difficult question, but hope instead to provide a useful framework for identifying certain distinguishing features of the mnemonic trace. Probably most important is recognition that there are at least two basically different means by which past action comes to be reflected in the performance of neurons. These differing processes produce differing forms of memory that, for brevity, I have designated "ionic" and "macromolecular" (Table 1).

The term "ionic" emphasizes the fact that transmembrane alterations in ionic concentrations or permeability affect the excitability of neurons, both directly and indirectly, by changing the resting and after-potentials, metabolism, availability of transmitter, etc. The prototype of such a mnemonic

TABLE 1. *Distinguishing characteristics of ionic versus macromolecular mnemonic processes*

	Ionic	Macromolecular
Prototype	Posttetanic potentiation	Conditioned reflex
Duration	Temporary	Permanent
Time relation[a]	Neurophysiological	Temporal paradox
Pathway	Limited to activated neurons	Stimulus generalization
Participating neurons	All, to varying degrees	Perhaps most prominent in specialized types

[a] See text.

process is posttetanic potentiation (PTP) (5a,23,39,62), but similar processes probably apply in other central facilitatory and refractory states (e.g., ref. 12), in the dominant focus (59), and in most instances of habituation. Although it is characteristic of these effects that they are temporary, their duration of minutes to days makes them unequivocally relevant to mnemonic phenomena. A number of studies show, for instance, that moderate stimulation of various neuronal systems in the hippocampus can produce a state of PTP lasting several hours or days (6,8,22,67,69), and these changes in excitability may be reflected in the morphology of dendritic spines for a comparable period of time (24). In a more natural situation, using the crossed phrenic phenomenon in dogs, potentiation commonly lasted 1 to 2 days, and in two animals lasted for 13 and 31 days (3). Persisting potentiation probably also underlies DiGiorgio's phenomenon (e.g., 11a,11b) in which postural asymmetry, induced by unilateral lesions of vestibular nuclei or cerebellum, survives for several hours after transection of the spinal cord. The asymmetry must endure for the order of 45 min in rats (9,29) prior to transection of the cord and requires the presence of the sensorimotor cortex during this "fixation" period (C. Giurgea, *personal communication;* but see 11b). Although the time for fixation may seem unduly long to be accounted for by PTP, such a time course can tentatively be ascribed either to some unknown characteristic of corticospinal effects or to the fact that physiologically generated activity is not nearly so intense, and hence not so effective, in generating potentiation as is the electrical tetanization commonly used for establishing PTP.

These principles probably also apply to several psychophysically measured, adaptive effects that appear to be good candidates for explanation on the basis of ionic memory. Among these are the maintenance of binocular depth perception, for if one eye is covered in man for as little as 24 hr, there is a significant decrease in the ability to estimate depth (70). In viewing random-dot stereograms, some practice is required before the patterns are perceived stereoscopically immediately on viewing them (58). Capacity for immediate stereoscopic fusion can be achieved by practice over a period of minutes or over several days (57), and the effect is specific to a given retinal location or orientation of the stimuli. A similar time course and specificity to the stimulated components are found for the McCollough effect (32), in which prolonged viewing of colored patterns produces aftereffects persisting for hours or days (32,42,43,63).

In contrast, the term "macromolecular" has been chosen to suggest that permanent memory traces involve an immunochemical process by which the effectiveness of particular neuronal interconnections is controlled. Such speculation has a certain appeal, for the mnemonic process then becomes analogous to those controlling the initial, embryonic selections of neural connectivity. In any event, there is a striking difference between the neurophysiological situation in PTP and that for conditioned reflexes (CRs) or associative learning (13,14, Table 1). For PTP it is the antecedent event (e.g., tetanization), the conditioning stimulus in neurophysiology, that alters the response to subsequent stimuli; whereas for establishing a CR, the conditional stimulus (CS) remains wholly ineffective unless a subsequent event, the unconditional stimulus (US), occurs. In other words, it is the subsequent event, the US, that changes the response to stimuli that precede it. It is surprising how often this fundamental and instructive peculiarity, the "temporal paradox" of CRs, is overlooked by those proposing explanations of the mnemonic process.

The temporal paradox suggests that after their activation by the CS certain neural components remain for a time susceptible to influence from subsequent activity arising in neighboring channels that, if it occurs, imparts to the previously activated components a permanent change in their effectiveness. This also implies that even prior to conditioning, the channels activated by CS and US must at some point impinge on or share to some degree the same neural entities. This requirement for preexisting overlap seems to impose a number of serious restrictions. First, the spontaneous, background discharge in the system must be extremely low, otherwise an inadmissable number of chance concatenations would occur. Second, conditioning would either be limited to a small number of possible channels, as is perhaps the case with nervous systems comprised of a relatively small number of neurons, or would require an extraordinarily profuse interconnectivity to assure the potential for concatenation of any possible combination of stimuli. Perhaps this latter possibility accounts for the wide degree of stimulus generalization found with certain CRs (e.g., 19). Finally, the greater part of human memory seems to be formed without a clear associative component, i.e., no US is identifiable, as would be needed were the temporal paradox and neuronal overlap an essential part of the macromolecular mnemonic process. However, this seeming lack of a US may be deceptive, since essentially all human memories are associative in that they are fixed in a coordinate system as to time and place. In other words, the subsequent fixating stimulus is here being continually provided by whatever system it is that registers the orientation of the individual in space and time. There is increasing reason to believe the hippocampus is involved in such spatial analysis (51,52), and this might offer, at last, some explanation for its seemingly critical role (55) in human memory. It has already been demonstrated (16) that simple temporal sequencing of stimuli, even those lacking a demonstrable motivational component, is sufficient for the establishment of enduring CRs.

The permanency of many forms of memory is extraordinary. A few years ago I visited for the first time in 40 years a town of about 20,000 population where I had spent the eighth year of my life. I drove unerringly through the center of town and about 1 km off into the side streets to arrive at my former home—garage, willow tree, sunken garden, all still extant, as pictured vividly in my mind's eye. More rigorous accounts of detailed recall are readily available (34,41,64). What is not generally appreciated, however, is the rapidity with which permanent mnemonic traces can be created. As few as two 4-sec episodes, consisting of a brief aversive experience (electric shock) and a 4-sec delay prior to onset of an electroconvulsive seizure, are sufficient for effective registration of those aversive experiences (37). After a single episode, i.e., punishment followed 4 sec later by seizure, the animal behaves as though it were entirely oblivious to the aversive nature of the situation, and one might easily conclude that all memory for it had been erased by the ensuing convulsion. The second occurrence, however, reveals that an incipient trace has survived and that, even as much as 2 weeks later, it can be effectively amalgamated with a second, equally truncated, trace (37). The experiments of Baldwin and Sołtysik (5) show that even complete interruption of the cerebral circulation does not extinguish memory traces formed just a few seconds earlier.

Such data suggest that the distinction often made between short-term and long-term memory is not applicable to the mnemonic process itself, but rather to some aspect in the effective retrieval of the trace. This is further indicated by such phenomena as transient global amnesia (25,26) or the gradual clearing of the retrograde amnesia that follows cerebral concussion (60). Obviously, in these instances the memory trace is not destroyed; it is simply inaccessible, as may be so-called short-term memory after similar traumatic occurrences. Additional evidence of confusion in the concept of short-term memory is found in research on "delayed-matching-to-sample" (DMS), a task in which an animal, e.g., a monkey, is shown a picture (the "sample") and then, following some delay, must select ("match") from a pair of pictures the one previously shown. Something of a world record was achieved by Mello (45) when, after months of training, some of her macaques could effect a correct match with a delay approaching 4 min. Most of her predecessors measured the monkeys' retention periods in seconds, and this was thus short-term memory. However, by making a slight change in the procedure, presenting the monkey with different sets of pictures for each trial rather than the same pictures over and over again, we found macaques could readily retain the sample for 1 to 4 days, and it has not been feasible to test longer intervals (54).

With such suspicions concerning the validity of the concept of short-term memory, it does not seem appropriate to suggest that in certain instances ionic memory represents a transitory phase in the process of developing a permanent, long-term macromolecular memory. However, some interaction between these two modes in neuronal retention of past events must be anticipated since there is, obviously, an ionic step in the neural activity postulated to lead to macromolecular memory. Equally uncertain is how to classify the now numerous demonstrations of "learning" by invertebrate preparations (see E. Kandel, *this volume,* and 1,2,7,10,11,27,31,46,68), or the important observations on modification of the vestibuloocular reflex (e.g., 30,47,48). The cerebellar-inferior olivary system appears to be critical to this and a number of other adaptive, compensatory motor performances (4,30,36,38). The cerebellar system is particularly interesting in relation to the proposals advanced herein because the climbing fiber input seems to be specifically augmented during a period of motor learning that, in turn, results in an altered firing of certain Purkinje cells in relation to the learned response (28). The powerful climbing fiber action could be ideally suited to serve as the subsequent stimulus in regard to the temporal paradox in the formation of macromolecular memory. There is, however, a very high level of continuing discharge present in Purkinje cells, and the most consistent relevant increase in climbing fiber action may occur too early to serve this role (28). Although modification of the vestibuloocular reflex can survive for a very impressive period of time, 2 weeks, in the absence of contravening experience (48), some doubt must still remain about whether this degree of permanency reflects macromolecular processes or whether some form of ionic memory might be involved (whatever these terms may mean in this context). The absence of stimulus generalization (47) also to some degree suggests an ionic mechanism.

Among the intriguing questions concerning neurons and memory is whether higher organisms have evolved specialized cell types to facilitate the storage and retrieval processes (15) or whether, instead, these processes reflect merely a sophistication of neuronal circuitry relatively independent of neuronal shape or accoutrement. Certainly ionic memory must be present in all neurons, albeit with much greater elicitability and duration in some types than others as, for instance, in the hippocampus (6,8,22,67,69). In cephalopods there do appear to be areas of the brain quite specifically involved with memory (see 46). The same seems to be true for vertebrates wherein the postoptic (35,71) or supraoptic (44, N. O'Connell, *unpublished observations*) decussation in fish and birds, respectively, is involved with interhemispheric mnemonic transfer, whereas other commissural systems do

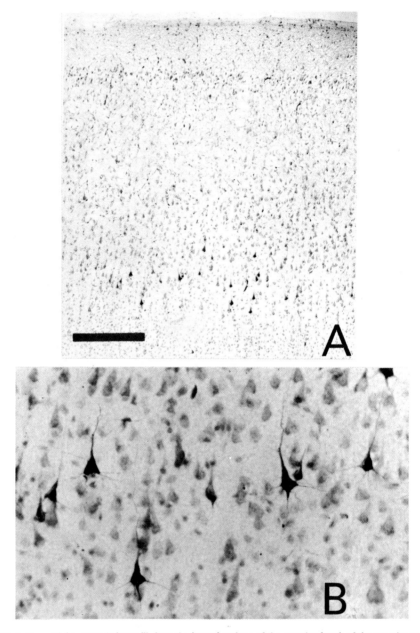

FIG. 1. Pyramidal neurons in layer III, from the lateral surface of the anterior fourth of the superior temporal gyrus, *Macaca fascicularis*, that have taken up horseradish peroxidase (HRP) after it was applied to the cut surface of the anterior commissure 36 hr prior to perfusion of the brain. The HRP in 50% concentration was held in a small piece of tubing stuffed with cottonoid, thus slowing its intraventricular diffusion. The monkey was kept anesthetized with allobarbital (Dial ®). Population of neurons shown here is somewhat more dense than usual. Labeled neurons were confined to layer III and were found only in sharply delimited areas. Calibration: A: 200 μm; B: 50 μm.

not seem capable of operating in this regard.[1] Although the cerebral cortex in mammals has long been considered the most likely site for registration of the changes essential to performance of a CR, recent data refute this in both cats and rabbits (49,50,61). Indeed, CRs established with neocortex intact survive its removal (50,61). Although evidence suggests an important role for the basal ganglia in this regard (e.g., 56), eyeblink CRs can be established in cats in the absence of both neocortex and basal ganglia (49). Some question may still remain, however, about whether CRs in the latter preparation would survive for a period of weeks without intervening training, i.e., whether they actually involve macromolecular memory even if the temporal paradox seems to be present.

In macaques we have shown that the anterior commissure has important access to mnemonic processing. Not only is it capable of providing information from one hemisphere to induce an engram in the other (17,20,66), but also its tetanization precludes both the acquisition and performance of CRs in either a simple lever-press on signal or in the DMS task (18,21,53). This interference with mnemonic performance is strictly phasic, i.e., it clears abruptly on cessation of tetanization and is thus unlike the interference seen within the same experiments on tetanization of the hippocampus, which commonly gives evidence of sustained electrical afterdischarge in such circumstance.

There is thus a basis for speculating that the neurons giving rise to the anterior commissure (Fig. 1) actually possess some special property in relation to memory although, of course, it may also be that they merely lie in an important "mnemonic path." In any event, they are rather sparsely distributed pyramidal cells in layer III (Fig. 1) of the rostral temporal area, which Zeki (72) found also to be their major area of projection. It is this area, the projection zone of the anterior commissure, that Horel and Misantone (33) have intersected to produce a total absence of visual learning in macaques, thereby reopening the question whether it actually is hippocampal rather than temporal lobe loss (55) that produces such profound mnemonic disturbance in man. It is possible that such experiments are pointing toward neurons that are specialized in the development of macromolecular memory.

SUMMARY

It is proposed that there are at least two distinguishably different mnemonic processes—ionic and macromolecular (Table 1). All neurons, in varying degree, display ionic memory, which is merely a consequence of their activa-

---

[1] In work still being pursued in this laboratory, however, N. O'Connell finds that if the supraoptic decussation is transected in newly hatched chicks, subsequent interocular transfer of a learned color discrimination is still possible; whereas if the transection is performed at 2 weeks of age, prior to training, there is no transfer. If it is cut after training, there is transfer.

tion. Such mnemonic effect is temporary, tends to be limited to the activated pathway, and probably underlies a rather large number of behavioral-psychophysical phenomena, such as habituation, dominant focus, McCollough effect, etc. Macromolecular memory, on the other hand, is permanent, can be substantially established in unerasable form within a few seconds, displays the temporal paradox of CRs in that it is the response to an antecedent neural event that ultimately becomes altered by subsequently occurring activity and it may be elicited over pathways not previously activated. It seems possible that macromolecular memory requires a significant degree of cellular specialization. The anterior commissure in macaques has been demonstrated to have exceptionally powerful access to some mnemonic system, and the neurons that give rise to this commissural pathway are herein identified as pyramidal cells in layer III of the rostral temporal cortex (Fig. 1).

ACKNOWLEDGMENT

Supported by Grant NS03606 from the National Institute of Neurological and Communicative Disorders and Stroke, National Institutes of Health. I am grateful to Dr. Manuel delCerro for assistance with the photomicrography and to Dr. William H. Overman and Nancy A. O'Connell for their contribution of work still unpublished.

REFERENCES

1. Alkon, D. L. (1975): Neural correlates of associative training in *Hermissenda*. *J. Gen. Physiol.*, 65:46–56.
2. Alloway, T. M., and Routtenberg, A. (1967): "Reminiscence" in the cold flour beetle (*Tenebrio molitor*). *Science*, 158:1066–1067.
3. Aserinsky, E. (1961): Effects of usage of a dormant respiratory nerve pathway upon its subsequent activity. *Exp. Neurol.*, 3:467–475.
4. Baizer, J. S., and Glickstein, M. (1974): Role of cerebellum in prism adaptation. *J. Physiol. (Lond.)*, 236:34p–35p.
5. Baldwin, B. A., and Sołtysik, S. S. (1969): Studies on the nature of recent memory. *Acta Neurobiol. Exp. (Warsz.)*, 29:293–318.
5a. Birks, R. I. (1977): A long-lasting potentiation of transmitter release related to an increase in transmitter stores in a sympathetic ganglion. *J. Physiol. (Lond.)*, 271:847–862.
6. Bliss, T. V. P., and Gardner-Medwin, A. R. (1973): Long-lasting potentiation of synaptic transmission in the dentate area of the unanaesthetized rabbit following stimulation of the perforant path. *J. Physiol. (Lond.)*, 232:357–374.
7. Borsellino, A., Pierantoni, R., and Schieti-Cavazza, B. (1970): Survival in adult mealworm beetles (*Tenebrio molitor*) of learning acquired at the larval stage. *Nature*, 225:963–965.
8. Bragin, A. G., Zhadina, S. D., Vinogradova, O. S., and Kozhechkin, S. N. (1977): Topography and some characteristics of the dentate fascia-field CA$_3$ relations investigated in hippocampal slices *in vitro*. *Brain Res.*, 135:55–66.
9. Chamberlain, T. J., Halick, P., and Gerard, R. W. (1963): Fixation of experience in the rat spinal cord. *J. Neurophysiol.*, 26:662–673.
0. Croll, R. P., and Chase, R. (1977): A long-term memory for food odors in the land snail, *Achatina fulica*. *Behav. Biol.*, 19:261–268.

11. Davidovich, A., Muñoz, M., and Luco, J. V. (1975): Modification of synaptic efficiency. Experiments in *Blatta orientalis*. *Acta Physiol. Lat. Am.*, 25:33–36.
11a. DiGiorgio, A. M. (1929): Peristenza, nell' animale spinale, di assimmetrie posturali e motorie di origine cerebellare. Nota 1, II e III. *Arch. Fisiol.*, 27: 519–580.
11b. DiGiorgio, A. M. (1943): Richerche sulla persistenza dei fenomeni cerebellari nell' animale spinale. *Arch. Fisiol.*, 43:47–63.
12. Doty, R. W. (1951): Influence of stimulus pattern on reflex deglutition. *Am. J. Physiol.*, 166:142–158.
13. Doty, R. W. (1961): General discussion. In: *Brain Mechanisms and Learning*, edited by A. Fessard, R. W. Gerard, J. Konorski, and J. F. Delafresnaye, p. 659. Blackwell, Oxford.
14. Doty, R. W. (1969): Electrical stimulation of the brain in behavioral context. *Ann. Rev. Psychol.*, 20:289–320.
15. Doty, R. W. (1975): Are there neurons specialized for memory? In: *Brain Mechanisms*, edited by T. N. Oniani, pp. 51–63. Metsniereba, Tbilisi. (In English, with summary in Russian.)
16. Doty, R. W., and Giurgea, C. (1961): Conditioned reflexes established by coupling electrical excitation of two cortical areas. In: *Brain Mechanisms and Learning*, edited by A. Fessard, R. W. Gerard, J. Konorski, and J. Delafresnaye, pp. 133–151. Blackwell, London.
17. Doty, R. W., and Negrão, N. (1973): Forebrain commissures and vision. In: *Handbook of Sensory Physiology*, edited by R. Jung, pp. 543–582. Springer-Verlag, Berlin.
18. Doty, R. W., and Overman, W. H., Jr. (1977): Mnemonic role of forebrain commissures in macaques. In: *Lateralization in the Nervous System*, edited by S. Harnad, R. W. Doty, J. Jaynes, L. Goldstein, and G. Krauthamer, pp. 75–88. Academic Press, New York.
19. Doty, R. W., and Rutledge, L. T. (1959): "Generalization" between cortically and peripherally applied stimuli eliciting conditioned reflexes. *J. Neurophysiol.*, 22:428–435.
20. Doty, R. W., Negrão, N., and Yamaga, K. (1973): The unilateral engram. *Acta Neurobiol. Exp. (Warsz.)*, 33:711–728.
21. Doty, R. W., Overman, W. H., Jr., and Negrão, N. (1978): Role of forebrain commissures in hemispheric specialization and memory in macaques. In: *Structure and Function of the Cerebral Commissures*, edited by I. S. Russell, M. W. van Hof, and G. Berlucchi. MacMillan, London. (*In press*).
22. Douglas, R. McK. (1977): Long lasting synaptic potentiation in the rat dentate gyrus following brief high frequency stimulation. *Brain Res.*, 126:361–365.
23. Eccles, J. C., and Rall, W. (1951): Effects induced in a monosynaptic path by its activation. *J. Neurophysiol.*, 14:353–376.
24. Fifkova, E., and van Harreveld, A. (1977): Long-lasting morphological changes in dendritic spines of dentate granular cells following stimulation of the entorhinal area. *J. Neurocytol.*, 6:211–230.
25. Flügel, K. A. (1975): Transitorische globale Amnesie—ein paroxysmales amnestisches Syndrom. *Fortschr. Neurol. Psychiatr.*, 43:471–485.
26. Fogelholm, R., Kivalo, E., and Bergström, L. (1975): The transient global amnesia syndrome. *Eur. Neurol.*, 13:72–84.
27. Gelperin, A. (1975): Rapid food-aversion learning by a terrestrial mollusk. *Science*, 189:567–570.
28. Gilbert, P. F. C., and Thach, W. T. (1977): Purkinje cell activity during motor learning. *Brain Res.*, 128:309–328.
29. Giurgea, C., and Mouravieff-Lesuisse, F. (1971): Pharmacological studies on an elementary model of learning—the fixation of an experience at spinal level: Part 1: Pharmacological reactivity of the spinal cord fixation time. *Arch. Int. Pharmacodyn. Ther.*, 191:279–291.
30. Haddad, G. M., Friendlich, A. R., and Robinson, D. A. (1977): Compensation of nystagmus after VIIIth nerve lesions in vestibulocerebellectomized cats. *Brain Res.*, 135:192–196.

31. Haralson, J. V., Groff, C. I., and Haralson, S. J., (1975): Classical conditioning in the sea anemone, *Cribrina xanthogrammica*. *Physiol. Behav.,* 15:455–460.
32. Holding, D. H., and Jones, P. D. (1976): Delayed one-trial extinction of the McCollough effect. *Q. J. Exp. Psychol.,* 28:683–687.
33. Horel, J. A., and Misantone, L. J. (1976): Visual discrimination impaired by cutting temporal lobe connections. *Science,* 193:336–338.
34. Hunter, I. M. L. (1977): An exceptional memory. *Br. J. Psychol.,* 68:155–164.
35. Ingle, D., and Campbell, A. (1977): Interocular transfer of visual discriminations in goldfish after selective commissure lesions. *J. Comp. Physiol. Psychol.,* 91: 327–335.
36. Ito, M., Shiida, T., Yagi, N., and Yamamoto, M. (1974): The cerebellar modification of rabbit's horizontal vestibulo-ocular reflex induced by sustained head rotation combined with visual stimulation. *Proc. Jpn. Acad.,* 50:85–89.
37. Kesner, R. P., McDonough, J. J., Jr., and Doty, R. W. (1970): Diminished amnestic effect of a second electroconvulsive seizure. *Exp. Neurol.,* 27:527–533.
38. Llinás, R., Walton, K., Hillman, D. E., and Sotelo, C. (1975): Inferior olive: Its role in motor learning. *Science,* 190:1230–1231.
39. Lloyd, D. P. C. (1949): Post-tetanic potentiation of response in monosynaptic reflex pathways of the spinal cord. *J. Gen. Physiol.,* 33:147–170.
40. Lucretius (ca 55 B.C.) (1957): *Of the Nature of Things,* translated by W. E. Leonard, p. 300. Dutton, New York.
41. Luria, A. R. (1968): *The Mind of a Mnemonist. A Little Book about a Vast Memory,* translated by L. Solotaroff, p. 160. Basic Books, New York.
42. MacKay, D. M., and MacKay, V. (1975): Dichoptic induction of McCollough-type effects. *Q. J. Exp. Psychol.,* 27:225–233.
43. MacKay, D. M., and MacKay, V. (1977): Retention of the McCollough effect in darkness: Storage or enhanced read-out? *Vision Res.,* 17:313–315.
44. Meier, R. E. (1971): Interhemisphärischer Transfer visueller Zweifachwahlen bei kommissurotomierten Tauben. *Psychol. Forsch.,* 34:220–245.
45. Mello, N. K. (1971): Alcohol effects on delayed matching to sample performance by Rhesus monkey. *Physiol. Behav.,* 7:77–101.
46. Messenger, J. B. (1973): Learning performance and brain structure: A study in development. *Brain Res.,* 58:519–523.
47. Miles, F. A., Braitman, D. J., and Eighmy, B. B. (1977): Vestibulo-ocular responses in the Rhesus monkey following prolonged optical reversal of vision. *Neurosci. Abstr.,* 3:545.
48. Miles, F. A., and Fuller, J. H. (1974): Adaptive plasticity in the vestibulo-ocular responses of the Rhesus monkey. *Brain Res.,* 80:512–516.
49. Norman, R. J., Villablanca, J. R., Brown, K. A., Schwafel, J. A., and Buchwald, J. S. (1974): Classical eyeblink conditioning in the bilaterally hemispherectomized cat. *Exp. Neurol.,* 44:363–380.
50. Oakley, D. A., and Russell, I. S. (1977): Subcortical storage of Pavlovian conditioning in the rabbit. *Physiol. Behav.,* 18:931–937.
51. O'Keefe, J. (1976): Place units in the hippocampus of the freely moving rat. *Exp. Neurol.,* 51:78–109.
52. Olton, D. S. (1977): Spatial memory. *Sci. Am.,* 236:82–98.
53. Overman, W. H., Jr., and Doty, R. W. (1977): Mnemonic disturbance in macaques from stimulation of anterior commissure versus limbic system or basal ganglia. *Neurosci. Abstr.,* 3:238.
54. Overman, W. H., Jr., and Doty, R. W. (1978): Visual memory in macaques versus man. *(In preparation).*
55. Penfield, W., and Mathieson, G. (1974): Memory. Autopsy findings and comments on the role of hippocampus in experiential recall. *Arch. Neurol.,* 31:145–154.
56. Prado-Alcalá, R. A., Grinberg, Z. J., Arditti, Z. L., García, M. M., Prieto, H. G., and Brust-Carmona, H. (1975): Learning deficits produced by chronic and reversible lesions of the corpus striatum in rats. *Physiol. Behav.,* 15:283–287.
57. Ramachandran, V. S. (1976): Learning-like phenomena in stereopsis. *Nature,* 262:382–384.

58. Ramachandran, V. S., and Braddick, O. (1973): Orientation-specific learning in stereopsis. *Perception,* 2:371–376.
59. Rusinov, V. S. (1973): *The Dominant Focus: Electrophysiological Investigations,* translated by B. Haigh, translation editor R. W. Doty, 220 pp. Consultants Bureau, New York.
60. Russell, W. R. (1959): *Brain Memory Learning: A Neurologist's View,* p. 140. Oxford Univ. Press (Clarendon), London and New York.
61. Russell, I. S., Kleinman, D., Plotkin, H. C., and Ross, R. B. (1969): The role of the cortex in acquisition and retention of a clasically conditioned passive avoidance response. *Physiol. Behav.,* 4:575–581.
62. Schulman, J. A., and Weight, F. F. (1976): Synaptic transmission: Long-lasting potentiation by a postsynaptic mechanism. *Science,* 194:1437–1439.
63. Skowbo, D., Gentry, T., Timney, B., and Morant, R. B. (1974): The McCollough effect: Influence of several kinds of visual stimulation on decay rate. *Perception and Psychophysics,* 16:47–49.
64. Smith, M. E. (1963): Delayed recall of previously memorized material after fifty years. *J. Genet. Psychol.,* 102:3–4.
65. Standing, L. (1973): Learning 10,000 pictures. *Q. J. Exp. Psychol.,* 25:207–222.
66. Sullivan, M. V., and Hamilton, C. R. (1973): Memory establishment via the anterior commissure of monkeys. *Physiol. Behav.,* 11:873–879.
67. Teyler, T. J., Alber, B. E., Bergman, T., and Livingston, K. (1977): A comparison of long-term potentiation in the *in vitro* and *in vivo* hippocampal preparations. *Behav. Biol.,* 19:24–34.
68. Tosney, T., and Hoyle, G. (1977): Computer-controlled learning in a simple system. *Proc. R. Soc. Lond. [Biol.],* 195:365–393.
69. Voronin, L. L. (1976): Cellular mechanisms of conditioned activity. *Zh. visshei nerv. deyatel'nosti,* 26:705–719. (In Russian.)
70. Wallach, H., and Karsh, E. B. (1963): Why the modification of stereoscopic depth-perception is so rapid. *Am. J. Psychol.,* 76:413–420.
71. Yeo, C. H., and Savage, G. E. (1976): Mesencephalic and diencephalic commissures and interocular transfer in the goldfish. *Exp. Neurol.,* 53:51–63.
72. Zeki, S. M. (1973): Comparison of the cortical degeneration in the visual regions of the temporal lobe of the monkey following section of the anterior commissure and the splenium. *J. Comp. Neurol.,* 148:167–176.

Brain Mechanisms in Memory and Learning:
From the Single Neuron to Man,
edited by M. A. B. Brazier.
Raven Press, New York © 1979.

Plastic and Dynamic Properties of Red Nucleus Neurons: A Physiological Study

Nakaakira Tsukahara

Department of Biophysical Engineering, Faculty of Engineering Science, Osaka University, Toyonaka, Osaka, Japan

It has long been suggested that the neural networks in the central nervous system (CNS) have an ability to store information in either short- or long-term range. This suggestion has been mainly based on the behavioral analysis of several species of animals. However, there is yet no detailed experimental evidence demonstrating the nature of the underlying neuronal mechanisms of learning and memory in CNS.

In approaching this problem, it is desirable to establish to what extent the neuronal networks undergo plastic changes in response to various kinds of environmental changes of the organism, even if these environmental changes are not directly related to behavioral learning and memory. We, therefore, attempted to analyze the possible plastic changes of corticorubral synapses in red nucleus (RN) neurons of adult cats in order to gain some insight into the neuronal mechanisms of plasticity in CNS. In this chapter, the synapto-genesis or sprouting of corticorubral synapses, after lesion of the nucleus interpositus (IP) of the cerebellum or after cross-innervation of the peripheral flexor and extensor nerves, are dealt with. Furthermore, a dynamic change of the neuronal excitability in RN neurons produced by impulse reverberation along the cerebelloreticular excitatory loops is presented.

SYNAPTIC PLASTICITY OF THE RED NUCLEUS NEURONS

In studying the problem of synaptic plasticity, RN neurons provide an excellent substrate, having unique and useful features of synaptic organization. They receive two kinds of synaptic inputs, one from the IP nucleus of the cerebellum on the somatic portion of RN cells and the other from the sensorimotor (SM) cortex on the distal dendrites (1). This synaptic organization characterizes several features of the postsynaptic potentials produced by these synaptic actions (14).

Taking advantage of this synaptic organization and the characteristics of the postsynaptic potentials, we have shown that the time to peak of the corticorubral excitatory postsynaptic potentials (EPSPs) in RN neurons induced from the SM cortex or their pathway at the cerebral peduncle (CP) became shorter two or more weeks after lesion of the IP nucleus, as illustrated in Fig. 1 (11–13). This result was taken to indicate that new and effective synapses formed at the proximal portion of the somadendritic membrane of RN neurons after IP lesion. This interpretation is based on the simplified assumption that the cable properties of dendrites of RN neurons have not changed drastically after IP lesions, a supposition that was tested experimentally and evaluated theoretically using Rall's compartment model (6,7). It was found that the observed slight change of the electrotonic length of RN neurons after IP lesion accounted for only a minor portion (less than 5%) of the observed decrease of the time to peak of the corticorubral EPSPs (13). Thus the major part of the change of the time to peak of the corticorubral EPSPs was interpreted as resulting from sprouting of the corticorubral fibers on the proximal portion of RN neurons. The subsequent electron microscopic study by Nakamura et al. (5) confirms this conclusion. Physiological studies by Murakami et al. (2,3) of the corticorubral unitary EPSPs

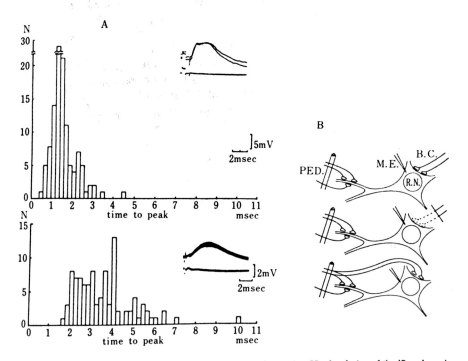

FIG. 1. Rise time of the corticorubral EPSPs induced by stimulating the CP after lesion of the IP nucleus. A: Frequency distribution of the time to peak of the CP-EPSPs in operated cats (*upper histogram*) and in normal cats (*lower histogram*). Specimen records of the intracellular and corresponding extracellular records are shown in the inset of each histogram. B: Diagram of the experimental arrangement. R.N., red nucleus neuron; B.C., input from IP through brachium conjunctivum; PED., input from cerebrum through CP; M.E., microelectrode. (Modified from Tsukahara et al., ref. 13.)

also support this by showing that two groups of the unitary EPSPs were recorded in cats with IP lesion; one is the corticorubral EPSPs with shorter time to peak and larger amplitude than in normal cats and the other is the unitary EPSPs of normal range (2,3).

The transfer characteristics of the newly formed corticorubral synapses showed the facilitation and posttetanic potentiation of normal corticorubral synapses. However, some quantitative difference between the newly formed and the normal synapses was found in the degree of facilitation and posttetanic potentiation (4).

Similar change in the time to peak of the corticorubral EPSPs was also found in cats whose flexor and extensor forelimb nerve were cross-innervated (8). For cross-innervation, the musculocutaneous, median, radial, and ulnar nerves were sectioned at the axillary region, and central stumps of the musculocutaneous, median, and ulnar nerves were united to the peripheral stump of the radial nerve by suturing the nerve sheath. In a similar procedure, the central stump of the radial nerve was united to the peripheral stumps of the musculocutaneous, median, and ulnar nerves. After a postoperative period varying from 2 to 6 months, the cats were prepared for intracellular recording from RN neurons contralateral to the cross-innervated muscles. It was found that the time to peak of the corticorubral EPSPs induced from the CP became shorter in chronic cross-innervated cats 2 to 6 months after operation than that of normal cats. This change is predominantly observed in RN cells innervating the upper spinal segments.

Experiments were also performed in cats with self-union of the forelimb nerves. For self-union of the forelimb nerves, above-mentioned forelimb nerves were sectioned and reunited without crossing by suturing the nerve sheath. The majority of CP-EPSPs of RN neurons had a time to peak in normal range, although in some cells, fast-rising EPSPs were also found.

The most attractive interpretation of these results is that new synapses were formed at the proximal portion of RN cells from corticorubral fibers, as in the case of IP lesion. In order to further substantiate this interpretation, a continuous exploration is still going on in our laboratory.

DYNAMICS OF THE REVERBERATING CIRCUIT

It has been well known that there are mutual connections between the cerebellar nuclei and the precerebellar reticular nuclei, such as the paramedian reticular nucleus, the nucleus reticularis tegmenti pontis, or the lateral reticular nucleus. It has also been established that these connections are mutually excitatory (1). Thus, a suggestion has been made that these connections represent reverberating circuits, which have long been postulated as the neuronal mechanism of the short-term memory as a dynamic circulation of neural signals. However, no clear demonstration of these reverberatory activities in the mammalian CNS has yet substantiated this postulate.

If the mutually excitatory connections actually constitute reverberating circuits, one would expect long-lasting depolarization and repetitive impulse discharges of the constituent neurons when one of these inputs is stimulated. However, the inhibitory action of Purkinje cells of the cerebellum, which act on the cerebellar nuclei, would prevent the reverberation of impulses.

Then, a question arises whether it is possible to demonstrate reverberatory activities of cerebellonuclear neurons if the Purkinje cell inhibition is eliminated experimentally. Since the IP nucleus innervates the RN neurons monosynaptically, it may also be possible to produce the reverberatory activities in RN neurons. If so, this provides a useful model with which to further analyze dynamic properties of the reverberating circuit. Therefore, an attempt was made to demonstrate impulse reverberation by eliminating the cerebellar cortical influences using (a) the pharmacological action of picrotoxin, which blocks the Purkinje cell inhibition, and (b) ablation of the cerebellar cortex (9,10).

Figure 2 illustrates the transmembrane potential changes of RN cells induced by stimulation of the ventrolateral nucleus of the thalamus, of brachium pontis, and of nucleus reticularis tegmenti pontis. After ventrolateral nucleus stimulation (Fig. 2B), a prominent depolarization could be produced after picrotoxin injection. Similar prolonged depolarization of RN

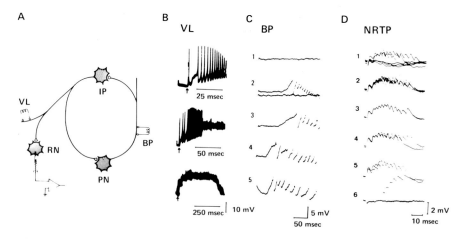

FIG. 2. A: Diagram of the experimental arrangement for study of the reverberating circuit between the IP nucleus and the precerebellar nuclei (PN). Stimulation was applied to the ventrolateral nucleus of the thalamus (VL), brachium pontis (BP), and nucleus reticularis tegmenti pontis (NRTP). B: Intracellular recording from a RN cell. A prolonged depolarization induced by a single shock to VL after picrotoxin injection. C: Picrotoxin-assisted depolarization of a RN cell evoked by BP stimulation of increasing stimulus intensities of 2, 2.8, 3, 4, and 5 V, respectively, from top to bottom. D: A prolonged depolarization elicited in a RN cell in a cat with chronic ablation of the intermediate cerebellar cortex by stimulating the NRTP. In this cat, the cerebral sensorimotor cortex was ablated chronically in addition to the ablation of the cerebellar cortex. The stimulus intensities to NRTP increased from top to bottom. The bottom trace of D indicates the extracellular field potential.

cells could also be produced in cats with chronic ablation of the cerebellar cortex as shown in Fig. 2D.

In order to exclude the possibility that the prolonged depolarization was produced by some loops via the spinal cord or the cerebral cortex, section of the spinal cord or ablation of the cerebral SM cortex was performed. These procedures did not abolish the prolonged depolarization.

The prolonged depolarization has a kind of threshold. Figure 2C shows the record of the depolarization by changing the stimulus intensities. At stimulus intensities of 2.8 V (Fig. 2C-2), the depolarization appeared in an all-or-none manner as noted in two traces with the same stimulus intensity. With further increase of stimulus intensity, the onset of the picrotoxin-assisted depolarization shortened. In addition, the rising time-course of the slow depolarization became faster as in Fig. 2C-4 and 2C-5 as compared to the traces in Fig. 2C-2 and 2C-3. These features of the prolonged depolarization could satisfactorily be reproduced by a mathematical model simulating the reverberating circuit (10). Indeed, the regenerative property with threshold phenomenon shown in Fig. 2C and D would be an important property of positive feedback systems. Because they have this property, we suggest that some of the mutual excitatory connections via the IP nucleus are reverberating circuits.

By this view, the postulated reverberating circuit can transform a millisecond electrical activity into neuronal firing lasting for several hundreds of milliseconds. It is tempting to suppose that these circuits in general act as a short-term memory storage, as has long been postulated. However, whether or not the reverberatory activities are related to real memory processes remains an open question. Similarly, the ability, postulated here, of central neurons in adult mammals to form new connections and synapses in various experimental conditions would be an important basis for understanding the neuronal mechanisms of long-term memory. It is hoped that these studies provide some insight into the brain mechanisms of learning and memory.

REFERENCES

1. Allen, G. I., and Tsukahara, N. (1974): Cerebrocerebellar communication systems. *Physiol. Rev.,* 54:957–1006.
2. Murakami, F., Fujito, Y., and Tsukahara, N. (1976): Physiological properties of the newly formed cortico-rubral synapses of red nucleus neurons due to collateral sprouting. *Brain Res.,* 103:147–151.
3. Murakami, F., Tsukahara, N., and Fujito, Y. (1978): Analysis of unitary EPSPs mediated by the newly-formed cortico-rubral synapses after lesion of the nucleus interpositus of the cerebellum. *Exp. Brain Res.,* 30:233–243.
4. Murakami, F., Tsukahara, N., and Fujito, Y. (1978): Properties of synaptic transmission of the newly formed cortico-rubral synapses after lesion of the nucleus interpositus of the cerebellum. *Exp. Brain Res.,* 30:245–258.
5. Nakamura, Y., Mizuno, N., Konishi, A., and Sato, M. (1974): Synaptic reorganization of the red nucleus after chronic deafferentation from cerebellorubral fibers: An electron-microscopic study in the cat. *Brain Res.,* 82:298–301.

6. Rall, W. (1964): Theoretical significance of dendritic trees for neuronal input-output relation. In: *Neural Theory and Modeling,* edited by R. F. Reiss, pp. 73–87. Stanford Univ. Press, Stanford.
7. Sato, S., and Tsukahara, N. (1976): Some properties of the theoretical membrane transients in Rall's neuron model. *J. Theor. Biol.,* 63:151–163.
8. Tsukahara, N., and Fujito, Y. (1976): Physiological evidence of formation of new synapses from cerebrum in the red nucleus neurons following cross-union of forelimb nerves. *Brain Res.,* 106:184–188.
9. Tsukahara, N., Bando, T., Kitai, S. T., and Kiyohara, T. (1971): Cerebello-pontine reverberating circuit. *Brain Res.,* 33:233–237.
10. Tsukahara, N., Bando, T., and Kiyohara, T. (1973): The properties of the reverberating circuit in the brain. In: *Neuroendocrine Control,* edited by K. Yagi and S. Yoshida, pp. 3–26. Tokyo Univ. Press, Tokyo.
11. Tsukahara, N., Hultborn, H., and Murakami, F. (1974): Sprouting of cortico-rubral synapses in red nucleus neurons after destruction of the nucleus interpositus of the cerebellum. *Experientia,* 30:57–58.
12. Tsukahara, N., Hultborn, H., Murakami, F., and Fujito, Y. (1975): Physiological evidence of collateral sprouting and formation of new synapses in the red nucleus following partial denervation. In: *Golgi Centennial Symposium: Perspectives in Neurobiology,* edited by M. Santini, pp. 299–303. Raven Press, New York.
13. Tsukahara, N., Hultborn, H., Murakami, F., and Fujito, Y. (1975): Electrophysiological study of formation of new synapses and collateral sprouting in red nucleus neurons after partial denervation. *J. Neurophysiol.,* 38:1359–1372.
14. Tsukahara, N., Murakami, F., and Hultborn, H. (1975): Electrical constants of neurons of the red nucleus. *Exp. Brain Res.,* 23:49–64.

Brain Mechanisms in Memory and Learning:
From the Single Neuron to Man,
edited by M. A. B. Brazier.
Raven Press, New York © 1979.

Intracellular Synaptic Mediators and the Endogenous Simulation of Neural Input to the Brain

Henry McIlwain

Department of Biochemistry, Institute of Psychiatry (British Postgraduate Medical Federation, University of London), London SE5 8AF, England

THE MOBILE MEDIATORS

The many stages now recognized in neurotransmitter action give additional scope to mechanisms for constructing and updating the internal model of environmental events that is believed to be necessary to perception and memory (9,25). Most synapses of the central nervous system act by chemical neurotransmission, and between liberation of neurotransmitter and modulation of cell firing, there are several chemical stages. Those stages that are illustrated in Table 1 are based on systems that act through cyclic nucleotides. There is much evidence that β-adrenergic actions and some actions of histamine and serotonin proceed through cyclic AMP, whereas adrenergic α receptors, some effects of acetylcholine, and others of serotonin and histamine proceed through cyclic GMP (10,32).

Taking cyclic nucleotide-mediated events as examples, the nucleotides themselves constitute one of the cytoplasmic components of complex systems distributed throughout most types of cells. The nucleotides act, either themselves or through intermediary components, on the functioning of the subsynaptic membrane, of cytoplasmic granules, and of microtubules and nuclei (29). One category of intermediaries, the protein kinases (no. 5 of Table 1) also include components that are cytoplasmic and mobile. The present account considers consequences likely to ensue when the cerebral actions of such mobile components, also, are distributed to cellular regions other than those of their formation, in particular, when they extend to other synaptic, and to nuclear, regions. These observations contrast with other proposals for a neural role of cyclic AMP, in which it is inactivated before leaving a limited postsynaptic site where it first acts and then is degraded (12). The present proposals are prompted by findings on the persistence of cyclic nucleotides in cerebral systems for 4 to 20 min after their generation, by electrical excitation or neurohumorally (3,21–23), together with the changes that take place in their cytological location during this time (26); and also by findings on

TABLE 1. Cyclic nucleotide systems of the mammalian brain

Component: forms of occurrence	Relationship among components	Further actions or properties
1. Cyclic nucleotides: cytoplasmic, free and bound, and membrane-attached	Specified neurotransmitters increase production of no. 1 by subsynaptic nucleotide cyclases	Persist for up to 4–20 min after formation; undergo translocation in tissue
2. Nucleotide cyclases: cytoplasmic, and subsynaptic, membrane-attached	Yield no. 1 when activated by neurotransmitters and by no. 4	Undergo axonal flow
3. Phosphodiesterases: cytoplasmic, and membrane-attached	Inactivate no. 1; activated by no. 4 when particle-attached	Undergo axonal flow
4. Activator protein: cytoplasmic	Augments turnover of no. 1 by activating both no. 2 and no. 3; requires Ca^{2+} for full activity	According to siting of nos. 2 and 3, no. 4 can increase no. 1 at particular sites and times
5. Protein kinases	Activated by no. 1, and then catalyses phosphorylation of no. 6 by ATP	Activated kinase can migrate to nucleus
6. Phosphoproteins: i, cell membrane ii, nucleus	Substrates of no. 5	Phosphorylation at i modifies membrane permeability, and at ii, genetic expression
7. Phosphoprotein phosphatases	Dephosphorylate no. 6	Terminate actions of no. 6
8. Kinase modulator proteins	Augment or inhibit the activity of no. 5; nucleotide-specific	The inhibitory modulator can oppose no. 1

For further details see text and refs. 12, 23, and 24.

activation and migration of protein kinase activity that follows cyclic nucleotide generation in related systems (15,17).

SHORT-TERM CONSEQUENCES ENVISAGED FROM THE PERSISTENCE AND MOVEMENT OF INTRACELLULAR SYNAPTIC MEDIATORS

1. Near the postsynaptic regions at which cyclic nucleotides have been formed, their actions may persist for appreciable times, dependent on the concentrations generated and their access to degrading enzymes and to the protein kinases through which the nucleotides act. This phenomenon has been suggested (23) as a means by which excitation can result in elevation or depression of firing rate for some seconds or minutes at the synaptic regions concerned.

2. Other instances have been noted in which a single brief period of stimulation results in a fluctuating firing rate, carrying, for example, multiple peaks of firing frequency during the subsequent 30 min (24). It is proposed that this action results from a bolus of synaptic mediator passing successive post-

synaptic sites or groups of sites at speeds of between 0.2 and 5 μm/sec, as observed for cytoplasmic transport (20,22,30) in anterograde and retrograde directions, axonally and dendritically.

3. Most nerve terminals in the brain end on dendritic processes, which are very richly covered with terminals. The observed ratio of nerve terminals to neurons in the human forebrain is 4×10^4, and over 90% of these are axodendritic or dendrodendritic (24,27). Terminals may be adjacent to or within 3 μm of each other; a given dendrite can extend for 1 mm or more. The time needed for these distances to be traversed by substances travelling by cytoplasmic transport at observed speeds of 0.25 to 5 μm/sec thus ranges from less than that 1 sec to several minutes, and these periods indicate the times available for modulation of cell firing by the nucleotides.

Neurons carrying large dendritic trees are capable of functioning in regional segments in initiating dendritic firing, Purkinje cells being able to initiate spikes at several points, with segments of the dendritic tree firing independently of one another (18). The excitability level of such a system behaves as though it can be accumulated over a period of time before firing is induced by climbing-fibre activation (19), a process that has been described as "reading" the state of the Purkinje cells and to which the accumulation of components of cyclic nucleotide systems appears likely to contribute.

4. It is a significant feature of present proposals that a mechanism is given for sequential action over a time period markedly longer than those of conducted action potentials. As an example of the time range available by conducted impulses, the parallel fibres of cerebella carry an array of presynaptic structures that can activate in succession the numerous Purkinje cells that each fibre innervates. Microelectrode studies have shown that this occurs (6,18) over periods of <1 to 5 msec. These time intervals accord with fibre length and velocity of conduction in the parallel fibres and with the fine-movement control they contribute to cerebellar function. Although similar distances are involved here and in item no. 3, below, the times concerned differ by factors of up to 10^6 and thus notably extend the sequential consequences of excitation.

PLACEMENT OF MEDIATOR-SENSITIVE POSTSYNAPTIC REGIONS

1. The cytoplasmic translocation of mediators active intracellularly gives added significance to the sequential order of entities positioned along nerve cell processes. Change initiated at the cell nucleus or perikaryon can be expected to reach the terminals of short axon branches before it reaches those of longer branches, and in dendrites, subsynaptic regions closest to the perikaryon will receive first a travelling modulator of similar origin. Conceivably flow route and rate may vary locally and alter these relationships,

but it appears inevitable that region *A* in Fig. 1 would receive such a modulator before region *B*. On the other hand, a modulator arising in a more distant region *D* would reach *B* before *A* and might not reach *A* or reach it only in attenuated form.

2. Consideration is therefore merited of instances of selective localization of terminal types on dendritic branches. It is emphasized that there "can be a very precisely ordered system of synaptic connections" (7) on dendrites; on granule cells, the synapses of commissural origin are segregated from those of entorhinal sources, with a group of different origin in another distinct location. The parallel fibres synapsed with cerebellar Purkinje cells at particular points of the dendritic tree, and spinal reflexes in cats operated through synapses at the proximal, dendrosomatic part of motoneurons (18,19). Competition for space on postsynaptic cell surfaces is suggested to occur among synapses, the areas occupied by terminals from a particular

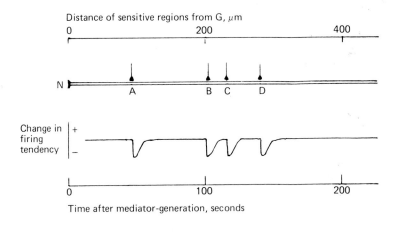

(1) *At a dendrite carrying many terminals,* A-D sensitive to mediator

Distance of sensitive regions from G, μm

N

Change in firing tendency

Time after mediator-generation, seconds

(2) *At the receptive field of a cortical neuron:*

M, cells activated by mediator
S, cells activated by sensory input

FIG. 1. Hypothetical placement of mediator-sensitive regions. Above: On a dendrite of a neuron N which carries many terminals; regions *A* to *D* and the change in firing tendency are referred to in the text. Below: Receptive field of a cortical neuron, consisting of points M at which cells are activated by a travelling or persisting mediator, and S at which they are activated by sensory input. The firing frequency of the neuron is considered to increase with increasing difference of activation at S and M, in the fashion in which "simple" cortical cells of Hubel and Wiesel (13; see 16) fire in response to different illumination of centre and surround, but do not fire, in response to uniform diffused light.

source shrinking or expanding by processes of pushing aside or displacement (34).

3. Such processes require chemically or enzymically understandable mechanisms; it has been proposed (33) that the formation of all such connections is initially a reversible process and that their maintenance is dependent on subsynaptic structures and products including cyclic nucleotides. The adjustments may occupy appreciable time; in the cortex of children 12 years old, Cajal type II neurons are still undergoing development (31). There is, ontogenically, a sequential formation of synapses open to limited modification (5,34). It is thus to be supposed that the positions occupied by terminals on dendrites carry significance and advantage in relation to sensory input and its cerebral organization.

4. It is now proposed that one aspect of this significance and advantage lies in the fashion in which a cytoplasmically moving mediator generates a change in firing tendency on passing a cognate subsynaptic region and simulates the sensory activation of that terminal. One fashion in which this may operate results in the autonomous firing rate of the cell concerned showing maxima and minima spaced at time intervals corresponding to the distances between the subsynaptic regions of its dendrites—the situation illustrated in Fig. 1. The activation of synapses at *A* is thus followed by processes that simulate the firing at *B* and *C;* if during the relevant times, terminals in these areas actually fire, their effects on neuron *N* will be augmented. Such augmentation expresses an expectancy based on terminal placement and thus (item no. 3 above) on the genetically and environmentally conditioned development of neuron *N*. If terminals at *A, B,* and *C* receive (directly or after local processing) input from sensory receptors spatially distributed at the skin, musculature, or retina, then their successive activation may be an essential part of the perception of motion, and the neuron *N* by mediator-flow may detect a previously experienced rate of motion.

SUGGESTED PARTICIPATION IN COMPARATOR-SYSTEMS: LONG-TERM CONSEQUENCES

1. Granted that mediator persistence and movement can result in the initiation and prolongation of temporally patterned cell firing, it may now be supposed that such cell firing can enter into systems of analysis similar to those involved in analysis of sensory input. Analogy to the processing of visual signals (13,14,16) suggests that if modulator-driven cells are regarded as supplying signals equivalent to one category of input to a retinal ganglion cell, the extent to which these signals differ from those of a surrounding group of normal, input-fired cells constitutes an effective trigger for activation of the ganglion-cell equivalent. Also, if mediator-driven cells are efferent to neurons equivalent to "simple" cells in the striate cortex, which receive also other (e.g., current sensory) input, the greater the contrast be-

tween the two types of input, the more activated this simple-cell equivalent will be. If, further, modulator-driven cells are efferent to neurons equivalent to "complex" cells of the visual cortex, the complex-cell equivalent would respond or not, according to the sequence in which signals arrived from the two sources. Analogy to cells in a different layer of the visual cortex suggests that arrays of complex cells receiving modulator-controlled output could supply a hypercomplex-cell equivalent that would respond in its firing pattern to the termination of such output as well as, differently, to its continuation.

2. Mediator-driven cells thus constitute an endogenous record that can be compared with new sensory input. Their situation is consistent with the view (8) that memory is a by-product of perceptual analysis, its persistence increasing with the depth of analysis, and that such records are widely distributed in the brain—by present ideas, within some of the same cells or cell categories as are concerned with perceptual analysis itself. It is consistent also with investigations in which long-term changes in cell firing and behaviour have been induced by brief localized electrical stimulation of the brain (4,11). This phenomenon of "kindling" was noted (28) to occur in areas postsynaptic to catecholamine systems, i.e., of known, or likely, relationship to systems in which cyclic nucleotides are the synaptic mediators (cf., MOBILE MEDIATORS above; Table 1). Noradrenergic innervation of the cerebral cortex has been found necessary for learning in rats (1).

3. Longer-term consequences of cyclic nucleotides as synaptic mediators were referred to in items no. 3 (p. 75) and no. 2 (above). Phenomena of long-term memory share characteristics with changes accompanying cell division in eukaryotes, which in several, but not all, instances involve cyclic nucleotides as "reporter molecules" (2). Such substances are required to reflect the functional or developmental state of a cell and to condition, by switch-like action at its nucleus, the synthesis of new effector proteins, e.g., enzymes. In the brain, also, cyclic nucleotides after their postsynaptic generation persist for sufficient time for arrival at the cell nucleus (MOBILE MEDIATORS). Modification of nuclear activity by a cyclic nucleotide-activated protein kinase originating in another part of a cell is proposed in explanation of transsynaptic induction of tyrosine hydroxylase in the adrenal medulla (15,17).

4. Such induction can understandably contribute to change in synaptic effectiveness; further mechanism is needed for the resulting change to be relevant to the cell firing that in neural systems generated the nucleotide. Thus one may note that a comparator cell (as Fig. 1–2) detecting no difference in firing between the endogenous mediator-driven cell and the cell giving current sensory input and consequently not itself being activated, does not generate mediator. When detecting difference and firing, the synaptic mediator is generated that is a reagent for alteration of the genome as well as of cell firing. The alteration, even if random, can be supposed ultimately to produce a matching pattern of cell firing; this is, however, only one of several

hypotheses that may be suggested at this stage, each requiring further specification in terms of the cellular array involved.

SUMMARIZING COMMENT

Synaptic mediators, exemplified by components of cyclic nucleotide systems, can be seen to participate as follows in input processing and retention in the brain. They are generated postsynaptically by the transmitters released by specific categories of neurons, and they mediate or modulate firing tendencies of the cells innervated. They persist beyond the period of their generation, for sufficiently long a period to account for several poststimulation phenomena. These include cell firing patterned temporally according to the linear sequence of regions sensitive to such mediators on the postsynaptic neuron: a sequence that thus constitutes a code "read" by the cytoplasmically travelling mediators. Components of cyclic nucleotide systems, on reaching the nuclei of such neurons, can alter genetic expression and thus effect long-term changes in their activities.

ACKNOWLEDGMENT

I am endebted to the Medical Research Council for support for cognate research.

REFERENCES

1. Anlezark, G. M., Crow, T. J., and Greenway, A. P. (1973): Evidence that noradrenergic innervation of the cerebral cortex is necessary for learning. *J. Physiol. (Lond.)*, 231:119–120.
2. Ashworth, J. M. (1976): Control of cell differentiation in the cellular slime mould, *Dictyostelium discoideum. Biochem. Soc. Trans.*, 4:961–964.
3. Barberis, C., McIlwain, H., and Newman, M. E. (1976): The persistence, translocation and metabolism of adenosine 3′:5′-cyclic monophosphate generated in isolated cerebral tissue by electrical stimulation. *Biochem. Soc. Trans.*, 4:748–749.
4. Bliss, T. V. P., and Gardner-Medwin, A. R. (1973): Long lasting potentiation of synaptic transmission in the dentate area of the unaesthetized rabbit following stimulation of the perforant path. *J. Physiol. (Lond.)*, 232:357–374.
5. Bodian, D. (1970): A model of synaptic and behavioural ontogeny. In: *The Neurosciences*, edited by G. C. Quarton, T. Melnechuk, and G. Adelman, pp. 129–140. Rockefeller Univ. Press, New York.
6. Braitenberg, V. (1967): Is the cerebellar cortex a biological clock in the millisecond range? *Prog. Brain Res.*, 25:334–346.
7. Cotman, C. W., and Banker, G. A. (1974): The making of a synapse. *Rev. Neurosci.*, 1:1–62.
8. Craik, F. I. M., and Lockhart, R. S. (1972): Levels of processing: Framework for memory research. *J. Verb. Learn. Verb. Behav.*, 11:671–684.
9. Craik, K. J. (1943): *The Nature of Explanation.* Univ. Press, Cambridge.
10. Daly, J. W. (1975): Role of cyclic nucleotides in the nervous system. In: *Handbook of Psychopharmacology*, Vol. 5, edited by L. L. Iversen, S. D. Iversen, and S. H. Snyder, pp. 47–130. Plenum Press, New York.
11. Douglas, R. M., and Goddard, G. V. (1975): Long-term potentiation of the

perforant path-granule cell synapse in the rat hippocampus. *Brain Res.*, 86:205–215.

12. Greengard, P. (1976): Possible role for cyclic nucleotides and phosphorylated membrane proteins in postsynaptic actions of neurotransmitters. *Nature*, 250:101–108.
13. Hubel, D. H., and Wiesel, T. N. (1962): Receptive fields, binocular interaction and functional architecture in the cat's visual cortex. *J. Physiol. (Lond.)*, 160:106–154.
14. Hubel, D. H., and Wiesel, T. N. (1968): Receptive fields and functional architecture of monkey striate cortex. *J. Physiol. (Lond.)*, 195:215–243.
15. Jungmann, R. A., Lee, S., and de Angelo, A. B. (1975): Translocation of cytoplasmic protein kinase and cyclic AMP-binding protein to intracellular acceptor sites. *Adv. Cyclic Nucleotide Res.*, 5:281–305.
16. Kuffler, S. W., and Nicholls, J. G. (1976): *From Neuron to Brain: A Cellular Approach to the Function of the Nervous System.* Sinauer, Sunderland, Mass.
17. Kurosawa, A., Guidotti, A., and Costa, E. (1976): Induction of tyrosine 3-monoxygenase in adrenal medulla: Role of protein kinase activation and translocation. *Science*, 193:691–693.
18. Llinás, R. (1970): Neuronal operations in cerebellar transactions. In: *The Neurosciences*, edited by F. O. Schmitt, pp. 409–425. Rockefeller Univ. Press, New York.
19. Llinás, R. (1975): Electroresponsive properties of dendrites in central neurons. *Adv. Neurol.*, 12:1–13.
20. Lubinska, L. (1975): On axoplasmic flow. *Int. Rev. Neurobiol.*, 17:241–296.
21. Lust, W. D., Goldberg, N. D., and Passonneau, J. V. (1976): Cyclic nucleotides in murine brain: The temporal relationship of changes induced in adenosine 3′, 5′-monophosphate and guanosine 3′, 5-monophosphate following maximal electroshock or decapitation. *J. Neurochem.*, 26:5–10.
22. McIlwain, H. (1976): An extended messenger role in the brain for cyclic AMP. *FEBS Lett.*, 64:271–273.
23. McIlwain, H. (1976): Translocation of neural modulators: A second category of nerve signal. *Neurochem. Res.*, 1:351–368.
24. McIlwain, H. (1977): Extended roles in the brain for second-messenger systems. *Neuroscience*, 2:357–372.
25. MacKay, D. M. (1970): Perception and brain function. In: *The Neurosciences*, edited by F. O. Schmitt, pp. 303–316. Rockefeller Univ. Press, New York.
26. Newman, M. E., and McIlwain, H. (1977): Adenosine 3′, 5′-cyclic monophosphate in nerve-terminal fractions from neocortical tissues: Its augmentation by a post-stimulation process. *Biochem. Soc. Trans.*, 5:1074–1075.
27. Pappas, G. D., and Waxman, S. G. (1972): Synaptic fine structure. In: *Structure and Function of Synapses*, edited by G. D. Pappas and D. P. Purpura, pp. 1–46. Raven Press, New York.
28. Phillips, A. G. (1976): Discussion. In: *Kindling*, edited by J. A. Wada, pp. 235–240. Raven Press, New York.
29. Robison, G. A., Butcher, R. W., and Sutherland, E. W. (1971): *Cyclic AMP*. Academic Press, New York.
30. Schubert, P., and Kreutzberg, G. (1975): Dendritic and axonal transport of nucleoside derivatives in single motoneurons and release from dendrites. *Brain Res.*, 90:319–323.
31. Sperry, R. W. (1971): How a brain gets itself properly wired for adaptive function. In: *The Biopsychology of Development*, edited by E. Tobach, L. R. Aronson, and E. Shaw, pp. 27–42. Academic Press, New York.
32. Triggle, D. J. (1976): The molecular basis of neurotransmitter-receptor interactions. In: *Chemical Pharmacology of the Synapse*, by D. J. Triggle, and C. R. Triggle, pp. 431–548. Academic Press, London.
33. Watson, W. E. (1976): *The Cell Biology of the Brain*, pp. 182–185. Chapman and Hall, London.
34. Wiesel, T. N., and Hubel, D. H. (1965): Comparison of the effects of unilateral and bilateral eye closure on cortical unit responses in kittens. *J. Neurophysiol.*, 28:1029–1040.

Brain Mechanisms in Memory and Learning:
From the Single Neuron to Man,
edited by M. A. B. Brazier.
Raven Press, New York © 1979.

Electrophysiology of Prefrontal Dorsolateral Cortex and Limbic Cortex Elucidating the Basis and Nature of Higher Nervous Associations in Primates

T. Desiraju

Neurophysiology Research Unit, Indian Council of Medical Research, and Department of Neurophysiology, National Institute of Mental Health and Neurosciences, Bangalore 560 029, India

The discovery of an organic substrate for certain psychological processes in the primate prefrontal cortex, made over 40 years ago by Jacobson (14), has opened up new fields and an ever expanding series of complex experiments and clinical findings in neuropsychology (5). These experimental studies and clinical observations on the prefrontal cortex have identified the dorsolateral sector of the prefrontal cortex as being involved in mechanisms of memory and learning. It has even been suggested that this cortex is concerned more with spatial than with temporal aspects of memory (13,29). Recent studies of the dorsolateral prefrontal cortex have also disclosed certain units whose discharges were found to undergo alterations with changes of psychic state (2,6). The prefrontal cortical units were also found to discharge in relation to steps of delays in "delayed alternation responses" and "delayed responses" (12,18).

The limbic or the cingulate cortex is another region that has for a long time attracted attention as being important for visceral and affective aspects of brain mechanisms and conscious behaviour (10,16,20,21,23,24,30,33, 34,35). The cingulate gyrus has been found to have two-way connections with the prefrontal cortex (15,25,26,30,36). Also, it has been reported that efferents of both prefrontal and cingulate cortices converge onto basal ganglia (15,30,36).

In the light of these links between the limbic cortex and the prefrontal cortex, it is only logical to expect that the two cortical subsystems work in association and mutually integrate the transactions of their neural codes and the underlying processes of higher nervous activities, including learning and memory. Just how far this assumption of the close operational association between the prefrontal and the limbic cortex is valid requires elucidation. Therefore, we have recently initiated attempts to investigate, first of all, the fundamental electrical characteristics of the communications between the limbic cortex and the dorsolateral prefrontal cortex in the primate (1,3,4, 7–9). The highlights of the observations made so far are summarised in this short report.

METHODS

The electrophysiological methods involving electrical stimulation and recording employed in this series of investigations have been published previously (1,5–7,20). Young rhesus monkeys weighing about 4 kg each were used for the experiments. All recordings and stimulations were carried on in the left cerebral hemisphere. Experiments were performed on monkeys lightly anaesthetised with pentobarbital, on *encéphale isolé* monkeys, and on conscious freely moving monkeys prepared with chronically implanted devices for microelectrode work (described in ref. 1,6). Further details are given below in the results section.

RESULTS

Associations Between Limbic Cortex and Neocortical Association Areas

In an initial preliminary survey made with chronically implanted semi-macroelectrodes in conscious animals in a monkey chair, it was found that stimulation of prefrontal cortex, parietotemporal association cortex, and midbrain reticular sites resulted in changes in the electrocorticogram of the cingulate cortex. In a reciprocal way, electrical stimulation of anterior cingulate white matter resulted in marked alterations of electrographical patterns of the prefrontal cortex as well as of the preoccipital cortex (7). These observations were followed by detailed microphysiological studies; the results so far collected on the prefrontal–cingulate relation are presented below.

Electrical Potentials of Prefrontal Cortex Evoked by Stimulation of Limbic Cortex

Electrical stimulations were made at different sites in the cingulum and its vicinity in the supracollosal anterior cingulate gyrus (7). Recordings of the evoked electrical waves were made with silver ball electrodes on the surface of the dorsolateral prefrontal cortex and of single unit discharges in the depths of cortex with stainless steel microelectrodes. Semimicroelectrodes were also used to make laminar recordings of focal slow waves together with the unitary potentials in the cortex.

Anterior cingulate stimulation evoked positive waves on the surface of the prefrontal cortex with a latency of 1 to 1.5 msec. These waves became isoelectric at depths between 0.3 and 0.6 mm and from thereon inverted to negativity. The evoked potentials were found to be distributed from the arcuate sulcus to two-thirds the distance on the surface of the cortex, rostrally. These results have been illustrated in previous publications (5,7).

Unit discharges of different latencies were also evoked by the stimulations. Short latency unit responses were in the range of 1.0 to 3 msec and were found usually in depths between 500 and 1,000 μm. Units with latencies of about 7 to 11 msec were also observed, often in the upper levels of the cortex. The number of impulses evoked was usually one per stimulus, concomitant with the rising phase of the negative focal slow potential. In addition to the units giving single impulse responses, other units were found that gave burst responses of long latency (11 to 16 msec) with impulse frequencies of 500 to 750/sec. Occurrence of such burst responses usually coincided with the falling phase of the negative focal slow potential.

The unit responses as well as the associated focal negative field potentials were sensitive to stimulus frequencies higher than 20/sec. Increasing the frequency of stimulation resulted in depression of the evoked potentials (5,7). The effects of cingulate stimulations on the evoked potentials of prefrontal cortex were not found to be affected by bilateral lesions of the dorsomedial thalamus (5,7).

Electrical Potentials of Limbic Cortex Evoked by Stimulation of Dorsolateral Prefrontal Cortex

The experiments were conducted in lightly anaesthetised monkey and also in the *encéphale isolé* monkey. About one cm of the anterior cingulate gyrus was exposed by making a window opening in the supralimbic premotor cortex to guide the recording electrodes into the cingulate under direct visual check (Fig. 1).

Concentric stimulating electrodes were positioned in the white matter of the prefrontal cortex on either side of the principal sulcus.

Electrical stimulation of the inferior frontal gyrus evoked unit discharges in cingulate cortex at latencies between 6 and 8 msec (Fig. 1). Stimulation of more ventrolateral or inferior frontal white matter, bordering the external capsule and putamen, evoked cingulate impulse discharges at much longer latencies, about 14 to 32 msec, riding on prominent negative waves of about 14 msec latency. Some units responded with delays of as much as 38 to 40 msec latency (Fig. 2). High-frequency stimulation resulted in decrease of amplitude of the focal negative waves, which were nearly blocked by stimuli of 45/sec (Fig. 3). Probably, the ventrolateral or inferior prefrontal cortical connection to the cingulate consists of fibres of small diameter; it is rather unlikely to be a polysynaptic connection as the responses could be evoked under light anaesthesia.

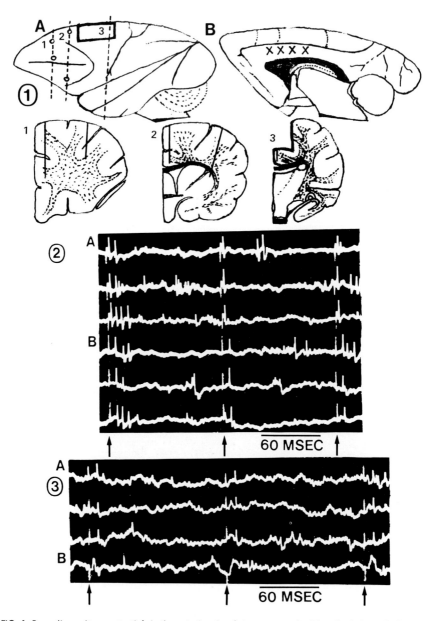

FIG. 1. Recording unitary potentials in the anterior cingulate cortex evoked by stimulations of white matter of FC and also by intracingulate stimulations. (1)A: Surface view of brain indicating the positions of common placements of stimulation electrodes at three levels (1, 2, 3) and the diagrams of coronal sections (1, 2, 3) corresponding to the three levels. The premotor cortical area bounded in the marked rectangle is excised to make a window to expose the cingulate. Positions of stimulation or recording electrode tracks in the cingulate are given in the three coronal sections. The prefrontal stimulating electrode track is in the white matter below the principal sulcus in section 1, whereas the track in section 2 is ending at the junction of inferior frontal white matter, external capsule, and putamen. (1)B: Extent (marked X) of anterior cingulate gyrus explored with recording microelectrodes. (2)A: Effect of anterior cingulate stimulation resulted in 1.5-msec latency unit discharges in another locus in the anterior cingulate about 1 cm caudal to the stimulation site. (2)B: FC stimulation also evoked impulses of the unit at 6 msec latency. (3)A: Another anterior cingulate unit giving 8-msec latency unit responses to FC stimulation. (3)B: Intracingulate stimulation has not produced a clear effect on this cingulate unit. FC: dorsolateral prefrontal cortex.

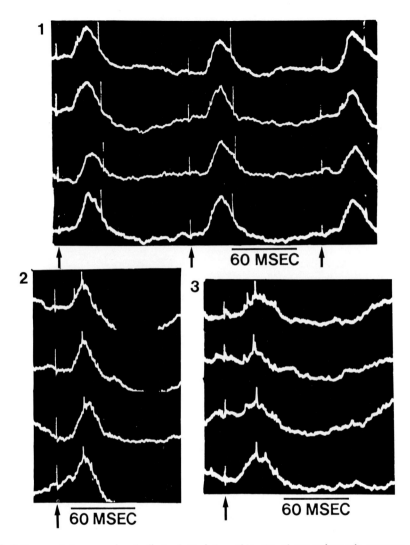

FIG. 2. Representative examples of effects of stimulations of junction of external capsule, putamen, and inferior frontal white matter on anterior cingulate gyrus. Note the evoked 14-msec latency prominent negative waves in the depth of the cingulate and unitary responses of different latencies. (1): Unit responses of about 40 msec latency. (2): Unit responses in the latency range of 18 to 32 msec. (3): Unit responses in the range of 14 to 40 msec latency.

Intracortical Interactions in Anterior Cingulate

In order to understand the intracingulate interactions, cingulate potentials evoked by stimulation of adjacent cingulate loci were also studied (Figs. 4 and 5). These stimulations, delivered about one cm rostral or caudal to the recording sites, were found to evoke unit responses of different latencies over a wide range, from as short as 2 to as long as 20 msec.

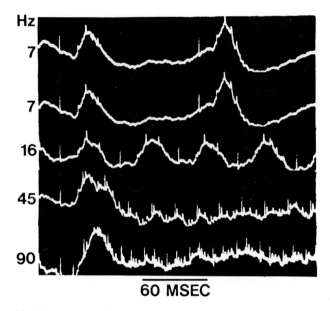

FIG. 3. Effects of high-frequency stimulations on the types of responses presented in Fig. 2. Note that the focal slow potentials undergo decrement when stimulus frequency is increased; with 45/sec the focal nega-tive waves have nearly disappeared and only unitary responses are left.

It was further observed that some cingulate units responded to both pre-frontal and intracingulate stimulation, illustrating convergence.

CONCLUSION

The observations reported here on reciprocal influences between the cingulate and the prefrontal cortex provide evidence for a fundamental mechanism of association by way of which neural codes of memory pro-grammes, learning sets, and innate tendencies governed by substrates of both archicortex and neocortex can be correlated, integrated, and trans-formed. Injuries of prefrontal cortex have been supposed to modify the ability for abstraction, parsing, and recall of information at the highest level as well as to alter the setting up of corollary cerebral interactions during conscious behaviour. Milner (22) has reported disturbances of memory re-sulting from injuries to the hippocampus, which is known to project to the cingulate via the anterior thalamus (28,36).

Learning and memory are experiential manifestations of reorganisations of information processing in the brain (11,19,27,31,32). The prefrontal cortex is closely connected to the other areas of association cortex of the parietal lobe and the temporal lobe. The cortex has also been found to re-ceive direct projections from the hypothalamus (17). The association cortices and the limbic system have been implicated in perceptual, motivational, and

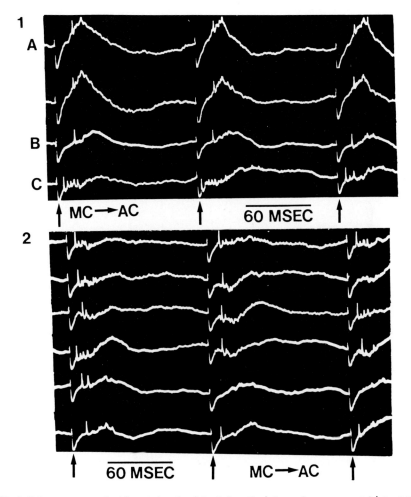

FIG. 4. Unit responses evoked in anterior cingulate during stimulations of a more caudal (about 1 cm) anterior cingulate locus. (1): A, B, and C represent traces recorded, respectively, near surface, near middle level, and in white matter (cingulum) of the anterior cingulate. Note the decrease of latency of unit potentials as the electrode is moved from the surface toward white matter. The latency of the earliest of the unit responses in A is 16 msec, whereas it is 4 msec in C. (2): Unit responses from another set evoked as in (1) above. Note that the latency of the early spike varies in the range of 6 to 12 msec.

other psychological aspects of learning and memory. Close functional links among the prefrontal and limbic cortices probably enrich the plasticity of recombinations of conditioned habits as well as the development of complex learning schemata and memory engrams of abstract logic, thereby helping man to cope with nature. These links (Fig. 6) may even offer scope for the evolution of better human beings, for the pathways may enable us voluntarily to cultivate potentialities for rechannelizing and transforming neural codes— those related to both body and mind in the regulation of somatic activities

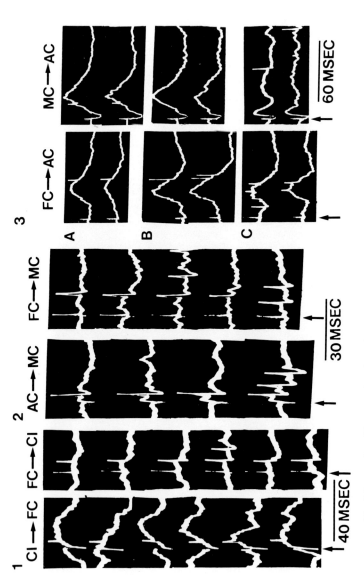

FIG. 5. Representative summary of the influences found between dorsolateral prefrontal cortex and anterior cingulate gyrus. FC, prefrontal cortex; CI and AC, rostral part of anterior cingulate; MC, caudal part of anterior cingulate. (1): Reciprocal relation between anterior cingulate and FC disclosed by interchanging the sites of stimulations and recordings. CI–FC: Stimulation of anterior cingulate evoked normally 3- to 4-msec latency unit potentials in the FC. FC–CI: Stimulations of FC evoked usually about 6- to 8-msec latency unit responses in anterior cingulate. (2): AC–MC: Anterior cingulate stimulation evoked about 2-msec latency unit spikes in another site located 1 cm caudally in the anterior cingulate. FC–MC: Stimulations of FC evoked about 6-msec latency unit potentials at the same locus of caudal anterior cingulate. (3): FC–AC: Long latency focal waves and unit responses evoked in anterior cingulate by stimulations of junction of putamen–external capsule–inferior frontal white matter. MC–AC: Effects on the same site in anterior cingulate of stimulations at a locus 1 cm caudally in the anterior cingulate. Note the short latency focal negative waves. A is a set of records obtained near the cingulate cortical surface, whereas B is from a little lower and C is from a still lower locus.

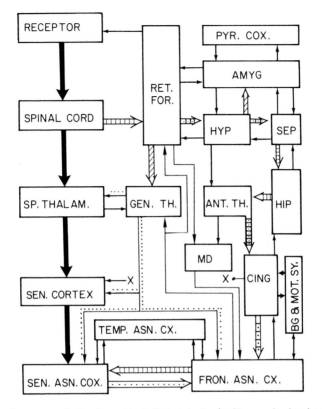

FIG. 6. Schematic summary of subsystems of brain likely to be involved in experiencing signals of external and internal worlds. The substrates of learning and memory are integrals of this scheme. The black arrow path is the primary channel of message transmission for sensing the external environment. The perception of the pattern of the message depends on associational interactions among the other major circuits. Processing through the segmented and dotted arrow path may generate the contents of affect (feelings) and judgment on the value of the information to self, inferred on the basis of innate knowledge and previously acquired frames of experiences. AMYG: amygdala; ANT TH: anterior thalamus; BG & MOT SY: basal ganglia and motor system; CING: cingulate cortex; FRON ASN CX: frontal association cortex; GEN TH: general thalamus; HIP: hippocampus; HYP: hypothalamus; MD: nucleus medialis dorsalis of thalamus; PYR COX: pyriform cortex; RET FOR: reticular formation; SEN ASN COX: sensory association cortex (parietal); SEP: septum; SP THALAM: specific thalamic nuclei; TEMP ASN CX: temporal association cortex.

as well as the affective and intellectual aspects of consciousness, of which learning and memory are but two processes. How to use these higher links to the best advantage has yet to be learned.

SUMMARY

By electrophysiological investigations in rhesus monkey, the fundamental transmission properties of a reciprocally communicating relation between the phylogenetically old limbic cortex (anterior cingulate) and the prefrontal dorsolateral association neocortex are described. It is suggested that this relation provides a substantial basis for integration of visceral and somatic sensorimotor codes and for transforming abstracts of affective and intellectual frames of neural organisations, which can be of great evolutionary significance not only for endowing man with uniquely advanced learning and memory capabilities but also for expanding his potentialities to the greatest biological extent possible.

ACKNOWLEDGMENT

The work of the author was supported by the Indian Council of Medical Research, New Delhi.

REFERENCES

1. Desiraju, T. (1973): Electrophysiology of the frontal granular cortex. I. Patterns of focal field potentials evoked by stimulations of dorsomedial thalamus in conscious monkey. *Brain Res.,* 58:401–414.
2. Desiraju, T. (1973): Electrophysiology of the frontal granular cortex. II. Patterns of spontaneous discharges of impulses of neurons in the cortex through states of sleep and wakefulness in the monkey. *Brain Res.,* 63:19–29.
3. Desiraju, T. (1973): Mechanisms for control of neural activity of the cerebral association cortex. I. The occurrence of augmenting potentials in the frontal granular cortex during stimulations of the nucleus medialis dorsalis. *Neurol. India,* 21: 145–151.
4. Desiraju, T. (1973): Mechanisms for control of neural activity of the cerebral association cortex. II. The occurrence of recruiting type of potentials in the frontal granular cortex during stimulations of medial thalamus. *Neurol. India,* 21:152–158.
5. Desiraju, T. (1975): Neural mechanisms of afferent projections in the organisation of dorsolateral prefrontal cortex. In: *Proc. Symp. Fifth Congr. Int. Primatol. Soc.,* (Symposium on Neurophysiology and Neuropsychology of the Primate Prefrontal Cortex), edited by S. Kondo, M. Kawai, A. Ehara, and S. Kawamura, pp. 423–443. Japan Science Press, Tokyo.
6. Desiraju, T. (1976): Reorganisation of neuronal discharges in the cerebral cortex through changing states of consciousness. In: *Mechanisms in Transmission of Signals for Conscious Behaviour,* edited by T. Desiraju, pp. 253–283. Elsevier, Amsterdam.
7. Desiraju, T. (1976): Electrophysiology of the frontal granular cortex. III. The cingulate-prefrontal relation in primate. *Brain Res.,* 109:473–485.
8. Desiraju, T. (1976): Electrophysiology of the mesogenetic limbic cortex of primate brain; anterior cingulate neuronal potentials evoked by stimulations of neogenetic prefrontal cortex. *Proc. 63rd Ind. Sci. Congr.,* 111:90.
9. Desiraju, T. (1977): Electrophysiology of the limbic cortex (cingulate gyrus) in primate. *Proc. Int. Union Physiol. Sci. XXVII Congr., Paris. (In press.)*
10. Desiraju, T. (1977): Mechanisms of cerebral functions and principles of organisation of primate brain. In: *Use of Non-human Primates in Biomedical Research,* edited by M. R. N. Prasad and T. C. Anand Kumar. Indian National Science Academy, New Delhi. *(In press.)*
11. Desiraju, T. (1977): Recent insights into understanding the problem of pattern generation and pattern recognition in the communication of coded information across nerve cells of brain. In: *Digital Techniques and Pattern Recognition.* Indian Statistical Institute, Calcutta. *(In press.)*
12. Fuster, J. M. (1973): Unit activity in prefrontal cortex during delayed-response performance: Neuronal correlates of transient memory. *J. Neurophysiol.,* 36:61–78.
13. Goldman, P. S., and Rosvold, H. E. (1970): Localization of function within the

dorsolateral prefrontal cortex of the rhesus monkey. *Exp. Neurol.,* 27:291–304.

14. Jacobsen, C. F. (1936): The functions of the frontal association areas in monkeys. *Comp. Psychol. Monogr.,* 13:3–60.

15. Johnson, T. N., Rosvold, H. E., and Mishkin, M. (1968): Projections from behaviorally-defined sectors of the prefrontal cortex to the basal ganglia, septum and diencephalon of the monkey. *Exp. Neurol.,* 21:20–34.

16. Kennard, M. (1955): The cingulate gyrus in relation to consciousness. *J. Nerv. Ment. Dis.,* 121:34–39.

17. Kievit, J., and Kuypers, H. G. J. M. (1975): Subcortical afferents to the frontal lobe in the rhesus monkey studied by means of retrograde horseradish peroxidase transport. *Brain Res.,* 85:261–266.

18. Kubota, K. (1976): Prefrontal programming of lever pressing reactions in the monkey. In: *Mechanisms in Transmission of Signals for Conscious Behaviour,* edited by T. Desiraju, pp. 61–80. Elsevier, Amsterdam.

19. Livingston, R. B. (1976): Sensory processing, perception, and behavior. In: *Biological Foundations of Psychiatry,* edited by R. G. Grenell and S. Gabay, pp. 47–143. Raven Press, New York.

20. MacLean, P. (1949): Psychosomatic disease and the "visceral brain." Recent developments bearing on the Papez theory of emotion. *Psychosom. Med.,* 11:338–353.

21. MacLean, P. D. (1975): On the evolution of three mentalities. *Man-Environment Systems,* 5:213–224.

22. Milner, B. (1958): Psychological defects produced by temporal lobe excision. In: *The Brain and Human Behavior,* edited by G. C. Solomon, S. Cobb, and W. Penfield, pp. 244–257. Williams & Wilkins, Baltimore.

23. Mirsky, A. F., Rosvold, H. E., and Pribram, K. H. (1957): Effects of cingulectomy on social behavior in monkeys. *J. Neurophysiol.,* 20:588–601.

24. Myers, R. E., Swett, C., and Miller, M. (1973): Loss of social group affinity following prefrontal lesions in free-ranging Macaques. *Brain Res.,* 64:257–269.

25. Nauta, W. J. H. (1971): The problem of the frontal lobe: A reinterpretation. *J. Psychiatr. Res.,* 8:167–187.

26. Pandya, D. N., Dey, P., and Butter, N. (1971): Efferent cortico-cortical projections of prefrontal cortex in the rhesus monkey. *Brain Res.,* 31:35–46.

27. Penfield, W. (1969): Consciousness, memory and man's conditioned reflexes. In: *On the Biology of Learning,* edited by K. H. Pribram, pp. 128–168. Harcourt, New York.

28. Powell, E. W. (1973): Limbic projections to the thalamus. *Exp. Brain Res.,* 17:394–401.

29. Rosvold, H. E. (1972): The frontal lobe system: Cortical-subcortical interrelationships. *Acta Neurobiol. Exp. (Warsz.),* 32:439–460.

30. Showers, M. J. (1959): The cingulate gyrus: Additional motor area and cortical autonomic regulator. *J. Comp. Neurol.,* 112:231–301.

31. Sperry, R. W. (1967): Split-brain approach to learning problems. In: *The Neurosciences,* edited by G. C. Quarton, T. Melnechuk, and F. O. Schmitt, pp. 714–722. Rockefeller Univ. Press, New York.

32. Thorpe, W. H. (1974): Learning, animal. In: *Encyclopaedia Britannica,* 15th ed., pp. 731–746. Encyclopaedia Britannica, Inc., Chicago.

33. Ward, A. A., Jr. (1948): The cingular gyrus: Area 24. *J. Neurophysiol.,* 11:13–23.

34. Watson, R. T., Heilman, K. M., Cauthen, J. C., and King, F. A. (1973): Neglect after cingulectomy. *Neurology (Minneap.),* 23:1003–1007.

35. Whitty, C. W. M. (1966): Some early and transient changes in psychological function following anterior cingulectomy in man. *Int. J. Neurol.,* 5:403–409.

36. Yakovlev, P. I., Locke, S., and Angevine, J. B., Jr. (1966): The limbus of the cerebral hemisphere, limbic nuclei of the thalamus, and the cingulum bundle. In: *The Thalamus,* edited by D. P. Purpura and M. D. Yahr, pp. 77–91. Columbia Univ. Press, New York.

DEVELOPMENTAL STUDIES

Brain Mechanisms in Memory and Learning:
From the Single Neuron to Man,
edited by M. A. B. Brazier.
Raven Press, New York © 1979.

Neuronal Activity of the Basal Ganglia Related to the Development of "Behavioral Sets"

N. A. Buchwald, C. D. Hull, and M. S. Levine

Mental Retardation Research Center, University of California Los Angeles,
Los Angeles, California 90024

There is still relatively little information available concerning how postnatal development of the mammalian nervous system contributes to the development of behavior. Seemingly, as behavior becomes more complex and differentiated, the accompanying neural developmental changes become increasingly difficult to identify. There is little reason to doubt that as an animal matures, experience with its external environment plays an increasingly important role in behavioral development. However, even late in development, there appear to be constraints on the importance of experience in behavioral development. These constraints are imposed by the immaturity of the developing nervous system.

As a means of determining some of the contributions of neural development to behavioral maturation, we have focused on the development of the basal ganglia, principally in the kitten. Justification for selection of the basal ganglia for study in this regard can be made on both practical and theoretical grounds. Practically, the basal ganglionic system in the adult cat is anatomically well defined, and many of its biochemical and electrophysiological properties have been determined. These data provide a good base line for assessing the degree of maturity of the basal ganglia in the developing brain. From a theoretical viewpoint, it might be expected that the basal ganglia are one of the brain systems that undergo a considerable degree of postnatal development. This view is based on the considerable evidence suggesting that the basal ganglia function importantly in the complex behaviors associated with maturity.

ANATOMY OF THE BASAL GANGLIONIC SYSTEM

Anatomy of the Adult

The basal ganglionic system consists of the neostriatum (caudate nucleus and putamen), the medial (nucleus entopeduncularis in carnivores) and lateral portions of the globus pallidus, the substantia nigra, and the sub-thalamic nucleus. Inputs to this system enter almost exclusively into the neostriatum. Striatal afferents come from the cerebral cortex, the intra-laminar thalamus (central medial and parafascicular regions), the pars com-pacta of the substantia nigra, and, more sparsely, from certain brainstem nuclei. The only known outputs of the striatum are to the globus pallidus and the pars reticulata of the substantia nigra. Two major output pathways of the pallidum go to the thalamus and the subthalamic nucleus (Fig. 1). Smaller pallidal outputs reach the habenula and the pons. A major output of the substantia nigra is to the ventral medial thalamus. Less prominent nigral projections reach the tectum and pons. The basal ganglionic system involves two major feedback loops and possibly one smaller loop. In one major loop the pallidum projects to the subthalamus, which, in turn, projects back to the pallidum. In the second, the striatum projects to the substantia nigra, which, in turn, projects back to the striatum. Less certainly these may be re-ciprocal connections between pallidum and nigra (5).

This brief anatomical description suggests certain general aspects of in-formation processing by the basal ganglionic system. Neural information enters via the striatum. This information is processed intranuclearly by way of the system's feedback loops, and the results of this processing are prin-cipally projected to the thalamus. The presence of the feedback loops sug-gests that timing of impulses in the system is important for it to work ef-ficiently. The internal structure of the nuclei that comprise the system also suggests another aspect of information processing. The ratio of output neurons to interneurons and the number of axon collaterals of neurons within the nucleus appear to be considerably higher for the neostriatum than for the other nuclei within the system (7,16–19,29); this indicates that most of the active information processing takes place within the caudate nucleus and putamen as opposed to the more passive relay of input to output that seems

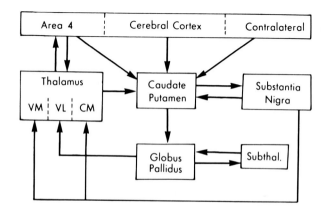

FIG. 1. Schematic representation of the connections of the basal ganglia. VM, VL, and CM are thalamic nuclei.

to be characteristic of the remaining nuclei of the basal ganglia. We return to these points in discussion of electrophysiological properties of the system.

Developmental Anatomy

What do we know of the postnatal anatomical development of the basal ganglionic system? Considerable information is available on the development of the caudate nucleus in the cat. Golgi studies indicate that a small- to medium-sized spiny neuron, the most common nerve cell in the striatum, develops rapidly within the first postnatal week at which time it seems to be mature in its appearance. Electron microscopic studies show that adult-like synapses are present by the fifth day of postnatal age (1). The major changes from day 5 onward are in the number of synapses per unit area. By the end of the first week the number of synapses has doubled. Between the first and fourth week the synaptic density again doubles. The period of rapid synaptic growth in the striatum during the first weeks of postnatal life is parallel to equally rapid growth reported for the cat visual cortex (6). Afferent fibers projecting from the kitten cortex to the caudate nucleus have been found as early as the fourth day postpartum. Studies of cortical and nigral projections to the caudate nucleus in monkeys and rabbits have shown that incoming axons can first be visualized as regional clusters of terminals (suggested in one instance to be columnar in projection) that tend to disperse with further development (10,11,32).

Available data do not provide direct evidence concerning late neuroanatomical development in the basal ganglionic system. Indeed, studies in the kitten of the early postnatal development of the output nuclei (pallidum and substantia nigra) have not yet been made. Provisionally, the data on caudate nucleus development suggest that new synapses continue to be added. Since the neostriatum continues to increase in size for 2 to 3 months postnatally and the synaptic density remains relatively constant, the total number of synapses in the caudate nucleus would have to increase. We return to this point after discussion of data on electrophysiological development.

ELECTROPHYSIOLOGICAL PROPERTIES
OF THE BASAL GANGLIA

Electrophysiology in the Adult

In the adult cat electrical stimulation of striatal inputs (cortical, thalamic, and nigral) evokes a rather uniform response in striatal neurons. Intracellular recordings of these responses show an initial excitatory postsynaptic potential (EPSP) that is ordinarily followed by an inhibitory postsynaptic potential (IPSP). The prevalence of this EPSP–IPSP sequence led to the construction of a structural-functional model. In this model nearly all inputs to the striatum are excitatory, and the inhibition is generated by neurons within the striatum (4,13). Incoming fibers not only excite the impaled neuron from which a recording is made but also excite its neighbors. Axon terminals of these latter cells in turn inhibit their neighboring neurons including the cell being recorded. Some of the neurons in the striatum are interneurons, others are output cells. Thus, the inhibitory contacts come either from interneuronal axons or from axon collaterals of striatofugal nerve cells. It might be expected that a nucleus, such as the striatum, that is structured so that its neurons mutually inhibit each other would show little spontaneous activity. In fact, this is the case for the striatum. In acute preparations, caudate neurons average about one spike every 2 sec (15). Even in behaving animals in which measurements are made with relationship to performance of a behavioral task and slowly firing neurons are less likely to be detected, average caudate neuronal firing rates are still only about 2/sec (30). In contrast, neurons in the globus pallidus in acute cats fire at a mean rate of 4/sec (21), and pallidal neuronal firing rates in behaving animals are 8/sec (30).

Available evidence indicates that many afferents to the caudate nucleus make direct contact with its output neurons (8). Thus, in the absence of the inhibitory modulation described above, the striatum would operate as a passive relay system transmitting its inputs to the pallidum and substantia nigra. Any "processing" of the input information would be limited to that which could be performed by the striatal output neuron itself as a result of its own membrane properties and of the nature of the transmitter released at its output terminal. As indicated below, there is evidence to suggest that the striatum does indeed tend to function as a relatively passive transmitter in early postnatal development.

Developmental Electrophysiology

A series of experiments has been conducted to assess the development of electrophysiological responses of caudate neurons to stimulation of its afferents. The first experiments utilized extracellular recording of action potentials of single neurons (22,24). This essentially limited our experimental analysis to assessment of excitatory responses since the spontaneous striatal firing was too slow to establish the presence of inhibitory responses to the stimulus. The results indicate that a large number of afferent connections are functional at birth. In a group of kittens with postnatal ages of 1 to 4 days, 56, 66, and 65% of all recorded cells responded to stimulation of frontal cortex, thalamus, and substantia nigra, respectively. These responses were, however, "immature" with respect to their ability to follow repetitive stimulation and in their latencies. The ability of immature striatal neurons to follow a 10-Hz stimulus did not, on the average, reach adult levels until the fourth week of age. As shown in Fig. 2, response latency values are

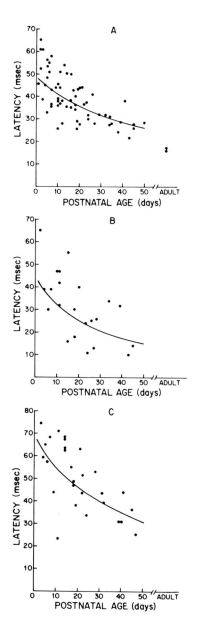

FIG. 2. Changes in latency of caudate unit responses to (A) precruciate cortex, (B) intralaminar thalamus, and (C) midbrain stimulation as a function of increasing age. Each point represents the mean of all responses in one animal. Curves are the best fit hyperbolic regression lines for each set of data. (From Morris et al., ref. 24. Copyright 1977 by Academic Press. Reprinted by permission.)

low and variable at birth, and although they decrease with postnatal age, they tend to remain lower in kittens than in adults even at the oldest ages tested (50 days postnatal) (24).

Several inferences might be drawn from these data. Morphologically, the increases in "synaptic security" represented by the developing striatal neurons' ability to follow repetitive stimulation may represent the effects of an increased number of synaptic contacts since increases in synaptic contacts and increasing ability to follow repetitive stimuli develop in parallel (1). The decrease in latency might reflect increased fiber diameter and myeliniza-tion.

The electrophysiological results also suggest constraints on the functioning of the basal ganglionic system in behavioral regulation. For the first 3 weeks postpartum, its ability to process information is limited by the inability of neostriatal cells to follow high repetition rates of inputs. The low and variable response latencies in early life make the system inefficient with respect to temporal integration of different inputs as well as impair possible temporal requirements for efficient operation of the feedback loops. This constraint is apparently still present to some degree through at least the second month of postnatal development.

An additional constraint can be inferred from a recently completed intra-cellular investigation of the development of inhibitory responses of caudate neurons to stimulation of striatopetal afferents (23). As indicated above, the most frequent response in the adult cat to such stimulation is an EPSP–IPSP sequence, and the extracellular studies of response development are not in-formative with respect to the IPSP component of the postsynaptic sequence. Intracellular recordings of responses evoked by stimulation of caudate in-puts have been made from kittens ranging in age from 1 to 72 days of post-natal age. The development of IPSPs lags considerably behind that of the EPSPs. Figure 3 shows the development of inhibitory responses to cortical stimulation. Although our data are less complete for nigral and thalamic stimulation, the results are in agreement with those found for the cortical stimulation. The inhibitory response does not usually resemble the adult inhibitory response until at least 2 months of age. This comparatively slow development of inhibition relative to excitation is apparently atypical for most forebrain structures. Prominent inhibitory responses have been found within the first 2 weeks of postnatal age for kitten neurons in the hippo-campus (27), thalamus (33), and motor (28) and visual cortex (14).

Within the context of the hypothetical model for structural-functional re-lationships in the striatum described above, we can account for the develop-ment of inhibition in the following ways. The model requires that the in-hibitory contacts on the recorded neuron come from neighboring neurons in the striatum itself and that the inhibition of the recorded neuron comes from the simultaneous excitation of these neurons by incoming impulses. From anatomical descriptions we know that input fibers make multiple con-tacts *en passant* with different dendrites and that there is a steady increase in the number of synapses in the developing caudate nucleus (1). Thus, a reasonable assumption is that a given input fiber may progressively develop contacts with dendrites of several different neurons in the heavily overlapping dendritic fields of caudate neurons. In addition, some of the increased synap-tic development may represent additional axonal contacts from intrinsic neurons that would be inhibitory.

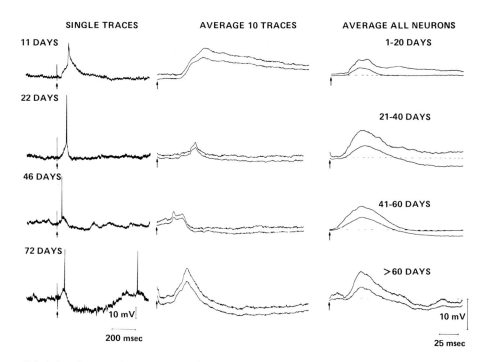

FIG. 3. Development of synaptic potentials in caudate neurons evoked by stimulation of pericruciate cortex. Left column shows single responses of individual caudate neurons recorded from 11-, 22-, 46-, and 72-day-old kittens. Center column shows the average and standard deviation of 10 single responses with the spike filtered off. The bottom trace of each pair represents the average response. The distance between the two traces represents the standard deviation. The right column shows the average and standard deviation for responses from all neurons recorded during the four age periods noted. For kittens 1 to 20 days of age the average response consists of only an EPSP. Over 20 days of age the IPSP of the EPSP–IPSP sequence begins to develop, but does not reach adult values until after about 40 days. Calibration on right refers to center and right columns.

Regardless of the correctness of our account of how development of inhibition takes place, the data suggest that the period of this development marks the time at which the striatum changes its mode of information processing from a passive relay system to one in which more active modulation of the input information takes place. The addition of inhibition to the earlier excitation engenders the possibility of much greater selection of which input impulses are transmitted to the striatal output nuclei, the pallidum, and the nigra. The spatiotemporal patterns of activation that are set up in these output structures should increase greatly with the addition of striatal inhibition.

CORRELATION OF BASAL GANGLIONIC FUNCTION WITH BEHAVIOR

Its relative size and position within the central nervous system suggest that the basal ganglionic system is part of a neural substrate normally associated with a broad spectrum of behaviors. Experiments designed to probe the role of the basal ganglia in behavior confirm this suggestion. Data have been provided to indicate involvement of the basal ganglia in behaviors as diverse as short-term memory performances (31,37) and contact-placing reactions (35). In attempting to abstract common elements from this diversity, we have suggested that the basal ganglia are part of a neural system whose functional role can be subsumed under the categories of "response set" or "cognitive set" (2). The term "set" represents our belief that the basal ganglia are more importantly involved in predisposing or enabling the animal to respond in a particular way than in directly evoking the performance. In the case of response set, we are referring to the underlying neural activity that enables the initiation and sequencing of movements that comprise a defined response. In the case of cognitive set, we refer to biasing of a decision to respond in a particular way on the basis of previously acquired information as might, for example, characterize performance in delayed-response paradigms. Data from lesion experiments generally suggest that the basal ganglia are importantly involved only in more complex responses or cognitive sets (2). The fact that single unit activity responses in basal ganglia and associated cortex and thalamus change significantly during behavioral performances in which response and cognitive sets are important components, lends credence to the idea that the basal ganglia are importantly involved in these behaviors (25, 26,30).

Although admittedly speculative, we believe that our recent findings concerning the relatively slow development of inhibition in caudate neuronal responses coupled with our structural-functional model of the basal ganglionic system point to an interesting transition point in behavioral development. Descriptively, the transition point is reflected in the ability of an animal to modify its set to perform in a particular way on the basis of information that it has recently acquired. For illustration of this kind of behavioral plasticity, three examples are cited.

The first example comes from an experiment performed in monkeys. It has been known for some time that lesions in the prefrontal cortex or in the caudate nucleus impair the ability of the monkey to perform delayed-response tasks. In this task a monkey is given a cue as to which of two or more incompatible responses is correct. The cue is removed, and after a delay period, the monkey is allowed to respond. Lesions of the prefrontal cortex made in infant monkeys appear to be less deleterious to delayed-response performance than those made at a later age (20). Lesions of the median dorsal nucleus of the thalamus (9) or of the head of the caudate nucleus (20) appeared to be equally deleterious whether made in infant or juvenile monkeys. Recently, Goldman and Rosvold (12) have brought these problems into sharper focus and suggested that a relative shift from subcortical to cortical dominance in regulating delay performance occurs with maturation. Goldman (11) then postulated that this cortical-subcortical shift reflected maturation of corticofugal fibers. She found, however, that there were abundant prefrontal-caudate fibers present in the infant monkey—a finding consistent with the histological and electrophysiological data from the cat discussed previously in this chapter. The account we provided for the development of IPSPs in caudate neurons would appear to be equally valid here. The neural maturation associated with this behavior would be reflected in increasing synaptic contacts to neighboring neurons in the caudate nucleus formed by a given input fiber rather than by additional input fibers entering the nucleus.

Our other two examples of changes in behavioral plasticity are drawn from observations of kittens that incurred bilateral ablations of the caudate nucleus ("acaudates") within 7 to 36 days of postnatal age. The first of these illustrates an inability to change a performance on the basis of recently acquired information (12). This could perhaps be equally well characterized as response perseveration or resistance to extinction. These acaudate kittens at 3 months of age learned to discriminate a visual cue in a T-maze about as well as their normal littermates and lesioned controls. However, when the discrimination was reversed, the control animals quickly reverted to a chance level of performance whereas the acaudate kittens made many more responses in the direction of the previously positive cue (3).

This type of response perseveration to a cue reversal is also characteristic of cats that have had their caudates removed as adults. In contrast to the early appearance of this perseverative deficit in the behavior of kittens is the effect of maturation on the "compulsory approach" syndrome seen in cats that have had their caudates removed as adults. This syndrome is one of the most characteristic behaviors of the adult acaudate cat in an open field situation (36). An outstanding feature of the syndrome is that the animal will select a prominent stimulus and persistently try to approach and make contact with it even when repeatedly rebuffed. In kittens, the compulsory approach syndrome is manifested 1 day after surgery and persists for about a week, after which it disappears. At about 4 to 6 months of age the constellation of behaviors comprising the syndrome begins to reappear and continues into adulthood. Although not as prominent as in cats lesioned as adults, the overall pattern of brain development apparently reaches a point at which the brain deficit becomes manifest again (34).

Examinations of the developing basal ganglionic system suggest there are patterns of neural development that place constraints on its plasticity. We believe that the determination of these constraints is better approached by examination of the development throughout the system rather than in a cortical-versus-subcortical framework.

ACKNOWLEDGMENTS

This work was supported by USPHS Grants HD-05058, MH-07097, and NS-12324

REFERENCES

1. Adinolfi, A. M. (1977): The postnatal development of caudate nucleus. A Golgi and electron microscopic study in kittens. *Brain Res.,* 133:251–266.
2. Buchwald, N. A., Hull, C. D., Levine, M. S., and Villablanca, J. (1975): The basal ganglia and the regulation of response and cognitive sets. In: *Growth and Development of the Brain,* edited by M. A. B. Brazier, pp. 171–189. Raven Press, New York.
3. Buchwald, N. A., Hull, C. D., Levine, M. S., and Villablanca, J. R. (1976): Developmental assessment of intact and brain-lesioned kittens. In: *Brain Dysfunctions in Infantile Febrile Convulsions,* edited by M. A. B. Brazier and F. Coceani, pp. 161–177. Raven Press, New York.
4. Buchwald, N. A., Price, D. D., Vernon, L., and Hull, C. D. (1972): Caudate intracellular responses to thalamic and cortical inputs. *Exp. Neurol.,* 38:311–323.
5. Carpenter, M. B. (1976): Anatomical organization of the corpus striatum and related nuclei. In: *The Basal Ganglia,* edited by M. D. Yahr, pp. 1–36. Raven Press, New York.
6. Cragg, B. G. (1972): The development of synapses in cat visual cortex. *Invest. Opthalmol.,* 11:377–385.
7. Fox, C. A., Andrade, A. N., LuQui, I. J., and Rafols, J. A. (1974): The primate globus pallidus: A Golgi and electron microscopic study. *J. Hirnforsch.,* 15:75–93.
8. Fuller, D. R. G., Hull, C. D., and Buchwald, N. A. (1976): Intracellular responses of caudate output neurons to orthodromic stimulation. *Brain Res.,* 96:337–341.
9. Goldman, P. S. (1974): An alternative to developmental plasticity: Heterology of CNS structures in infants and adults. In: *Plasticity and Recovery of Function in the Central Nervous System,* edited by D. G. Stein, J. J. Rosen, and N. Butlers, pp. 149–174. Academic Press, New York.
10. Goldman, P. S., and Nauta, W. J. H. (1977): Columnar distribution of cortico-cortical fibers in frontal association, limbic and motor cortex of the developing rhesus monkey. *Brain Res.,* 122:393–413.
11. Goldman, P. S., and Nauta, W. J. H. (1977): An intricately patterned prefronto-caudate projection in the rhesus monkey. *J. Comp. Neurol.,* 171:369–386.
12. Goldman, P. S., and Rosvold, H. E. (1972): Effects of selective lesions in infant and juvenile rhesus monkeys. *Brain Res.,* 43:53–66.
13. Hull, C. D., Bernardi, G., Price, D. D., and Buchwald, N. A. (1972): Intracellular responses of caudate neurons to temporally and spatially combined stimuli. *Exp. Neurol.,* 38:324–336.
14. Hull, C. D., and Fuller, D. R. G. (1975): Development of postsynaptic potentials recorded from immature neurons in kitten visual cortex. In: *Brain Mechanisms in Mental Retardation,* edited by N. A. Buchwald and M. A. B. Brazier, UCLA Forum in Medical Sciences, Vol. 18, pp. 179–184. Academic Press, New York.
15. Hull, C. D., Levine, M. S., Buchwald, N. A., Heller, A., and Browning, R. A. (1974): The spontaneous firing pattern of forebrain neurons. I. The effects of dopamine and nondopamine depleting lesions on caudate unit firing patterns. *Brain Res.,* 73:241–262.
16. Kemp, J. M., and Powell, T. P. S. (1971): The structure of the caudate nucleus of the cat: Light and electron microscopy. *Philos. Trans. R. Soc. Lond. [Biol.],* 262: 383–401.
17. Kemp, J. M., and Powell, T. P. S. (1971): The synaptic organization of caudate nucleus. *Philos. Trans. R. Soc. Lond. [Biol.],* 252:403–412.
18. Kemp, J. M., and Powell, T. P. S. (1971): Site of termination of fibers in the caudate nucleus. *Philos. Trans. R. Soc. Lond. [Biol.],* 262:413–427.
19. Kemp, J. M., and Powell, T. P. S. (1971): Termination of fibers from cerebral cortex and thalamus upon dendritic spines in the caudate nucleus: A study with the Golgi method. *Philos. Trans. R. Soc. Lond. [Biol.],* 262:429–439.
20. Kling, A., and Tucker, T. J. (1967): Effects of combined lesions of frontal granular cortex and caudate nucleus in neonatal monkey. *Brain Res.,* 6:428–439.
21. Levine, M. S., Hull, C. D., and Buchwald, N. A. (1974): Pallidal and entopeduncu-

lar intracellular responses to striatal, cortical, thalamic and sensory inputs. *Exp. Neurol.,* 44:448–460.

22. Lidsky, T. I., Buchwald, N. A., Hull, C. D., and Levine, M. S. (1976): A neurophysiological analysis of the development of cortico-caudate connections in the cat. *Exp. Neurol.,* 50:283–292.

23. Morris, R., Cherubini, E., Hull, C. D., Levine, M. S., and Buchwald, N. A. (1977): Postsynaptic potentials evoked in developing caudate nucleus neurons by activation of their afferents. *Neurosci. Abstr.,* 3:128.

24. Morris, R., Fuller, D. R. G., Hull, C. D., and Buchwald, N. A. (1977): Development of caudate neuronal responses to stimulation of the midbrain, thalamus and cortex in the kitten. *Exp. Neurol.,* 57:121–131.

25. Neafsey, E. J., Hull, C. D., and Buchwald, N. A. (1978): Preparation for movement in the cat. I. Unit activity in the cerebral cortex. *Electroenceph. clin. Neurophysiol.,* 40:706–713.

26. Neafsey, E. J., Hull, C. D., and Buchwald, N. A. (1978): Preparation for movement in the cat. II. Unit activity in the basal ganglia and thalamus. *Electroenceph. clin. Neurophysiol.,* 40:714–723.

27. Purpura, D. P., Prelevic, S., and Santini, M. (1968): Postsynaptic potentials and spike variations in the feline hippocampus during postnatal ontogenesis. *Exp. Neurol.,* 22:408–422.

28. Purpura, D. P., Schofer, R. J., and Scarff, T. (1965): Properties of synaptic activities and spike potentials of neurons in immature cortex. *J. Neurophysiol.,* 28:925–942.

29. Rinvik, E., and Grofova, I. (1970): Observations on the fine structure of the substantia nigra in the cat. *Exp. Brain Res.,* 11:229–248.

30. Soltysik, S., Hull, C. D., Buchwald, N. A., and Fekete, T. (1975): Single unit activity in basal ganglia of monkeys during performance of a delayed response task. *Electroenceph. clin. Neurophysiol.,* 39:65–78.

31. Stamm, J. S. (1969): Electrical stimulation of monkeys prefrontal cortex during delayed response performance. *J. Comp. Physiol. Psychol.,* 67:535–546.

32. Tennyson, V. M., Mytilineou, C., Heikkila, R., Barrett, R. E., Cohen, G., Cote, L., Duffy, P. E., and Marcs, L. (1975): Dopamine-containing neurons of the substantia nigra and their terminals in the neostriatum. In: *Brain Mechanisms in Mental Retardation,* edited by N. A. Buchwald and M. A. B. Brazier, UCLA Forum in Medical Sciences, Vol. 18, pp. 227–264. Academic Press, New York.

33. Thatcher, R. W., and Purpura, D. P. (1972): Maturational studies of inhibitory and excitatory synaptic activities of thalamic neurons in neonatal kittens. *Brain Res.,* 44:661–665.

34. Villablanca, J. R. (1978): Comparative effects of neonatal and adult striatal and frontal lesions in cats. In: *Proceedings of a Symposium on Basal Ganglia—Cellular and Functional Aspects,* Frankfurt, July 1977, edited by R. Hassler, N. A. Buchwald, and S. Kitai, *Applied Neurophysiol. (In press.)*

35. Villablanca, J. R., Marcus, R. J., Olmstead, C. E., and Avery, D. L. (1976): Effects of caudate nuclei or frontal cortical ablations in cats. III. Recovery of limb placing reactions including observations in hemispherectomized animals. *Exp. Neurol.,* 53:289–303.

36. Villablanca, J. R., Olmstead, C. E., and Marcus, R. J. (1976): Effects of caudate nuclei or frontal cortical ablations in cats. I. Neurology and gross behavior. *Exp. Neurol.,* 52:389–420.

37. Wyers, E., and Deadwyler, S. (1971): Duration and nature of retrograde amnesia produced by stimulation of caudate nucleus. *Physiol. Behav.,* 6:840–846.

Brain Mechanisms in Memory and Learning:
From the Single Neuron to Man,
edited by M. A. B. Brazier.
Raven Press, New York © 1979.

Maturation of Cortical Function: A Comparison Between Physiological Activity and Anatomical Findings

Kihumbu Thairu

Department of Medical Physiology, University of Nairobi, Nairobi, Kenya

One of the parameters widely used by neurophysiologists for the measurement of the maturation of cortical function is the primary evoked potential. In work using this parameter, studies of the single or averaged evoked potentials have been used. The changes that take place in the evoked potential during the maturation of brain function have been demonstrated in the rabbit (11), in the cat and the rabbit (13), in man (8,12), in sheep (14), and in the albino rat (15).

The anatomical correlates of the cortical evoked potential have been described by Chang and Kaada (3), Eccles (6), Cragg (4), and Amassian et al. (1). According to these workers the diphasic adult primary evoked potential recorded at the surface of the cortex is composed of, first, a positive wave P_1 followed by the first negative wave N_1. This diphasic potential results when afferent impulses reach the pyramidal and multiform cells in the cortex thus causing a depolarisation that travels to the surface. For the immature brain, the evoked P_1, when present, is supposed to arise from anatomical structures similar to those in mature brains (14,15), whereas N_1 is supposed to be caused by primary superficial depolarisation, which is caused by special afferents that terminate in the superficial cortical layer in immature brains (2,5). These authors have shown that these afferents increase and then decrease in density during ontogenesis, thus explaining the evoked potential changes described during ontogenesis. The work presented in this chapter shows how the maturing cortex responds to repetitive stimulation under certain conditions.

MATERIALS AND METHODS

The experiments were done under halothane (fluothane) anaesthesia on rats aged between a few hours and 12 days. All the animals were carefully wrapped in cotton wool and kept warm (temperatures 36 + 1°C), using a

105

pad thermostatically heated. A stereotaxic head-holder was used for immobilising the heads of rats older than 7 days, but for younger ones, whose skulls are very soft, the immobilisation was effected by strapping the head firmly to the anaesthetic mask with adhesive tape. The somatosensory cortex was exposed and kept moist and warm with liquid paraffin saturated with physiological saline. The dura was left intact. The stimuli had a duration of 0.05 msec and were delivered by an insulated stimulator. They were applied to the contralateral forepaw once every minute for the control response and at faster repetitive rates for the experimental ones. However, in the latter case a resting period of 3 to 5 min was always allowed between successive barrages of stimulation. The stimulus strength necessary for eliciting cortical potentials with the largest peak-to-peak voltage (maximal stimulus) was used in every case. The recording electrode, a "weightless silver ball," diameter about 0.5 mm, was placed on the relevant forepaw area of the rat's somatosensory cortex. The indifferent electrode was placed in the conjunctival sac. The recorded signal was fed into an oscilloscope via a preamplifier time-constant 0.2 sec. A photographic record of the evoked potentials was made.

RESULTS

For rats younger than 5 days, increasing the frequency of the stimulus caused an increase in the latency (from the stimulus artefact to "take off") of the responses as well as shrinkage of the first positive wave P_1. Various frequencies were tried from 1/min and more, with the same results. In rats aged between 5 to 12 days whose evoked potentials show a large negative wave N_1, when the stimulus frequency was increased to about 2 to 4/sec, the first negative wave N_1 shrank whereas P_1 grew in size, instead of shrinking as it did for lower frequencies, and the latency was increased. At times the shrinkage of N_1 and the concomitant growth of P_1 made the potentials assume the configuration of adult diphasic potentials. If the stimulation was maintained at the frequency of 2 to 4/sec for over 20 sec or so, P_1 eventually shrank and in the end disappeared, leaving only a small N_1 that in turn disappeared much later. Rats aged between 8 and 12 days showed the above effects most vividly because N_1 is very much larger than P_1 in the control responses elicited in such rats. One marked difference between P_1 and N_1 is that during repetitive stimulation it was always observed that the N_1 gradually diminished in size, without going through a phase of potentiation, until it disappeared. It was also observed that N_1 was always the last to disappear in such circumstances.

DISCUSSION

The primary somatosensory evoked potentials in rats less than 13 days of age have been shown to be immature (16). The results presented here have shown that repetitive stimulation in such rats can produce potentials that have a similar configuration to those of adult potentials. The basic change in the configuration of the immature potentials is the facilitation or potentiation of the first positive wave P_1 and the shrinkage or inhibition of the first negative wave N_1. The N_1 mechanisms are thus inhibited by repetitive stimulation. The exact anatomical site of the inhibition is not yet determined although cortical inhibition studies using γ-aminobutyric acid (17) suggest that the site is in the superficial cortical layers of the cortex. Repetitive cortical stimulation has been shown to potentiate cerebellar conduction (9). Synaptic potentiation by repetitive stimulation has also been shown (7). It is therefore possible that repetitive stimulation causes synaptic potentiation of the synaptic activities in the pyramidal and multiform cells of layers V and VI, which activity is thought to give rise to P_1. Repetitive stimulation has been used to obtain an averaged evoked potential in ontogenetic studies (8,10). It is therefore important to take into consideration the differences in the behaviour of the two components of the primary evoked potential when such studies are carried out. The differences in behaviour of these two components further support the theory that the components are caused by the electrophysiological phenomena arising out of different anatomical structures in the cortex.

SUMMARY

Intermittent barrages of subcutaneous electrical stimulation applied to the contralateral forepaw have been used for eliciting primary somatosensory evoked responses in immature rats. This mode of stimulation had the following effects on the responses:

1. The latency was increased in all rats.
2. For rats younger than around 5 days, at first the first positive wave P_1 gradually disappeared and then the first negative wave followed suit.
3. In rats aged 5 to 12 days, for repetitive frequencies of about 2 to 4/sec, firstly P_1 was enhanced while N_1 was concomitantly diminished. This change made the responses assume the shape of mature responses.
4. Even in such rats, stimulation using frequencies lesser or greater than about 2 to 4/sec produces the effects mentioned under no. 2 as did stimulation at 2 to 4/sec if it was maintained for more than about 20 sec. The results support the theory that in the immature cortex the two main components of the primary evoked potential arise from different anatomical structures.

REFERENCES

1. Amassian, V. E., Waller, H. J., and Macy, J., Jr. (1964): Neural mechanism of the primary somatosensory evoked potential. *Ann. NY Acad. Sci.,* 112:5–32.
2. Ata-Muradova, F., and Chernyvskaya, I. (1967): Morphological correlates of evoked potentials in rabbit sensorimotor cortex during postnatal ontogenesis. *Neurosci. Transl.,* 2:143–152.

3. Chang, H. T., and Kaada, B. (1950): An analysis of the primary response of visual cortex to optic nerve stimulation in cats. *J. Neurophysiol.,* 13:305–318.
4. Cragg, B. G. (1954): The electrical responses of mammalian cerebral cortex. *J. Physiol.,* 124:254–268.
5. Eayrs, J. T., and Goodhead, B. (1959): Postnatal development of the cerebral cortex in the rat. *J. Anat.,* 93:385–402.
6. Eccles, J. C. (1951): Interpretation of action potentials evoked in the cerebral cortex. *Electroenceph. clin. Neurophysiol.,* 3:449–464.
7. Eccles, J. C., Llinás, R., and Sasaki, K. (1966): Parallel fibre stimulation and responses induced thereby in the Purkinje cells of the cerebellum. *Exp. Brain Res.,* 1:17–39.
8. Ellingson, R. J. (1960): Cortical electrical responses to visual stimulation in the human infant. *Electroenceph. clin. Neurophysiol.,* 12:663–677.
9. Gardner-Medwin, A. R. (1971): An extreme supernormal period in cerebellar parallel fibres. *J. Physiol. (Lond.),* 222:357–371.
10. Hrbek, A., Karlberg, P., and Olson, T. (1973): Development of visual and somatosensory evoked potentials in pre-term newborn infants. *Electroenceph. clin. Neurophysiol.,* 34:225–232.
11. Hunt, W. E., and Goldring, S. (1951): Maturation of the evoked responses of the visual cortex in the postnatal rabbit. *Electroenceph. clin. Neurophysiol.,* 3:465–471.
12. Manil, J., Desmedt, J. E., and DeBecker, H. (1967): Maturation of the somatosensory evoked potentials in man. *Electroenceph. clin. Neurophysiol.,* 23:578.
13. Marty, R. (1962): Développement post-natal des réponses sensorielles du cortex cérébral chez le chat et le lapin. *Arch. Anat. Microsc. Morphol. Exp.,* 51:129–264.
14. Molliver, M. E. (1967): An ontogenetic study of evoked somesthetic cortical responses in the sheep. *Prog. Brain Res.,* 26:78–91.
15. Thairu, B. K. (1971): Post-natal changes in the somaesthetic evoked potentials in the albino rat. *Nature (New Biol.),* 231:30–31.
16. Thairu, K. (1976): Comparative depth recordings of the somatosensory cortical potentials evoked in immature and adult rats. *East Afr. J. Med. Res.,* 3:75–81.
17. Thairu, K. (1972): Effects of topically applied γ amino butyric acid (GABA) on the primary somatosensory evoked responses in the cortex of the immature rat. *J. Physiol. (Lond.),* 224:42P–43P.

Brain Mechanisms in Memory and Learning:
From the Single Neuron to Man,
edited by M. A. B. Brazier.
Raven Press, New York © 1979.

Genetic and Environmental Factors in the Ontogeny of Learning

Alberto Oliverio

Laboratorio di Psicobiologie e Psicofarmacologie, Rome; and Istituto di Psicologie, Universitá Roma, Rome 00198, Italy

In recent years a number of symposia have been devoted to memory and learning, to their biochemical or neurophysiological correlates, and to a series of environmental effects that modify these two processes in animals, as in man. Almost 10 years ago, a meeting held in Geneva on this topic and organized by Piaget (28) pointed out that from an ontogenetic viewpoint it is almost impossible to distinguish clearly between the mechanisms of memory and those of learning, and that memory represents a basic step in the development of learning and, therefore, of intelligence. At that time, seemingly the golden age of research on memory, most studies were based on a molecular approach, and it seemed that thorough biochemical researches might solve the enigma of the behavioral black box.

The present volume treats a number of topics including "simple" cellular models, maturational mechanisms, drug or hormone effects, neurochemical correlates, neurophysiological mechanisms, and, finally, a topic that complicates a little bit the theoretical models, namely, the role played by the environment and by cultural factors on the memory and learning processes in man. This large number of approaches contrasts with the specificity of the earlier researches, mostly centered on consolidation mechanisms and on biochemical analyses of macromolecules or nucleic acids. The latter approaches, stemming from the discoveries of the molecular biology, suggested that the mechanisms of transactional memory were similar to those of the genetic code. Thus, memory and learning were studied in their simplest forms in unicellular organisms and in invertebrates. Since then a number of neurophysiological and psychobiological studies have pointed out the differences existing between the behavioral systems of invertebrates and vertebrates, indicating that it is rather difficult to generalize between the mechanisms and strategies characterizing a paramecium, an insect, and an octopus. In this regard Altman (1) has indicated that a phylogenetic approach to learning must consider the structure of the nervous system and that different mechanisms characterize the spinomedullary level typical of protochordates like the amphioxus, the paleoencephalic level typical of protovertebrates like amphibia, and the mesencephalic level typical of protomammalian behavior.

Obviously a psychobiological approach to memory is today more complex than it was 10 to 15 years ago. The mechanisms of the black box appear to be rather more complicated, or at least the inputs and the outputs more numerous; the initial optimistic approach has become skeptical or even pessimistic. In a recent review on the study of the molecular psychobiology of memory, Gaito (14) speaks about its appearance, contribution, and decline and contrasts the initial period, characterized by early developments in research and vigorous research, with the present period, initiated in the seventies and characterized by decline (Table 1).

During the period of vigorous research—but also today— the approaches to memory were based on a number of strategies, ranging from studies of the morphological background to analyses of macromolecular storage, chemical transfer, neurotransmitters, or electrophysiological correlates. An even larger number of treatments have characterized the approaches to memory consolidation—the electroconvulsive shock, anesthesia, spreading depression, antibiotics, and anticholinergic agents or central nervous system (CNS) stimulants, an example of classic methodological strategies. This large array of studies indicates that the problem is really complex and that there are a number of systems of subsystems to be investigated, a fact that also appears from a recent review by Will (38), which analyses the main correlational studies between learning and neurochemistry. The majority of the studies aim at correlations between the cholinergic system and learning; a second group is devoted to the analysis of cholinergic or adrenergic enzymes; research into the serotoninergic, noradrenergic, and, more recently, the dopaminergic sys-

TABLE 1. *Molecular psychobiology of memory*

Period 1—Prior to molecular biology (1950)
  Halstead: Nuclear proteins and memory

Period 2—Early development in research (1958–1964)
  Cameron: Yeast RNA to patients
  Roy John: RNase in cats and planarians
  Hydén: RNA and RNA base ratios in training
  McConnell: Transfer in planarians
  Agranoff; Barondes; Chamberlain; Flexner: RNA or
    protein synthesis inhibitors
  Gaito: Theories on DNA modification

  Period 3—Vigorous research (1965–1970)
  Ungar: Jacobson: Transfer
  Glassman: RNA precursors

Period 4—Decline (1971–   )
  Hydén: Ca^{2+} and specific proteins
  Agranoff and Barondes: RNA or protein synthesis in-
    hibitors

From Gaito, ref. 14.

TABLE 2. Correlational studies between learning and neurochemistry

Parameter	No. of studies
Cholinergic system	29
"Enzymes"	28
Serotoninergic system	10
Noradrenergic system	8
Proteins + nucleic acid	8
Dopaminergic system	5

Total studies on inbred mice, 12. From Will,
ref. 38.

tems occupies third place; and proteins and nucleic acids are in last place (Table 2). These are the main studies up to 1977, but there is today a body of research dealing with naturally occurring peptides that, with no doubt, have a role in memory and learning mechanisms.

It is difficult to state whether all the chemicals listed above have a main or a secondary role in these behavioral states, and whether a given biochemical response is stimulation related, acquisition related, or experience related. Entingh et al. (12), in discussing the relationships of biochemical changes to behavioral states, specify that four different questions should be answered: Is the neurochemical response necessary for learning? Do other behavioral states produce those neurochemical changes? Does memory formation always produce that neurochemical response? Does a particular change directly code for memory or is it an intermediate in the chain of events? The last question is probably the most difficult one and seems to be related to the role of neurotransmitters in learning. However, it is also rather difficult to answer the second question, i.e., how to select an appropriate behavioral parameter and an appropriate test. In this regard a number of studies have been centered on different types of behavioral stimulation and memory-related processes based on environmental enrichment, on a number of learning tasks, or on imprinting (Table 3).

I have given a schematic picture of the situation up to this point. It is difficult to say which of the different approaches is the most promising, and it is impossible to indicate when the picture will be almost complete. Perhaps the main result of all these efforts is the shower of findings on the brain mechanisms that regulate behavior. However I would like to underline another point, that the existence of contrasting findings and the number of species or individual differences in relation to learning and memory are not negative points and must be thoroughly considered; they indicate the presence of a large intraspecific individual variability or the presence of species-specific mechanisms that have their roots in the genetic and environmental mechanisms that modulate these complex abilities. A second research strategy may

TABLE 3. *Behavioral stimulation and memory-related processes*

Parameter	Study
Environmental enrichment	Bennett and Rosenzweig, 1964; Greenough, 1970
Wire climbing	Hydén, 1967
Reversal situations	Hydén, 1967; Hydén and Lange, 1968; Elias and Eleftheriou, 1972
Active avoidance	Zemp, Wilson, and Glassman, 1967; Entingh et al., 1974; Carreres et al., 1971; Pohle and Matthies, 1971; Beach et al., 1969
Imprinting and exposure to light	Horn et al., 1973

From Entingh et al., ref. 12.

find its roots in the existence of this variability, and the question, What are the psychological and neurochemical correlates of learning and memory? may be turned into another question, What are the neurophysiological and neurochemical bases of behavioral individuality? This problem rests on long-continuing work on behavior genetics based in its first approach on artificial selection experiments. Since the first experiments on the selection of maze learning in the mouse at the beginning of this century, a large number of behavioral abilities have been identified in rodents (Table 4).

Research into the genetic determinants of individual differences through a comparative approach is justified by the similarities existing between many neurophysiological processes within mammals. In particular many learning mechanisms, such as short- or long-term memory, consolidation processes, and different learning abilities, present many interspecies similarities. It is therefore possible that a comparative behavioral genetic study will be a fruit-

TABLE 4. *Behavioral selection in rodents*

Behavior	Species	Author
Alimentary preference	Rat	Nachman, 1959
Spontaneous activity	Mouse	Vicari, 1929
	Rat	Rundquist, 1923
Aggression	Mouse	Lagerspetz, 1961
Emotionality	Rat	Hall, 1938
		Broadburst, 1958
Audiogenic seizures	Rat	Maier, 1943
	Mouse	Frings & Frings, 1953
Maze learning	Mouse	Bagg, 1915
	Rat	Tolman, 1924
		Thryon, 1922
		Heron, 1935
		Thompson, 1954
Avoidance learning	Rat	Bignami & Bovet, 1965
		Oliverio, 1969

From Oliverio, ref. 24.

ful approach to the organic foundations of behavioral individuality, to individual learning abilities, and to a number of conditions resulting in mental retardation.

In the comparative approach, the laboratory mouse has gained an outstanding place; Lindzey and Thiessen (19) suggested a few years ago that the mouse represents a prototype in behavior-genetic analyses. A large number of experiments have been conducted in recent years by using different lines, strains, and mutations of mice in order to determine their aptitudes in a number of learning tasks, ranging from active and passive avoidance to maze learning and lever-press instrumental learning. The reviews on this topic (22,34) indicate that much useful information has been collected in this area during recent years. An indication of the growing attention devoted to the behavior of genetically defined mice exists in a recent bibliography (33) listing 1,222 references dealing with a number of behavioral categories. Table 5, based on the study of Sprott and Staats (33), indicates that almost 150 studies concentrated on the learning abilities of genetically defined mice, a lower number, 26, was devoted to memory mechanisms, and an incredibly low number of experiments, only 15, deal with neurochemical mechanisms.

If we consider in detail the field of learning, one basic step in behavioral experiments was the demonstration that whereas individual mice belonging to random-bred populations attain disparate learning levels, inbred strains are characterized by homogeneous performances within each strain. In a large number of learning situations ranging from positively rewarded maze learning to negatively rewarded active avoidance, different strains of mice were

TABLE 5. *Behavioral studies using inbred or selected strains of mice*

Category	No. of studies
Activity (wheel running, exploratory)	100
Aggression	121
Audiogenic seizures	162
Communication (vocalization, pheromonal)	44
Emotionality	47
Feeding (eating, drinking, taste)	60
Learning	144
Maternal	34
Memory	26
Psychomotor	20
Reproduction	72
Biorhythms	15
Social	47
CNS: manipulations + measurements	106
Neurochemistry	15

From Sprott and Staats, ref. 33.

ranked for their high-, intermediate-, and low-learning patterns (4). For example, by comparing the overall performance attained by nine strains of mice, Bovet et al. (4) were able to show that their strains were very poor in avoidance performance in shuttle box and that in Lashley III maze situations two other strains (DBA/2J and C57Br/cdJ) attained a very high level of performance whereas other strains showed intermediate values. These behavioral differences were demonstrated to be qualitative also, since the study of distributed versus massed practice in avoidance and maze learning showed that under the same training conditions some strains were characterized by good short-term performance, whereas other strains showed more efficient memory storage mechanisms. A number of behavioral measures have been assessed in some of these strains that have been used in diallele studies and intercrossed up to the F2 and F3 generation in order to assess genetic correlations (25). For example, the high-avoiding strains of mice SEC1/ReJ and DBA/2J, which are also good maze learners, are characterized by low levels of exploratory behavior and running activity, whereas the C57BL/6J strain presents poor avoidance and maze levels, but is very active (25). By using inbred strains, researchers have also shown that the mode of inheritance of a given behavioral measure depends on the crosses considered; crossing the C57 strain with SEC mice resulted, in fact, in SEC-like progeny, whereas crossing DBA with C57 yielded an offspring similar to the C57 genotype (Fig. 1). A similar behavioral pattern was evident for avoidance and maze learning.

As previously noted, a number of studies are concentrated on the biochemical differences that characterize the various inbred strains of mice. The rationale for these investigations is to try to correlate the observed behavioral differences with given biochemical mechanisms at the level of the brain. Pryor et al. (30) have measured, for example, acetylcholinesterase activity in five strains of mice and observed that the high-avoiding strains, A and DBA/2,

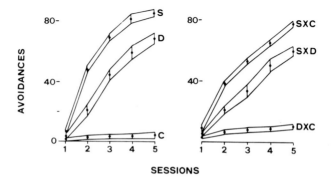

FIG. 1. Mean percentage avoidances (± 95% confidence limits of the mean) during sessions 1 to 5 in the three strains of inbred mice and in their F1 offspring. C, C57BL/6; D, DBA/2; S, SEC/1Re. [From Oliverio et al., ref. 25. Copyright (1972) by the American Psychological Association. Reprinted by permission.]

also showed a higher acetylcholinesterase activity than the two low-avoiding strains, C3H/He and C57BL/6. Mice belonging to the DBA/2 and C57BL/6 strains were subjected to detailed analyses by Ebel et al. (10), and Mandel et al. (21). The data indicate that DBA/2 are characterized by higher acetylcholinesterase and choline-acetyltransferase activities in the frontal and temporal lobe than C57BL/6 mice. These findings were interpreted as suggesting a more active acetylcholine metabolism in this strain.

As for the adrenergic system, Kempf et al. (18), in experiments carried out on C57BL/6J, DBA/2J, and SEC/ReJ mice, have demonstrated that the two high-avoiding strains (SEC and DBA) present a higher norepinephrine (NE) turnover in their hypothalamus than do C57BL/6 mice. On the contrary a lower NE turnover is evident in the first two strains when the pons and the medulla oblongata are considered. In line with these findings, Eleftheriou (11) has demonstrated that DBA/2 mice exhibit the highest turnover rate of NE whereas C57BL/6 (and C3H) mice display a lower activity in all brain regions examined.

In addition to inbred strains a number of recombinant inbred lines and a number of mutations characterized by different behavioral, neuroanatomical, or neurochemical abilities are today available; the advantages deriving from their use have been discussed in a recent book on genetics and environment and intelligence (23).

There is a relatively low number of examples of the advantages of using a strategy resting on a behavioral genetic approach in the study of learning and memory. A second approach, however, deserves consideration—the study of the ontogeny of memory. A number of studies have demonstrated that capacity for long-term memory increases during postnatal development; a variety of mechanisms, both behavioral and neurological, may account for the increase of memory and learning during ontogenesis, as appears very clearly from a comprehensive review by Campbell and Spear (7).

As for the psychogenetic approach, the ontogenetic approach to learning and memory may also be based on a less direct strategy. Instead of looking for the direct correlates of specific memorization, a study of the neurological and neurochemical ontogeny that parallel memory and learning development may prove very fruitful. In addition to a number of behavioral changes taking place during development (reflex activities, locomotor activities, mother-offspring relationships, memory, and a number of complex adaptive behaviors), there are in fact a number of changes in the CNS that might also influence memory; myelinization, cell differentiation, development of electrical activity, neural transmission, nucleic acid content, protein synthesis, and metabolic rate are just a few examples of the developmental changes that parallel the development of memory.

This type of approach can also analyze the role exerted by genetic and environmental factors on behavioral ontogenesis. If we consider human infants, the importance of gestational and early postnatal environment has been stressed by Soviet psychologists, chiefly by Luria (20), who suggests that a heterogeneous number of gestational and perinatal factors results in mental retardation. Similarly, interest in the early determinants of behaviour is increased since a number of studies have indicated that infants react to environmental differences from the first days or weeks of life (28, 31,37). This approach has raised interest in a number of scales, measures, and physiological tests that can be applied from the first days of life. Whereas Soviet psychologists are more inclined toward a number of electrophysiological measures that can be assessed in the newborn, the trend in the United States is oriented more toward scales in which a number of reflex activities and behavioural postures are quantified (3,5,6,39).

We would like to stress that the experiments conducted on animal models may represent a useful step toward a better knowledge of the role of the environment on behavioral ontogenesis. Similarly, we would like to show that a number of pharmacological, nutritional, and environmental factors may affect the postnatal development of behavior and interact with the genetic make-up of the individual. Reflex responses found in newborn mice such as rooting, head orientation, labial suckling, and positive and negative thermotaxis may be considered behavioral mechanisms that ensure the survival as well of mice, dogs, and humans. The disappearance of these reflexes and the maturation of other neuromuscular reflex activities connected to myelination have similar developmental patterns in these species, the age of a 1- to 2-week-old mouse being equivalent to that of a 3- to 4-week-old dog or a 3-month-old baby for some behavioral features (13).

A number of studies conducted in cats, dogs, mice, and rats have been devoted to an analysis of the development of different measures of postnatal behavior ranging from electrocortical activity to motor reflexes, sleep patterns, locomotor behavior, and mother-offspring relationships (2,13,32,35,36). These studies indicate, in general terms, that in nonprecocious mammals the postnatal maturation of the cortex and of myelinized structures is paralleled by a maturation of a number of behavioural activities necessary for more complex adaptive behaviors. The existence of this period of postnatal brain maturation is important in relation to the different environmental factors that may positively or negatively affect this critical period and act on the development of behavior. In this regard, the electrocorticographic (ECoG) activity of the mouse seems to be an important measure since it parallels the different stages of maturation of the cortex. The maturation of the ECoG activity and the effects of *in utero* treatments with CNS-stimulating drugs were assessed in C57 and SEC mice, which, as previously noted, are characterized by opposite levels of activity, learning abilities, and brain chemistry (25). From the ECoG analysis in both strains a progressive postnatal maturation of the electrical patterns was clearly evident that reached the adult level the 12th day after birth. When the patterns corresponding to the first day of age were considered, clear differences were evident between the two strains (Fig. 2).

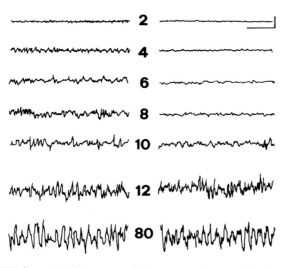

FIG. 2. ECoG in C57BL/6 and SEC/1Re mice at different ages after birth. Samples of polygraphic re-cordings during waking indicate that the development of ECoG activity occurs at earlier stages in C57BL/6 strain. The tracings are almost identical at age 12 days. Scale, 1 sec/200 μV. [From Oliverio et al., ref. 27. Copyright (1975) by Elsevier/North Holland Biomedical Press. Reprinted by permission.]

In fact, whereas in the C57 mice a regular rhythmic electrical activity was recorded from the first day of age and was characterized at 4 days of age by a regular activity, at a higher voltage (6 to 10 cycles/sec) the SEC strain showed a barely detectable electrical activity before the eighth day after birth. Thus, it was evident that slower patterns of postnatal cortical maturation characterize the SEC strain, which shows high levels of avoidance and maze learning as compared with the C57 strain. This result presents slower learning patterns and higher levels of exploratory and wheel-running activity. It is important to underline that no significant difference was evident between brain and body weights in the two strains considered.

A growing number of experimental and clinical findings suggest that mal-nutrition during pregnancy affects brain growth and exerts negative effects on postnatal behavioral development; a negative relationship between malnu-trition, on the one hand, and brain development and learning ability in the adult, on the other, has been suggested (27).

The use of inbred strains of mice seems to be a fruitful tool in the study of the effects of early malnutrition on electrophysiological and behavioral de-velopment (27). In a recent study, mice from random-bred mice and from mice derived from SEC/1Re and C57BL/6 strains were used, and the effects of malnutrition were assessed by artificially altering the littersize at birth, using small (four pups), intermediate (eight pups), or large (16 pups) litters. An analysis of the effects of early malnutrition on brain and body weight showed that clear deficits were evident from the first weeks after birth. Mice from the large litters were characterized at 16 and 24 days of age by body and brain weights that were, respectively, 50 and 30% lower than those evident in mice belonging to the small litters. This deficit was still evident in adult 60-day-old mice.

When the development of a number of reflex activities was considered, it was evident that in well-nourished mice reflexes such as the rooting reflex were mature from the first day in all strains and other reflexes such as cliff aversion or righting appeared on the third day, whereas still other reflexes appeared at a later age. Early malnutrition exerted a negative effect on the development of some of these reflexes; although the rooting reflex was unaffected, cliff aversion, righting, placing, and grasping appeared at a later age in the large litters. Some differences were evident between C57BL/6 and SEC/1Re mice; reflexes such as righting and placing, for example, were more affected in C57 mice than in the SEC strain.

The measures of ECoG activity showed that the postnatal maturation of the ECoG activity was delayed by malnutrition in all strains. For example, random-bred mice belonging to well-nourished litters showed a rhythmic pattern (6 to 10 cycles/sec) from the fourth day of age, and the tracing increased in voltage at 16 days and reached the highest amplitude by the 24th day. In contrast, the electrical activity was extremely reduced at 4 or 8 days in the large litters, which showed, only after 16 days of age, a pattern similar to that evident at 4 days in well-nourished mice. When inbred mice were considered, it was evident that ECoG maturation was more precocious in well-nourished C57 mice than in SEC mice; thus a delay in the ECoG maturation was evident at an earlier stage (day 4 to 8) in the C57 strain, for small litters from the SEC strain showed barely detectable ECoG activity at this stage. However, the ECoG maturation of the mice belonging to the intermediate and to the large litters of both strains reached an adult level only at 24 to 30 days of age, without showing those intermediate patterns evident in the small litters at 8 (C57BL/6) or 16 days (5SEC/1Re).

The detrimental effects of malnutrition on brain development were evident when locomotor activity and avoidance learning were assessed in adult mice malnourished during the suckling period. These measurements were taken in 60-day-old mice following dietary rehabilitation. With respect to the locomotor activity, the C57BL/6 mice belonging to small litters were more active than SEC/1Re mice, as previously demonstrated (25); a general trend toward an increased exploratory activity, independently of the strain considered, was observed as litter size increased. In contrast, avoidance learning of Swiss and SEC mice was greatly impaired in early malnourished mice. No obvious effect following dietary deprivation was detectable in the C57BL/6 mice, which were already characterized by poor avoidance levels even when reared in small litters.

A more selective and interesting type of malnutrition is that derived from diets deprived of essential fatty acids (EFA). It must be emphasized that the advantage of this method is that the use of EFA malnutrition during pregnancy avoids the possible pitfalls connected with an altered mother-offspring ratio, as in experiments in which malnutrition is obtained by varying the litter size.

The results showed that brain and body growth patterns were only slightly affected in mice born from females fed EFA-deprived diets during pregnancy. However, a number of reflexes, for example, placing reflex, appeared later in the EFA group than in control mice; similarly, grasping and bar holding were also delayed by 2 to 3 days, as in mice malnourished during the suckling period (8,26). The reflexes delayed in their maturation (righting, placing, grasping, and bar holding reflexes) were those involving motor abilities normally evident during the first 2 weeks after birth, suggesting that the administration of an EFA-deprived diet affects the myelinization of the nervous motor system tracts.

The ECoG recordings also showed a clear delay in the maturation of the brain electrical activity of EFA-deprived mice, compared with the controls. However, the ECoG of control and EFA-deprived animals was similar, starting from the third week of age. By using this type of malnutrition, it was also possible to show that the avoidance-learning ability was impaired after 2 months of rehabilitation, in mice fed by females that were EFA deprived during pregnancy. The selective deprivation of fatty acids seems therefore to affect the patterns of brain development permanently (9,15). A morphological analysis of brain maturation has indicated that in the animals fed EFA-deprived diets there is a delay of myelination processes in a number of myelinated structures that may result in long-lasting effects on learning ability (16) (Fig. 3).

If it is possible to stunt or delay the development of the brain and learning abilities through the use of diets deprived of free fatty acids, it is also possible to accelerate the development of a number of reflex activities and of the ECoG by feeding diets characterized by odd-chain fatty acids during pregnancy and lactation (17). Some of the reflexes considered appeared from 4 to 6 days earlier than in control mice. Similarly a clear-cut acceleration in the maturation of the cortical activity was also evident. These findings are particularly interesting because they indicate that it is possible to alter—in one direction or the other—brain and behavioral ontogeny and to modify learning ability as assessed in the adult.

Finally, to return to the role of the genetic make-up and the environment in relation to learning, it is interesting to note the effects that early environmental enrichment or impoverishment exert on different genotypes, e.g., the two strains of mice (C57BL/6 and SEC/1Re) that are characterized by opposite learning abilities.

Litters derived from C57 or SEC dams were assigned to three different laboratory conditions: (a) standard laboratory rearing, (b) enriched cages, and (c) impoverished cages. All mice were kept until testing (6 weeks) in the three different conditions and then subjected to shuttle-box learning (100

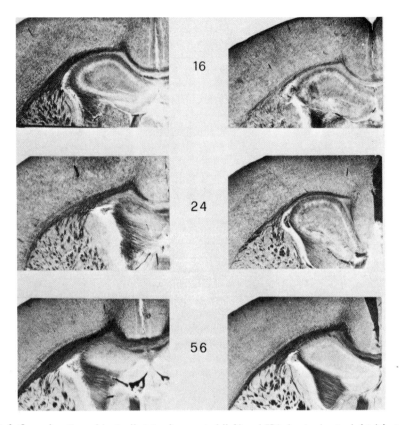

FIG. 3. Coronal sections of brains deriving from control (*left*) and EPA-deprived animals (*right*) at comparable levels at the age of 16, 24, and 56 days (*middle*). Baker staining. ×30. (From Gozzo and D'Udine, ref. 16.)

trials/day during 5 consecutive days) and Lashley III maze learning (three trials/day during 5 consecutive days). The results indicate that early environmental differences may be able to modify the learning abilities as measured in the adults. Figure 4 indicates that impoverished and enriched mice belonging to the SEC strain attained in the two tasks a lower and higher learning performance, respectively. In contrast, the effects connected with an impoverished or enriched environment were less evident in the C57 strain, which is more mature at birth and therefore is probably less sensitive to drastic environmental differences. In fact, only impoverished C57 mice differed in their performance from the other groups belonging to the same strain (24).

In conclusion, the mouse represents a good model for an analysis of the genetic, gestational, or postnatal factors that result in a number of complex patterns of learning. The study of the psychobiological processes that are the ground for a number of genetic and ontogenetic differences and stages may

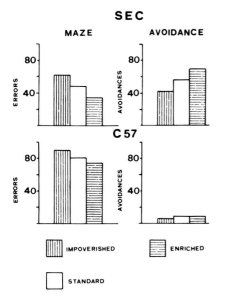

FIG. 4. Performances of C57BL/6 and SEC/1Re mice raised in a standard, enriched, or impoverished environment from birth to testing. Each group consisted of 24 mice. The numbers refer to mean percent avoidances or to mean maze errors. Differences between impoverished and enriched environments were at the 1% level in SEC mice, whereas in C57·mice the differences were evident only for the impoverished groups tested in the maze. [From Oliverio, ref. 24. Copyright (1977) by Elsevier/North Holland Biomedical Press. Reprinted by permission.]

serve in making a catalog of the different learning abilities and neurochemical correlates of a given phenotype. This approach may appear a longer strategy to the study of learning and memory, but may prove to be a more rewarding one.

REFERENCES

1. Altman, J. (1966): *Organic Foundations of Animal Behavior.* Holt, New York.
2. Altman, J., and Sundarshan, K. (1975): Postnatal development of locomotion in the laboratory rat. *Anim. Behav.,* 23:896–920.
3. Bailey, N. (1969): *Manual for the Bailey Scales of Infant.* Psychological Corp., New York.
4. Bovet, D., Bovet-Nitti, F., and Oliverio, A. (1969): Genetic aspects of learning and memory in mice. *Science,* 163:139–149.
5. Brazelton, T. B. (1973): *Neonatal Behavioral Assessment Scale.* Heinemann, London.
6. Broman, S. H., Nichols, P. L., and Kennedy, W. A. (1975): *Preschool IQ: Prenatal and Early Developmental Correlates.* Lawrence Earlbaum Assoc., Hillsdale, New York.
7. Campbell, B. A., and Spear, N. E. (1972): Ontogeny of memory. *Psychol. Rev.,* 79:215–236.
8. Castellano, C., and Oliverio, A. (1976): Early malnutrition and postnatal changes in brain and behavior in the mouse. *Brain Res.,* 101:317–325.
9. D'Udine, B., and Oliverio, A. (1976): Lipid malnutrition and early development. *Behav. Processes,* 1:183–190.
10. Ebel, A., Hermetet, J., and Mandel, P. (1973): Comparative study of acetylcholinesterase and choline-acetyltransferase enzyme activity in brain of DBA and C57 mice. *Nature [New Biol.],* 242:56–57.
11. Eleftheriou, B. E. (1971): Regional brain norepinephrine turnover rates in four strains of mice. *Neuroendocrinology,* 7:329–336.
12. Entingh, D., Dunn, A., Glassman, E., Wilson, J. E., Hogan, E., and Damstrat, T.

(1975): Biochemical approaches to the biological basis of memory. In: *Handbook of Psychobiology*, edited by M. S. Gazzaniga and C. Blakemore, pp. 201–238. Academic Press, New York.

13. Fox, M. W. (1965): Reflex ontogeny and behavioral development of the mouse. *Anim. Behav.*, 13:234–241.
14. Gaito, J. (1976): Molecular psychobiology of memory: Its appearance, contributions and decline. *Physiol. Psychol.*, 4:476–484.
15. Galli, G., Messeri, P., Oliverio, A., and Paoletti, R. (1975): Deficiency of essential fatty acids during pregnancy and avoidance learning in the progeny. *Pharmacol. Res. Commun.*, 7:71–80.
16. Gozzo, S., and D'Udine, B. (1977): Lipid malnutrition and postnatal brain myelination ontogeny. *Neurosci. Lett.* (*In preparation.*)
17. Gozzo, S., Oliverio, A., Salvati, S., Serlupi-Crescenzi, G., Tagliamonte, B., and Tomassi, G. (1977): Nutritional studies of the lipid fraction of n-alkane grown yeast. IV. Effects on behavioral development. *Nutr. Rep. Intl.* (*In press.*)
18. Kempf, E., Greilshamer, J., Mack, G., and Mandel, P. (1974): Correlation of behavioral differences in three strains of mice with differences in brain amines. *Nature*, 247:483–485.
19. Lindzey, G., and Thiessen, D. D. (1970): *Contributions to Behavior-Genetic Analysis. The Mouse as a Prototype.* Appleton, New York.
20. Luria, A. R. (1972): *L'enfant Retardé Mental.* Privet, Paris.
21. Mandel, P., Ebel, A., Hermetet, J. C., Bovet, D., and Oliverio, A. (1973): Etudes des enzymes du système cholinergique chez les hybrides F_1 de souris se distinguant par leur aptitude au conditionnement. *CR Acad. Sci. Paris*, 276:395–398.
22. Oliverio, A. (1974): Genetic and biochemical analysis of behavior in mice. *Prog. Neurobiol.*, 3:191–215.
23. Oliverio, A. (editor) (1977): *Genetics, Environment and Intelligence.* Elsevier/North-Holland, Amsterdam.
24. Oliverio, A. (1977): Unpublished results quoted in article titled "Strain differences and learning in the mouse," by D. Bovet. In: *Genetics, Environment and Intelligence*, edited by A. Oliverio. Elsevier/North-Holland, Amsterdam.
25. Oliverio, A., Castellano, C., and Messeri, P. (1972): A genetic analysis of avoidance, maze and wheel running behavior in the mouse. *J. Comp. Physiol. Psychol.*, 79:459–473.
26. Oliverio, A., Castellano, C., and Puglisi-Allegra, S. (1975): Effects of genetic and nutritional factors on post-natal reflex and behavioral development in the mouse. *Exp. Agric. Res.*, 1:41–56.
27. Oliverio, A., Castellano, C., and Renzi, P. (1975): Genotype or prenatal drug experience affect brain maturation in the mouse. *Brain Res.*, 90:357–360.
28. Papoušek, H. (1967): Conditioning during early postnatal development. In: *Behavior in Infancy and Early Childhood*, edited by Y. Brackbill and G. Thompson, pp. 259–274. The Free Press, New York.
29. Piaget, J. (1970): Mémoire et intelligence. In: *Le Mémoire*, edited by D. Bovet, A. Fessard, C. Flores, N. H. Frijda, B. Inhelder, B. Milner, and J. Piaget, pp. 169–184. Presses Universitaires de France, Paris.
30. Pryor, G. T., Schlesinger, K., and Calhoun, W. H. (1966): Differences in brain enzymes among five inbred strains of mice. *Life Sci.*, 5:2105–2111.
31. Scarr-Salapatek, S., and Williams, M. L. (1973): The effect of early stimulation on low-birth-weight infants. *Child Dev.*, 44:94–101.
32. Scott, J. P. (1953): The process of primary socialization in canine and human infants. *Sociol. Res. Child Dev. Monogr.*, 28:1–34.
33. Sprott, R. L., and Staats, J. (1975): Behavioral studies using genetically defined mice. A bibliography. *Behav. Genet.*, 5:27–82.
34. Van Abeelen, J. H. F. (editor) (1974): *The Genetics of Behaviour.* North-Holland, Amsterdam.
35. Van Abeelen, J. H. F. (1966): Effects of genotype on mouse behavior. *Anim. Behav.*, 14:218–225.
36. Verlay, R., Garma, L., and Scherrer, J. (1969): Aspects ontogénétiques des états de veille et de sommeil chez les mammifères. *Bord. Méd.*, 4:877–885.

37. White, B. L. (1971): *Human Infants: Experience and Psychological Development.* Harvard Univ. Press, Cambridge.
38. Will, B. E. (1977): Neurochemical correlates of individual differences in animal learning capacity. *Behav. Biol.,* 19:143–171.
39. Yarrow, L. J., Rubenstein, J. L., and Pedersen, F. W. (1975): *Infant and Environment: Early Cognitive and Motivational Development.* Halsted, New York.

EXPERIMENTAL ELECTRICAL AND
NEUROCHEMICAL STUDIES

Brain Mechanisms in Memory and Learning:
From the Single Neuron to Man,
edited by M. A. B. Brazier.
Raven Press, New York © 1979.

Neurophysiological Analysis of Conditioned Taste Aversion

Jan Bureš and O. Burešová

Institute of Physiology, Czechoslovak Academy of Sciences, Prague, Czechoslovakia

Although research into the mechanism of conditioning at the level of single neurons and neural networks has brought important discoveries as reviewed in other contributions to this volume, it has not yet solved the fundamental enigma of conditioning, that is, how the originally ineffective (neutral) input to a neuron changes into an effective one, the conditioned stimulus (CS), when associated with the subsequent activation of this neuron by the unconditioned stimulus (US). The obvious requirement for a feedback from the neurons activated by the US to the previously stimulated CS input can be implemented by impulse flow through neural loops (4,10,16) or by direct chemical interaction between the postsynaptic and presynaptic elements involved (2,15,28). The investigation of the putative feedback mechanism is hindered by the difficulty of separating its manifestations from the neural changes induced by the isolated CS or US. This is particularly true for conditioned reactions, the formation of which requires close contiguity of the CS and US. According to Gormezano (14), conditioned eye blink in the rabbit is most rapidly established at a CS–US delay of 250 msec. Although delays of similar duration are optimal for most types of conditioning, trace conditioning seems to provide a better opportunity for the isolation of events underlying the actual establishment of new connections. Unfortunately, proficiency of trace conditioning is inversely related to the duration of the CS–US interval, because the simple "post hoc, propter hoc" concept of causality, forming the basis of anticipatory behaviour, makes the relationship of remote events improbable.

There are exceptions to this rule, however, for example, in the neural control of feeding (25), which must bridge the inherent delay between the exteroceptive signals of food (appearance, odor, taste) and the delayed visceral consequences of its ingestion (satiation and alleviation of specific deficiencies as opposed to absence of nutritive value or even to poisoning). Owing to the high survival value of the anticipatory rejection of poisons or inadequate diets, natural selection has equipped higher organisms with efficient learning mechanisms allowing association of food-related CS with the ingestion-induced US over hour-long delays. The conditioned food aversion (CFA) represents a unique model of conditioning (22,24) in which various phases of CS and US processing are so spread in time that they can be separately subjected to interfering procedures and examined for electrical or chemical concomitants (9). The present chapter reviews a series of experiments that take advantage of these possibilities and dissect the apparently uniform mechanism of conditioning into components with surprisingly different properties.

CONDITIONED FOOD AVERSION PARADIGM

CFA, known to rat ecologists and pest fighters for decades (11), had to be modified in order to meet the requirements of laboratory experimentation (13). In a typical CFA [or more specifically conditioned taste aversion, (CTA)] paradigm, rats are exposed to a standardised drinking situation until the daily water intake becomes so stabilized as to make it possible to assess deviations from the expected values as manifestations of preference or of aversion. After this habituation period, usually lasting for several days, the animal is offered a flavoured liquid (CS, e.g., sodium saccharin solution) and poisoned after an appropriate interval (tens of minutes to several hours) with a sublethal dose of a drug, eliciting severe but fully reversible gastrointestinal distress [US, e.g., 0.15 M lithium chloride (LiCl), 2 to 4% body

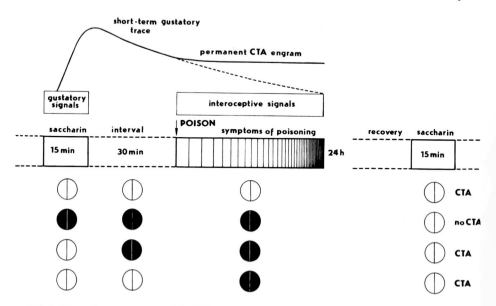

FIG. 1. Schematic representation of the CTA experiments and summary of conditions interfering with CTA acquisition. Above: The experimental paradigm and the hypothetical brain processes. Below: Brain conditions during various phases of the experiment. Black indicates bilateral cortical spreading depression (CSD), anesthesia, or hypothermia. For details, see text.

weight]. After normalization of water intake, the presence of CTA is tested by offering the animal the CS again. Aversion is expressed by the ratio of the CS intake during the retention test to the CS consumption during acquisition.

Many alternatives to this basic paradigm usually preserve its fundamental features, that is, the association of the sensory properties of food with the delayed visceral effects. For purposes of experimental analysis, CTA acquisition can be divided into three phases (Fig. 1): (a) processing of the gustatory stimulus and formation of the short-term gustatory trace, (b) persistence of the short-term gustatory trace, and (c) association of the short-term gustatory trace with the visceral signals of poisoning and consolidation of the permanent CTA engram. These phases are mutually separated by intervals that are sufficiently long to allow their differential influencing by experimental interventions.

Whereas features of classic conditioning prevail during CTA acquisition, CTA retrieval is usually tested in an operant situation and expressed by behavioural suppression in a way resembling passive avoidance or conditioned emotional reactions. Retrieval can be tested also in a classic conditioning situation when the taste stimulus is applied by forced feeding or by intraperitoneal injection (1), and the aversive reaction is expressed by the intensity of the conditioned stress (27). Each presentation of the gustatory CS not accompanied by poisoning represents an extinction trial. Since extinction is directly proportional to the amount of the CS consumed, forced application of the CS usually yields faster extinction than does spontaneous intake.

CONDITIONED TASTE AVERSION ACQUISITION

The temporal separation of the three phases of CTA acquisition made it possible to examine their resistance to conditions interfering with the normal brain function. Cortical spreading depression (CSD), anesthesia, hypothermia, and electroconvulsive shock (ECS) were tested with CTA, using saccharin as the CS and LiCl poisoning as the US. Since all the above interfering procedures prevent spontaneous drinking, their influence on the first phase of acquisition had to be examined by forced feeding of saccharin (0.1% solution) (CSD, ECS) or by intraperitoneal injection of saccharin (2% solution, 1% body weight) (anesthesia, hypothermia). All four procedures brought essentially similar results (Fig. 1): they prevented CTA acquisition when applied before and during processing of the gustatory stimulus, but had little effect on the persistence of the gustatory trace and on formation of the permanent CTA engram when applied after saccharin administration. The differential effect was best expressed in the case of anesthesia (5) and hypothermia (17), which fully suppressed CTA when applied before intraperitoneal saccharin injection, but even enhanced CTA when elicited in the CS–US interval (26) or simultaneously with the US. Bilateral CSD had a similar effect (6), but unlike anesthesia, it accelerated the decay of the gustatory trace in the CS–US interval (7). ECS interfered with all three stages of CTA acquisition, but its effect was most pronounced when the shock preceded saccharin drinking. This last finding, which mirrors the well-known ECS effects on memory consolidation (21), is illustrated in Fig. 2.

In order to achieve a strong CTA, control animals were forced fed saccharin and subsequently poisoned by LiCl on days 3 and 4. In the experimental group, ECS either preceded saccharin administration by 15 to 120 min or was applied during the 30 min CS–US interval. The retention test performed on day 5 showed strong saccharin aversion in the untreated control group and absence of CTA in rats that received ECS 15 and 30 min before saccharin drinking. The anterograde amnesia evoked by ECS lasted for about 60 min since almost normal CTA was formed in rats receiving saccharin with a 120-min post-ECS delay. ECS applied immediately after saccharin

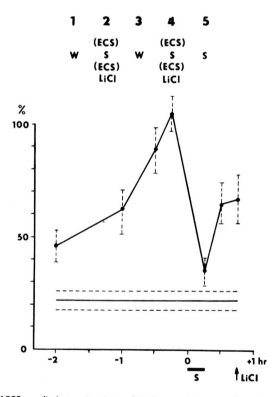

FIG. 2. The effect of ECS, applied at various intervals before or after onset of saccharin drinking (*abscissa*), on CTA acquisition. Ordinate represents Consumption of saccharin during retention testing expressed in percentages of saccharin intake of naïve animals. The horizontal line shows saccharin consumption in CTA-trained rats without ECS. The vertical lines indicate the values for the standard error of the mean. The experimental paradigm is illustrated in the upper part of the figure. 1 to 5, Days of experiment; W or S water or saccharin drinking; LiCl, intraperitoneal injection of 0.15 M lithium chloride.

drinking did not cause significant impairment of CTA acquisition. The amnesic effect of ECS was better expressed when ECS approached the LiCl injection. These last results are consonant with the studies by Nachman (23), Kral (18,19), and Kral and Beggarly (20), who have demonstrated partial disruption of CTA by ECS applied in the CS–US interval and immediately before and after poisoning. The striking difference between the effects of ECS applied 15 min before and immediately after saccharin drinking indicates that processing of the gustatory stimulus and formation of the gustatory trace require a high degree of postconvulsive recovery, whereas the gustatory trace formed by the normal brain is more resistant to ECS treatment.

The differential effects of the interfering procedures employed indicate that the first phase of CTA acquisition is an active process equally impaired by cessation of activity (anesthesia, hypothermia), by excessive activity (ECS), and by procedures combining both the above effects (CSD). Once the short-term gustatory trace has been formed, it is probably maintained by passive means (metabolic or morphologic changes of the synapses) that are little affected by inactivity, but can be disrupted by massive chaotic discharge induced by ECS and by CSD. The fact that CSD only slightly reduces the persistence of the short-term gustatory trace is probably due to the spatially restricted effect of CSD and may indicate that the essentially subcortical short-term trace requires only limited cortical support. Such a subcortical trace is more sensitive to the all-pervading effects of ECS, but is not completely wiped out even by the strongest ECS treatment (19). The increased amnesic effect of ECS applied immediately before LiCl injection indicates that the association of the gustatory trace with poisoning is another active link in CTA acquisition. The underlying processes must be confined to subcortical regions, however, that are not reached by CSD and whose activity is preserved during anesthesia and hypothermia.

The unimpaired association of the CS trace with the US under anesthesia, which seems to be radically different from other conditioning paradigms, is perhaps not unique to CTA acquisition, but cannot be easily established in the case of conditioned reflexes requiring close temporal contiguity of the CS and US. The fact that the second and third phase of CTA acquisition proceeds even when higher nervous functions are seriously disturbed has a high adaptive value; it permits the organism to associate the food-related signals processed with intact brain with the consequences of food ingestion even when such ingestion induced severe coma. This may be the reason why evolution equipped the CFA mechanism almost as well as respiration and other homeostatic functions with circuits protected against possible failure.

The above analysis of CTA acquisition represents the gustatory trace as a short-term trace, but this is not quite accurate. As pointed out by Kral (18), gustatory traces unaccompanied by poisoning do not disappear, but turn into long-term engrams, labeling the corresponding flavours as safe. This is expressed by decreased neophobia towards familiar flavours. Kral (18) suggests that the inverse relationship between CTA strength and the duration of CS–US interval is not due to the decay of the gustatory trace but to its decreasing association with poisoning. According to this concept, ECS causes the so-called disassociation, i.e., it blocks the process underlying the CS–US association without interfering with the persistence of the gustatory trace, which can be regarded as transient only with respect to its association with poisoning.

CONDITIONED TASTE AVERSION RETRIEVAL

Active CTA retrieval requires spontaneous behaviour of the animal and therefore, cannot be tested, under anesthesia, hypothermia, and bilateral CSD. There are experimental conditions, however, that indicate mechanisms of CTA retrieval are more resistant to interference than the first phase of CTA acquisition. Thus rats subjected to ECS before CTA retrieval show rejection of the aversive stimulus as soon as they resume spontaneous drinking 20 to 30 min after ECS, that is, at a time when they are still unable to acquire new CTAs. The differential effect on CTA acquisition and retrieval is still more striking in the case of paradoxical sleep deprivation. As shown by Danguir and Nicolaidis (12) and by Bhatt et al. (3), rats deprived for 24 hr of paradoxical sleep by being forced to stay on small pedestals (7 cm in diameter) are unable to acquire CTA to the flavour of fluids drunk shortly after termination of deprivation. On the other hand, the same paradoxical sleep deprivation does not prevent retrieval of the earlier acquired CTA (Fig. 3). Although both CTA acquisition and retrieval involve processing of gustatory signals, retrieval does not require modification of synaptic connections and can be considered, therefore, the more simple and more resistant process.

On the other hand, every application of the CS influences the neural circuits of the conditioned reaction, which are either strengthened by the new CS–US association or weakened by extinction, when CS has been presented alone. Since extinction does not require active behaviour of the animal during presentation of the gustatory stimulus and can be tested days later, it can be subjected to the same interfering procedures as CTA acquisition. The experimental evidence based on experiments employing CSD and anesthesia indicates that the plastic processes mediating CTA extinction are different from those of CTA acquisition.

The first results pointing in this direction were obtained in rats with strong CTA to saccharin who were force fed with the aversive fluid under bilateral CSD (8). Whereas intact rats resisted drinking the saccharin solution and attempted to remove it from their mouths by spitting and head shaking, functionally decorticate rats swallowed the intraorally infused solution as readily as naïve animals. CTA retrieval tested on the next day in the rats with intact brain revealed considerably weakened aversion, comparable to or even ex-

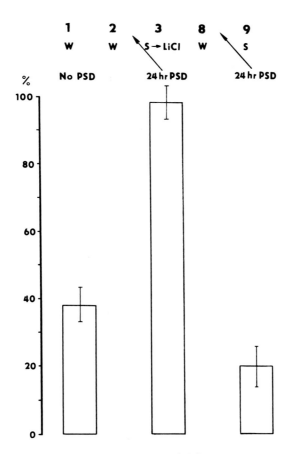

FIG. 3. The effect of 24-hr paradoxical sleep deprivation (PSD) on CTA acquisition or retrieval. Above: Scheme of the experiment. Arrows indicate the PSD treatment. The columns represent saccharin consumption during retention testing expressed in percentages of saccharin intake of naïve animals. Further description, as in Fig. 2.

ceeding extinction attained by force-feeding saccharin to intact rats (Fig. 4). The differential effect of CSD on CTA acquisition was demonstrated most clearly when forced feeding of saccharin to CTA trained animals was followed by LiCl injection. This treatment enhances CTA in normal rats, but induces extinction in functionally decorticate animals, obviously because CSD blocks the formation of the short-term gustatory trace essential for CTA acquisition, but does not prevent readout of the already established CTA engram necessary for CTA extinction.

Similar results were obtained with anesthesia (9). Intraperitoneal injection of 2% sodium saccharin (1% body weight) to CTA-trained rats caused significant CTA extinction in both unanesthetized and anesthetized (40 mg/kg pentobarbital) animals (Fig. 4). This result indicates that the processing of the gustatory information continues in the anesthetized animals. Electroen-

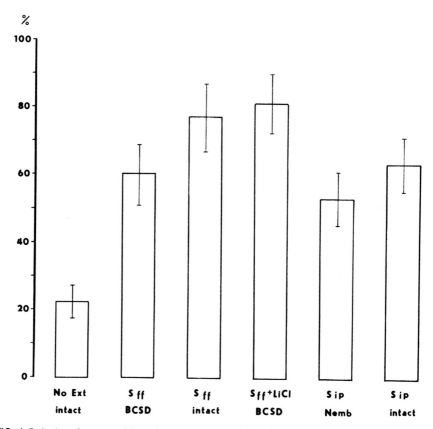

FIG. 4. Extinction of a strong CTA under control conditions (intact), bilateral cortical spreading depression (BCSD), or pentobarbital anesthesia (Nemb.). The columns indicate saccharin consumption expressed in percentages of saccharin intake in naïve animals. Sff, extinction induced by forced feeding of 0.1% saccharin; Sip, extinction induced by intraperitoneal injection of 2% saccharin (1% body weight); No Ext., nonextinguished controls. Other description, as in Fig. 2.

cephalographic arousal elicited in CTA-trained rats anesthetized with urethane by intraperitoneal administration of saccharin is probably an electrophysiological concomitant of the readout process.

Whereas in the intact brain, gustatory stimuli can lead either to formation or to extinction of CTA, under CSD or anesthesia they can only elicit CTA extinction. This dissociation made it possible to study the mutual relationship of the acquisition and extinction mechanisms in experiments in which saccharin drinking in intact naïve rats was followed by anesthesia, poisoning, and intraperitoneal injection of saccharin. It was expected that the gustatory stimuli received under anesthesia would interfere with the CTA-forming mechanism and weaken the resulting CTA. This assumption was only partly confirmed by the results shown in Fig. 5.

Intraperitoneal injection of saccharin did not significantly decrease CTA

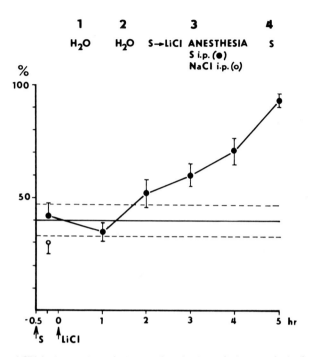

FIG. 5. Extinction of CTA by intraperitoneal injection of saccharin applied to anesthetized rats at different intervals (*abscissa*) after saccharin drinking and poisoning. Ordinate represents Saccharin consumption during the retention test expressed in percentages of saccharin intake of naïve animals. Full horizontal line, retention test in unextinguished control animals; dashed lines, standard error of the mean.

when applied in the middle of the 30-min CS–US interval or 1 hr after LiCl poisoning. With longer LiCl–saccharin injection intervals, extinction gradually increased, reached a peak 5 hr after poisoning, and slightly decreased again at 24 hr. Analogous results were obtained in unanesthetized rats, although extinction was less pronounced at longer acquisition–extinction intervals.

The gradually increasing efficiency of extinction in the above experiments can be attributable to the corresponding alleviation of the symptoms of poisoning or to the decay of the short-term gustatory trace, induced by saccharin drinking in the intact animals. To decide between these two possibilities, in another experimental series CTA-trained rats were anesthetized, injected with LiCl and 60 min later with saccharin. This treatment did not decrease the efficiency of extinction in comparison with controls receiving NaCl instead of LiCl; during retention testing, saccharin consumption increased to 73% of normal intake in the experimental animals and to 73% in the controls. The failure to extinguish CTA by saccharin injection in anesthetized rats 1 hr after saccharin–LiCl association is not due to persisting symptoms of poisoning but rather to the fact that at this time the short-term memory file still contains the strong gustatory trace formed during intact brain processing of the taste signals. It seems that in the processing of gustatory information, CTA-forming mechanisms are given priority over the CTA-extinguishing processes. The CTA engram is formed or enhanced whenever a short-term memory trace is associated with the visceral signals of poisoning. CTA is extinguished either by gustatory stimuli not followed by poisoning or by taste signals not recorded in the short-term memory file (stimuli received under anesthesia) even when they overlap with poisoning.

CONCLUSION

The above results provide further support for the hypothesis (8) schematically illustrated in Fig. 6. According to this concept, there are two levels of gustatory signal processing. At the lower level they are evaluated according to their immediate palatability and trigger corresponding unconditioned consummatory reactions. The higher level processing enters all gustatory stimuli into a short-term memory file, where they wait several hours for visceral signals of the metabolic consequences of food ingestion. Association of the short-term gustatory trace with the visceral input leads to formation of permanent memory traces, which label various taste stimuli as desirable, neutral, or aversive. This labeling permits the organism to anticipate the consequences of food consumption; if its taste corresponds to an aversive gustatory engram, the conditioned aversive response overrules the immediate palatability of the food. Conversely, anticipation of positive consequences may stimulate ingestion of diets that would otherwise be rejected as unpalatable.

The remarkable peculiarity of CTA is that gustatory stimuli elicit immedi-

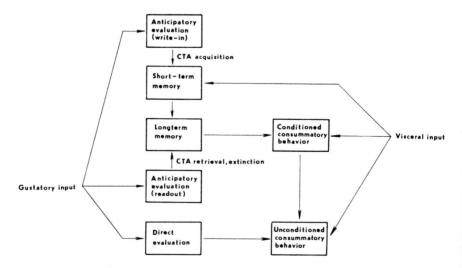

FIG. 6. Scheme of the hypothetical mechanisms of CTA acquisition and retrieval. For details, see text.

ate retrieval, but delayed formation, of CTA engrams. Since activation of the conditioned reflex in absence of the US leads to extinction, the CTA engram is weakened by each readout proportional to the intensity and duration of the gustatory stimulation. In intact animals association of subsequent poisoning with the short-term gustatory trace counteracts the initial extinction and may increase the CTA strength, as is the case in the CTA overtraining. This biologically important mechanism enables the animal to establish the maximum amount of a particular food that can be consumed without adverse consequences. Rapid eye movement sleep deprivation, anesthesia, hypothermia, ECS, and CSD prevent formation of the short-term gustatory trace, but do not interfere with the association of the already established short-term gustatory trace with poisoning, nor do they block the readout of the permanent gustatory engram. This is the reason why administration of the aversive stimulus under anesthesia or CSD causes CTA extinction despite subsequent poisoning, which cannot be associated with the taste stimulus in absence of the short-term gustatory trace.

The analysis of the neural mechanisms of CTA raises the question whether its unusual properties are specific for this conditioned reaction or whether they can also occur in a less conspicuous form in other types of learning. The most important points to be verified by further research are:

1. Is the short-term memory mediating other conditioned reactions with shorter CS–US delays similarly resistant to interfering procedures?

2. Can such a short-term trace be associated with other types of US (e.g., electrocutaneous shock) applied under brain states otherwise incompatible with learning?

3. Are experimental conditions preventing acquisition of a conditioned response compatible with extinction of the same reaction?

These problems have not yet been seriously tackled by neurophysiological research, because there has been no reason to suspect the existence of such phenomena. Although their investigation will be seriously hindered by the rapid decay of the short-term traces and by the possible blockade of the nonvisceral US by the interfering procedures, it may eventually show that the dissociation of the CS identification mechanisms during acquisition and retrieval and of the CS–US association mechanisms is not limited to CTA. At the same time, CTA serves as a convenient model of conditioning, allowing dissection of the underlying neural processes into isolated components that can be examined by localized functional ablation or interfering procedures, or both.

REFERENCES

1. Baum, M., Foidart, D. S., and Lapointe, A. (1974): Rapid extinction of a conditioned taste aversion following unreinforced intraperitoneal injection of the fluid CS. *Physiol. Behav.*, 12:871–873.
2. Baumgarten, R. J. von (1970): Plasticity in the nervous system at the unitary

level. In: *The Neurosciences,* Second Study Program, edited by F. O. Schmitt, pp. 260–271. Rockefeller Univ. Press, New York.

3. Bhatt, V. H., Bureš, J., and Burešová, O. (1978): Differential effect of paradoxical sleep deprivation on acquisition and retrieval of conditioned taste aversion in rats. *Physiol. Behav.,* 20:101–107.

4. Brindley, G. S. (1969): Nerve nets of plausible size that perform many simple learning tasks. *Proc. R. Soc. Lond. [Biol.],* 174:173–191.

5. Bureš, J., and Burešová, O. (1977): Physiological mechanisms of conditioned food aversion. In: *Food Aversion Learning,* edited by N. W. Milgram, L. Krames, and T. M. Alloway. Plenum Press, New York.

6. Burešová, O., and Bureš, J. (1973): Cortical and subcortical components of the conditioned saccharin aversion. *Physiol. Behav.,* 11:435–439.

7. Burešová, O., and Bureš, J. (1974): Functional decortication in the CS–US interval decreases efficiency of taste aversion learning. *Behav. Biol.,* 12:357–364.

8. Burešová, O., and Bureš, J. (1975): Functional decortication by cortical spreading depression does not prevent forced extinction of conditioned saccharin aversion in rats. *J. Comp. Physiol. Psychol.,* 88:47–52.

9. Burešová, O., and Bureš, J. (1977): The effect of anesthesia on acquisition and extinction of conditioned taste aversion. *Behav. Biol.,* 20:41–50.

10. Burke, W. (1966): Neuronal models for conditioned reflexes. *Nature,* 210:269–270.

11. Chitty, D., (editor) (1954): *Control of Rats and Mice,* Vol. 1, 2. Clarendon Press, Oxford.

12. Danguir, J., and Nicolaidis, S. (1976): Impairment of learned aversion acquisition following paradoxical sleep deprivation in the rat. *Physiol. Behav.,* 17:489–492.

13. Garcia, J., and Ervin, F. R. (1968): Gustatory-visceral and telereceptor-cutaneous conditioning: Adaptation in internal and external milieus. *Commun. Behav. Biol.,* 1:389–415.

14. Gormezano, I. (1966): Classical conditioning. In: *Experimental Methods and Instrumentation in Psychology,* edited by J. B. Sidowski, pp. 385–420. McGraw-Hill, New York.

15. Griffith, J. S. (1966): A theory of the nature of memory. *Nature,* 211:1160–1163.

16. Horn, G. (1970): Changes in neuronal activity and their relationship to behaviour. In: *Short Term Changes in Neural Activity and Behavior,* edited by G. Horn, and R. A. Hinde, pp. 567–606. Cambridge Univ. Press, London.

17. Ionescu, E., and Burešová, O. (1977): The effects of hypothermia on the acquisition of conditioned taste aversion in rats. *J. Comp. Physiol. Psychol.,* 91:1297–1307.

18. Kral, P. A. (1971): Electroconvulsive shock during the taste-illness interval: Evidence for induced disassociation. *Physiol. Behav.,* 7:667–670.

19. Kral, P. A. (1971): ECS between tasting and illness: Effects of current parameters on a taste aversion. *Physiol. Behav.,* 7:779–782.

20. Kral, P. A., and Beggarly, H. D. (1973): Electroconvulsive shock impedes association formation: Conditioned taste aversion paradigm. *Physiol. Behav.,* 10:145–147.

21. Mc Gaugh, J. L., and Herz, M. J. (1972): *Memory Consolidation.* Albion, San Francisco.

22. Milgram, N. W., Krames, L., and Alloway, T. M. (1977): *Food Aversion Learning.* Plenum Press, New York.

23. Nachman, M. (1970): Limited effects of electroconvulsive shock on memory of taste stimulation. *J. Comp. Physiol. Psychol.,* 73:31–37.

24. Riley, A. L., and Baril, L. L. (1976): Conditioned taste aversions: A bibliography. *Animal Learning & Behavior,* 4(1B):1S–13S.

25. Rozin, P., and Kalat, J. W. (1971): Specific hungers and poison avoidance as adaptive specializations of learning. *Psycholog. Rev.,* 78:459–486.

26. Rozin, P., and Ree, P. (1972): Long extension of effective CS–US interval by anesthesia between CS and US. *J. Comp. Physiol. Psychol.,* 80:43–48.

27. Smotherman, W. P., Hennessy, J. W., and Levine, S. (1976): Plasma corticosterone levels during recovery from LiCl produced taste aversions. *Behav. Biol.,* 16:401–412.

28. Szilard, L. (1964): On memory and recall. *Proc. Natl. Acad. Sci. USA,* 51:1092–1099.

Brain Mechanisms in Memory and Learning:
From the Single Neuron to Man,
edited by M. A. B. Brazier.
Raven Press, New York © 1979.

Modulation of Memory Processes by Neuropeptides of Hypothalamic-Neurohypophyseal Origin

D. de Wied and B. Bohus

Rudolf Magnus Institute for Pharmacology, Medical Faculty, University of Utrecht, Utrecht, The Netherlands

Neuropeptides are hormones that affect the nervous system. Various pituitary and hypothalamic hormones function as neuropeptides. Examples are adrenocorticotropic hormone (ACTH) and the related melanocyte-stimulating hormones α-MSH and β-MSH. The influence of these pituitary hormones on the nervous system is localised in a few amino acids of the molecule and thus independent of the classic endocrine effects of these hormones, which may act as prohormones (48). Neuropeptides derived from ACTH and α-MSH (ACTH 4–7, ACTH 4–10, ACTH 4–16) affect motivational, learning, and memory processes in the rat (50) and motivation, attention, and concentration in man (21). Lysine pituitary hormone (β-LPH) generates neuropeptides with opiate-like activity (10,18). Neuropeptides that originate in the brain are releasing hormones like thyrotropin-releasing hormone (TRH) and luteinizing-releasing hormone (LRH) (see, for review, 25) and the neurohypophyseal hormones vasopressin and oxytocin.

The presence of neurohypophyseal hormones in the cerebrospinal fluid (CSF) (13,19,23,42) suggests an important role for these neuropeptides in brain functions. The aim of the present survey is to review some basic data on the central action of these hormones within the framework of the hypothesis that neurohypophyseal hormones modulate memory processes. Memory is defined here as the consolidation, reproduction (retrieval), and repression of newly acquired experience.

The possibility that the pituitary is involved in acquisition, consolidation, and maintenance of learned behavior was first suggested by observations in partially and totally hypophysectomized rats. Whereas the extirpation of the anterior pituitary or the whole gland leads to an impairment in the acquisition of a shuttle box-avoidance response (46), the removal of the posterior pituitary does not materially affect acquisition, but does interfere with the maintenance of such a response (47). These abnormalities can be readily corrected by treatment with various pituitary hormones such as ACTH, α-MSH, and vasopressin (7,47,48).

In intact rats, vasopressin may affect acquisition of avoidance behavior, however, extinction is a more sensitive parameter for its effect. The injection of relatively small amounts of vasopressin and related peptides increases resistance to the extinction of shuttle box- and pole jumping-avoidance behavior. This effect is long term (49,52) (Fig. 1) and has led to the suggestion that vasopressin and related peptides influence memory processes. The long-term behavioral effect of vasopressin is independent of its vasopressor or antidiuretic activities since desglycinamide[9] lysine[8] vasopressin (DG-LVP), which is practically devoid of classic endocrine effects (55), has a similar behavioral effect to that of the whole molecule. Further evidence for an effect of vasopressin on memory processes can be derived from studies on retrograde amnesia. Vasopressin and related peptides were found to protect against both puromycin-induced amnesia in mice (22,44) and amnesia for a passive avoidance response in rats induced by CO_2 inhalation or electroconvulsive shock (27). These peptides do not affect the maintenance of a food running-approach response in hungry rats (17). However, vasopressin is active in sexually motivated approach behavior. Male rats trained in a

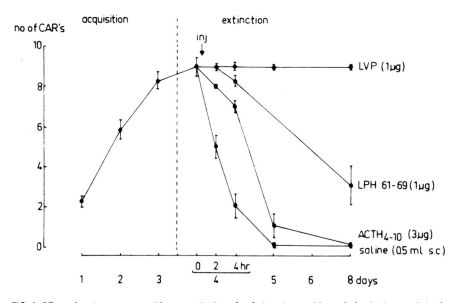

FIG. 1. Effect of various neuropeptides on extinction of pole jumping-avoidance behavior in rats. Animals were trained for 3 days (10 trials each session) to jump onto a pole following 5 sec presentation of the conditioned stimulus (CS), which was a light on top of the box. Electric footshock was used as the unconditioned stimulus (UCS) (For a detailed description of the procedure, see ref. 49). After 3 days of training, extinction was studied in which the UCS did not follow the CS when the animal failed to respond. Those animals that made eight or more avoidances during the first extinction session on day 4 were injected subcutaneously with lysine[8] vasopressin (LVP) (60 mU), β-LPH 61–69 (0.3 μg), ACTH 4–10 (3 μg), or saline (0.5 ml) and run again at 2 and 4 hr after injection on day 4 and on days 5 and 8. Note the long-term effect of LVP in contrast to that of ACTH 4–10. The effect of β-LPH 61–69 might be of longer duration than that of ACTH 4–10, but extinction was not studied on day 5 in rats treated with this peptide. Mean ± standard error of four to five rats. CAR, conditioned avoidance response.

T-maze to run for a receptive female choose the correct arm of the maze in a higher percentage following treatment with DG-LVP than do saline-treated controls. Copulation reward is essential for this effect of the peptide (4).

That vasopressin is physiologically involved in memory processes has been demonstrated in rats with hereditary hypothalamic diabetes insipidus. A homozygous variant of the Brattleboro strain lacks the ability to synthetize vasopressin (34). The heterozygous littermates have a relatively normal water metabolism, whereas the other homozygous variant is completely normal in synthetizing vasopressin. The vasopressin content of the posterior pituitary of homozygous diabetes insipidus rats (HO-DI) is hardly detectable, and the oxytocin content is also low. This is not caused by a defective synthesis, but is a result of augmented release in plasma and CSF (13). The animals also lack arginine vasotocin (AVT) (29). HO-DI rats are inferior in acquiring and maintaining active and passive avoidance behavior (9). Extinction of shuttle box and pole jumping behavior is facilitated. Celestian et al. (11) found that HO-DI rats are inferior in acquiring shuttle box-avoidance behavior. Not more than 30% of the rats achieved the criterion of learning 80% or more avoidances in these studies. However, retention of the response in the remaining rats was markedly enhanced.

Severe memory impairment can be observed when HO-DI rats are subjected to a step-through one-trial avoidance test (53). Absence of passive avoidance behavior was found 24 hr or later after the learning trial even after exposing the animals to electric footshocks of high intensity and long duration. In contrast, heterozygous (HE-DI) or homozygous normal (HO-NO) rats exhibited passive avoidance behavior already after a much milder punishment. Treatment of HO-DI rats with AVP or DG-LVP facilitated passive avoidance behavior. Avoidance latencies of thus treated HO-DI rats were indistinguishable from those of the HE-DI and HO-NO rats. Restoration of memory function is therefore not related to normalisation of water metabolism since DG-LVP is practically devoid of antidiuretic activities although it retained its behavioral potency. HO-DI rats do avoid without treatment if tested immediately or 1 hr after the learning trial. These observations suggest that in the absence of vasopressin memory rather than learning processes are at fault.

Essentially the same results were found in intact rats treated intraventricularly with specific vasopressin antiserum (40). Such treatment neutralizes centrally circulating vasopressin. Vasopressin antiserum administered immediately after the learning trial into one of the lateral ventricles prevents passive avoidance behavior when tested 6 hr or more after the trial. This is not so if tested at 2 min or 1 or 2 hr after administration of the antiserum, indicating again that the consolidation of information is disturbed in the absence of vasopressin (37).

Resistance to extinction of pole jumping-avoidance behavior in rats was used to relate structural aspects of neurohypophyseal peptides and their

TABLE 1. *Amino acid sequences of neurohypophyseal hormones and related neuropeptides*

Arginine[8] vasopressin (AVP)	H-Cys-Tyr-Phe-Gln-Asn-Cys-Pro-Arg-Gly-NH_2
Lysine[8] vasopressin (LVP)	H-Cys-Tyr-Phe-Gln-Asn-Cys-Pro-Lys-Gly-NH_2
Pressinamide (PA)	H-Cys-Tyr-Phe-Gln-Asn-Cys-NH_2
Prolyl-argyl-glycinamide (PAG)	H-Pro-Arg-Gly-NH_2
Oxypressin (OXP)	H-Cys-Tyr-Phe-Gln-Asn-Cys-Pro-Leu-Gly-NH_2
Oxytocin (OXT)	H-Cys-Tyr-Ile-Gln-Asn-Cys-Pro-Leu-Gly-NH_2
Tocinamide (TA)	H-Cys-Tyr-Ile-Gln-Asn-Cys-NH_2
Prolyl-leucyl-glycinamide (PLG)	H-Pro-Leu-Gly-NH_2
Arginine[8] vasotocin (AVT)	H-Cys-Tyr-Ile-Gln-Asn-Cys-Pro-Arg-Gly-NH_2

analogs and fragments of these hormones to their effect on learned behavior (Table 1). AVP appeared to be the most potent peptide, followed by LVP. Removal of the C-terminal glycinamide (DG-LVP and DG-AVP) decreases the potency somewhat. Such peptides, however, lack almost all activities on blood pressure, antidiuresis, ACTH release, etc. (55). The covalent ring structure of vasopressin is only slightly effective as is the C-terminal tripeptide following subcutaneous administration. Intraventricular administration of vasopressin increases resistance to extinction in much lower amounts than systemic injection (51). The covalent ring of vasopressin pressinamide (PA) is also highly active following this route, whereas the C-terminal tripeptide prolyl-argyl-glycinamide (PAG) is much less effective, indicating that the covalent ring structure contains the essential requirements for the behavioral effect although a second activity site may be present in the C-terminal tripeptide. These considerations are in accord with further structure activity studies in the pole-jumping test in which it was found that certain residues in the 20-membered covalent ring are critical for the behavioral effect of vasopressin. Successive modifications of the positions 2, 3, 4, and 5 all markedly reduced the potency of vasopressin on resistance to extinction (45). In contrast, the behavioral activity of vasopressin is more tolerant to changes in positions 8 and 9, indicating that the most striking dissociation of potencies in learned and endocrine responses are found in those peptides with substitution in the linear peptide portion.

Oxytocin, like vasopressin, increases resistance to extinction of pole jumping-avoidance behavior, but is less active than vasopressin (54). However, Schulz et al. (30) found that oxytocin had the reverse effect of vasopressin and facilitated extinction of active avoidance behavior. Replication of the experiments of Schulz et al. (30) failed to confirm their results (8). Oxytocin either had no effect or increased resistance to extinction, depending on the dose used. However, the results apparently depend on the route of administration. Injection of 1 ng of oxytocin given intraventricularly immediately after each acquisition session did tend to facilitate extinction of pole jumping-avoidance behavior (8). Conversely, injection of 1 μl oxytocin antiserum after each acquisition session increased resistance to extinction of pole jumping-avoidance behavior. Thus, in our hands, centrally administered oxytocin led to behavioral effects opposite to those of vasopressin.

As mentioned before, vasopressin markedly affects passive avoidance behavior of HO-DI rats. In intact rats, a single injection of vasopressin immediately after the learning trial in the same paradigm also facilitates passive avoidance behavior. The effect is of a long-term nature (1,5). Passive avoidance behavior was used in subsequent experiments to study the influence of neurohypophyseal hormones in more detail. AVP induced facilitation of passive avoidance behavior. When AVP was given systemically immediately after the learning trial, the strength and duration of the facilitation of passive avoidance behavior was found to increase with the AVP dose. Injection of 1 μg per rat markedly increased avoidance latency not only at the first (24 hr) retention test but also at the second (48 hr) and third (72 hr). To determine the critical period of the effect of AVP, the hormone was administered at various intervals after the learning trial. Intraventricular administration of 10 ng of AVP immediately after the learning trial appeared to be most effective. If administration was postponed until 3 hr after the learning trial, the effect was greatly reduced, and 6 hr after the trial the effect of AVP was abolished. Thus administration in the first hours after the learning trial is essential for AVP to affect memory consolidation. This is in agreement with previous studies in the pole-jumping test (49). If AVP was given 23 hr after the learning trial, e.g., 1 hr prior to the first retention trial, passive avoidance behavior again was facilitated. Thus, AVP affects not only the consolidation but also the retrieval of information.

Structure activity studies on passive avoidance behavior following intraventricular administration revealed that the effect of vasopressin on consolidation is located in the covalent ring structure PA, as was also found in the studies with the pole-jumping test. A second activity site, however, might be present in the linear portion of the molecule since PAG had a slight effect on passive avoidance behavior. Oxytocin given intraventricularly had an effect opposite to that of AVP. Passive avoidance behavior was attenuated following the injection of 0.1 and 1 ng oxytocin. This neuropeptide reduces the consolidation of information and may thus be regarded as an amnesic neuropeptide (Fig. 2). The whole molecule is needed for this effect since the covalent ring structure of oxytocin—tocinamide (TA)—in a dose of 0.1 ng had a slight inhibitory effect on passive avoidance behavior, but in a dose of 1 ng markedly facilitated passive avoidance responding. It acted even stronger than AVP. The C-terminal tripeptide prolyl-leucyl-glycinamide (PLG) was inactive. Thus, for the amnesic effect, the whole oxytocin molecule is needed. The related peptides oxypressin and vasotocin had an effect similar to that of, respectively, vasopressin and oxytocin. This is in accord with the previous findings since oxypressin has the same covalent ring structure as vasopressin, vasotocin the same as oxytocin (Table 1).

As mentioned before, vasopressin and related peptides protect against both

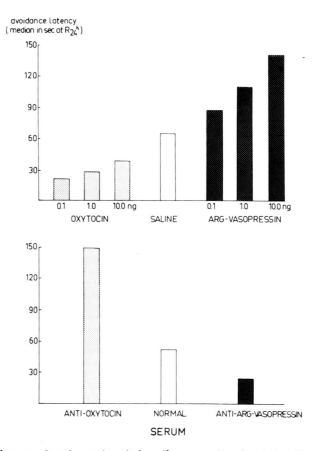

FIG. 2. Effect of vasopressin and oxytocin and of specific vasopressin and oxytocin antiserum on passive avoidance behavior. Passive avoidance behavior was studied by using a one-trial learning paradigm in a step-through type situation as described by Ader and de Wied (1). The apparatus consisted of a large, dark compartment equipped with a grid floor and a mesh-covered, brightly illuminated runway attached to the front center of the dark chamber. After adaptation the rats were placed in the runway facing away from the dark compartment and allowed to enter the chamber on day 1. Three more trials were given on day 2. The last of these trials was followed by a single footshock of 2 sec duration (0.25 mA, AC), immediately after entering the dark compartment. Retention was tested at 24 and 48 hr after the learning trial. Materials were injected through a permanent polyethylene cannula in a lateral ventricle immediately after the learning trial. Latency to enter the dark compartment was recorded up to 300 sec. The figure depicts median scores of eight to 10 rats. Note the opposite effects of vasopressin and oxytocin and their respective antisera on avoidance latencies.

puromycine-induced amnesia of mice in a Y-maze (22,44) and amnesia for a passive avoidance response induced by CO_2 inhalation or electroconvulsive shock in rats when injected immediately after the training (27). Interestingly, vasopressin is active in this respect but not oxytocin. However, the linear tripeptide of oxytocin PLG is highly effective in protecting against amnesia in contrast to the ring structures of vasopressin and oxytocin. It is possible therefore that different brain structures are involved in memory formation and in memory loss. It is also possible that resistance to extinction and retrograde amnesia represent different memory processes. Retrograde amnesia is a temporary disturbance in reproduction or retrieval of recent information, whereas resistance to extinction of avoidance behavior concerns the consolidation of information. As we have seen, the covalent ring structures of vasopressin and oxytocin PA and TA facilitate the consolidation of information, whereas the C-terminal tripeptides PLG and PAG are the sites of the molecules that protect against amnesia. These parts of the molecules may therefore be involved in the retrieval of information. The whole oxytocin or vasotocin molecule is needed for the repression of information.

The different behavioral effects of the neurohypophyseal hormones and their fragments suggest that they act as precursor molecules for neuropeptides that modulate memory processes. If this is true, one would expect specific enzymes that generate the linear and the ring portion of these molecules to be present in the brain. It has been found that a membrane-bound hypothalamic exopeptidase is able to generate MSH-inhibiting factor, (MIF I) (PLG)[1] from oxytocin that inhibits the release of MSH (12). Such enzymes have not been detected for vasopressin. There are enzymes present in the brain that inactivate vasopressin by hydrolysis of peptide bonds in the acyclic position of the molecule (43), but no enzymes have been identified so far that remove the proline residue to yield PA.

Brain catecholamines are implicated in memory functions. These amines have a profound influence on consolidation and retrieval of active and passive avoidance behavior (see for review 35). The memory-blocking effect of protein synthesis inhibitors can be modulated with drugs that alter adrenergic function (26,28). Conversely, inhibition of catecholamine synthesis produces amnesia (26). In fact, amnesia caused by protein synthesis inhibition may be due to blockade of enzymes involved in the synthesis of catecholamines (15). It is possible, therefore, that the neurohypophyseal hormones modulate memory processes through alterations in amine metabolism in certain areas in the brain. Indeed, intracerebroventricular administration of AVP increases the nerve impulse flow in noradrenergic neurons in the hypothalamus, the thalamus, and the medulla oblongata (32). It appeared that AVP alters catecholamine metabolism in a restricted number of sites within these and other brain structures (32,33). Norepinephrine disappearance was accelerated in the dorsal septal nucleus, the nuclei of the dorsal hippocampus, the parafascicular nucleus, the medial forebrain bundle, the anterior hypothalamic nucleus, the dorsal raphe nucleus, the locus coeruleus, the nucleus tractus solitarii, and the A_1-region. A decreased norepinephrine disappearance was found in the supraoptic nucleus and the nucleus ruber. Dopamine disappearance was accelerated in the caudate nucleus, the median eminence, the dorsal raphe nucleus, and the A8-region. PLG mimicked the effect of AVP in the

---

[1] PLG, prolyl-leucyl-glycinamide.

caudate nucleus, the supraoptic nucleus, and the nucleus ruber, e.g., accelerated dopamine disappearance in the caudate nucleus and decreased the disappearance of norepinephrine in the supraoptic nucleus and the nucleus ruber. In addition, PLG increased norepinephrine disappearance in the A8-region and the nucleus commissuralis and decreased norepinephrine and dopamine disappearance in the A9-region (41). It thus appears that AVP increased norepinephrine impulse flow in the dorsal septal nucleus, the dorsal hippocampus, and the parafascicular nucleus. These structures play an essential role in behavioral performance and are implicated in learning and memory processes (2,3,6,20,31). Destruction of septal or hippocampal structures prevents the consolidating effect of vasopressin (36,39) and microinjection of vasopressin into the posterior thalamic area, including the parafascicular nucleus, facilitates the retention of active avoidance behavior (38). Thus, the increased norepinephrine impulse flow in these areas following intraventricular AVP and the involvement of these structures in the consolidating effect of vasopressin on avoidance behavior may be related. PLG does not affect catecholamine metabolism in these regions or the retention of active and passive avoidance behavior. The most prominent effect of this tripeptide on catecholamine metabolism is observed in the substantia nigra, in particular the A8- and A9-regions, and in the nucleus caudatus. This points to a specific action of PLG on the nigrostriatal system. PLG increases the synthesis of dopamine in striatal tissue (16), and it potentiates L-DOPA-induced behavioral changes (24). Evidence has been presented for a specific role of dopamine in amnesia (14,56). The protective effect of PLG on amnesia may therefore be mediated by nigrostriatal dopamine. Data on the effect of oxytocin on amine metabolism are not yet available to relate the amnesic effect of this neurohypophyseal hormone to a specific transmitter system.

The present data indicate that neurohypophyseal hormones interfere directly with brain tissue. Their most important action is to modulate memory processes. The covalent ring structure of the neurohypophyseal hormones is involved in the consolidation of newly acquired behavior, the linear part in the reproduction of stored information, and oxytocin and vasotocin both have amnesic properties. These effects may be mediated by different neurotransmitter systems—limbic midbrain norepinephrine in case of consolidation of avoidance behavior, nigrostriatal dopamine in case of the reproduction of stored information (retrieval).

REFERENCES

1. Ader, R., and de Wied, D. (1972): Effects of vasopressin on active and passive avoidance learning. *Psychon. Sci.*, 29:46–48.
2. Albert, D. J., and Mah, C. J. (1972): An examination of conditioned reinforcement using a one-trial learning procedure. *Learning and Motivation*, 3:369–388.
3. Altman, J., Brunner, R. L., and Bayer, S. A. (1973): The hippocampus and behavioral maturation. *Behav. Biol.*, 8:557–596.

4. Bohus, B. (1977): Effect of desglycinamide-lysine vasopressin (DG–LVP) on sexually motivated T-maze behavior in the male rat. *Horm. Behav.*, 8:52–61.
5. Bohus, B., Ader, R., and de Wied, D. (1972): Effects of vasopressin on active and passive avoidance behavior. *Horm. Behav.*, 3:191–197.
6. Bohus, B., and de Wied, D. (1967): Failure of α-MSH to delay extinction of conditioned avoidance behavior in rats with lesions in the parafascicular nuclei of the thalamus. *Physiol. Behav.*, 2:221–223.
7. Bohus, B., Gispen, W. H., and de Wied, D. (1973): Effect of lysine vasopressin and ACTH 4–10 on conditioned avoidance behavior of hypophysectomized rats. *Neuroendocrinology*, 11:137–143.
8. Bohus, B., Urban, I., van Wimersma Greidanus, Tj. B., and de Wied, D. (1978): Opposite effects of oxytocin and vasopressin on avoidance behavior and hippocampal theta rhythm in the rat. *Neuropharmacology*, 17:239–247.
9. Bohus, B., van Wimersma Greidanus, Tj. B., and de Wied, D. (1975): Behavioral and endocrine responses of rats with hereditary hypothalamic diabetes insipidus (Brattleboro strain). *Physiol. Behav.*, 14:609–615.
10. Bradbury, A. F., Smyth, D. G., Snell, C. R., Birdsall, N. J. M., and Hulme, E. C. (1976): C-fragment of lipotropin has a high affinity for brain opiate receptors. *Nature*, 260:793–795.
11. Celestian, J. F., Carey, R. J., and Miller, M. (1975): Unimpaired maintenance of a conditioned avoidance response in the rat with diabetes insipidus. *Physiol. Behav.*, 15:707–711.
12. Celis, M. E., Taleisnik, S., and Walter, R. (1971): Regulation of formation and proposed structure of the factor inhibiting the release of melanocyte-stimulating hormone. *Proc. Natl. Acad. Sci. USA*, 68:1428–1433.
13. Dogterom, J. (1977): The Release and Presence of Vasopressin in Plasma and Cerebrospinal Fluid as Measured by Radioimmunoassay: Studies on Vasopressin as a Mediator of Memory Processes in the Rat. Thesis, University of Utrecht, Utrecht, The Netherlands.
14. Fibiger, H. C., and Phillips, A. G. (1976): Retrograde amnesia after electrical stimulation of the substantia nigra: Mediation by the dopaminergic nigro-neostriatal bundle. *Brain Res.*, 116:23–33.
15. Flexner, L. B., and Goodman, R. H. (1975): Studies on memory: Inhibitors of protein synthesis also inhibit catecholamine synthesis. *Proc. Natl. Acad. Sci. USA*, 72:4660–4663.
16. Friedman, E., Friedman, J., and Gershon, S. (1973): Dopamine synthesis: Stimulation by a hypothalamic factor. *Science*, 182:831–832.
17. Garrud, P., Gray, J. A., and de Wied, D. (1974): Pituitary-adrenal hormones and extinction of rewarded behaviour in the rat. *Physiol. Behav.*, 12:109–119.
18. Guillemin, R., Ling, N., and Burgus, R. (1976): Endorphines, peptides d'origine hypothalamique et neurohypophysaire à activité morphinomimetique. Isolement et structure moleculaire d'α-endorphine. *CR Acad. Sci. (Paris)*, Ser. D., 282:783–785.
19. Heller, H., Hasan, S. H., and Saifi, A. Q. (1968): Antidiuretic activity in the cerebrospinal fluid. *J. Endocrinol.*, 41:273–280.
20. Hirsch, R. (1974): The hippocampus and contextual retrieval of information from memory: A theory. *Behav. Biol.*, 12:421–444.
21. Kastin, A. J., Sandman, C. A., Stratton, L. O., Schally, A. C., and Miller, L. H. (1975): Behavioral and electrographic changes in rat and man after MSH. In: *Progress in Brain Research, Vol. 42: Hormones, Homeostasis and the Brain*, edited by W. H. Gispen, Tj. B. van Wimersma Greidanus, B. Bohus, and D. de Wied, pp. 143–150. Elsevier, Amsterdam.
22. Lande, S., Flexner, J. B., and Flexner, L. B. (1972): Effect of corticotropin and desglycinamide⁹-lysine vasopressin on suppression of memory by puromycin. *Proc. Natl. Acad. Sci. USA*, 69:558–560.
23. Pavel, S. (1970): Tentative identification of arginine vasotocin in human cerebrospinal fluid. *J. Clin. Endocrinol. Metab.*, 31:369–371.
24. Plotnikoff, N. P., and Kastin, A. J. (1976): Neuropharmacology of hypothalamic releasing factors. *Biochem. Pharmacol.*, 25:363–365.
25. Prange, A. J., Jr., Nemeroff, C. B., Lipton, M. A., Breese, G. R., and Wilson, I. C.

(1977): Peptides and the central nervous system. In: *Handbook of Psychopharmacology*, edited by L. L. Iversen, S. D., Iversen, and S. H. Snyder. Plenum Press, New York. (*In press.*)

26. Quartermain, D., and Botwinick, C. Y. (1975): Role of the biogenic amines in the reversal of cycloheximide-induced amnesia. *J. Comp. Physiol. Psychol.*, 88:386–401.

27. Rigter, H., van Riezen, H., and de Wied, D. (1974): The effects of ACTH and vasopressin analogues on CO_2-induced retrograde amnesia in rats. *Physiol. Behav.*, 13:381–388.

28. Roberts, R. B., Flexner, J. B., and Flexner, L. B. (1970): Some evidence for the involvement of adrenergic sites in the memory trace. *Proc. Natl. Acad. Sci. USA*, 66:310–313.

29. Rosenbloom, A. A., and Fisher, D. A. (1975): Radioimmunoassayable AVT and AVP in adult mammalian brain tissue: Comparison of normal and Brattleboro rats. *Neuroendocrinology*, 17:354–361.

30. Schulz, H., Kovács, G. L., and Telegdy, G. (1976): The effect of vasopressin and oxytocin on avoidance behaviour in rats. In: *Cellular and Molecular Bases of Neuroendocrine Processes*, edited by E. Endröczi, pp. 555–564. Akadémiai Kiadó, Budapest.

31. Segal, M., and Olds, J. (1972): Behavior of units in hippocampal circuit of the rat during learning. *J. Neurophysiol.*, 35:680–690.

32. Tanaka, M., de Kloet, E. R., de Wied, D., and Versteeg, D. H. G. (1977): Arginine[8]-vasopressin affects catecholamine metabolism in specific brain nuclei. *Life Sci.*, 20:1799–1808.

33. Tanaka, M., Versteeg, D. H. G., and de Wied, D. (1977): Regional effects of vasopressin on rat brain catecholamine metabolism. *Neurosci. Lett.*, 4:321–325.

34. Valtin, H., and Schroeder, H. A. (1964): Familial hypothalamic diabetes insipidus in rats (Brattleboro strain). *Am. J. Physiol.*, 206:425–430.

35. van Ree, J. M., Bohus, B., Versteeg, D. H. G., and de Wied, D. (1977): Neurohypophyseal principles and memory processes. *Biochem. Pharmacol.* (*In press.*)

36. van Wimersma Greidanus, Tj. B., and de Wied, D. (1976): Dorsal hippocampus: A site of action of neuropeptides on avoidance behavior? *Pharmacol. Biochem. Behav.*, 5(Suppl. 1):29–33.

37. van Wimersma Greidanus, Tj. B., and de Wied, D. (1976): Modulation of passive-avoidance behavior of rats by intracerebroventricular administration of antivasopressin serum. *Behav. Biol.*, 18:325–333 (Abstr. No. 6122).

38. van Wimersma Greidanus, Tj. B., Bohus, B., and de Wied, D. (1973): Effects of peptide hormones on behavior. In: *Progress in Endocrinology, Int. Congr. Series No. 273*, edited by C. Gual and F. J. G. Ebling, pp. 197–210. Excerpta Medica, Amsterdam.

39. van Wimersma Greidanus, Tj. B., Bohus, B., and de Wied, D. (1975): CNS sites of action of ACTH, MSH and vasopressin in relation to avoidance behavior. In: *Anatomical Neuroendocrinology*, edited by W. F. Stumpf and L. D. Grant, pp. 284–289. S. Karger A. G., Basel.

40. van Wimersma Greidanus, Tj. B., Dogterom, J., and de Wied, D. (1975): Intraventricular administration of antivasopressin serum inhibits memory consolidation in rats. *Life Sci.*, 16:637–644.

41. Versteeg, D. H. G., Tanaka, M., de Kloet, E. R., van Ree, J. M., and de Wied, D. (1977): Prolyl-leucyl-glycinamide (PLG): Regional effects on α-MPT-induced catecholamine disappearance in rat brain. *Brain Res.*, 143:561–566.

42. Vorherr, H., Bradbury, M. W. B., Hoghoughi, M., and Kleeman, C. R. (1968): Antidiuretic hormone in cerebrospinal fluid during endogenous and exogenous changes in its blood level. *Endocrinology*, 83:246–250.

43. Walter, R., Griffiths, E. C., and Hooper, K. C. (1973): Production of MSH release-inhibiting hormone by a particulate preparation of hypothalami: Mechanisms of oxytocin inactivation. *Brain Res.*, 60:449–457.

44. Walter, R., Hoffman, P. L., Flexner, J. B., and Flexner, L. B. (1975): Neurohypophyseal hormones, analogs, and fragments: Their effect on puromycin-induced amnesia. *Proc. Natl. Acad. Sci. USA*, 72:4180–4184.

45. Walter, R., van Ree, J. M., and de Wied, D. (1977): Memory consolidation in the rat by neurohypophyseal hormones and analogues. *Proc. Natl. Acad. Sci. (In press.)*
46. de Wied, D. (1964): Influence of anterior pituitary on avoidance learning and escape behavior. *Am. J. Physiol.,* 207:255–259.
47. de Wied, D. (1965): The influence of the posterior and intermediate lobe of the pituitary and pituitary peptides on the maintenance of a conditioned avoidance response in rats. *Int. J. Neuropharmacol.,* 4:157–167.
48. de Wied, D. (1969): Effects of peptide hormones on behavior. In: *Frontiers in Neuroendocrinology,* edited by W. F. Ganong and L. Martini, pp. 97–140. Oxford Univ. Press, London/New York.
49. de Wied, D. (1971): Long-term effect of vasopressin on the maintenance of a conditioned avoidance response in rats. *Nature,* 232:58–60.
50. de Wied, D. (1974): Pituitary-adrenal system hormones and behavior. In: *The Neurosciences, Third Study Program,* edited by F. O. Schmitt and F. G. Worden, pp. 653–666. MIT Press, Cambridge.
51. de Wied, D. (1976): Behavioral effects of intraventricularly administered vasopressin and vasopressin fragments. *Life Sci.,* 19:685–690.
52. de Wied, D., and Bohus, B. (1966): Long term and short term effects on retention of a conditioned avoidance response in rats by treatment with long-acting pitressin and α-MSH. *Nature,* 212:1484–1486.
53. de Wied, D., Bohus, B., and van Wimersma Greidanus, Tj. B. (1975): Memory deficit in rats with hereditary diabetes insipidus. *Brain Res.,* 85:152–156.
54. de Wied, D., and Gispen, W. H. (1977): Behavioral effects of peptides. In: *Peptides in Neurobiology,* edited by H. Gainer, pp. 397–448. Plenum Press, New York.
55. de Wied, D., Greven, H. M., Lande, S., and Witter, A. (1972): Dissociation of the behavioral and endocrine effects of lysine vasopressin by tryptic digestion. *Br. J. Pharmacol.,* 45:118–122.
56. Yokel, R. A., and Wise, R. A. (1975): Increased lever pressing for amphetamine after pimozide in rats: Implications for a dopamine theory of reward. *Science,* 187:547–549.

Brain Mechanisms in Memory and Learning:
From the Single Neuron to Man,
edited by M. A. B. Brazier.
Raven Press, New York © 1979.

Altering Memory by Electrical and Chemical Stimulation of the Brain

James L. McGaugh, Paul E. Gold,* Mark J. Handwerker,**
Robert A. Jensen, Joe L. Martinez, John A. Meligeni, and
Beatriz J. Vasquez

Department of Psychobiology, University of California, Irvine, California 92717

As the chapters in this volume amply demonstrate, a variety of approaches are used in research into the brain mechanisms underlying learning and memory. Numerous studies have examined anatomical, electrophysiological, and chemical changes in the brain that are correlated with various aspects of learning and memory, including acquisition, storage, and retrieval (34, 43,51). Other studies have examined changes in learning and memory associated with development, brain injury, and disease as well as changes produced by experimental treatments that alter brain functioning (1,3,5,6,10,32, 41,50).

Our research focuses on treatments that modulate the storage or consolidation of newly acquired responses. The guiding hypothesis is that an understanding of effects of experimental treatments on memory, together with an understanding of the neurobiological bases of the treatments, will provide important leads to the neural bases of memory. It is also assumed that the findings of such studies will add to knowledge provided by correlational studies of the neurobiology of memory.

In our studies, rats or mice are trained on a simple learning task and then, shortly after training, are administered a treatment that alters brain functioning. A retention test is administered later to determine whether the retention is altered by the posttraining treatment. We use tasks such as one-trial inhibitory avoidance, one-way active avoidance, or Y-maze brightness discrimination because training in these tasks requires only a few seconds or minutes and we can vary rather precisely the time between acquisition and posttraining treatment. Ordinarily the retention test is given within a week after training. Most studies have used a 1- to 3-day retention interval.

Using such procedures, we examined the effects of a variety of experimental treatments (14,44,45,47). This chapter reviews some of our recent studies

---

* *Present address:* Department of Psychology, University of Virginia, Charlottesville, Virginia 22901; ** Laboratory of Neurobiology, San Juan, Puerto Rico 00901.

examining the effects, on retention, of posttraining administration of electrical brain stimulation, hormones, and drugs affecting catecholamines. The findings, in general, provide strong evidence that memory storage processes are time dependent (2,13,46). Both retrograde amnesia and retrograde enhancement of memory can be produced by posttraining treatments. The effects can be obtained in a variety of learning tasks. However, the effects vary with the training conditions, the experimental treatment, and the animals' "state" at the time of training. We regard these treatments as producing modulating influences because the same treatment may either enhance or impair retention depending on the training conditions used.

MODULATING EFFECTS OF ELECTRICAL STIMULATION OF THE BRAIN

It is well known that retention is impaired by posttraining administration of electroconvulsive shock (46). It is also known that retention can be impaired or enhanced by more moderate electrical stimulation of specific brain regions including the mesencephalic reticular formation (3,7,37), substantia nigra (52), caudate nucleus (27), entorhinal cortex (42), hippocampus (8,27,36,40,53), and amygdala (19,20,22) (for reviews, see 35,38,45). Electrical stimulation can produce retrograde amnesia with current intensities that do not elicit either behavioral convulsions or electrical brain seizure activity. It is clear from these studies that brain seizures are neither necessary nor sufficient conditions for producing alterations in memory following electrical stimulation of the brain.

The amygdala is a particularly effective site for altering retention with posttrial low-intensity electrical stimulation. The results of a series of studies (17–23) indicate that, in rats, retrograde amnesia is produced by either unilateral or bilateral amygdala stimulation consisting of a 25 to 30 μA stimulation train (0.1 msec, 100 Hz) lasting for 10 sec. Comparable effects are found when the animals are trained in a variety of tasks including inhibitory avoidance, one-way active avoidance, and Y-maze discrimination (22,23,26). Further with all three tasks, the effects vary with the region of the amygdala stimulated. When stimulation is administered to rats shortly after they are trained, stimulation in or near the basomedial nucleus produces the greatest degree of amnesia (17). However, if the stimulation is administered several hours after training, other regions of the amygdala are more effective (18). The brain regions in which posttrial electrical stimulation is most effective in altering memory appear to vary with the time that the stimulation is administered.

The stimulation appears to alter memory by modulating processes initiated by the training experience. The effects depend on many conditions, including the time since training and the nature of the training experience. In most studies, amygdala stimulation produced retrograde amnesia. However, facilitation of retention can also be produced. The findings, summarized in Fig. 1,

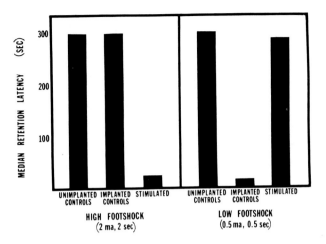

FIG. 1. Effect of posttrial amygdala stimulation on retention of inhibitory avoidance training. Note that implanted controls had a retention deficit for training with low but not high footshock. Furthermore, relative to the implanted control groups, amygdala stimulation facilitated retention of low footshock training, but interfered with retention of high footshock training. (From Gold et al., ref. 17.)

indicate that, in rats, the effect of the same type of stimulation depends on the level of footshock used in training (20). When a high footshock was used as punishment in a one-trial inhibitory avoidance task, good retention was seen in both unimplanted controls and unstimulated controls with implanted electrodes. Further, with high footshock, immediate posttraining amygdala stimulation impaired retention. However, with low footshock the retention performance of nonstimulated controls with implanted electrodes was poor, whereas that of rats given immediate posttrial amygdala stimulation was comparable to that of unimplanted controls. These findings are consistent with other evidence that posttraining electrical stimulation can compensate for retention deficits produced by brain lesions or other treatments affecting brain functioning (2,4,7,40). More generally, however, these findings suggest that under conditions where retention would otherwise be good, posttrial brain stimulation produces impairment, and under conditions where retention would otherwise be poor, stimulation produces enhancement of retention. It is clear that brain stimulation does not simply disrupt neuronal activity, it appears to have more general modulating influences. It might act by directly altering neuronal activity in other brain regions or by affecting hormone release. This latter possibility is of interest because of evidence that learning and retention can be altered by hormones (9,10,14).

MODULATING EFFECTS OF HORMONES

De Wied and his colleagues have provided extensive evidence that learning and extinction are altered by adrenocorticotrophic hormone (ACTH) and peptide analogs of ACTH. ACTH and peptide fragments also alter retention when administered shortly after training (9,10). Thus ACTH acts in some way(s) to modulate consolidation. The effects of ACTH on memory are comparable to those obtained with other treatments including electrical stimulation of the brain (16). As the findings in Fig. 2 indicate, the effects of posttraining administration of ACTH are dose dependent and vary with the level of footshock used in training. In saline-treated controls, the retention of an inhibitory avoidance task varied directly with footshock level. With low footshock, two doses of ACTH (3.0 and 6.0 IU) enhanced retention. With a slightly higher footshock, only the lower dose enhanced retention. With the highest footshock, both doses impaired retention. These findings are similar to those obtained with electrical stimulation of the amygdala (Fig. 1). They provide further support for the view that posttraining treatments act by modulating processes initiated by training. Their effects depend on the consequences of the training experience. If the training conditions yield poor retention, the posttraining treatment can enhance retention.

These findings support the general view (13) that the efficiency of storage of recently acquired responses depends on the hormonal responses initiated by the training experience. Experimentally administered hormones may act simply by adding to endogenously released hormones and thus amplifying the processes involved in storage. Posttraining treatments such as brain stimulation may act by releasing hormones. Treatments producing memory impair-

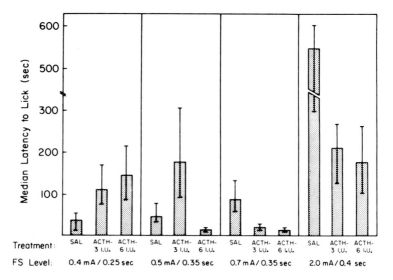

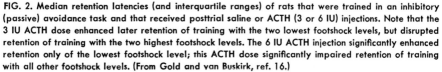

FIG. 2. Median retention latencies (and interquartile ranges) of rats that were trained in an inhibitory (passive) avoidance task and that received posttrial saline or ACTH (3 or 6 IU) injections. Note that the 3 IU ACTH dose enhanced later retention of training with the two lowest footshock levels, but disrupted retention of training with the two highest footshock levels. The 6 IU ACTH injection significantly enhanced retention only of the lowest footshock level; this ACTH dose significantly impaired retention of training with all other footshock levels. (From Gold and van Buskirk, ref. 16.)

ment may do so by supplying or releasing abnormally high levels of hormones. However, it remains to be determined whether other modulators of memory storage act by influencing hormonal mechanisms. Further, as yet, little is known about the basis or bases of the modulating influence of hormones on memory. Hormones, or peptide fragments of hormones, might act directly on neuronal processes to affect storage, or hormonal release might produce other effects that influence neuronal activity involved in memory storage. It is important to determine whether hormonal release is central to the effects of various treatments known to influence memory storage.

EFFECTS OF TREATMENTS AFFECTING CATECHOLAMINES

Training experiences cause the endogenous release of numerous substances besides ACTH. Kety (39) proposed that processes associated with affective states such as the release of biogenic amines modulate synaptic processes in ways that selectively strengthen recently activated neuronal circuits. Evidence from studies of posttraining administration of brain stimulation and ACTH are, of course, consistent with this general hypothesis. Studies of the effects, on memory consolidation, of treatments affecting monoamines also support this general view. A number of studies demonstrated that retention of newly learned responses is impaired by either pre- or posttraining parenteral administration of drugs, such as diethyldithiocarbamate (DDC) and fusaric acid, that interfere with the synthesis of norepinephrine (24,31). Studies in our laboratory showed that DDC causes anterograde and retrograde amnesia in several learning tasks (29,54). In general the degree of memory impairment varies directly with the dose and inversely with the time—pre- or posttraining—of drug administration. We, as well as other investigators, also found retrograde enhancement with DDC in one task (two-way shuttle response) (6,28).

It is usually assumed that these memory effects are due to alteration in brain catecholamines. In support of this view, we found that, in mice, retention is enhanced by posttraining intracerebroventricular administration of catecholamines (30). Recently we also found that, in rats, retention impairment is produced by direct intracerebroventricular administration of DDC (33). In these experiments DDC was administered into the lateral ventricle either before or after they were trained on a one-trial inhibitory avoidance task. In the studies cited above the typical parenterally administered doses of DDC were from 300 to 700 mg/kg. In our intracerebroventricular studies, we have used doses ranging from 0.4 to 4.0 mg in volumes of 1 to 10 μl. Figure 3 shows the retention latencies of animals given intracerebroventricular DDC shortly before they were trained. Retention was tested 3 days after the training trial. Retention was markedly impaired by 5 or 10 μl (i.e., 2.0 or 4.0 mg) doses administered 15 min prior to training. Administration of DDC 24 hr before training did not affect retention latencies. Control animals

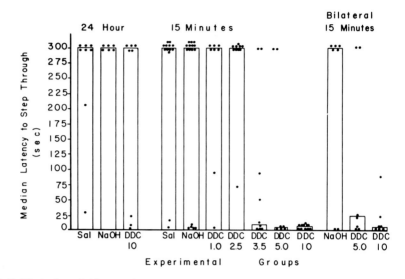

FIG. 3. Effect of pretrial intracerebroventricular administration of DDC on retention of rats. Black dots indicate scores of individual animals. Doses are in μl (0.4 mg/μl). (From Jensen et al., ref. 33.)

given 10 μl of NaCl or NaOH displayed good retention. Figure 4 shows the retention latencies of animals given posttraining unilateral intracerebroventricular DDC. Significant retention impairment was produced only by the 10 μl dose. Impairment was produced by administration immediately after training but not 6 or 24 hr after training. Thus, the effects of intracerebroventricularly administered DDC on retention are dose dependent and time dependent. The finding that the retention effects can be produced by such low doses (in comparison with the typical parenteral doses) supports the view that DDC effects on memory are due to central, rather than peripheral,

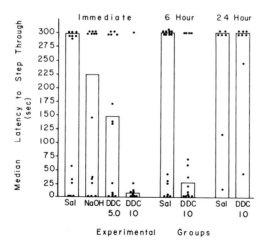

FIG. 4. Effect of posttraining intracerebroventricular administration of DDC on retention in rats. Black dots indicate scores of individual animals. Doses are in μl (0.4 mg/μl). (From Jensen et al., ref. 33.)

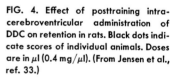

effects of the drug. Whether the effects are due to influences on brain catecholamines or other influences (6) remains to be determined.

Stein et al. (55) provided additional evidence suggesting that central
catecholamines are involved in modulating memory storage processes. In
their experiment rats were given parenteral injections of DDC shortly prior
to training, and they showed impaired intention when tested several days
later. The retention impairment was attenuated by intracerebroventricular
administration of norepinephrine shortly after training. These findings suggest that the retention deficit and its attenuation are due to reduction and
replenishment of brain norepinephrine. In recent experiments we have replicated and extended these experiments. However, our findings question the
view that replenishment of central norepinephrine is required for attenuating
DDC-induced retention deficits.

Rats in our studies (48) were given a Ringers control solution or DDC
(680 mg/kg) intraperitoneally approximately one-half hour before they
were trained on a one-trial inhibitory avoidance task. Two footshock levels
used—a low footshock (0.5 mA, 1 sec) and a high footshock (2 mA, 2 sec).
These footshock levels were similar to those used in studies of brain stimulation and ACTH described above. Immediately or 4 hours after training, either
a Ringers solution or norepinephrine was administered intracerebroventricularly by means of implanted cannulae. A retention test was given 1 week later.
The effects of immediate posttraining administration of norepinephrine are
shown in Fig. 5. With low footshock, DDC produced retention impairment
in all groups, and posttraining norepinephrine did not attenuate the effects
of DDC. With high footshock, DDC produced amnesia in animals given
Ringer's solution after training, as well as in animals given the high dose of
norepinephrine (100 μg). However, DDC did not produce amnesia in animals given the lower doses of norepinephrine immediately after training. Attenuation of DDC amnesia was not produced at any dose when the norepinephrine was administered 4 hr after training. Thus, these findings are quite
consistent with those reported by Stein et al. (55) and provide additional
support for the view that the behavioral effects are caused by alterations in
central norepinephrine.

However, other recent experiments have demonstrated that, in rats, retention can be enhanced by parenteral injections of norepinephrine and epinephrine (16,20). It is unlikely that these effects are due to a direct action of
these amines in the brain since there is no evidence that they pass the blood-
brain barrier. In view of these findings, we examined the effects of posttraining parenteral administration of norepinephrine and epinephrine on retention of rats given DDC before training. Except for doses and route of
administration, the procedures were identical to those used in the experiment
described above. The effects of norepinephrine are shown in Figs. 6 and 7. As
can be seen, when low footshock was used (Fig. 6), the DDC injections produced retention impairment in rats given either posttraining Ringer's solution

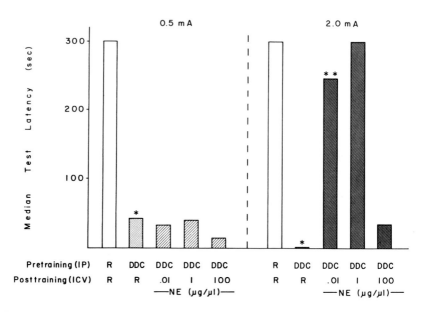

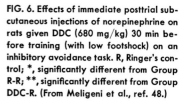

FIG. 5. Effects of immediate posttraining intracerebroventricular administration of norepinephrine on retention of rats given i.p. DDC (680 mg/kg) 30 min before training (with high or low footshock) on an inhibitory avoidance task. R, Ringer's control; *, significantly different from R-R group; **, significantly different from DDC-R group. (From Meligeni et al., ref. 48.)

or a low dose of norepinephrine (5 μg/kg) subcutaneously. Significant impairment was not found in animals given higher posttraining doses of norepinephrine (50 and 500 μg/kg). In groups given the higher footshock (Fig. 7), significant attenuation of DDC-induced amnesia was found only at the lowest dose of norepinephrine (5 μg/kg). No effects were produced by norepinephrine administered 4 hr after training. Clearly, the dose of norepinephrine

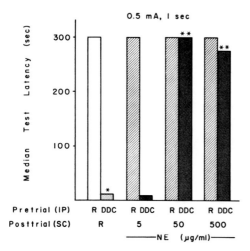

FIG. 6. Effects of immediate posttrial subcutaneous injections of norepinephrine on rats given DDC (680 mg/kg) 30 min before training (with low footshock) on an inhibitory avoidance task. R, Ringer's control; *, significantly different from Group R-R; **, significantly different from Group DDC-R. (From Meligeni et al., ref. 48.)

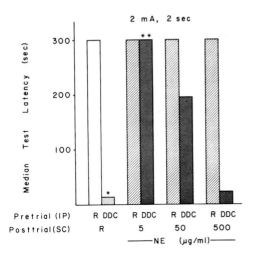

FIG. 7. Effects of immediate posttrial subcutaneous injections of norepinephrine on
rats given DDC (680 mg/kg) 30 min before training (with high footshock) on an
inhibitory avoidance task. R, Ringer's control; *, significantly different from Group
R-R; **, significantly different from Group
DDC-R. (From Meligeni et al., ref. 48.)

required to attenuate the impairing effects of DDC depended on the footshock
level. With high footshock only the lowest dose attenuated the DDC effect.
With a low footshock, higher doses of norepinephrine were required to attenuate the DDC effect. Given these results, it is puzzling that when norepinephrine was given intracerebroventricularly, no dose was effective in attenuating the DDC effect in animals trained with low footshock (Fig. 5). It

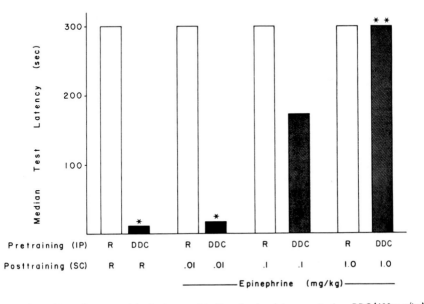

FIG. 8. Effects of immediate posttrial subcutaneous injection of epinephrine on rats given DDC (680 mg/kg)
30 min before training (with high footshock) on an inhibitory avoidance task. R, Ringer's control; *, significantly different from Group R-R; **, significantly different from Group DDC-R. (From Meligeni et al.,
ref. 49.)

might be, of course, that inappropriate doses were used. For example, a dose of greater than 1 and less than 100 μg might well have been effective.

The effects of parenterally administered epinephrine are comparable to those produced by norepinephrine. The results of a study of the effects of subcutaneously administered epinephrine, using procedures identical to those used in the above experiment except that only the high footshock was used, are shown in Fig. 8 (49). DDC administered one-half hour before training impaired retention in rats given subcutaneous injections of a Ringer's solution or the lowest dose (0.01 mg/kg) of epinephrine. Good retention was displayed by rats given Ringer's solution or DDC followed immediately by subcutaneous injections of epinephrine at a dose of 1.0 mg/kg. No effects were found with epinephrine injections given 4 hr after training. This finding is interesting in view of the findings of Gold and van Buskirk (15) that in otherwise untreated or normal rats, that is, rats not given DDC, retention is enhanced by immediate posttraining subcutaneous doses of 0.01 and 0.10 mg/kg of epinephrine. Therefore, when poor retention is produced by DDC, a higher dose of epinephrine is required to enhance retention or, in this case, to attenuate the DDC-induced amnesia.

BASES OF THE EFFECTS OF PERIPHERALLY ADMINISTERED HORMONES

There is now substantial evidence that retention can be modulated by posttraining peripheral administration of several substances that are normally released by emotional experiences. ACTH, norepinephrine, and epinephrine affect retention when administered subcutaneously. Norepinephrine and epinephrine attenuate DDC-induced amnesia. The peptide fragment $ACTH_{4-10}$ attenuates amnesia produced by anisomycin (12), an inhibitor of protein synthesis. Since none of these hormones is known to pass the blood-brain barrier, it seems unlikely that they act directly on the brain when administered peripherally. However, it is worth noting that the doses of norepinephrine injected subcutaneously in our experiment were extremely high in comparison with those doses found to be effective when administered intracerebroventricularly (50 and 500 μg/μg versus 0.01 and 1 μg). Thus, the possibility that the effects are due to small amounts of the hormone passing through the blood-brain barrier cannot be completely ruled out. There is, of course, substantial evidence that these substances affect the brain when they are administered into the brain or ventricles (11). Thus, when these substances are present in the brain, they may act directly to modulate neuronal processes involved in memory storage, as Kety (39) suggested.

However, the peripherally administered hormones might also act indirectly through influences on the cardiovascular system. The modulating influences of peripherally administered hormones might be due to the activating influences of such changes on brain systems involved in arousal. Peripherally induced changes in arousal may act just as electrical stimulation of the mesencephalic formation (2) to produce brain changes that modulate memory storage processes. Whatever the bases of the effects, however, the results of these recent experiments clearly show that retention is altered by centrally as well as peripherally administered hormones. It remains to be determined whether effects obtained with the two routes of administration are due to a common effect on the brain.

EFFECTS OF LOCUS COERULEUS LESIONS

A number of recent experiments investigated the effects, on learning and memory, of brain lesions that alter levels of brain catecholamines. Lesions of the locus coeruleus produce a marked decrease in forebrain norepinephrine levels. The findings of studies using drugs that reduce brain norepinephrine suggest that such lesions should impair learning and memory. Recently Zornetzer et al. (56) found that although lesions of the locus coeruleus do not impair retention in mice, they greatly extend the gradient of retrograde amnesia produced by posttraining electrical stimulation of the brain. Experiments in our laboratory confirmed this effect (25). Rats were given bilateral lesions of the locus coeruleus and then trained on an inhibitory avoidance task. Immediately after training they were given 0.5 sec electrical stimulation of the frontal cortex at current intensities of 2, 4, and 8 mA. On a retention test 2 days later the retention performance of lesioned rats was comparable to that of the unlesioned controls at all current intensities. Each intensity produced amnesia in both lesioned and unlesioned animals. Other groups of rats were given cortical stimulation (4.0 mA) either immediately after training or 3, 6, or 24 hr after training. The immediate posttrial treatments produced amnesia in both lesioned and control animals. However, retention was impaired by the 3-hr and 6-hr posttraining stimulation only in the rats with locus coeruleus lesions. These findings indicate that locus coeruleus lesions do not necessarily have effects that impair learning or retention. However, such lesions greatly increase the time period following training during which the animal remains susceptible to the impairing effects of electrical stimulation of the brain on memory storage. Thus, our findings are consistent with the view that forebrain norepinephrine may play some role in the stabilization of recently acquired memories.

CONCLUDING COMMENTS

These findings, as well as those reported in several other chapters in this volume, indicate that memory storage processes are readily modulated by a variety of treatments administered shortly after training. The fact that retrograde enhancement and disruption of memory is produced by treatments affecting substances ordinarily released when animals are stimulated provides support for the view that such substances serve to modulate neuronal processes underlying memory (13,39). Further study of the ways in which posttraining treatments influence ACTH and monoamines as well as the ways in which hormones affect neuronal activity should provide some important leads to understanding how the brain acts to store experiences.

ACKNOWLEDGMENTS

This work has been supported by Research Grant MH 12526, Fellowships MH 05429 and MH 05358, and Training Grant MH 14599 from the National Institute of Mental Health, as well as Research Grant AG 00469 from the National Institute of Health, Research Grant BNS 76–17370 from the National Science Foundation, and a grant from the McKnight Foundation.

REFERENCES

1. Bechtereva, N. P. (1979): Bioelectric expression of long-term memory activation and possible mechanisms of this process. *This volume.*
2. Bloch, V. (1970): Facts and hypotheses concerning memory consolidation. *Brain Res.,* 24:561–575.
3. Bloch, V., Hennevin, E., and Leconte, P. (1979): Relationship between paradoxical sleep and memory processes. *This volume.*
4. Bloch, V., Hennevin, E., and Leconte, P. (1977): Interaction between posttrial reticular stimulation and subsequent paradoxical sleep in memory consolidation processes. In: *Neurobiology of Sleep and Memory,* edited by R. R. Drucker-Colin and J. L. McGaugh (associate editors, R. A. Jensen and J. L. Martinez, Jr.), pp. 255–272. Academic Press, New York.
5. Bureš, J. (1979): Neurophysiological analysis of conditioned taste aversion. *This volume.*
6. Danscher, G., and Fjerdingstad, E. J. (1975): Diethyldithiocarbamate (antabuse): Decrease of brain heavy metal staining pattern and improved consolidation of shuttle box avoidance in goldfish. *Brain Res.,* 83:143–155.
7. Denti, A., McGaugh, J. L., Landfield, P. W., and Shinkman, P. (1970): Effects of posttrial electrical stimulation of the mesencephalic reticular formation on avoidance learning in rats. *Physiol. Behav.,* 5:659–662.
8. Destrade, C., Soumireu-Mourat, B., and Cardo, B. (1973): Effects of posttrial hippocampal stimulation on acquisition. *Behav. Biol.,* 8:713–724.
9. De Wied, D. (1974): Pituitary-adrenal system, hormones and behavior. In: *The Neurosciences,* edited by F. O. Schmitt and F. G. Worden, pp. 653–666. MIT Press, Cambridge.
10. De Wied, D. (1979): Modulation of memory processes by neuropeptides of hypothalamic-neurohypophyseal origin. *This volume.*
11. Dunn, A. J., and Gispen, W. H. (1977): How ACTH acts on the brain. *Biobehav. Rev.,* 1:15–23.
12. Flood, J. F., Jarvik, M. E., Bennett, E. L., Orme, A. E., and Rosenzweig, M. R. (1977): Effects of ACTH peptide fragments on memory formation. *Pharmacol. Biochem. Behav.,* 5(Suppl. 1):41–51.
13. Gold, P. E., and McGaugh, J. L. (1975): A single-trace, two-process view of memory storage processes. In: *Short-Term Memory,* edited by D. Deutsch and J. A. Deutsch, pp. 355–378. Academic Press, New York.
14. Gold, P. E., and McGaugh, J. L. (1977): Hormones and memory. In: *Neuropeptide Influences on the Brain and Behavior,* edited by L. H. Miller, C. A. Sandman, and A. J. Kastin. Raven Press, New York. (*In press.*)

15. Gold, P. E., and van Buskirk (1975): Facilitation of time-dependent memory processes with posttrial epinephrine injections. *Behav. Biol.,* 13:145–153.
16. Gold, P. E., and van Buskirk, R. B. (1976): Enhancement and impairment of memory processes with posttrial injections of adrenocorticotrophic hormone. *Behav. Biol.,* 16:387–400.
17. Gold, P. E., Edwards, R. M., and McGaugh, J. L. (1975): Amnesia produced by unilateral, subseizure, electrical stimulation of the amygdala in rats. *Behav. Biol.,* 15:95–105.
18. Gold, P. E., Hankins, L. L., and Rose, R. P. (1977): Time-dependent changes in optimal sites for producing amnesia with posttrial amygdala stimulation in rats. *Behav. Biol.,* 20:32–40.
19. Gold, P. E., Hankins, L. L., and Rose, R. P. (1977): Time-dependent post-trial changes in the localization of amnestic electrical stimulation sites within the amygdala of rats. *Behav. Biol.,* 20:32–40.
20. Gold, P. E., Hankins, L., Edwards, R. M., and Rose, R. P. (1978): Enhancement of disruption of memory storage with posttrial unilateral amygdala stimulation: Interaction with footshock level. (*In preparation.*)
21. Gold, P. E., Hankins, L., Edwards, R. M., Chester, J., and McGaugh, J. L. (1975): Memory interference and facilitation with posttrial amygdala stimulation: Effect on memory varies with footshock level. *Brain Res.,* 86:509–513.
22. Gold, P. E., Macri, J., and McGaugh, J. L. (1973): Retrograde amnesia produced by subseizure amygdala stimulation. *Behav. Biol.,* 9:671–680.
23. Gold, P. E., Rose, R. P., Hankins, L. L., and Spanis, C. (1976): Impaired retention of visual discriminated escape training produced by subseizure amygdala stimulation. *Brain Res.,* 118:73–85.
24. Gorelick, D. A., Bozewicz, T. R., and Wagner, W. H. (1975): The role of catecholamines in animal learning and memory. In: *Catecholamines and Behavior,* Vol. 2, edited by A. J. Friedhoff, pp. 1–30. Plenum Publ., New York.
25. Handwerker, M. J. (1976): The Role of the Nucleus Locus Coeruleus in Avoidance Learning and Retention Stability in Rats. Doctoral Dissertation, University of California, Irvine.
26. Handwerker, M. J., Gold, P. E., and McGaugh, J. L. (1974): Impairment of active avoidance learning with post-training amygdala stimulation. *Brain Res.,* 75:324–327.
27. Haycock, J. W., Deadwyler, S. A., Sideroff, S. I., and McGaugh, J. L. (1973): Retrograde amnesia and cholinergic systems in the caudate-putamen complex and dorsal hippocampus of the rat. *Exp. Neurol.,* 41:201–213.
28. Haycock, J. W., van Buskirk, R., and McGaugh, J. L. (1976): Facilitation of retention performance in mice by posttraining diethyldithiocarbamate. *Pharmacol. Biochem. Behav.,* 5:525–528.
29. Haycock, J. W., van Buskirk, R., and McGaugh, J. L. (1977): Effects of catecholaminergic drugs upon memory storage processes in mice. *Behav. Biol.,* 20:281–310.
30. Haycock, J. W., van Buskirk, R., Ryan, J. R., and McGaugh, J. L. (1977): Enhancement of retention with centrally administered catecholamines. *Exp. Neurol.,* 54:199–208.
31. Hunter, B., Zornetzer, S. F., Jarvik, M. E., and McGaugh, J. L. (1977): Modulation of learning and memory: Effects of drugs influencing neurotransmitters. In: *Handbook of Psychopharmacology,* edited by L. Iverson, S. Iverson, and S. Snyder. Plenum Press, New York.
32. Izquierdo, I., and Elisabetsky, E. (1979): Physiological and pharmacological dissection of the main factors in the acquisition and retention of shuttle behavior. *This volume.*
33. Jensen, R. A., Martinez, Jr., J. L., Vasquez, B., McGaugh, J. L., McGuiness, T., Marrujo, D., and Herness, S. (1977): Amnesia produced by intraventricular administration of diethyldithiocarbamate. *Neurosci. Abstr.,* 3:235.
34. Kandel, E. R. (1979): Cellular aspects of learning. *This volume.*
35. Kesner, R. (1973): A neural system analysis of memory storage and retrieval. *Psychol. Bull.,* 80:177–203.

36. Kesner, R. P., and Connor, H. S. (1972): Independence of short- and long-term memory: A neural systems approach. *Science,* 176:432–434.
37. Kesner, R. P., and Conner, H. S. (1974): Effects of electrical stimulation of rat limbic system and midbrain reticular formation upon short- and long-term memory. *Physiol. Behav.,* 12:5–12.
38. Kesner, R. P., and Wilburn, M. W. (1974): A review of electrical stimulation of the brain in the context of learning and retention. *Behav. Biol.,* 10:259–293.
39. Kety, S. (1972): Brain catecholamines, affective states, and memory. In: *The Chemistry of Mood, Motivation, and Memory,* edited by J. L. McGaugh, pp. 65–80. Plenum Publ., New York.
40. Landfield, P. W., Tusa, R., and McGaugh, J. L. (1973): Effects of posttrial hippocampal stimulation on memory storage and EEG activity. *Behav. Biol.,* 8:485–505.
41. Mark, R. F. (1979): Sequential biochemical steps in memory formation: Evidence from the use of metabolic inhibitors. *This volume.*
42. Martinez, Jr., J. L., McGaugh, J. L., Hanes, C. L., and Lacob, J. S. (1977): Modulation of memory processes induced by stimulation of the entorhinal cortex. *Physiol. Behav.,* 19:139–144.
43. Matthies, H. (1979): Biochemical, electrophysiological, and morphological correlates of brightness discrimination in rats. *This volume.*
44. McGaugh, J. L., and Dawson, R. G. (1971): Modification of memory storage processes. In: *Animal Memory,* edited by W. K. Honig and P. H. R. James. Academic Press, New York; also revised for *Behav. Sci.,* 16:45–63 (1971).
45. McGaugh, J. L., and Gold, P. E. (1976): Modulation of memory by electrical stimulation of the brain. In: *Neural Mechanisms of Learning and Memory,* edited by M. R. Rosenzweig and E. L. Bennett, pp. 549–560. MIT Press, Cambridge.
46. McGaugh, J. L., and Herz, M. J. (1972): *Memory Consolidation.* Albion, San Francisco.
47. McGaugh, J. L., Gold, P. E., van Buskirk, R. B., and Haycock, J. W. (1975): Modulating influences of hormones and catecholamines on memory storage processes. In: *Progress in Brain Research, Vol. 42: Hormones, Homeostasis and the Brain,* edited by W. H. Gispen, Tj. B. van Wimersma Greidanus, B. Bohus, and D. de Wied, pp. 151–162. Elsevier, Amsterdam.
48. Meligeni, J. A., Ledergerber, S. A., and McGaugh, J. L. (1978): Norepinephrine attenuation of amnesia produced by diethyldithiocarbamate. *Brain Res.,* 149:155–164.
49 Meligeni, J. A., Ledergerber, S. A., and McGaugh, J. L. (1978): Peripheral epinephrine attenuation of amnesia produced by diethyldithiocarbamate. (*Submitted for publication.*)
50. Oliverio, A. (1979): Genetic and environmental factors in the ontogeny of learning. *This volume.*
51. Rose, S. L. (1979): Transient and lasting biochemical responses to visual deprivation and experience in the rat visual cortex. *This volume.*
52. Routtenberg, A., and Holzman, N. (1973): Memory disruption by electrical stimulation of substantia nigra, pars compacta. *Science,* 181:83–86.
53. Sideroff, S., Bueno, O., Hirsch, A., Weyand, T., and McGaugh, J. L. (1974): Retrograde amnesia initiated by low-level stimulation of hippocampal cytoarchitectonic areas. *Exp. Neurol.,* 43:285–297.
54. Spanis, C. W., Haycock, J. W., Handwerker, M. J., Rose, R. P., and McGaugh, J. L. (1977): Impairment of retention of avoidance responses in rats by posttraining diethyldithiocarbamate. *Psychopharmacology,* 53:213–215.
55. Stein, L., Belluzzi, J. D., and Wise, C. D. (1975): Memory enhancement by central administration of norepinephrine. *Brain Res.,* 84:329–335.
56. Zornetzer, S. F., Gold, M. S., and Boast, C. A. (1977): Neuroanatomic localization and the neurobiology of sleep and memory. In: *Neurobiology of Sleep and Memory,* edited by R. R. Drucker-Colin and J. L. McGaugh (associate editors, R. A. Jensen and J. L. Martinez, Jr.), pp. 185–226. Academic Press, New York.

Brain Mechanisms in Memory and Learning:
From the Single Neuron to Man,
edited by M. A. B. Brazier.
Raven Press, New York © 1979.

Transient and Lasting Biochemical Responses to Visual Deprivation and Experience in the Rat Visual Cortex

Steven P. R. Rose

Brain Research Group, Biology Department, The Open University,
Milton Keynes MK7 6AA, England

In this chapter, I consider, first, the general nature of the plastic neuronal modifications we may expect to underlie behavioural changes in response to experience, of which learning is a special case; second, the biochemical techniques available for the study of such neuronal modifications and their presumed correlations with the changed behaviour; and, third, some recent evidence for transient and longer term modifications in neurochemical systems underlying axonal flow and synaptic transmission in response to experience. These approaches are examined in one model situation—that of the first exposure of dark-reared animals to the light. I also try to relate this model to events in analogous situations involving specific and measurable learning.

PLASTICITY AT THE NEURONAL LEVEL

Not all neurons or ensembles of neurons[1] are plastic in the sense of being modifiable by experience. Excluding the category of regeneration following destruction of cells or their connections, which seems to be so drastic a procedure that the term plasticity must itself be stretched beyond usefulness to encompass the responses to it (but see the discussion in ref. 1), it would appear that a proportion of all neurons in the central nervous system (CNS) are hardwired during ontogeny and relatively unmodifiable by experience. An example is the relative irrelevance of visual experience to the greater part of the wiring of the eye–brain pathways in all the species so far studied. Such neurons and their connections can be regarded as epigenetically specific, and it may also be suggested (with some support from empirical studies)

---

[1] In this section, I use the term "neuron" to mean a theoretical neuron; the events described may actually be expressed in terms of changed relationships within an ensemble of neurons, and any actual, physical neuron within the brain may participate in all the conditions described here—hardwired, transient, and long-term plastic—in some of its characteristics (7).

that the proportion of such hardwired, specific neurons to the total number of CNS neurons shows phylogenetic variation, being lowest in species, such as the human, with the greatest learning ability and the least "wired-in" behaviour.

To turn from hardwired to "plastic" neurons, there are at least two senses in which the word plasticity is used in the context of neuronal modification. The first type of plasticity sees the cell as analogous to a rubber ball, which deforms on bouncing but reverts to its original rest state thereafter. If we use the word "state" to refer to the global statement of the biochemical or physiological condition of the cell, then the normal state of a neuron is its "ground state," Ng. New inputs produce a transient change to some more activated state, Na, from which it subsequently reverts:

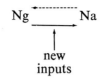

These transient changes may be the correlates of temporarily changed behaviour in the organism or, in the special case of learning, they may represent the condition in which an ensemble of neurons "holds" short-term memory, or both.

The second sense in which plasticity is used refers to a lasting modification to the properties of the neuron (or ensemble) as a result of developmental experience or learning. Here, the event is analogous to the moulding of thermostable plastic: once the modification is imposed, it is durable. Such long-term plastic changes are the results of differing types of experience and therefore may be of several sorts. The most general may be those imposed by nutritional or hormonal deficits or imbalances during early development, which have known behavioural and biochemical sequelae, although these may be of a rather broad nature and not precisely determined by the experience itself. Of more interest perhaps is the evidence for classes of cells within the nervous system that are primed, so to speak, to respond with a thermostable plastic change at a given developmental stage. The exact nature of the change, however, is experientially determined. The example here is the phenomenon of imprinting, which is "ready to go" in the precocial bird within the first posthatch days, but in which the object of the imprinting is determined by environmental chance. Here we may envisage a class of neurons, Ng, that arrive at an epigenetic choice point at which they switch to one of a number of possible alternative stable states.

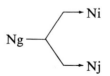

The stability (within limits, ref. 2) of imprinting subsequently implies that once this choice has been made, it is essentially irreversible.

As behavioural modification and learning continue into adulthood, we must envisage a further class of neurons that remain plastic or potentially plastic throughout life, capable at any time, as a result of the appropriate constellation of inputs, of undergoing a stable modification of state:

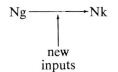

new
inputs

Note that, as explained in the footnote to the first page, there is no *a priori* reason why the same actual physical neuron should not, in some aspect of its properties and at some time in its career, take part in several or all of these classes of response. The problem for the cell neurobiologist is to use model systems for these supposed classes of change and to attempt to map their cellular correlates in real biochemical, morphological, and physiological events. To this end, a number of simplifying assumptions are generally made, notably a biochemical parsimony principle that cellular changes that occur in response to such general developmental modulators as environmental enrichment or sensory deprivation and stimulation will be similar to those involved in the:

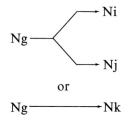

transformations, the distinction being afforded not by a different biochemical process, but by the number, addresses, and connectivity of the cells involved in the response. Since only disconfirmatory experiments can test such an assumption and we are far from having a complete cellular model for any transient or stable plastic response as yet, it may at present rest.

BIOCHEMICAL APPROACHES

Having reviewed the range of biochemical options and their limitations recently (26,27), I merely summarise here the approaches available in the study of transient or long-term effects in any model system. They include: (a) correlative studies in which the measurement of changes in enzyme activities and in the absolute levels of substances such as RNA, protein, and small metabolites or the indirect measurement of levels of macromolecules or of rates of turnover by isotopic techniques is made during or after experience; and (b) interventionist studies in which biochemical systems are disrupted by drug treatment and the consequence for the animal's behaviour (e.g., failure to learn, failure to recall) is observed.

Both approaches are liable to ambiguities of interpretation. At the behavioural level, exposure to novel experience results in a range of events in the organism (e.g., stress, sensory stimulation, arousal) as well as learning. Any one of these may be the behavioural correlate of the observed biochemical response. Intervention at the biochemical level, for instance by drugs, results in a complex sequence of primary and secondary biochemical effects [for instance, the inhibition of protein synthesis by cycloheximide also produces large pools of free amino acids (14), and which of these is primarily responsible for the inhibition of learning is not necessarily clear]. The choice of adequate controls (3) and a combination in the same experiential situation of correlative and interventionist strategies is essential, although I know of only one experimental situation in which this combined approach has been fully developed, that of imprinting in the chick (25).

NEUROCHEMICAL CORRELATES OF DARK-REARING AND LIGHT EXPOSURE IN THE RAT

I will review the biochemical correlates of the properties of the model system (i.e., visual deprivation and stimulation). The visual system is a useful model because of the relative ease with which input can be controlled (by comparison, for example, with auditory stimuli), of the extent to which, at least in the mammals, its physiology and anatomy have been mapped, and of the observation of the relatively hardwired nature of many of its neurons. Rats deprived of light from birth show, within seconds of first exposure in young adulthood, the full normal behavioural repertoire, including startle responses, depth discrimination, and the ability to learn visual tasks. Dark-reared or light-deprived animals may be compared with light-exposed littermates, with "normals," or with animals deprived of sight by eyelid suturing or enucleation. Both the nature and extent of the light stimulus can be controlled and "visual" and "nonvisual" regions of the brain compared. In some experiments using light stimulation in birds in which the optic tract shows complete decussation, one-half of the brain can be used as a control for the other (4–6,15). However, without behavioural controls, which have not been attempted, the observed biochemical changes must be regarded as measuring transient and longer term sequelae of plasticity to experience in general rather than of learning *per se.*

Dark-rearing and subsequent light exposure have been shown to result in measurable morphological changes in the visual pathways and also frontal cortex in several rodent species, studied either with Golgi methods or at the level of electron microscopy. According to Valverde (37,38), there is a reduction of dendritic spines on the apical dendrites of visual cortex pyramidal cells during dark-rearing in mice, with a sprouting of spines taking place on exposure to light. Cragg (8,9) has shown changes in synaptic number and density in the visual cortex and lateral geniculate in dark-reared rats subsequently exposed to light, whereas Vrensson and de Groot (39,40) have claimed that dark-rearing for 7 months in the rabbit results in a 40% deficit of synaptic vesicles but no change in the number of synaptic zones. Subsequent light exposure did not reverse this deficit, which remained even after a year of normal visual experience.

Mares et al. (18) have followed DNA metabolism autoradiographically with ^{3}H-thymidine and have shown that in rats the normal decline in the rate of glial proliferation that occurs during development proceeds more rapidly during visual deprivation in the lateral geniculate and visual cortex. Dewar and his co-workers (11,12) found a lower rate of incorporation of precursor into RNA in blind than in sighted rats and in dark-reared than in light-exposed rats. Thus, there is morphological and biochemical evidence from other laboratories for lasting plastic responses in metabolic state to dark-rearing and light exposure.

In our experiments, pregnant Wistar rats are placed in light-proof wooden boxes housed within an otherwise normal animal house environment, and the male offspring are reared in the dark until weaning. At this stage the mother and one-third of the offspring are removed, to live in a normal 12-hr-light-12-hr-dark animal house regime until 50 days (normals, N). Half of the remaining dark-reared animals are then removed and subjected to normal laboratory illumination for varying periods of time (light-exposed, L), while the remainder stay in the dark (dark controls, D). For incorporation studies, isotope (generally ^{3}H- or ^{14}C-lysine) is injected intraperitoneally, normally 1 hr before killing. Drugs or inhibitors may also be injected at varying times prior to killing. Visual and motor cortices are then dissected out and prepared for cellular or subcellular fractionation, enzyme or protein assay by methods described in more detail in the papers from which the results to be discussed are derived.

Effects on Rate of Protein Synthesis

Our initial studies with this system (reviewed in ref. 25) were devoted to the demonstration that light exposure results in a transiently enhanced rate of protein synthesis or turnover in the visual cortex, lateral geniculate, and retina compared with dark controls (21,23,24). The elevation lasts 1 to 3 hr after light exposure and is of about 20% in magnitude (longer periods of exposure result in a depression in incorporation rate). The next questions were whether the apparent elevation is a real effect on protein metabolism or reflects merely changes in precursor pools consequent on blood flow changes (which are known to occur), and whether we were observing a generalised elevation in synthesis of all cell proteins or a particular response in a limited number.

To approach these questions, we labeled the proteins of 1-hr L and D animals as before and, following the labeling, separated the proteins from visual cortex into soluble and insoluble fractions. Each group was then further subdivided, using polyacrylamide gel electrophoresis and a double-labeling procedure (22). Six out of 41 visual cortex protein fractions showed reliable elevations in incorporation of up to 2 to 300% in Ls compared with Ds; one fraction showed a depression. Thus it does seem as though incorporation into only a limited number of proteins is affected by the light exposure or dark-reared animals.

But, which proteins, and located where within the cell? Gel fractionation of whole tissue homogenate is not the best way of approaching this question. An alternative was to attempt a subcellular fractionation followed by further column separation procedures. An initial fractionation revealed that 1 hr after onset of light exposure much of the elevation in the visual cortex is ribosomally bound (16), but attempts to fractionate further the ribosomal pellet have not been successful. On the other hand, the soluble cytoplasmic fraction, on passage through a Sephadex G200 column, yields at least three differentially enriched peaks in the light, compared to the dark, animals (A. Jones-Lecointe, *unpublished experiments*). The further identification of these fractions is described in the section on the tubulin system below.

Cellular Locus of Effects

In cerebral cortex from normal animals, the rate of synthesis of protein is higher in neurons than in glia or neuropil, whether measured by autoradiography (13), direct electron microscopy (20), or biochemically following the gradient separation of neuronal, perikaryal, and neuropil fractions (28). A significant proportion of the labeling of neuronal perikaryal proteins, at least from lysine and phenylalanine as precursors, is into a rapidly labeling protein (RLP) fraction that is transported out of the perikarya over a 1- to 4-hr period, apparently into dendrites, axons, and synapses. This exported fraction includes glycoprotein, as demonstrated by the use of ^{3}H-fucose as a precursor, and its export from the perikarya is blocked by intraperitoneally administered colchicine, which inhibits axonal flow. The synthesis of RLP also seems to be particularly sensitive to the administration of cycloheximide (30). It seemed sensible to examine the effect of dark-rearing and light exposure on protein synthesis in neuronal perikaryal and neuropil fractions from the rat visual cortex, and this comparison showed that the elevation of incorporation that occurs on light exposure is entirely neuronal (31). Synthesis of RLP is apparently suppressed in dark-reared animals compared with normals, but is switched on within an hour of the onset of light exposure (29). Thus, although the major elevation of incorporation of precursor into proteins that occurs on the onset of visual stimulation is apparently transient, the switching on of the production of the neuronal RLP, by comparison with its suppression in the visual cortex of the dark-reared animal, appears to be a lasting effect.

Involvement of the Tubulin System in the Response to Onset of Visual Stimulation

The apparent involvement in the visual cortex response to the onset of light stimulation of a component of axonally or dendritically transported material led us to consider the possible role of the microtubule system and its major component, tubulin. In this context, I should like to describe two experiments. The first compares the rate of labeling of polymerisable tubulin derived from the soluble cytoplasmic fraction of the visual cortex, in N, D, and L rats. The second measures the total quantity of tubulin present as determined by colchicine binding in the three conditions.

In the first experiment animals were injected with ^{3}H-lysine and killed after 1 hr of exposure. Polymerised tubulin was prepared from the cytoplasm by the method of Shelanski et al. (34). Figure 1 shows that although in the total homogenate there is a 43% elevation of incorporation in L over D, as expected from our earlier work, in the polymerized tubulin (P_2) fraction, incorporation in both N and L animals was double that in Ds. This effect is

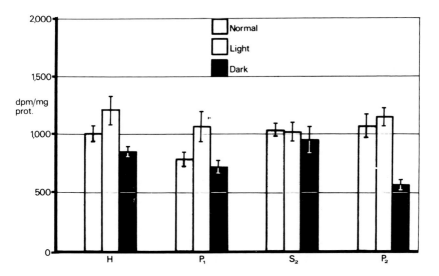

FIG. 1. Incorporation of ^{3}H-lysine into tubulin-enriched fraction in N, L, and D rat visual cortex. Results are normalised means $\pm$ SEM for seven L, eight D, and nine N animals. Dark bars, D; grey bars, N, open bars, L; H, total homogenate; P_1, particulate pellet; P_2, polymerised tubulin; S_2, supernatant after tubulin removal by the method of Shelanski (34). D versus L is significant at $p < 0.02$ in H, P_1, and D versus L and D versus N significant at $p < 0.001$ in the tubulin fraction. (From Rose et al., ref. 32.)

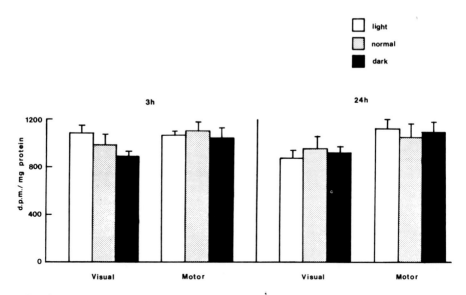

FIG. 2. ³H-colchicine binding in visual and motor cortex of N, L, and D rats at 3 and 24 hr. ³H-colchicine binding was measured as described in ref. 36. Results are from 12 animals in each condition ± SEM. Code as in Fig. 1. Elevation in visual cortex L versus D at 3 hr is significant (p < 0.05). (From Stewart and Rose, ref. 36.)

limited to the visual cortex and is absent in the motor regions. There is, thus, a lasting increase in the rate of synthesis of tubulin in the visual cortex on light exposure, and it is tempting to relate this to the neuronal RLP fraction referred to above. Moreover, the molecular weight of tubulin makes it an appropriate candidate for one of the peaks of cytoplasmic protein fractionated on Sephadex G200 referred to in the section above on the effects on the rate of protein synthesis (32).

The total quantity of tubulin present in N, L, and D motor and visual cortices was estimated by the *in vivo* intraperitoneal injection of ³H-colchicine. The drug is taken up into the brain and binds to tubulin. The tubulin ³H-colchicine complex can be precipitated from tissue homogenates with trichloracetic acid. The colchicine binding shows saturable kinetics, and although tubulin is not the only protein that binds the drug, it is the major component, as control experiments with an analog of colchicine, lumicolchicine, which does not bind to tubulin, show. L animals were exposed for 3 or 24 hr and 1 hr before killing were injected with ³H-colchicine. Figure 2 shows the results of this experiment. There are no changes in ³H-colchicine binding in the motor cortex at either 3 or 24 hr in L, D, or N animals, but in the visual cortex after 3 hr, there is a 23% elevation in L compared with D. There are no differences between N and D animals, and by 24 hr the elevation in L animals has disappeared. When lumicolchicine was substituted for colchicine, there was no difference in binding between the conditions, and vinblastine precipitation experiments help confirm that much of the colchicine radioactivity is in fact bound to tubulin (36).

Thus, by contrast with the lasting alteration in its synthetic rate, the amount of tubulin present appears to show only a transient elevation. One possible explanation is that the newly synthesised tubulin was converted into a form inaccessible to colchicine, perhaps by incorporation into membrane structures (19). However, an alternative possibility is provided by the observation, in another set of studies of the effects of light exposure, that dark-rearing results in a deficit in the level of activity (defined in terms of maximal specific activity, or units/mg protein) of several cerebral acid hydrolases. These include glucosidase and galactosidase (35). Three hours of light exposure elevates the visual cortex enzyme activities to levels similar to those found in normal animals. Although we have not measured protease activity, if it follows the pattern of the other degradative enzymes and increases on light exposure, we could account for our observations if the effect of light exposure were to increase the turnover rate of tubulin by speeding both the synthetic and the degradative steps, but the mobilisation of the degradative side of the process were to lag behind that of synthesis. Hence there is an initial "overshoot" in total tubulin production that is subsequently stabilized. (The slightly lower amount of colchicine binding present in the visual cortex after 24 hr of light exposure, shown in Fig. 2, fits this hypothesis). These observations are also compatible with the observations of Cronly-Dillon and Perry concerning tubulin levels and synthesis over the period of eye-opening in the hooded rat (10).

Involvement of the Acetylcholine Transmitter System

The models of neuronal plasticity under discussion all imply that the outcome of the modulation of perikaryal metabolism is a modification of synaptic connectivity. Although there are a variety of ways this can occur, a probable one is a change in transmitter efficacy. Unfortunately, the visual system transmitter(s) are not known with any degree of certainty, although one candidate, certainly present in quantity, is acetylcholine (ACh). Hence a study of ACh metabolism in dark-rearing and light exposure could be revealing. The activity of acetyl cholinesterase (AChE) in the avian visual system has been shown responsive to visual stimulation (5,6). In our first series of experiments (35) we measured choline acetyltransferase (CAT) and AChE in N, D, and L animals and found that 3 hr of light exposure resulted in a significant elevation of enzyme-specific activity above both D and N levels. The existence of specific ligand binding methods for the measurement of the ACh-receptor protein provides perhaps a more meaningful marker for synaptic function than do enzyme activities. The nicotinic ACh receptor is scarcely present in the cerebral cortex, but the muscarinic receptor (mAChr) is present in considerable amounts (17) and may be as-

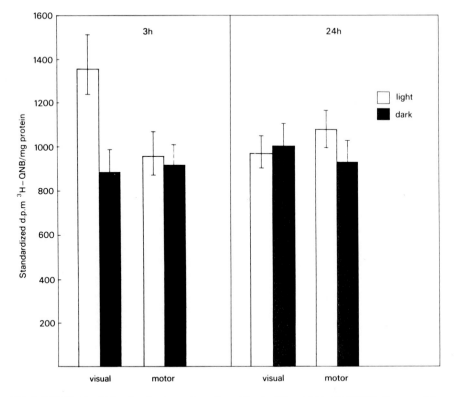

FIG. 3. QNB-binding in visual and motor cortex of L and D rats at 3 and 24 hr. ³H-QNB binding was determined as described in ref. 33. Results are means of ⩾ 16 animals in each case ± SEM. Standardised results mean that 1,000 dpm ≃ 1.0 pmole QNB-bound, but 3- and 24-hr values are not directly comparable. Dark bars, D; open bars, L; visual cortex L versus D at 3 hr p < 0.01. (From Rose and Stewart, ref, 33.)

sayed using the specific ligand ³H-quinuclidinyl benzilate (QNB) in the presence and absence of atropine, which abolishes the specific binding (41).

Figure 3 shows the results of such an assay on the visual and motor cortex of D and 3- and 24-hr L animals. For comparison purposes, Fig. 4 shows the results of the AChE measurement on visual and motor cortices of N, D, and 3- and 24-hr L animals. Three hours after the onset of light exposure, there is a 54% increase in QNB binding in the visual cortex of L compared with D animals; by 24 hr the elevation has vanished. The motor cortex is unaffected at either time. There is also no difference (not shown in the figure) between QNB binding in D and N animals. The events in AChE match those in mAChr; the 3-hr L activity is elevated by 24% above that in D or N, and by 24 hr it is back to control values once more. Again, the effect is specific to the visual cortex (33).

These observations indicate that a permanent increase in the ACh transmitter system/mg cortex protein does not occur following the onset of light exposure, but that there is a transient increase in the activity of all three

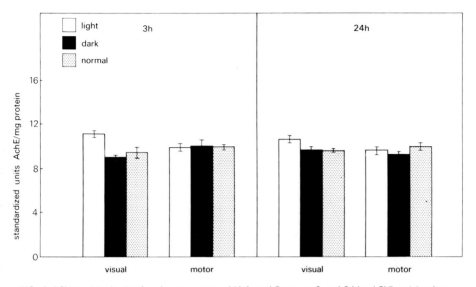

FIG. 4. AChE activity in visual and motor cortex of N, L, and D rats at 3 and 24 hr. AChE activity determined as described in ref. 33. Results are means of $\geq$ 10 animals in each case $\pm$ SEM. Three- and twenty-
four-hour values not directly comparable. Code as in Fig. 1. At 3 hr, in the visual cortex elevation in L v D
and L v N are significant ($p < 0.001$; $p < 0.02$).

components of the system—CAT, AChE, and mAChr. This concordance
would seem more likely to be a result of a modulated rate of synthesis of the
three proteins concerned than a coordinated unmasking of enzyme and receptor sites, but the latter possibility cannot be ruled out at this stage. In
addition, the fact of a CAT/AChE/mAChr response of this type is pre-
sumptive, although not final, evidence for the involvement of the system in
synaptic transmission in the visual cortex.

INTERPRETATION OF THE MODEL IN CELLULAR TERMS

The results of the previous section may now be considered in the light of
the general considerations with which this chapter commenced. Although a
substantial proportion of the visual system of the rat is hardwired and not
dependent on functional stimulation for cellular organisation to occur, the
onset of visual experience, at least in the adolescent/young adult animal,
can still occasion plastic neuronal responses both of the form

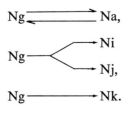

or perhaps, $Ng \longrightarrow Nk.$

We cannot distinguish here between the two types of long-term plastic response that may occur, corresponding roughly, at the behavioural level, to the generalized sharpening of visual responses as a consequence of stimulation (neuronal differentiation) and to the learning of specific responses (connectivity changes between particular neurons). To do this would require the sort of behavioural controls we have carried out in our imprinting studies on the chick (25). Although these studies are not discussed here, it is worthy of note that in the imprinting system biochemical changes rather analogous to those described here have been found relatively (though not completely) unambiguously to underlie learning. So far as the cell biology of first exposure to light in the rat is concerned, we may deduce from our data that there is a transient potentiation of acetylcholinergic synapses in the visual cortex by increased activity of the CAT/AChE/mAChr system, perhaps by way of *de novo* synthesis. This transient response lasts on the order of hours and is accompanied by an elevation of protein synthesis and a transient increase in the amount of the tubulin available for colchicine binding. More permanent changes include the switching on of the synthesis of a neuronal (glyco-) protein that participates in cellulofugal flow, and a doubling of the rate of synthesis (and possibly of degradation) of polymerizable tubulin. These changes must carry others in their train; for instance, increased protein turnover makes increased demands on energy metabolism and hence, possibly, on local blood flow, known to be affected in some species by visual stimulation (4). If the more lasting changes result in a permanent, as opposed to transient, modification of synapses, they must do so without involving the ACh system. Perhaps the changes occur at other, noncholinergic synapses, or perhaps the permanent modification of a synapse involves other changes than those in transmitter metabolism and receptor-binding sites. The known presence of membrane-bound tubulin in the postsynaptic density may be significant in this regard.

I believe that the biochemical techniques now exist for the further analysis of both transient and permanent plastic responses in the rat first-exposure model, and, further, that the model may produce an understanding of the cellular bases of plasticity that is applicable more widely, and indeed more directly, to the special case of learning.

ACKNOWLEDGMENTS

The work described in this chapter has, at various times, involved the collaboration of the following co-workers: Dr. Altheia Jones-Lecointe, Dr. Ken Richardson, Dr. Arun Sinha, and Dr. Michael Stewart. I am grateful to them for discussion and comment, although they are not responsible for the synthesis presented here. Part of the work has been supported under grants from the Medical Research Council.

REFERENCES

1. Barlow, H., and Gaze, M. (editors) (1977): Plasticity in the nervous system. *Philos. Trans. R. Soc. Lond. (Biol.)*, 278:241–436.
2. Bateson, P. P. G. (1966): The characteristics and context of imprinting. *Biol. Rev.*, 41:177–220.
3. Bateson, P. P. G. (1970): Are they really products of learning? In: *Short-Term Changes in Neural Activity and Behaviour*, edited by G. Horn and R. Hinde, pp. 553–564. Cambridge Univ. Press.
4. Bondy, S. C., Lehman, R. A. W., and Purdy, J. L. (1974): Visual attention affects brain blood flow. *Nature*, 248:440–441.
5. Chakrabarti, T., and Daginawala, H. F. (1975): Effect of unilateral visual deprivation and visual stimulation on activities of alkaline-phosphatase, acid-phosphatase, Na^+ and K^+ activated Mg_2^+ catalysed adenosine-triphosphate and on content of sodium and potassium-ions of optic lobe of adult pigeon. *J. Neurochem.*, 24:983–988.
6. Chakrabarti, T., Dias, P. D., Roychowdury, D., and Daginawala, H. F. (1974): Effect of unilateral visual deprivation on activities of acetylcholinesterase, cholinesterase and carbonic-anhydrase of optic lobe of adult pigeon. *J. Neurochem.*, 22:865–867.
7. Changeux, J. P., and Danchin, A. (1976): Selective stabilization of developing synapses as a mechanism for specification of neuronal networks. *Nature*, 264:705–712.
8. Cragg, B. G. (1967): Changes in visual cortex on first exposure of rats to light. *Nature*, 215:251–253.
9. Cragg, B. G. (1970): Synapses and membranous bodies in experimental hypothyroidism. *Brain Res.*, 18:297–307.
10. Cronly-Dillon, J. R., and Perry, G. W. (1976): Tubulin synthesis in developing rat visual cortex. *Nature*, 261:581–583.
11. Dewar, A. J., and Reading, H. W. (1973): Comparison of RNA metabolism in visual cortex of sighted rats and rats with retinal degeneration. *Exp. Neurol.*, 40:216–231.
12. Dewar, A. J., Reading, H. W., and Winterburn, K. (1973): RNA metabolism in subcellular-fractions from rat cerebral cortex and from visual-cortex in rats with retinal degeneration. *Exp. Neurol.*, 41:133–139.
13. Droz, B., and Koenig, H. L. (1970): Localization of protein metabolism in neurons. In: *Protein Metabolism of the Nervous System*, edited by A. Lajtha, pp. 93–108. Plenum Press, New York.
14. Hambley, J. W., and Rogers, L. J. (1977): Some neurochemical correlates of permanent learning deficits associated with intracerebral injections of amino acids in young chick brain. *Proc. Int. Soc. Neurochem.*, 6:359.
15. Hambley, J., and Morgan, I. (1977): *Abstracts Australian Biochemical Society*, Brisbane.
16. Jones-Lecointe, A., Rose, S. P. R., and Sinha, A. K. (1976): Subcellular localisation of enhanced lysine incorporation into cerebral cortex proteins in dark-reared and light-exposed rats. *J. Neurochem.*, 26:929–933.
17. Kuhar, M. J., and Yamamura, H. I. (1976): Localization of cholinergic muscarinic receptors in rat brain by light microscopic autoradiography. *Brain Res.*, 110:229–243.
18. Mareš, V., Bruckner, G., Narovec, T., and Biesold, D. (1977): The effect of different light regimes on DNA synthesis and cell division in the rat visual centres. *Life Sci.*, 21:727–732.
19. Matus, A. I., Walters, B. B., and Mughal, S. (1975): Immunohistochemical demonstration of tubulin associated with microtubules and synaptic junctions in mammalian brain. *J. Neurocytol.*, 4:733–744.
20. Palay, S., and Chan-Palay, V. (1972): In: *Metabolic Compartmentation in the Brain*, edited by R. Balazs and J. E. Cremer, pp. 287–304. Macmillan, London.

21. Richardson, K., and Rose, S. P. R. (1972): Changes in ³H-lysine incorporation following first exposure to light. *Brain Res.,* 44:299–303.
22. Richardson, K., and Rose, S. P. R. (1973): Differential incorporation of ³H-lysine into visual cortex protein fractions during first exposure to light. *J. Neurochem.,* 21:531–537.
23. Rose, S. P. R. (1967): Changes in visual cortex on first exposure of rats to light. *Nature,* 215:253–255.
24. Rose, S. P. R. (1972): Changes in amino acid pools in the rat brain following first exposure to light. *Brain Res.,* 38:171–178.
25. Rose, S. P. R. (1977): Early visual experience, learning and neurochemical plasticity in the rat and the chick. *Phil. Trans. R. Soc. Lond. (Biol.),* 307–318.
26. Rose, S. P. R., Hambley, J., and Haywood, J. (1975): Neurochemical approaches to developmental plasticity and learning. In: *Neural Mechanisms of Learning and Memory,* edited by M. R. Rosenzweig and E. Bennett, pp. 293–309. MIT Press, Cambridge.
27. Rose, S. P. R., and Haywood, J. (1977): Experience, learning and brain metabolism. In: *Biochemical Correlates of Brain Structure and Function,* edited by A. N. Davison, pp. 249–292. Academic Press, London.
28. Rose, S. P. R., and Sinha, A. K. (1974): Incorporation of amino acids into proteins in neuronal and neuropil fractions of rat cerebral cortex: Presence of a rapidly labelling fraction. *J. Neurochem.,* 23:1065–1076.
29. Rose, S. P. R., and Sinha, A. K. (1974): Incorporation into a rapidly-labelling neuronal protein fraction in visual cortex is suppressed in dark reared rats. *Life Sci.,* 15:223–230.
30. Rose, S. P. R., and Sinha, A. K. (1976): Rapidly labelling and exported neuronal protein: ³H-fucose as precursor and effects of cycloheximide and colchicine. *J. Neurochem.,* 27:963–967.
31. Rose, S. P. R., Sinha, A. K., and Broomhead, S. (1973): Precursor incorporation into cortical protein during first exposure of rats to light: Cellular localisation effects. *J. Neurochem.,* 21:539–546.
32. Rose, S. P. R., Sinha, A. K., and Jones-Lecointe, A. (1976): Synthesis of a tubulin-enriched fraction in rat visual cortex is modulated by dark rearing and light exposure. *FEBS Lett.,* 65:135–139.
33. Rose, S. P. R., and Stewart, M. G. (1978): Transient increase in muscarinic ACh receptor and AChE in visual cortex on first exposure of dark reared rats to light. *Nature,* 271:169–170.
34. Shelanski, M. L., Gaskin, F., and Cantor, C. R. (1973): Microtubule assembly in absence of added nucleotides. *Proc. Natl. Acad. Sci. USA,* 70:765–768.
35. Sinha, A. K., and Rose, S. P. R. (1976): Dark rearing and visual stimulation in the rat: Effect on brain enzymes. *J. Neurochem.,* 27:921–926.
36. Stewart, M. G., and Rose, S. P. R. (1978): Increased binding of ³H-colchicine to visual cortex proteins of dark-reared rats on first exposure to light. *J. Neurochem.* 30:595–599.
37. Valverde, F. (1967): Apical dendrite spines of the visual cortex and light deprivation in the mouse. *Exp. Brain Res.,* 3:337–352.
38. Valverde, F. (1971): Rate and extent of recovery from dark rearing in the visual cortex of the mouse brain. *Brain Res.,* 33:1–11.
39. Vrensson, G., and de Groot, D. (1974): The effect of dark rearing and its recovery on synaptic terminals in the visual cortex of rabbits: A quantitative e.m. study. *Brain Res.,* 78:263–278.
40. Vrensson, G., and de Groot, D. (1975): The effect of monocular deprivation on synaptic terminals in the visual cortex of rabbits: A quantitative e.m. study. *Brain Res.,* 93:15–24.
41. Yamamura, H. I., and Snyder, S. H. (1974): Muscarinic cholinergic binding in rat-brain. *Proc. Natl. Acad. Sci. USA,* 71:1725–1729.

Brain Mechanisms in Memory and Learning:
From the Single Neuron to Man,
edited by M. A. B. Brazier.
Raven Press, New York © 1979.

Effects of Binocular Deprivation and Specific Experience in Cats: Behavioral, Electrophysiological, and Biochemical Analyses

Bogusław Zernicki

Department of Neurophysiology, Nencki Institute of Experimental Biology,
02–093 Warsaw, Poland

Depriving animals of visual stimulation from birth and giving them specific visual experience during early periods of life are essential methods for studying the effects of environmental factors on the development of the visual system. Recently, these methods have been used successfully in cats. Although some data conflict (see ref. 1), it has been clearly established that both deprivation and early experience influence the visually guided behavior of cats as well as the physiology and morphology of their visual system (for review see refs. 1,4). In the present review, recent data in this field from the Nencki Institute are summarized. The findings represent available portions of a long-term study.

METHODS

Both deprivation and training were done binocularly. Thus we avoided the role of competitive elements, which are responsible in part for the changes from monocular procedures (e.g., see 18). The only exception to this procedure involved investigations of biochemical correlates of visual training when utilizing a subject as its own control was particularly critical.

An original technique of visual deprivation was employed. On the eighth postnatal day, before eye opening, kittens had white double *hoods* fitted closely around their heads. The hood prevented pattern vision, but allowed access to scattered light on both retinae. The advantage of this method over eyelid suturing is that the hood can be temporarily removed to offer the cat some visual experience. The details of this technique may be found elsewhere (25).

For chronic experiments, three-dimensional objects were used as visual stimuli. A pair of objects usually consisted of a black ping-pong ball and a three-dimensional cross of the same size and color. In acute experiments, either the same objects were used (they were moved automatically in front of the cat's head, see 54) or light stimuli were presented.

With the exception of biochemical investigations, adult cats were used for the experiments. Four categories of cats, differing in visual experiences, were mainly used.

1. *N cats:* control cats that came to the laboratory as adults or in the third month of life. The cats were not from rearing facilities and were usually not pets; the majority of them had lived freely in the city or in the country-side.

2. *C cats:* control cats born in the laboratory and reared with unshielded eyes.

3. *Hc cats, Hb cats, Hcb, Hs cats:* hood-reared cats with visual experience, during critical periods, with the cross, ball, both, or stick. From 2 to 15 weeks of age, the kittens were maintained individually with hoods taken off for 20 min daily while they played in a small box with crosses, balls, both, or sticks. Thus during this pretraining, the kittens received not only visual but also visuomotor experience. Moreover, the visual stimuli presumably became associated with the reduction of the drive to play.

4. *H cats:* inexperienced hood-reared cats. Some of these cats were observed when remaining in hoods and were denoted then as *hooded cats.*

In the hood-reared cats used for the acute experiments, the hoods were removed during the experiment. In cats used for the chronic experiments, the hoods were off during experimental sessions only (i.e., they were removed about 10 min before a session and replaced immediately after) or the hoods were removed 2 weeks before the first session.

For acute experiments, the brainstems of the cats were transected at the pretrigeminal level (2,52,56). The isolated cerebrum of the pretrigeminal cat is in an *awake* state, as shown by such evidence as the presence of ocular-orienting reflexes to visual stimuli and the possibility of the elaboration of ocular-conditioned reflexes. Since the pretrigeminal preparation is presumably without pain to the subject, cats may be easily restrained in a stereotaxic apparatus, which facilitates the precise presentation of the visual stimuli at different points of the visual field and the recording of ocular and single-unit responses.

In the pretrigeminal cat, horizontal eye movements are absent, since the presumed center for horizontal eye movements is located behind the transection, but vertical eye movements remain intact (52). In the majority of experiments, eye movements were not abolished by gallamine, and the vertical position of the eye was monitored. For this purpose an original tensometric method was used (15). Under these conditions the presence of ocular fixation reflexes to visual stimuli indicated that (a) the preparation was in a good state and (b) the cat attended to the stimulus presented. However, the interpretation of single-unit responses was then somewhat difficult, since some of them are eye movement-related (29).

BEHAVIORAL RESULTS

Hooded Cats

The behavior of hooded cats in their home cages was observed by Korda (24a). The cages consisted of two compartments, each 90 × 50 × 40 cm. In the first month of life, the behavior of the hooded kittens did not seem to differ from that of their littermates reared with eyes opened, but the hooded kittens left the nest for the first time 2 or 3 days later than did the kittens without eye shields.

At the age of 3 to 7 months in eight of the 23 hooded kittens observed, episodes of stereotypic behavior appeared. The kittens walked in a pendulum-like fashion along the front wall of a cage compartment (distance of 90 cm). These episodes lasted usually several minutes, covered from 18 to 34% of the observation sessions, and became longer lasting and more frequent with the increasing age of the kittens. Such stereotypic behavior has been observed often in captive wild animals (e.g., in a zoo), but was not found in our control kittens reared with open eyes. It was also not observed in hooded kittens reared in a large group cage (3 × 1 × 3 m), with objects available for climbing. It follows that episodes of stereotypic behavior occur only both when vision is eliminated and when kinesthetic stimulation is reduced (by placing the kittens in relatively small cages).

The behavior of hooded cats was also tested in a situation described by Santibañez (38). Four visible loudspeakers were located in the upper corners of a box. In experiment 1 orienting reflexes evoked by tones were compared in four hooded cats and four C cats. On the first trials, clear-cut reflexes consisting of movement of pinnas and head movements toward the proper loudspeaker were observed in all cats (10). However, in hooded cats the resistance to habituation of the orienting reflexes was about three times less than in C cats. Experiment 2 attempted to transform orienting reflexes into alimentary conditioned reflexes by rewarding a reflex to a correct loudspeaker with food. Four hooded cats, four H cats (hood-reared cats without hoods), and four C cats were used. H cats and C cats easily mastered the task, the mean number of sessions to the criterion being 10 in H cats and 11 in C cats. On the other hand, none of the hooded cats met the criterion within 20 sessions. In the hooded cats, however, conditioned reflexes were easily elaborated when the hoods were removed. The results show that deprivation of visual feedback affects orienting and conditioned reflexes toward the visible source of the auditory stimulus.

General Behavior of Hood-Reared Cats

Relieved of their hoods in the home cage, some cats became very active, whereas others "froze." When moved to a new place (e.g., onto the floor of the experimental room), the cats displayed extreme caution. They sought to avoid every collision with objects by touching them with their snout, withdrawing the head, and touching again. They seemed to be even more cautious than hooded cats placed in the same room. The cats descended with difficulty from an elevation of 30 cm and did not show visual placing.

These deficits disappeared quickly, and after 2 weeks H cats did not seem to behave differently from C cats, but a long-lasting deficit in depth perception remained. In contrast, such postdeprivation deficits in dark-reared (3,46) and lid-sutured (6) cats are longer lasting; according to van Hof-van Duin (46), they disappear gradually only within 2 months.

Ocular-Following Reflex

This reflex was studied carefully in eight H cats and 14 N cats (25,31). The recording was performed in pretrigeminal preparations where horizontal

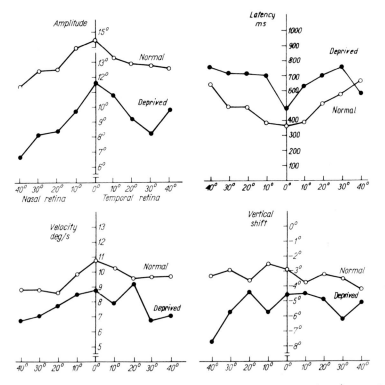

FIG. 1. The comparison of ocular-following movement properties in normally reared cats (*open circles*) and visually deprived cats (*solid circles*). The stimulus was applied with different horizontal eccentricity. Mean data for 14 N cats and eight H cats for four stimulus varieties (slit and stick, upward and downward movement). Smooth movements appearing after stimulus offset are not included. For the vertical shift of the following movements (*last graph*), the negative values represent the lag of the eye movement with respect to the stimulus movement. The differences between N cats and H cats were statistically significant except for the latency of movements obtained from 40° peripheral sites. (From Kossut et al. ref. 25, by permission.)

eye movements were absent. A black stick or a light slit ($1° × 4°$) was moved with $10°$/sec speed for 2 sec along the vertical meridian or parallel up to $40°$ in the nasal or temporal hemifield. In both groups, the reflexes of following objects were evoked from the entire area (although the pursuit movements had longer latencies and lower velocities at the periphery than in the center of the retina) and showed similar resistance to habituation. In H cats, however, irrespective of the place of stimulation, the latencies of the pursuit movements were longer, their velocities lower, and the course less regular than in N cats (Fig. 1). It, therefore, appears that in H cats the ocular-following reflex is only moderately impaired.

In contrast to our results, it has been reported (3,39,46) that in dark-reared or lid-sutured cats the ocular-following reflex is seriously impaired or even absent during the first postdeprivation days, and Sherman (39,40) found that lid-sutured cats did not notice the objects in the contralateral hemifield. The reasons for these discrepancies are unclear. The average light reduction produced by the hood is comparable to that produced by the cat's eyelid (27,31). Ikeda et al. (22) reported that strabismus alone can produce similar visual field loss in normal cats, and possibly in lid-sutured cats the strabismus was more pronounced than in H cats. However, some H cats show marked convergent or divergent strabismus that was maintained for several months.

Simultaneous Object Discrimination Learning

Four groups of cats were used: H cats, Hcb cats (the cats had experience with the cross and ball stimuli), and the two control groups of C cats and N cats. The cats were trained in a two-choice discrimination apparatus. The pair of objects consisted of a cross and a ping-pong ball. The right-left position of the objects was changed randomly, and correct responses were rewarded with food. Two experiments with different subjects were performed. In experiment 1 (50) hood-reared cats had their hoods off only during sessions, and the cross-versus-ball discrimination task was immediately introduced. In experiment 2 (49a), hoods were taken off 2 weeks before training, and the first task involved simply object-versus-no-object discrimination.

Results are shown in Table 1 and may be summarized as follows:

1. In H cats object-discrimination learning was clearly impaired. In contrast to the control groups, these cats were unable to meet the criterion within 60 sessions for the cross-versus-ball discrimination task when learned in one stage (experiment 1), and they met the criterion slowly when trained in two stages (experiment 2). The impairment seems to be comparable to that reported by Ganz et al. (17) for form-discrimination learning in cats deprived by lid suturing.

2. Surprisingly almost the same impairment was observed in Hcb cats.

TABLE 1. *Cross-versus-ping-pong-ball discrimination learning in cats with different visual experiences*

	Sequence of tasks					
Group	Cross or ball vs. no object	Cross vs. ball	Cross or ball vs. no object	Stick vs. ball	Cross vs. ball	No. of cats
Experiment 1[a]						
N		13				10
C		24				8
Hcb		⎰ 36				2
		⎱ (60)	25	9	5	7
H1		(60)	16	8	2	4
H2	⎰ 26	6				2
	⎨ 55	(60)				1
	⎱ (60)					1
Experiment 2[b]						
N	4	12				8
C	11	11				7
H	17	22				10

Mean number of sessions to criterion are given (criterion sessions are excluded). Parentheses indicate the cases when criterion was not reached in 60 sessions. In experiment 1 the hoods were off only during sessions, whereas in experiment 2 they were taken off 2 weeks before training.

[a] From Zablocka et al., ref. 50.
[b] From T. Zablocka and B. Żernicki, ref. 49a.

Poor behavioral consequences of selective visual experience (vertical or horizontal strips) were also reported by Muir and Mitchell (33).

3. Some impairment was observed also in the C cats, reared with open eyes in the laboratory, as compared with N cats that spent the early period of life outside the laboratory.

4. Removal of the hoods 2 weeks before training in H cats (experiment 2) seemed to reduce their deficit in discrimination learning.

The second result suggests that visual and visuomotor experience with the objects did not improve discrimination learning with food reward. We may speculate that the experience of utilization of visual cues for food reward is more important. Such experience was certainly obtained by cats with their hoods removed 2 weeks before training and was particularly abundant in N cats that spent the early period of life under normal conditions of searching and fighting for food.

Go-No-Go-Object-Discrimination Learning

In this task visual stimuli comprised a single stick and two sticks composing an angle (49). Three groups of cats were used: seven C cats, three Hs cats (having pretraining with a stick), and three Hb cats (having pretraining with a ball). Within 16 sessions six of seven cats met criterion, but only one Hs cat and none of the Hb cats reached criterion. The deficit in go-no-go-discrimination learning in hood-reared cats seemed to be comparable to that described above for simultaneous discrimination learning and to that reported by Chow and Stewart (6) for go-no-go-form discrimination learning in cats deprived by lid suturing.

Retention of Simultaneous Object Discrimination after Visual Cortex Ablation

A discrimination task was elaborated in five hood-reared cats (three H cats and two Hcb cats) and in four N cats (51). In the hood-reared cats,

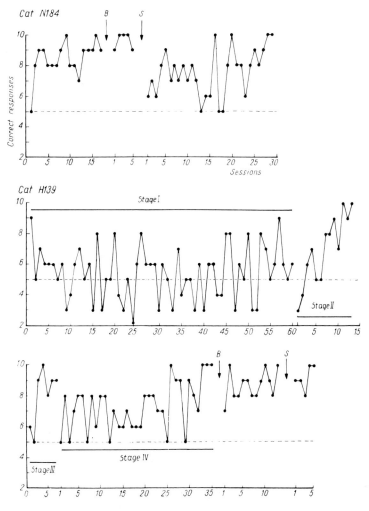

FIG. 2. Retention of cross-versus-ball simultaneous discrimination after visual cortex ablation in cats N184 and H139. In these cats lesions were similar, but their effects contrasting. In both cats the cross was the positive stimulus. Four stages of initial learning in H139 are indicated with horizontal lines (cross versus ball, cross versus no cross, cross versus stick, and cross versus ball). Criterion sessions are included. B, preoperative retention break; S, surgery. (From Zablocka et al., ref. 51, by permission.)

learning was much slower than in controls (83 versus 10 mean sessions to the criterion; with four stages of training for hood-reared cats, see above), and retraining was necessary after a preoperative retention period (mean of four sessions). In both groups, the cortical projection of central vision was removed in areas 17, 18, and 19. In hood-reared cats the deficit following the cortical lesion was less than in N cats (Fig. 2). Mean sessions for relearning was eight in hood-reared cats and 15 in N cats.

These results suggest that hood-reared cats used visual cortex to a lesser degree than controls in the discrimination task and that the role of the visual cortex has been replaced perhaps by the superior colliculus–pretectum system and its cortical representation in areas 21 and 20 and the Clare-Bishop area. This suggestion might explain all of the behavioral characteristics of the hood-reared cats: slow initial learning, forgetting after the preoperative period, and the small postoperative deficit.

RESULTS OF SINGLE-UNIT RECORDING

Visual Cortex: Areas 17 and 18

Inexperienced hood-reared cats (H cats) and cats having visual pretraining with a cross (Hc cats), ball (Hb cats), or stick (Hs cats) were used (54). C cats or N cats served as controls. In experiment 1 the effects of cross-versus-ball pretraining were studied, and experiment 2 examined the effects of stick-versus-ball pretraining. Recordings were made in adult cats with pretrigeminal brainstem transections. The vertical positions of the eyeballs were monitored. Unit responses were recorded in areas 17 and 18 within the projection of area centralis.

In all groups of cats, about 60% of the cells were responsive, nearly all of them to both objects tested. This finding contrasts with the observations of other authors (26,41) that the number of visually responsive cells in area 17 is reduced in deprived cats. It is possible that this discrepancy is caused in part by differences in methods; our recordings were made in the awake pretrigeminal preparation with a preserved ocular-following reflex.

The object available in the play box evoked stronger responses on the average than the control object (Table 2). For a pair of objects of a more different shape (stick versus ball), the dominance of the exposed stimulus seemed to be stronger. Thus in the visual cortex, unit responses to natural objects were modified by early visual experience. However, the effect of pretraining was rather moderate. Possibly during recording, the differences in the form of the objects were overshadowed by the identity of other features of the stimuli (the objects moved in the same direction and with the same speed in front of the cat). The effect of visual pretraining seems indeed to depend greatly on procedural details. Some authors (5,36,45) reported a positive effect of specific visual experience lasting only a few hours,

TABLE 2. *Stimulus-dominance distributions (%) of responsive units and points with multiunit responses in areas 17 and 18 in cats with different visual experiences*

Group		Stimulus dominance				No. of	No. of
Experiment 1	c	c > b	c = b	c < b	b	cats	recorded points
C	1	24	58	16	1	5	134
H	1	17	64	18	0	4	113
Hc	2	34	52	12	0	3	92
Hb	0	12	62	26	0	3	99
Experiment 2	s	s > b	s = b	s < b	b		
N	0	22	52	26	0	2	63
Hs	0	48	38	14	0	1	29
Hb	0	17	34	49	0	3	85

The recording was within the projection of the area centralis. Symbols for stimulus dominance indicate that the response was evoked only to one stimulus (cross, ball, or stick), that the response to one stimulus was stronger, or that the responses to both stimuli were equal. In both experiments the differences were statistically significant.

b, ball; c, cross; s, stick.

From Żernicki and Michalski, ref. 54.

whereas other authors (28,44) failed to obtain any effect after long-lasting pretraining (see also 9,11,35).

Visual Cortex: Area 19

Four groups of cats were used: four Hc cats, four Hb cats, four H cats, and eight N cats (30). Unit responses to the cross and the ball were recorded in area 19 within the projection of the area centralis. Stimulus dominance of the object used in the play box was manifested weakly. Interestingly, both objects activated significantly more units in the experienced hood-reared cats than in H cats and N cats. The percentage of reactive units in different groups were as follows: Hc group, 51%; Hb group, 57%; H group, 39%; and N group, 26%. Moreover, in the experienced hood-reared cats the average responses were stronger. One can speculate that in H cats many cells were "uncommitted," and in normal cats many cells were engaged specifically by various stimuli, so that in both groups they were unresponsive to the standard stimuli employed. Compared with previous findings, the present results indicate that early visual experience affects area 19 differently than areas 17 and 18.

Superior Colliculus

Four groups of cats were used: (a) N cats, (b) H cats, (c) cats with extensive visual cortex ablation (lateral suprasylvian, suprasplenial, and

TABLE 3. *Comparison of percentage of units with particular features in superior colliculus of different groups of cats*

Group	Direction selective	Speed selective	Preferring low-speed	Preferring high-speed	Responsive to diffuse flash	No. of cats	No. of units
N	66	50	25	25	66	8	32[a]
H	39	85	67	18	55	6	33[a]
Visually decorticated	22	50	44	6	75	7	32[b]
Isolated colliculus	36	69	33	33	67	9	70[c]

[a] From Dec et al., ref. 12.
[b] From Dec and Tarnecki, ref. 11a.
[c] From Dec et al., ref. 11b.

splenial gyri) on the homolateral side to recording, and (d) cats with isolated midbrain (55). The midbrain was isolated from the pons and forebrain by two brainstem transections, pretrigeminal and preoptic. The latter passed along the rostral border of the optic tract, leaving it and the chiasm intact. Thus direct visual input into the isolated tissue was maintained. In all groups single-unit response to a moving spot and diffused flash were investigated.

Two important results were as follows:

1. Compared to N cats, in the remaining groups the number of direction-selective units was reduced by about half (Table 3, Fig. 3). The impairment of direction selectivity of collicular units in visually deprived cats has also been noted by other authors (13,14,20,48). Accordingly, the input from the normal visual cortex seems to be critical for preservation of about half of the direction-selective units in the cat's superior colliculus.

2. In contrast to the N group and isolated colliculus group, the units of visually deprived or decorticated cats preferred low-speed stimuli. In visually deprived cats, such a preference has also been noted by Hoffmann and Sherman (20). It is interesting to consider to what extent these deficits of collicular units are responsible for the above described impairment of the ocular-following reflex in H cats.

BIOCHEMICAL RESULTS

An attempt was made to assess the differences in protein content and composition in the cerebral cortex of visually deprived, and control, 1-month-old kittens (32). Electrophysiological (5,23,34) and morphological (7,8) studies showed that in deprived kittens at this age, as compared to controls, the specificity of unit responses of the visual cortex to some stimuli characteristics (particularly stimulus orientation) is diminished and the number of synapses per neuron is reduced. Insoluble proteins in area 17 and in the

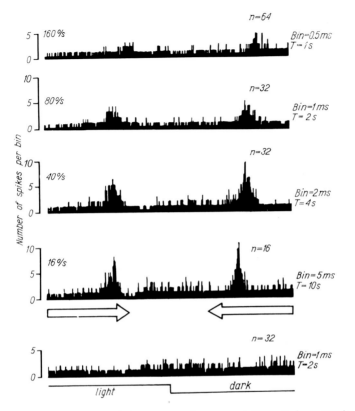

FIG. 3. Poststimulus time histograms of the responses of a representative collicular neuron in a visually deprived cat. The responses to the light spot moving with different speeds (*four upper records*) and to the diffuse flash (*lower record*) are shown. The neuron did not show direction selectivity; it preferred the low-speed spot movements and did not respond to diffuse flash. (From Dec et al., ref. 12, by permission.)

somatic sensory cortex were investigated in seven H kittens and four C kittens. We found that visual deprivation did not affect the total protein content or electrophoretic pattern of insoluble proteins, but deprivation did change their percentage distribution in certain zones of electrophoretograms (Fig. 4). The changes appeared in both cortices investigated, but one change was observed in the visual cortex only. The effect of visual deprivation on nonvisual cortex has been observed also by Ryugo et al. (37), who found that the number of spines in the auditory cortex of rats was increased after bilateral eye enucleation.

Another set of pilot experiments dealt with the changes of protein metabolism after the first visual experience (31a). We again used H kittens that were 1 month old. Thus, they were at the peak of susceptibility to visual experience when, it is believed, (5,36,45) they may respond to a few hours of visual stimulation with dramatic changes in the receptive field properties of cortical units. The kittens had the brainstem transected at the pretrigeminal level, one

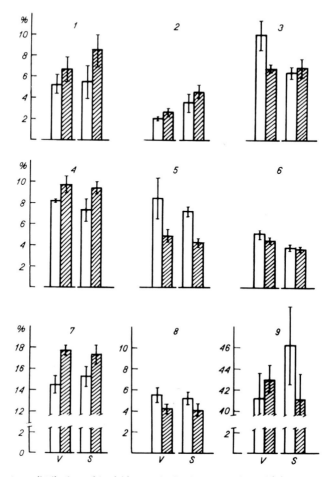

FIG. 4. Percentage distributions of insoluble proteins in nine zones of visual (V) and somatic sensory (S) cortex of normally reared (*plain bars*) and deprived (*striped bars*) kittens. The amount of protein in each zone was expressed as a percentage of the total content in the gel. Data from four C kittens and seven H kittens (mean ± SEM). In H kittens the protein content was significantly higher in zone 4 and zone 7 and lower in zone 5 for both visual and somatic cortex. In zone 3 the protein content for the visual cortex of C kittens was higher than in the other cortices. (From Mitros et al. ref. 32, by permission.)

eye occluded, and peripheral nasal retina of the other eye stimulated with black moving objects (36). In this way visual input was restricted to one hemisphere while the other hemisphere was used as a control. Electroencephalogram activity and the ocular-following reflex were monitored, and cortical samples taken out of the waking brain. The duration of visual training and period of incorporation of radioactive leucine (given intravenously) varied in different series of experiments. Generally, an increase of leucine incorporation into total proteins of the stimulated visual cortex was observed. Sometimes the insoluble proteins were responsible for this increase. In the paradigm with 1.5 hr of stimulation and 30 min of incorporation beginning 1 hr after the onset of stimulation, when the subcellular fractionation was performed, the increase of crude mitochondrial fraction in some cases and the microsomal fraction in other cases were observed. Four cats out of five had higher radioactivity of homogenate proteins on the stimulated side, an effect that was not observed in somatosensory cortex.

It could be argued that the increase in incorporation of the labeled substance is evoked simply by an increase of cerebral blood flow (CBF) in the visually stimulated hemisphere. Recently we have investigated the effect of visual stimulation on the CBF in the adult pretrigeminal cat (42,43). The CBF was measured in the occipital and frontal lobes by external monitoring of the clearance of ^{133}Xe. In the pretrigeminal preparation a strong visual stimulus (a feather duster that was moved for 3 min in front of the cat's eyes) evoked an average increase of the CBF of 44% in the occipital lobe and 24% in the frontal lobe. However, this response habituated rapidly within a few trials. Thus, the CBF response could not contribute significantly to the increase of labeled leucine incorporation in these animals when it was injected some time after the onset of visual stimulation. So far we have not been able to compare the CBF in two hemispheres while only one of them is visually stimulated.

CONCLUSIONS

1. Our results and the majority of results of other authors indicate that binocular deprivation and specific experience in cats lead to rather moderate behavioral and neural deficits. In this respect it is instructive to compare behavioral deficits shown by visually deprived cats with those of humans after surgery for congenital cataracts in adulthood (47). Deprived cats eventually master all behavioral tasks, whereas human patients show dramatic deficits in the utilization of visual cues. It follows that the development of the cat's visual system is controlled predominantly by the genetic factor.

2. In visually deprived cats not only the visual system itself but obviously also the associations between the visual system and motor, limbic, and other sensory systems do not develop normally, and we know (24,53) that such associations play a substantial role in behavior. Several lines of evidence suggest the important role of the deficit in the development of such associations in the mechanism of behavior impairment of deprived animals. Hein and Held (16,19) showed that kittens who were reared with a collar that prevented sight of limbs and torso showed deficiencies in eye-paw coordination. After cataract removal, humans see the objects from the beginning (in fact, they are confused by an abundance of impressions), but they do not know their meaning (47). Our biochemical investigations revealed some

changes in distribution of protein in the nonvisual cortex of deprived animals. Finally, it is tempting to think (see above) that in our discrimination learning situation the main problem of a visually deprived cat was not to distinguish the cross and the ball, but to utilize them as cues for finding food.

3. Our results have shown that after visual cortex ablation, the retention of visual discrimination is better in deprived cats than in controls. This result can be explained by a hypothesis that deprived cats use less visual cortex in learning than normals, and the role of the visual cortex is replaced by the superior colliculus–pretectum system and its cortical representation. Accordingly, recent results of Sherman (40) indicated that in visually deprived cats the superior colliculus plays a predominant role in visually guided orienting behavior. Electrophysiological results also indicated that impairment of collicular unit responses in deprived cats seems to reflect only the changes in the visual cortex and hence in the corticotectal projection. If our hypothesis is correct after superior colliculus–pretectum lesions, the retention of a discrimination task should be more affected in deprived cats than in controls. This possibility is being tested in our laboratory.

4. In accordance with Konorski's hypothesis (24), which is an extension of Hubel and Wiesel's (21) concept of hierarchical organization of the visual system, in the visual cortex of hood-reared cats having pretraining with a given object, there should exist *gnostic units* reacting specifically to this object. However, we have not found such units either in visual areas 17 and 18 or in area 19. It is an interesting question whether or not gnostic units could be found in other visual cortical areas. Conclusion 3 above may suggest that in visually deprived cats gnostic units should rather be looked for in the cortical representation of the superior colliculus–pretectum system.

5. The last comments concern methodological problems. It is generally accepted that in cats the deficits following dark-rearing or bilateral lid suturing are similar. Some of deficits observed in hood-reared cats (e.g., impairment of discrimination learning) seem also to be of a similar degree to those observed in dark-reared or lid-sutured cats. On the other hand, in some other aspects H cats are less impaired. The most striking example is that in H cats the ocular-following reflex is present immediately after a deprivation period. The problem of effectiveness of different methods of visual deprivation needs further investigation.

In contrast to the majority of other studies, we examined *awake* cats for single-unit recordings, utilizing the pretrigeminal preparation for this purpose. Moreover, in some experiments we controlled the cat's attention to a visual stimulus by recording ocular fixation reflexes. Our experimental material is not as yet satisfactory to evaluate these procedures. It is predicted, however, that they may be critical during recording in higher order cortical areas where the information from many polysynaptic pathways can be drastically reduced by narcosis or inattention of the animals.

ACKNOWLEDGMENTS

I thank Dr. W. Ławicka and Dr. M. Kossut for comments. Some of the reviewed investigations from the Nencki Institute were supported by Project 10.4.1.01 of the Polish Academy of Sciences and by Foreign Research Agreement 05.001.0, annex 280-A of the U.S. Department of Health, Education and Welfare under PL-480.

REFERENCES

1. Barlow, H. B. (1975): Visual experience and cortical development. *Nature,* 258: 199–204.
2. Batini, C., Moruzzi, G., Palestini, M., Rossi, G. F., and Zanchetti, A. (1959): Effects of complete pontine transections on the sleep-wakefulness rhythm: The midpontine pretrigeminal preparation. *Arch. Ital. Biol.,* 97:1–12.
3. Baxter, B. L. (1966): The effect of visual deprivation during postnatal maturation on the electroretinogram of the cat. *Exp. Neurol.,* 14:224–237.
4. Blakemore, C. M. A. (1974): Development of functional connexions in the mammalian visual system. *Br. Med. Bull.,* 30:152–157.
5. Blakemore, C., and Van Sluyters, R. C. (1975): Innate and environmental factors in the development of the kitten's visual cortex. *J. Physiol. (Lond.),* 248:663–716.
6. Chow, K. L., and Stewart, D. L. (1972): Reversal of structural and functional effects of long-term visual deprivation in cats. *Exp. Neurol.,* 34:409–433.
7. Cragg, B. G. (1975): The development of synapses in kitten visual cortex during visual deprivation. *Exp. Neurol.,* 46:445–451.
8. Cragg, B. G. (1975): The development of synapses in the visual system of the cat. *J. Comp. Neurol.,* 160:147–166.
9. Cynader, M., Berman, N., and Hein, A. (1975): Cats raised in a one-directional world: Effects on receptive fields in visual cortex and superior colliculus. *Exp. Brain Res.,* 22:267–280.
10. Czihak, E. (1977): Audio-visual targeting reflex in cats deprived of pattern vision from birth. *Acta Neurobiol. Exp. (Warsz.),* 37. *(In press.)*
11. Daw, N. W., and Wyatt, H. J. (1976): Kittens reared in a unidirectional environment: Evidence for a critical period. *J. Physiol. (Lond.),* 257:155–170.
11a. Dec, K., and Tarnecki, R. (1978): *In preparation.*
11b. Dec, K., Tarnecki, R., and Zernicki, B. (1978): *Acta Neurobiol. Exp. (Warsz.),* 38:103–112.
12. Dec, K., Sarna, M., Tarnecki, R., and Żernicki, B. (1976): Effects of binocular deprivation of pattern vision on single unit responses in the cat superior colliculus. *Acta Neurobiol. Exp. (Warsz.),* 36:687–692.
13. Flandrin, J. M., and Jeannerod, M. (1975): Superior colliculus: Environmental influences on the development of directional responses in the kitten. *Brain Res.,* 89:348–352.
14. Flandrin, J. M., Kennedy, H., and Amblard, B. (1976): Effect of stroboscopic rearing on the binocularity and directionality of cat superior colliculus neurons. *Brain Res.,* 101:576–581.
15. Folga, J., Michalski, A., Turlejski, K., and Żernicki, B. (1973): Eye-movement recording with a tensometric method in the pretrigeminal cat. *Acta Neurobiol. Exp. (Warsz.),* 33:655–658.
16. Ganz, L. (1975): Orientation in visual space by neonates and its modification by visual deprivation. In: *The Developmental Neuropsychology of Sensory Deprivation,* edited by A. H. Riesen, pp. 169–210. Academic Press, New York.
17. Ganz, L., Hirsch, H. B., and Tieman, S. B. (1972): The nature of perceptual deficits in visually deprived cats. *Brain Res.,* 44:547–560.
18. Guillery, R. W. (1972): Binocular competition in the control of geniculate cell growth. *J. Comp. Neurol.,* 144:117–130.

19. Hein, A., and Held, R. (1967): Dissociations of the visual placing response into elicited and guided components. *Science,* 158:390–392.
20. Hoffmann, K. P., and Sherman, S. M. (1975): Effects of early binocular deprivation on visual input to cat superior colliculus. *J. Neurophysiol.,* 38:1049–1059.
21. Hubel, D. H., and Wiesel, T. N. (1965): Receptive fields and functional architecture in two nonstriate visual areas (18 and 19) of the cat. *J. Neurophysiol.,* 28: 229–289.
22. Ikeda, H., Jacobson, S. G., Plant, G., and Tremain, K. E. (1976): Behavioural, neurophysiological and morphological evidence for a nasal visual field loss in cats reared with monocular convergent squint. *J. Physiol. (Lond.),* 260:48P–49P.
23. Imbert, M., and Buisseret, P. (1975): Receptive field characteristics and plastic properties of visual cortical cells in kittens reared with or without visual experience. *Exp. Brain Res.,* 22:25–36.
24. Konorski, J. (1967): *Integrative Activity of the Brain. An Interdisciplinary Approach,* p. 531. Univ. Chicago Press, Chicago.
24a. Korda, P. (1978): *Acta Neurobiol. Exp. (Warsz.),* 38 *(In press.)*
25. Kossut, M., Michalski, A., and Żernicki, B. (1977): The ocular following reflex in cats deprived of pattern vision from birth. *Brain Res. (In press.)*
26. Kratz, K. E., and Spear, P. (1976): Effects of visual deprivation and alterations in binocular competition on responses of striate cortex neurons in the cat. *J. Comp. Neurol.,* 170:141–152.
27. Loop, M. S., and Sherman, S. M. (1977): Visual discrimination during eyelid closure in the cat. *Brain Res.,* 128:329–339.
28. Maffei, L., and Fiorentini, A. (1974): Geniculate neural plasticity in kittens after exposure to periodic gratings. *Science,* 186:447–449.
29. Michalski, A., and Moroz, B. (1977): The effect of pursuit eye movements on single unit activity in cat visual cortex. *Acta Neurobiol. Exp. (Warsz),* 37. *(In press.)*
30. Michalski, A., Kossut, M., and Żernicki, B. (1975): Single unit responses to natural objects in area 19 of cats with different early visual experiences. *Acta Neurobiol. Exp. (Warsz),* 35:77–83.
31. Michalski, A., Kossut, M., and Żernicki, B. (1977): The ocular following reflex elicited from the retinal periphery in the cat. *Vision Res.,* 17:731–736.
31a. Mitros, A., et al. (1978): *Acta Neurobiol. Exp. (Warsz.),* 38 *(In press.)*
32. Mitros, K., Niemierko, S., Kossut, M., and Żernicki, B. (1976): Electrophoretic patterns of insoluble proteins in the sensory cerebral cortex of visually deprived and normal kittens. *Acta Neurobiol. Exp. (Warsz),* 36:407–416.
33. Muir, D. W., and Mitchell, D. E. (1975): Behavioral deficits in cats following early selected visual exposure to contours of a single orientation. *Brain Res.,* 85:459–477.
34. Pettigrew, J. D. (1974): The effect of visual experience on the development of stimulus specificity by kitten cortical neurones. *J. Physiol. (Lond.),* 237:49–74.
35. Pettigrew, J. D., and Freeman, R. D. (1973): Visual experience without lines: Effect on developing cortical neurons. *Science,* 182:599–601.
36. Pettigrew, J. D., and Garey, L. J. (1974): Selective modification of single neuron properties in the visual cortex of kittens. *Brain Res.,* 66:160–164.
37. Ryugo, D. K., Ryugo, R., Globus, A., and Killackey, H. P. (1975): Increased spine density in auditory cortex following visual or somatic differentiation. *Brain Res.,* 90:143–146.
38. Santibañez-H., G. (1976): The targeting reflex. *Acta Neurobiol. Exp. (Warsz),* 36:181–203.
39. Sherman, S. M. (1973): Visual field defects in monocularly and binocularly deprived cats. *Brain Res.,* 49:25–45.
40. Sherman, S. M. (1977): The effect of cortical and tectal lesions on the visual fields of binocularly deprived cats. *J. Comp. Neurol.,* 172:231–246.
41. Singer, W., and Tretter, F. (1976): Receptive-field properties and neuronal connectivity in striate and parastriate cortex of contour-deprived cats. *J. Neurophysiol.,* 39:613–630.
42. Skolasińska, K., Królicki, L., and Żernicki, B. (1977): A blood flow increase to a

visual stimulus in the occipital lobe of the cat with brainstem transection at the pretrigeminal level. *Acta Neurobiol. Exp. (Warsz)*, 37:5–14.

43. Skolasińska, K., Królicki, L., and Żernicki, B. (1977): *Acta Neurol. Scand.*, Suppl. 64:256–257.
44. Stryker, M. P., and Sherk, H. (1975): Modification of cortical orientation selectivity in the cat by restricted visual experience: A reexamination. *Science*, 190:904–905.
45. Tretter, F., Cynader, M., and Singer, W. (1975): Modification of direction selectivity of neurons in the visual cortex of kittens. *Brain Res.*, 84:143–149.
46. van Hof-van Duin, J. (1976): Development of visuomotor behavior in normal and dark-reared cats. *Brain Res.*, 104:233–241.
47. Von Senden, M. (1960): *Space and Sight. The Perception of Space and Shape in the Congenitally Blind Before and After Operation*. Methuen, London.
48. Wickelgren-Gordon, B. (1972): Some effects of visual deprivation on the cat superior colliculus. *Invest. Ophthalmol.*, 11:460–467.
49. Zabłocka, T. (1975): Go-no go differentiation to visual stimuli in cats with different early visual experiences. *Acta Neurobiol. Exp. (Warsz)*, 35:399–402.
49a. Zabłocka, T., and Żernicki, B. (1978): *Acta Neurobiol. Exp. (Warsz)*, 38:63–70.
50. Zabłocka, T., Konorski, J., and Żernicki, B. (1975): Visual discrimination learning in cats with different early visual experiences. *Acta Neurobiol. Exp. (Warsz)*, 35:389–398.
51. Zabłocka, T., Żernicki, B., and Kosmal, A. (1976): Visual cortex role in object discrimination in cats deprived of pattern vision from birth. *Acta Neurobiol. Exp. (Warsz)*, 36:157–168.
52. Żernicki, B. (1974): Isolated cerebrum of the pretrigeminal cat. *Arch. Ital. Biol.*, 112:350–371.
53. Żernicki, B. (1975): Drive-controlled reflexes: A theory. *Acta Neurobiol. Exp. (Warsz)*, 35:475–490.
54. Żernicki, B., and Michalski, A. (1974): Single unit responses to natural objects in visual areas 17 and 18 of cats reared under different visual experiences. *Acta Neurobiol. Exp. (Warsz)*, 34:697–712.
55. Żernicki, B., Doty, R. W., and Santibanez-H., G. (1970): Isolated midbrain in cats. *Electroenceph. clin. Neurophysiol.*, 28:221–235.
56. Żernicki, B., Kossut, M., Slósarska, M., and Rokicka, J. (1976): Pretrigeminal kitten. *Acta Neurobiol. Exp. (Warsz)*, 36:389–392.

Note added in proof: Our recent results (presented at the II Europ. Neurosci. Meeting) show that following the lesions of the superior colliculus-pretectum the retention of visual discrimination was indeed less in hand-reared cats than in controls.

Brain Mechanisms in Memory and Learning:
From the Single Neuron to Man,
edited by M. A. B. Brazier.
Raven Press, New York © 1979.

Biochemical, Electrophysiological, and Morphological Correlates of Brightness Discrimination in Rats

H. Matthies

Institut für Pharmakologie und Toxikologie, Medizinische Akademie Magdeburg, Magdeburg, German Democratic Republic

The acquisition and consolidation of a new behavior resulting in a more or less permanent memory trace make up a very complex process and may include the activity and the functional changes of a large number of cells of many structures of the brain. It can be assumed that, until the permanent trace has been formed, a series of events subsequently occurs, distinguishable by the different underlying cellular mechanisms, by their time course, and by the effects of various chemical and physiological influences.

By reason of this complexity of processes and mechanisms, it probably would be impossible to explain and to understand the biological basis of learning and memory formation by studying only one correlate by a single method. It seems necessary to consider a multidisciplinary approach, investigating *one* model of learning and memory formation by various morphological, biochemical, physiological, and behavioral methods. Such research would also be very helpful in overcoming the limitations of each of the applied methods.

I report here some of our results obtained in this research, which may demonstrate some interesting correlations, making possible the outline of a working hypothesis, even if still disposing of only a small piece of the whole picture.

In the laboratories of our institute at Magdeburg, in cooperation with some other groups at Berlin and Leipzig, we investigated the correlates of the acquisition and consolidation of a shock-motivated brightness discrimination in rats; this model was chosen as suitable for the different methods.

The behavioral task was performed in a Y maze, using throughout the parameters shown in Figs. 1 and 2.

The retention of the memory trace in our behavioral task was tested by a relearning procedure. The analysis of the experimental results obtained with different training-relearning intervals and training-electric conditioning shock (ECS) intervals and considering the particular stages of relearning showed the occurrence of two deficits in the time course of retention—the

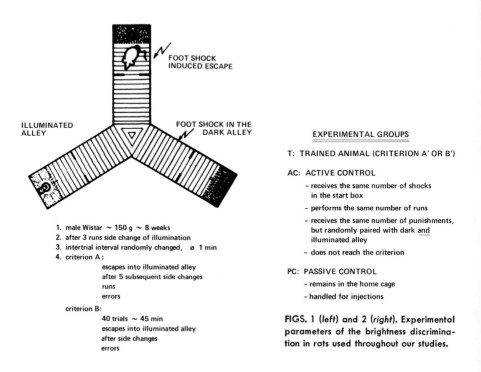

FOOT SHOCK
INDUCED ESCAPE

ILLUMINATED
ALLEY

FOOT SHOCK IN THE
DARK ALLEY

1. male Wistar ~ 150 g ~ 8 weeks
2. after 3 runs side change of illumination
3. intertrial interval randomly changed, ø 1 min
4. criterion A :

      escapes into illuminated alley
      after 5 subsequent side changes
      runs
      errors

   criterion B:

      40 trials ~ 45 min
      escapes into illuminated alley
      after side changes
      errors

EXPERIMENTAL GROUPS

T: TRAINED ANIMAL (CRITERION A' OR B')

AC: ACTIVE CONTROL

- receives the same number of shocks
  in the start box

- performs the same number of runs

- receives the same number of punishments,
  but randomly paired with dark and
  illuminated alley

- does not reach the criterion

PC: PASSIVE CONTROL

- remains in the home cage
- handled for injections

FIGS. 1 (*left*) and 2 (*right*). Experimental
parameters of the brightness discrimination in rats used throughout our studies.

first, 1 hr, and the second, 4 hr after completion of training (Fig. 3). These
two subsequent memory deficits suggest the existence of at least three different mechanisms ensuring retention—a short-term, an intermediate, and a
long-term memory. Our methods did not allow us to determine the existence
of a very short transient memory assumed by several authors.

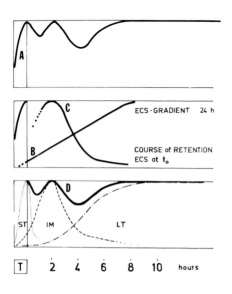

ECS·GRADIENT   24 h

COURSE of RETENTION
ECS at t_o

ST   IM   LT

T   2   4   6   8   10   hours

FIG. 3. Behavioral feature of the brightness discrimination in rats. A: Time course of retention.
B: Gradient of the amnestic effect of ECS. Different interval between training and ECS, retention
test 24 hr after training. C: Time course of retention after an ECS immediately after training.
D: Assumed sequence of three storage mechanism, short-term (ST), intermediate (IM), and long-
term (LT) storage. Retention deficits result from
insufficient overlapping of the different storage
mechanisms.

The application of an ECS immediately after training revealed that the intermediate memory seems to be resistant to ECS, whereas the formation of the long-term memory is inhibited. An effect on the short-term memory was not detectable by reason of the postconvulsive depression following the shock.

ECS application at different intervals after training and determination of the retention 24 hr later showed the well-known gradient of the amnestic effect of ECS—a nearly complete amnesia if the shock was given immediately after training and an increasing ineffectiveness of the ECS with prolongation of the training–ECS interval up to 8 hr.

This short introductory survey of the phenomenology of the retention of the memory trace in our behavioral paradigm demonstrates that this model of learning and consolidation may be suitable for comparing and correlating different stages of memory formation and the time course of parameters obtained by biochemical, morphological, and physiological methods.

We began our investigations with autoradiographic studies on the incorporation of ribonucleic acid (RNA) and protein precursors during learning, in order to obtain, first, topographic and semiquantitative information on the involvement of macromolecular synthesis during the acquisition and consolidation of a memory trace. Tritium-labeled uridine or uridine nucleotides were injected intraventricularly or intraperitoneally prior to training; the radioactive pulse lasted 2 hr.

Trained animals showed significantly increased incorporation of labeled material into hippocampal cells over passive and active controls (Fig. 4). An enhanced labeling was also observed in the visual and cingular cortex. Other cortical as well as thalamic and hypothalamic structures showed no

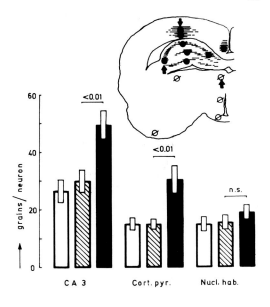

FIG. 4. Incorporation of ³H-uridine monophosphate into the brain regions of the rat during and after training. ●, Significant increase of incorporation in trained rats over active controls; Ø, no significant differences; white columns, passive controls; shadowed columns, active controls; black columns, trained animals.

differences between the experimental groups (Fig. 4). The increased incorporation during learning was mainly found in neurones. The comparison of hippocampal pyramids in the CA3 and CA4 sectors with their satellite glia cells is shown in Fig. 5. The neuronal cells show a higher rate of incorporation of the labeled RNA precursor. An increased incorporation correlated with the training procedure was observed only in the neuronal cells.

This observation also suggests that the increased incorporation during learning is not due to circulatory changes or alterations of extracellular conditions, for if so, similar changes in the neighbouring cells would be expected.

Analogous experiments with tritium-labeled leucine (Fig. 6) showed very similar results. The main sites of incorporation changes were again found in the hippocampus and in the visual cortex of trained animals as compared with passive and active controls. In order to prove that the increased incorporation of the labeled amino acid indicates an increased protein synthesis, radiochemical methods were used to measure the specific activity of the precursor pool and to calculate the rate of protein synthesis in the hippocampus. The results confirmed our assumption of an increased macromolecular synthesis correlated to learning. Furthermore, a quantitative electron microscopic analysis of neuronal ribosomes in different hippocampal pyramidal cells, which showed an increased incorporation of labeled precursors in trained animals, also revealed an increased number of ribosomes (Fig. 7), mainly of membrane-bound particles. On comparing CA3 and CA1 pyramidal cells, the former also exhibited significant increases in active controls, but the latter showed specific significant changes only in trained animals, an observation that is mentioned again later.

In further investigations, we considered not only the period of acquisition

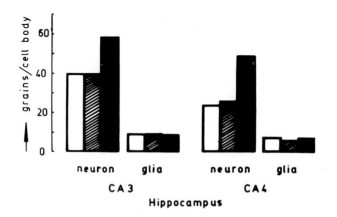

FIG. 5. Incorporation of ³H-uridine monophosphate into CA3 and CA4 pyramids and their satellite glia during acquisition. White columns, passive controls; shadowed columns, active controls; black columns, trained animals.

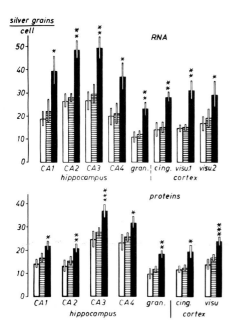

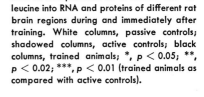

FIG. 6. Incorporation of ^{3}H-uridine and ^{3}H-leucine into RNA and proteins of different rat brain regions during and immediately after training. White columns, passive controls; shadowed columns, active controls; black columns, trained animals; *, $p < 0.05$; **, $p < 0.02$; ***, $p < 0.01$ (trained animals as compared with active controls).

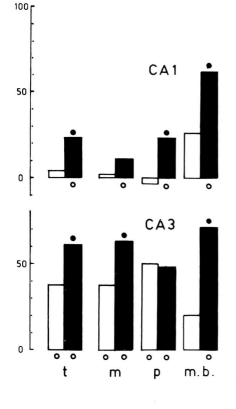

FIG. 7. Electron microscopic evaluation of the ribosomes of CA1 and CA3 pyramids 70 min after acquisition of a brightness discrimination test in rats. Ordinate: Increase of ribosomes as compared to passive controls, 100%. White columns, active controls; black columns, trained animals; t, total ribosomes; m, monosomes; p, polysomes; m.b., membrane-bound ribosomes; O, $p < 0.05$ as compared to passive controls; ●, $p < 0.05$ difference between active controls and trained animals.

during training and the short period following it, but also studied the macro-molecular processes during the consolidation in the subsequent hours. The radioactive nucleotides or aminoacids were injected at different intervals after training, and the incorporation rate was measured during a constant pulse time.

It was shown again that an increased incorporation rate of aminoacids into proteins occurred during and immediately after training (Fig. 8), which could be characterized as increased protein synthesis in hippocampal structures of trained animals as compared with active and passive controls. After this training period, the incorporation rate returned to control values. But 5 hr after training, when the animals had already been in their home cage for a long time, a new increase of the incorporation rate occurred in the hippocampus of trained animals, lasting 4 to 6 hr. This biphasic meta-bolic activity could be observed with regard to the RNA, as well as to the protein synthesis, and was not due to circadian rhythms of brain metabolism. If the incorporation was separately measured in soluble and insoluble pro-teins, we observed, during the first peak of synthetic activity, a stronger and significant increase of incorporation into soluble proteins, whereas the second peak was characterized by a significant increase of incorporation into insoluble proteins.

For further elucidation of the functional changes developing during con-solidation of a memory trace, we tried to characterize more precisely the newly synthesized proteins. Because glycoproteins are supposed to play a

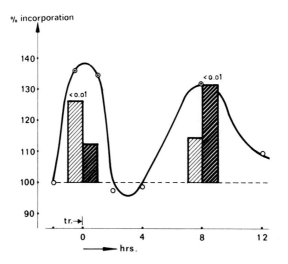

FIG. 8. Incorporation rate of ^{3}H-leucine into proteins of the rat hippocampus at different times during and after acquisition of a brightness discrimination. Ordinate: % incorporation into proteins of trained animals as compared with active controls. Radiochemical determination. Pulse duration, 2 hr. Intraventricular in-jection of ^{3}H-leucine. —O—, Incorporation into total proteins; —⊙—, $p < 0.02$; light shadowed columns, incorporation into soluble proteins; dark shadowed columns, incorporation into insoluble proteins.

particular role in the regulation and determination of intercellular relationships, we investigated the formation of glycoproteins in our learning paradigm. Tritium-labeled or ^{14}C-fucose was used as labeled precursor, because this carbohydrate moiety of glycoproteins is hardly catabolized in the brain of rats and becomes predominantly incorporated into proteins, but not into gangliosides. Autoradiographic studies demonstrated that the labeled fucose penetrates easily into the brain after intraventricular application. In the first hours after injection, the labeled material was mainly found in the perikarya, but in the course of 4 to 10 hr, it was transported into the dendritic and axonal trees.

If tritium-labeled fucose was injected before training, an increased incorporation of this carbohydrate was found in the hippocampal proteins of trained animals over active and passive controls. But this enhanced incorporation into total proteins was not significant. Only after separation of soluble and insoluble proteins were significant differences found in the insoluble fraction.

The visual cortex of trained animals showed no difference from that of active controls during training, either in total proteins or after separation into soluble and insoluble proteins.

In a subsequent series of experiments, we investigated the time course of glycoprotein formation during acquisition and consolidation, in analogy to our previous studies on the rate of protein synthesis. We examined the incorporation of tritium-labeled fucose on our three experimental groups at different times during and after acquisition. In each of the rat brains, labeling was determined by densitometric evaluation of autoradiograms as well as by extraction and separation of insoluble proteins on polyacrylamide gel according to the scheme demonstrated in Fig. 9. The radiochemical investigation included also the visual cortex.

As an example, the results obtained on the CA3 sector are presented.

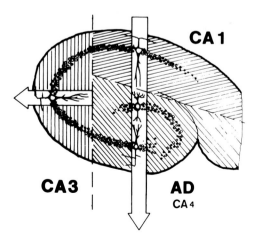

FIG. 9. Schematic illustration of the dissection of the hippocampal structure for biochemical studies (*shadowed areas*) and of the tracks of densitometric measurement of autoradiograms.

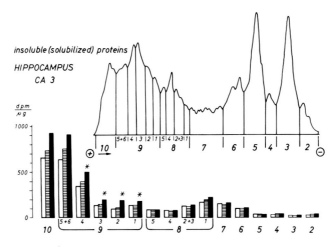

FIG. 10. Incorporation of ³H-fucose into insoluble proteins of the CA3 region of the rat during acquisition of a brightness discrimination. Separation after solubilization by polyacrylamide (PAA)-gel electrophoresis. Top: The densitogram after staining with amido black and the scheme of slicing the gels into groups and subgroups of bands for determination of protein content and incorporation of ³H-fucose. Bottom: The incorporation into proteins of the three experimental groups. White columns, passive controls; shadowed columns, active controls; black columns, trained animals; *, differences between trained animals and active controls p < 0.05.

The quantitative measurement of fucose incorporation into the bands of separated insoluble proteins was only possible in the slowly migrating, high molecular weight protein groups 6 to 10. Figure 10 shows the incorporation during 2 hr, including the training and the posttraining period. Significant differences between trained animals and active controls were obtained in gel bands 9–4 to 9–1. The whole picture of the time course of the radiochemical results of CA3 (Fig. 11) demonstrates significant incorporation changes in trained animals compared with active controls, during acquisition and 7 to 9 hr after training only in the same protein bands of group 9, but not of groups 10 or 8.

The autoradiographic method (Fig. 12) also shows significant increases of the incorporation into the structures of the CA3 cells during acquisition as well as 7 to 9 hr after training. It can also be seen that the fiber structures show a tendency to higher incorporation over the neuronal cell body, indicating the beginning of the transport of the labeled material into the dendritic and axonal trees already after a pulse time of 2 hr.

The further analysis of all data, thus obtained, resulted in a valuation matrix and a derived scheme of the time course of incorporation for each of the structures under investigation. A generalized survey summarizes the data (Fig. 13).

According to these results, the biphasic time course of macromolecular production during our learning experiment, as obtained by the determination of protein synthesis, has also been found on the formation of glycoproteins,

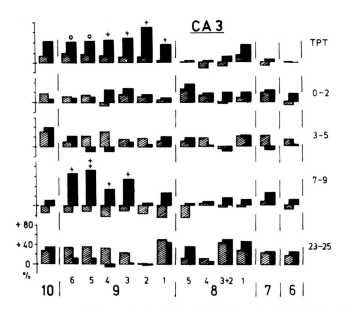

FIG. 11. Incorporation rate of ^{3}H-fucose into insoluble solubilized proteins of CA3 region of the rat at different times during and after acquisition of a brightness discrimination test. Intraventricular injection of ^{3}H-fucose, pulse duration 2 hr. Separation by PAA-gel electrophoresis. Ordinate: percent increase of incorporation into protein bands (according to Fig. 12) of active controls (*shadowed columns*) and trained animals (*black columns*), passive controls, 100%. Differences between active controls and trained animals: O, $p < 0.05$; +, $p < 0.02$; ‡, $p < 0.01$. TPT, training-posttraining period, application of the labeled precursor 15 min before training; 0–2, application of labeled precursor immediately after training; 3–5, application 3 hr after training; 7–9, application 7 hr after training; 23–25, application 23 hr after training.

supporting, therefore, our earlier findings. But the more subtle analysis of hippocampal and cortical substructures clearly revealed a more differentiated pattern of biochemical processes. Whereas granular cells of the area dentata of trained animals showed, only during the acquisition period, an increased formation of glycoproteins mainly of group 9, and CA1 and CA3 cells demonstrated a second peak of glycoprotein formation after a silent period. They differed from each other, however, by the protein groups involved— the protein group 9 mainly in CA3 pyramids and the protein groups 8 and 9 in the CA1 neurons. Furthermore, the CA1 cells seemed to start the second period of glycoprotein formation quite a lot earlier than the CA3 cells.

Very different from the observations on hippocampal pyramids are the results in the visual cortex; there is no significant difference in any case between trained animals and active controls. But, during the silent period of the hippocampal neurons, a significant increase of glycoprotein formation occurred in the visual cortex of both trained animals and active controls. Therefore, these changes may not be understood as correlates of the training process but only as correlates of sensory and motor activation provoked

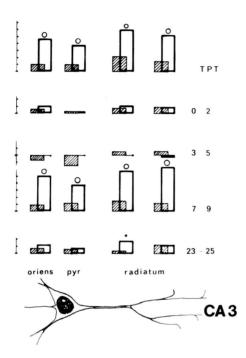

FIG. 12. Densitometric measurement of autoradiograms from the same animals, as in Fig. 13. Ordinate: percent increase of density (arbitrary units) in slices of active controls (*shadowed columns*) and trained animals (*white columns*), passive controls, 100%. Graduation of scale, 10%. Difference between trained animals and active controls: ○, *p* < 0.05. See Fig. 11 for further explanation of figure.

by footshocks, escapes, and visual information independent of their contiguity in the different experimental conditions of trained animals and active controls. It seems remarkable that this probably unspecific neuronal activation involves all groups of glycoproteins from 6 to 10.

What may we conclude from these observations?

1. During the time course of learning and consolidation, characteristic behavioral and neurophysiological patterns related to brain structures seem to occur, as well as biochemical patterns characteristic with respect to their temporal, spatial, and material distribution.

2. It is stimulating to speculate on some relationship between the functional structure of the hippocampus as a cascade circuit and the above findings. Assuming an increased filtering of information and the resulting formation of new connections from dentate area via CA3 to CA1 cells, we should expect to observe an increasing significance of the differences between trained animals and active controls. And as a matter of fact, we have found an increase of differences in the augmentation of ribosomal units and in the glycoprotein formation, in comparing dentate area CA3 and CA1 cells. It is obviously too early to make more conclusions, but we believe it would be interesting to look further into this problem.

Even if our results as well as those of other authors support the assumption of characteristic biochemical correlates related to learning and memory

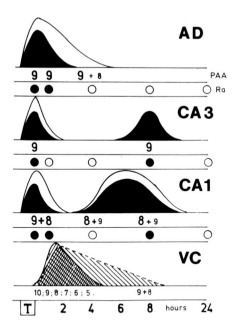

FIG. 13. Schematic representation of the radio-chemical and autoradiographic results of the investigation of fucose incorporation during and after acquisition of brightness discrimination in rats. Curves, time course of intensity of incorporation; black areas, significant changes in protein bands of trained animals as compared with active controls; white areas, changes in trained animals more than 40%, but not significant; PAA, involvement of protein groups according to the classification of protein bands in PAA gels of Fig. 10 in significant changes of trained animals; ●, significant changes in trained animals in the autoradiographic study; ○, no changes observed in the autoradiographic study; AD, area dentata; CA3, CA1, sectors of the hippocampus; VC, visual cortex.

formation, they seem not to be conclusive enough. Therefore, we tried to get some more facts on the nature of the macromolecular changes by comparing our biochemical parameters under conditions of a relatively unspecific hippocampal activation. We investigated, therefore, the protein synthesis and the glycoprotein formation after septal stimulation of the hippocampus via the mainly cholinergic septohippocampal pathway (Figs. 14 and 15).

In our learning paradigm, as already mentioned before, labeled leucine as well as labeled fucose was increasingly incorporated, and a true enhancement of protein synthesis could be calculated from the specific activity of the precursor pool and of the macromolecules.

After 15 to 30 min of septal stimulation with 7 cycles/sec, which induced a rhythmic, slow activity in the hippocampus, the incorporation of fucose into proteins remained, however, unchanged, whereas the incorporation of leucine was increased, as in our learning experiment. More precise investigations indicate that after septal stimulation, contrary to learning, mainly fast migrating proteins seem to be involved in the induced protein synthesis.

Thus, the macromolecular changes in the hippocampus, after a relatively unspecific neuronal activation, qualitatively differ from those observed in the learning paradigm. Nevertheless, septal stimulation immediately after acquisition of the brightness discrimination was able to improve the retention of this learned behavior after 24 hr.

These observations suggested more detailed investigation into the neuronal processes at the cellular level that induce macromolecular changes in different experimental conditions and that may be determined by the nature of

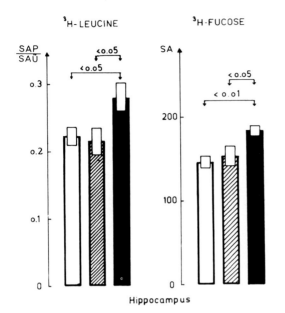

FIG. 14. Incorporation of ³H-leucine and of ³H-fucose into total proteins of rat hippocampus during and immediately after acquisition of a brightness discrimination (radioactive pulse 2 hr). SAP, specific activity of proteins; SAU, specific activity of supernatant after ³H-leucine application; SA, specific activity of proteins after ³H-fucose application, white bars, passive controls; shadowed bars, active controls; black bars, trained animals.

the chemical transmitters so far involved during acquisition. Because the activation of the hippocampal, rhythmic activity by septal stimulation was assumed to be mediated by cholinergic links, we expected similar effects to occur after intrahippocampal application of cholinergic agonists. Therefore, we examined the effects of oxotremorine, a potent muscarinergic drug, after injection into the dorsal hippocampus by chronically implanted cannulas (Fig. 16). We observed the occurrence of a lasting rhythmic, slow activity, that

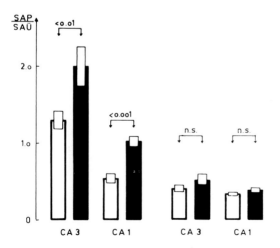

FIG. 15. Incorporation of ³H-leucine and of ³H-fucose into rat hippocampal regions after 15 min stimulation of septum (7 cycles/sec) leading to hippocampal, rhythmic, slow activity (radioactive pulse 2 hr). White bars, nonstimulated controls; black bars, stimulated animals. SAP, specific activity of proteins; SAU, specific activity of supernatant.

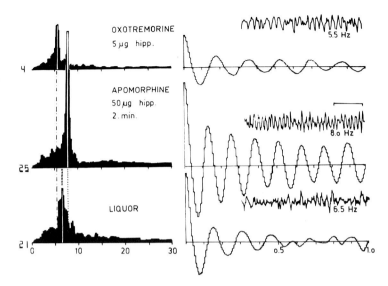

FIG. 16. Power spectrum and autocorrelation of hippocampal electroencephalogram (dorsal hippocampus) after intrahippocampal injection of drugs. Liquor: control after injection of artificial cerebroventricular fluid. Abscissa: Power spectrum, cycles/sec; autocorrelograms, 1 sec.

was moreover characterized by a shift of the dominant frequency from 7 cycles/sec in control periods to 5.5 cycles/sec after oxotremorine. The effect of this substance could be inhibited by scopolamine.

If oxotremorine was intrahippocampally injected immediately after the acquisition of brightness discrimination test, the retention of the learned behavior 24 hr later was significantly improved, as after septal stimulation. The effect was more pronounced in animals with incomplete training. The intrahippocampal application of scopolamine after training resulted in a significant impairment of the retention.

In order to test whether the influence of local cholinergic activation on retention depended on protein synthesis, we studied the effect of oxotremorine after inhibition of protein synthesis by anisomycin in a dosage inhibiting the incorporation of leucine by 80%. It was found that oxotremorine alone only slightly increased the aminoacid incorporation, evoked the rhythmic, slow activity, and improved the retention, as already mentioned. When the protein synthesis in the hippocampus was partially inhibited to a degree that resulted in an impaired retention, the improving effect of oxotremorine was also diminished to control values. However, the occurrence of the rhythmic, slow activity after oxotremorine was not dependent on protein synthesis. We may conclude that cholinergic receptor activation in hippocampal structures does induce synchronization and macromolecular changes by different ways. The results after septal stimulation, which was not able to induce an increased incorporation of fucose and which showed increased incorporation of leucine mainly into fast migrating proteins, indicate, however, that qualitative differences seem to exist between metabolic changes after learning and after cholinergic stimulation, respectively. Thus additional factors may function in learning that complete the metabolic processes necessary for the reconstruction of the neuronal network during consolidation of a memory trace.

Therefore, we examined other transmitter systems in our experimental task. In order to stimulate dopaminergic receptors, we applied apomorphine into the dorsal hippocampus (Fig. 16). We observed also the occurrence of rhythmic, slow activity, but contrary to the effect of oxotremorine, the dominant frequency shifted to the right in the power spectrum from 6.5 in the control period to 8.0 cycles/sec after apomorphine application. The intrahippocampal injection of this drug, immediately after acquisition, nevertheless, also resulted in a significant improvement of retention after 24 hr (Fig. 17). The dopaminergic antagonist haloperidol, on the other hand, impaired the retention when injected into the hippocampus after the acquisition of the new behavior. Thus, quite similar effects were obtained by activation of different transmitter systems. The frequency of the evoked synchronization seems to be less relevant than the rhythmic activity in general.

In order to obtain comparable and more lucid conditions for the investigation of the influence of putative transmitters on macromolecular processes,

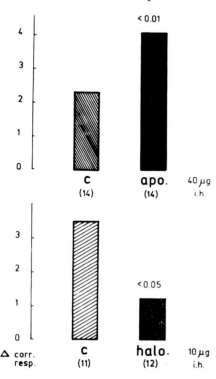

FIG. 17. Effect of intrahippocampal injection of drugs immediately after acquisition of a brightness discrimination on its retention after 24 hr. Ordinate: difference of correct responses of training and of relearning, respectively. c, Control (saline); apo, apomorphine; halo, haloperidol.

we used a simpler system—hippocampal slices *in vitro*. On this model, the muscarinergic agonists oxotremorine, arecoline, and pilocarpin did not clearly increase the protein synthesis in lower concentrations, but diminished the incorporation of leucine at higher concentrations (Fig. 18). The incorporation of fucose was not affected at all over a wide range of concentrations. Similar results were obtained with the nicotinergic agonist 1,1-dimethyl-4-phenyl-piperazine, but already in lower doses, suggesting that the effects of the muscarinergic drugs in higher doses are also nicotinergic in nature. The incubation of the hippocampal slices in the presence of dopamine revealed also an impairment of protein synthesis, but the incorporation of fucose was markedly enhanced.

These results did not completely fit our expectations, mainly in relation to the influence on protein synthesis. We do not yet have an explanation for this discrepancy, but we know the limited metabolism of brain tissue *in vitro*, with regard not only to the quantitative, but also to the qualitative abilities. Nevertheless, the differences, according to the fucose incorporation when comparing cholinergic and dopaminergic influences, seem to support the assumption that the complex pattern of macromolecular changes occurring during learning and consolidation are due to the action of several different transmitters. Therefore, the stimulation of one of the transmitter systems would hardly result in the occurrence of the complete pattern of molecular changes whether *in vivo* or *in vitro*, but may nevertheless improve the retention *in vivo*, when the other necessary factors are functioning.

And that is a matter of course if we consider the neurophysiological conception of learning and conditioning. The formation of a memory trace, of

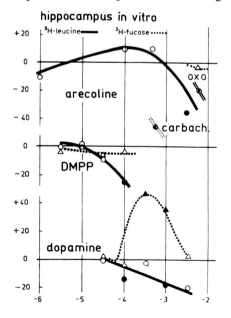

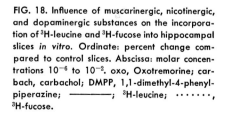

FIG. 18. Influence of muscarinergic, nicotinergic, and dopaminergic substances on the incorporation of ^{3}H-leucine and ^{3}H-fucose into hippocampal slices *in vitro*. Ordinate: percent change compared to control slices. Abscissa: molar concentrations 10^{-6} to 10^{-2}. oxo, Oxotremorine; carbach, carbachol; DMPP, 1,1-dimethyl-4-phenyl-piperazine; ———, ^{3}H-leucine; ·······, ^{3}H-fucose.

a temporary connection, supposes the temporal and spatial convergence of more than two informational channels, in the simplest form of an unconditioned, a conditioned, a motivational, and an emotional one. These channels are obviously mediated by different transmitter systems that not only carry the actual information in a neurophysiological sense through the pathways, but also may change the interneuronal connections and their efficiency by the induction of complex biochemical reactions and subsequent reconstruction of the integrating neuronal cells. We can construct a heuristic model of these neuronal processes (Fig. 19). A conditioned input to an integrative cell induces a short-lasting facilitation of postsynaptic membranes, probably by conformational changes of their proteins due to ionic shifts or some other reversible processes. The immediately following unconditioned input leading to a depolarization of the neuronal membrane and a following action potential may sustain the facilitated conditioned synapse for a longer period. Depending on the activity of motivational and emotional inputs, probably mediated by aminergic transmitters, a chain of different syntheses of macromolecules may be activated that are transported into the dendritic tree and incorporated in these postsynaptic structures, the state of which has been changed by the specific conditioned and unconditioned inputs. The incorporation of the newly synthesized material, probably glycoproteins, on these sites holds the facilitated state of the synapses, thus forming one of the numerous new connections distributed in the brain that may be regarded as the biological basis of a memory trace.

This model may also direct our attention to the search for correlations of the different memory stages (short-term, intermediate, and long-term storage) to related cellular mechanisms. We began with the long-term processes as connected with macromolecular syntheses; then we were engaged with the period in which these events developed. But during this time, memory already exists, and we had to look for mechanisms that would hold the trace during induction, and the slow development of permanent neuronal changes. Because synaptic structures might be candidates for transient alterations during short-term as well as intermediate storage, we investigated, by electron microscopy and morphometric methods, the synaptic structures in some hippocampal regions during the early periods after acquisition of the brightness discrimination. We observed, during the first hour after training, an increase in the number of electron microscopically detectable synapses in the stratum radiatum of the CA3 and CA1 sector (Fig. 20). These changes disappeared slowly during the following day. The enlarged number of synapses was accompanied by an increase in the thickness and the areas of postsynaptic densities in the same regions of trained animals as in active controls. At the same time, the acetylcholine content changed in the hippocampus. The free acetylcholine increased during training and decreased immediately thereafter; the vesicular-bound transmitter increased during the first hour after training, indicating the involvement of cholinergic terminals in these proc-

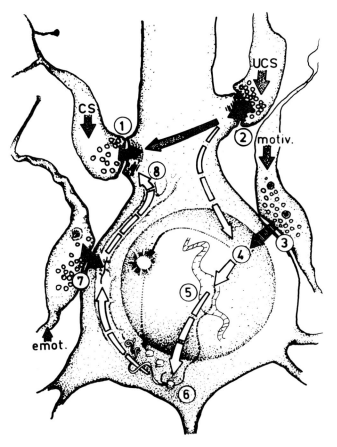

FIG. 19. Hypothetical model of neuronal processes underlying a change of connectivity during formation of a permanent memory trace. 1: Conditioned specific sensory input: "inactive" synapse, only inducing local conformational changes of postsynaptic membrane structures without subsequent action potential. Repetition leads to a facilitated state of the synapse. 2: Unconditioned specific memory input: "active" synapse, inducing postsynaptic potential followed by action potential, which also prolongs conformational change at the conditioned input. The receptor activation induces also intracellular processes leading together with 3 to a changed synthesis of neuronal proteins. 3: Motivational input mediated by aminergic transmitter leading together with 2 to a changed synthesis of neuronal proteins via activation of protein kinases. 4: Transport of phosphorylated proteins regulating gene expression into nuclear compartment. 5: Change of gene expression. 6: Quantitative or qualitative change, or both, of formation of polypeptide chains. 7: Emotional input, mediated by aminergic or other putative transmitter stimulating formation of glycoproteins. 8: Transport of glycoproteins into the dendritic tree to the inactive, but still conformational changed postsynaptic structure of the conditioned synapse. Incorporation of glycoproteins into the altered postsynaptic structure irreversibly transforms the inactive but facilitated synapse into an active synapse.

esses. These observations clearly demonstrate that synaptic structures, as detected by electron microscopic techniques, are very dynamic entities and that considerable short-lasting functional changes in the synaptosomal units, probably serving as holding mechanisms for short-term and intermediate storage, can be determined with appropriate methods.

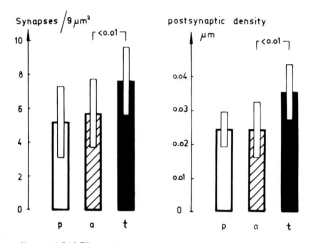

FIG. 20. Stratum radiatum of CA3 70 min after training. Early changes of synaptic structures in the rat hippocampus after acquisition of a brightness discrimination. Electron microscopic study. Left: Ordinate, number of synapses/9 μm^2. Right: Thickness of postsynaptic densities. p, Passive controls; a, active controls; t, trained animals; BD, brightness discrimination.

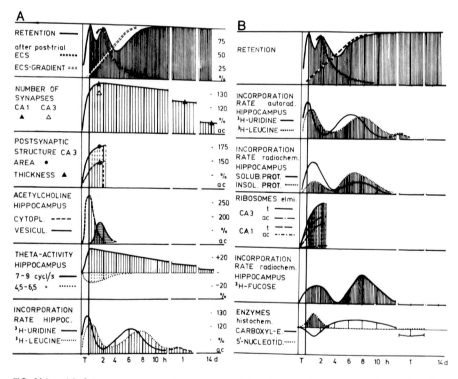

FIG. 21A and B. Schematic representation of the correlates of the posttraining period (consolidation) of brightness discrimination in rats. Abscissa: time after completion of training. Ordinate: retention: %; ac, active controls = 100%; theta activity, portion of the relative power spectrum—change in percent of the pretrial control period.

If we summarize our results in a scheme (Fig. 21A and B) that allows us to compare the time course of the correlates of our learning paradigm as so far determined, we can distinguish two groups of observations. First, one group is mainly related to synaptic processes, showing early changes probably important for the induction of long-term changes as well as for mechanisms of an intermediate storage until the long-term trace has been completed. The increase of the number of synapses has a time course similar to that of the increased synchronous activity of the hippocampus, suggesting a particular role of enhanced rhythmic activity for the stimulation of macromolecular syntheses occurring in neurons, which were involved already during acquisition.

Second, another group of correlates is connected with the increased macromolecular processes themselves, probably enabling the formation of new stable interneuronal synapses. Glycoproteins seem to play an important role. The biphasic time course of macromolecular changes seems to indicate two qualitatively different processes, occurring either in the same neuronal population or in two or more different sets of neurons. If they are located in the same cells, one could speculate that the first increase of macromolecular synthesis is mainly related to the formation of ribosomal and regulatory proteins. This assumption would be supported by the observed increase of ribosomes during this period. The second increase, however, could mainly reflect the formation of specific proteins and glycoproteins necessary for the reconstruction of postsynaptic structures involved in the development of the functional memory trace.

Altogether we have only a few pieces of a jig-saw puzzle in our hands, and it is too early to recognize the whole picture of memory. It has been my intention in this chapter to show that its understanding would be facilitated if pieces from only one puzzle are studied to complete the picture (and not from very different objects). I believe that the multimethodical approach to one single experimental model of memory formation is very helpful to a better understanding of the problem that originally brought together the contributors to this very exciting volume.

ACKNOWLEDGMENTS

The research work of this report was done in cooperation with T. Ott, N. Popov, E. Kammerer, B. Lössner, W. Wetzel, W. Pohle, R. Jork, Gisela Grecksch (Institute of Pharmacology, Medical Academy Magdeburg), J. Wenzel, M. Frotscher, M. Joschko (Institute of Anatomy, Humboldt-University Berlin), H. Luppa, and H. G. Bernstein (Sektion Biowissenschaften, Karl-Marx-University, Leipzig, DDR).

Brain Mechanisms in Memory and Learning:
From the Single Neuron to Man,
edited by M. A. B. Brazier.
Raven Press, New York © 1979.

Sequential Biochemical Steps in Memory Formation: Evidence from the Use of Metabolic Inhibitors

Richard Mark

Department of Behavioural Biology, Research School of Biological Sciences,
Australian National University, Canberra, Australia

EXPERIMENTAL BASIS: LONG-TERM MEMORY

Information on which learning is based comes into the central nervous system of animals as patterns of nerve impulses and goes out to execute behaviour in the same electrical code. Learning, from the physiological point of view, is nothing more than a change in the spatial and temporal pattern of impulses in nerve networks that form the response to a particular kind of stimulus; or the converse, a change in the kind of stimulus that evokes a particular pattern of response. The physiological basis of memory is the way in which the correspondence between patterns of stimulus and response can be varied. Knowledge of this is rudimentary and controversial. All one can say is that well-learned patterns of action are stored in the brain in an extremely stable state by a mechanism that probably involves protein synthesis and as such becomes part of the structure of the brain (3).

There is, of course, an extremely large literature on the pharmacology of learned behaviour. Very many substances, some of which are endogenous to the brain and may act as neurotransmitters, modify learning or the behavioural responses required for learning in characteristic ways. None of this work has yet reached a point at which we can affirm that any particular chemical reaction, with perhaps the exception of those required for protein synthesis, serves an absolutely essential link in the formation of memory.

Nevertheless, it is reasonable to assume that there are chemical steps to the formation of the memory record that are similar in different animals and similar no matter what behavioural context the learned behaviour occupies. If there is to be a stable and perhaps structural store of memory, there must be a translation mechanism whereby the ephemeral code of the nerve impulse is changed into a form that can produce a permanent record. Knowledge of such steps in translation between functional and structural codes would be an important step in understanding the physiology of memory, even if it fell short of revealing the final store.

I now review experiments on the use of certain metabolic inhibitors on learned behaviour in young chickens that have allowed us to piece together a sequence of biochemical events that could bridge some of the gaps between electrical signaling and macromolecular metabolism in the initiation of memory. We began this work from a neurophysiological point of view by considering what changes in the metabolism of nerve cells could produce a record of their previous activity that might be the basis of their electrophysiological differentiation from inactive neurons. Since most cells lose potassium ions and gain sodium ions after the passage of many impulses, this seemed a good place to start. The transient ionic imbalance has no significant effect by itself on the electrophysiological properties of cells, but does activate the enzyme sodium/potassium adenosine triphosphatase (Na/K ATPase), which restores resting concentrations with some accompanying increase of membrane potential. Such a change, which can outlast by far the period of intense impulse activity, might be recognizable in nerve networks concerned with memory and could provide the basis for a short-duration electrophysiological memory. This enzyme may be inhibited in different ways by several compounds; of these, we have used lithium ions, ouabain, and ethacrynic acid.

We tested the effects on memory formation in young chickens with intracerebral injections of these substances. The main behavioural task used was the one-trial passive-avoidance task of Cherkin (1b) in which chickens learn to avoid pecking an attractive target, a small shiny bead, when it is coated with an aversant chemical, methyl anthranilate. The proportion of birds that do not peck the same uncoated lure on subsequent presentation gives a quantitative measure of memory retention in the population tested. Two significant findings were made. Inhibitors of Na/K ATPase, ouabain lithium and ethacrynic acid, produced amnesia when injected into the brain before or a few minutes after learning, but not later, whereas inhibitors of protein synthesis blocked memory when injected up to a half hour after the one-trial learning (8). Secondly, ouabain given shortly before learning resulted in a more rapid decline of learned response over the subsequent hour then did cycloheximide (10). In fact, a dose of cycloheximide that produces complete amnesia in birds tested a day later has no effect on the level of memory retention for the first half-hour after learning. A chemically diverse group of substances with a common known biochemical effect on active ion transport also has a common behavioural action on memory different from the effects of cycloheximide. Both the fact that they are only effective if injected within a few minutes of learning and that they cause a more rapid decline of memory than does cycloheximide suggest that they are operating on an earlier stage in the formation of the memory record than the one that is thought to involve protein synthesis. This is sufficient evidence to suggest that somehow the initiation of memory is linked to activation of membrane Na/K ATPase. All agents that inhibit ionic metabolism, by their effects, produce changes in the extracellular ionic environment of nerve cells. Could this be the basis of their action? Recent experiments by Gibbs and Ng (4) show this not to be so and have given evidence of a still earlier phase of memory formation. Injection of K^+ into chick brains, K^+ being the most likely ion to affect neurones, produces memory inhibition but only under different circumstances. K^+ inhibits memory on the above task only when injected 5 min before or up to 2.5 min after learning, whereas the Na/K ATPase inhibitors work up to 10 min after learning. Also the maximum inhibitory effect is produced by 2 mM K^+, 0 mM or up to 7 mM being quite ineffective. Gibbs & Ng (4) have used this as evidence that there is an initial short-term storage phase, closely following the impulse activity of training, that is in some way related to ionic changes but precedes the activation of Na/K ATPase. But they also show that the effects of inhibiting the enzyme can be separated from the ionic changes that its inhibition might be expected to have on the immediate environment of nerve cells.

Is there a way in which activity of Na/K ATPase could be linked in turn with a permanent store? We have previously suggested one way in which the transmembrane transport of ions could influence macromolecular metabolism (5). It is a departure from an older idea that protein synthesis on which memory is to be based may be sensitive to intracellular ion concentrations. In particular we proposed that one important step was the accumulation of small organic building blocks such as amino acids, taken up preferentially in recently active cells by a transport process that perhaps needs activity of the Na/K ATPase. If it is possible to interfere with the uptake of such molecules in the absence of block of Na/K ATPase, it should, on the above theory, be possible to block the formation of long-term structural memory without interfering with the short-term modifiability of behaviour. The behavioural effect should mimic that of cycloheximide but via a different biochemical mechanism.

Gibbs et al. (6) have just published this experiment, and the results follow precisely these predictions. Amino acid transport may be disorganised by supplying a high concentration of amino-isobutyrate (AIB), a nonmetabolizable amino acid that shares uptake mechanisms with some classes of amino acids. High concentration of AIB competes for transmembrane transfer with small neutral amino acids resulting in a deficit in their uptake. When injected into the brains or into the circulation of chickens 5 min before they are trained on the one-trial passive-avoidance task described above, there is no effect on learning or on memory retention for the first 30 min after training. Then there is a sudden fall off, which is exactly the time course of memory loss after injection of cycloheximide. The same effects follow the injection of proline, which has a similar biochemical effect.

The biochemical consequences of injecting AIB are quite different from those of cycloheximide. The uptake of ^{14}C-leucine into the chick brain can be shown to be inhibited, but the overall rate of incorporation into protein is not changed significantly. In contrast, an amnesic dose of cycloheximide produces an almost complete inhibition of protein synthesis. Assuming that new protein synthesis is really required for permanent memory, we can say that it must be a very small fraction of the total ongoing protein synthesis of the brain and that it is peculiar in that it requires a pool of amino acids recently taken up into the brain.

In addition, the above authors found that AIB is ineffective in inhibiting memory when injected more than 10 min before or after learning. That there are limits on the time of effectiveness of the drug when injected *before* learning simply reflects the time after a single injection for which an effective concentration is maintained at its site of action before becoming dispersed by various means. That there are limits on the time of effectiveness when injected *after* learning is of greater significance. At this time the memory is in a form not susceptible to cycloheximide, and therefore is in the physiological short-term or labile state. During this period, we deduce from the argument above that it is possible to produce an effect of AIB of about 10-min duration. Yet the action on memory occurs only with interference with the early parts of the short-term period, not the later. The inhibitory effects of AIB are, therefore, on metabolic events about the time of learning, but are not expressed behaviourally until about 30 min later. If the real amnesic action of AIB is on amino acid uptake, we can conclude that the change on which the eventual memory depends requires amino acids accumulated within a few minutes of learning, but that the memory is held in a non-susceptible physiological short-term store for about another 30 min.

If the structural modification that is to form a memory store takes time to become effective, what is going on during this time and why should it be so long? One possibility is that, even though it takes only seconds to make a protein, the time may be required to accumulate an effective quantity. Another possibility is that time is required for the intracellular transport of the molecules from their site of manufacture, presumably ribosomes in the cell body to their site of action, which is almost certainly in the cell membrane and probably either pre- or postsynthesis membrane. The accumulation theory seems less likely because of the short time of action of AIB, and since we do not know the nature of memory molecules, they cannot be measured and the theory is not easily testable. Intracellular transport can be studied through its inhibition by agents that disrupt intracellular microtubules. One such is colchicine, which has already been shown to interfere with the acquisition of new behavioural responses in goldfish (2).

Bell and Hambley (1a) have now tested the effect of injecting colchicine into chickens brains a few minutes after learning of the one trial avoidance task. There is a clear and dose-dependent block of memory tested 24 hr after learning, at doses comfortably removed from those that cause other behavioural side effects or mortality. Preliminary experiments show that the onset of amnesia is delayed, so the short-term store is not affected significantly.

In this kind of learning where a behavioural response changes within seconds, the long-lasting changes in the brain still take many minutes to become established and pass through at least three pharmacologically separable stages. The common finding is that a consolidation period is required for long-term memory, presumably, from the above results, because the synthetic process triggered off at the time of learning requires both the synthesis and transport of proteins. It is obvious that if the cellular events for the formation of a long-lasting memory record have an irreducible time course that is very long in behavioural terms, it is essential that there be an interim memory mechanism equally powerful in directing behaviour to bridge the period required for structural change.

EFFECTS OF INHIBITORS ON SHORT-TERM MODIFIABILITY OF BEHAVIOUR

We, therefore, come to the question whether behaviour that is dependent on a short-range memory is susceptible to differential effects of these various inhibitors. For these experiments, we used multitrial learning tasks and tested the effect of injections given before the learning trials on short-term performance. The main test was that of visual discrimination of food grains from pebbles of similar size, shape, and colour, stuck at random to a perspex floor. A hungry chicken placed on such a floor will peck eagerly, usually showing an initial slight preference for pebbles. Since the pebbles will not come up, it soon shifts its preference to the food grains, which are distinguishable mainly by their coarser texture and more constant colour. By watching the birds and recording each peck with an event recorder, the proportion of pecks at grain and pebbles can be calculated. Plotting the proportions in each consecutive group of 20 pecks gives a learning curve that normally decreases to only three or four errors (pecks at pebbles) between the 40th and 60th peck. Cycloheximide given into the brain before training does not impair learning, but the acquired behaviour does not last and the task must be learned anew when presented the next day. Both ethacrynic acid and ouabain have a similar effect on the performance of this task that is quite different from the action of cycloheximide. In chickens injected intracranially before training, learning does not occur. The initial preference for pebbles is not lost, and in 60 pecks, no statistically significant tendency to peck at grain emerges. This is quite compatible with ouabain and ethacrynic acid's having an inhibitory effect on the initial phases of memory formation. If performance is to improve in a multitrial learning task such as this, the choice made on each peck must be conditioned by the outcome of the previous trials. If access to a short-term memory store is blocked, no learning can occur. This contrasts with the effect of the protein synthesis inhibitors in which learning is normal but retention fails.

One most unexpected effect showed up when testing birds that had been injected with ouabain or ethacrynic acid for memory retention at intervals after the training. Birds tested as early as 30 min after training showed some initial preference for grain even though no such preference had been expressed in training. Chickens tested 1 hr after training showed an immediate preference for grains making only three or four errors in the first 20 pecks, which is the level of performance of birds trained with no drug treatment. Apparently in this task, ouabain or ethacrynic acid had blocked access to memory as it was being formed so that modification of behaviour was not possible, but had not prevented the formation of permanent memories of the kind susceptible to disruption by inhibitors of protein synthesis. Control experiments showed this to be so. Why it is possible to get a comparatively isolated effect on the short-term modification of behaviour in this task while both short- and long-term memory are affected with one-trial passive avoidance is not yet understood.

Chickens were also trained in an operant task for heat reward. They were placed in a refrigerator at 4°C and provided with two beads of different colours. Pecks at one turned a heat lamp on for a fixed period, whereas pecks at the other had no effect. Groups of chickens injected with either saline or ouabain were then trained in a procedure in which they obtained 20 rewards irrespective of the number of errors. Both sets of birds were then tested 20 min later by extinction. Those injected with saline showed no extinction in the first 10 pecks (pecking almost exclusively at the bead paired with the reward). Those trained under the influence of ouabain pecked at random. This also is compatible with the idea that ouabain prevents ongoing access to forming memory so that short-term modification of behaviour is impossible.

Another task in which the effects of Na/K ATPase inhibitor has a comparable effect is observational learning. Chickens were trained to feed from a novel, bright blue food dish by watching, through a perspex partition, two teacher birds already familiar with the dish feeding from it. Normally, when the teachers are removed and the partition lifted, after a delay the learner bird rushes straight for the dish and begins feeding within seconds. A bird that has not watched others feeding from a novel dish initially shows an alarm response when first confronted with the object and does not approach it for at least 5 min. Chickens injected with saline show the normal observational learning; those injected with ethacrynic acid show evident interest in the feeding teachers, but when given access to the bowl after a 5-min delay, fail to approach it (9).

We have failed in one kind of learning in chickens to show an amnesic action of ouabain. This is in poison-based food aversions (8a). Chickens form visual food aversions over long delays when a novel food is paired with poisoning by a subsequent intraperitoneal injection of a toxin. We had hoped to be able to prevent this association by presenting the visually novel food to chickens under the influence of ouabain. Run straight, this experiment appears to work, and birds pretreated with ouabain before the initial exposure show no aversion to the new kind of food when they are re-presented with it some days later. If, however, they are reinjected with ouabain or even saline before testing, the aversion becomes apparent. Intracranial injection in association with a novel food that is subsequently paired with sickness, produces yet another variety of state-dependent learning, something that had not appeared in previous experiments using these inhibitors. Our failure, therefore, was due to the potency of intracranial injection of a small volume of fluid as a stimulus readily associated with food and sickness that prevented further pharmacological analysis of this kind of learning by our present techniques.

SUMMARY OF BEHAVIOURAL EXPERIMENTS

In all of the above tasks where learning occurs over many trials and several minutes, inhibitors of Na/K ATPase impair performance. Behavioural control experiments, reported in detail elsewhere, leave us with the conclusion that the common action is on the way that a memory store, with a duration measured in minutes, can direct behaviour. Thus far, the idea that access to a temporary store cannot exist without the action of Na/K ATPase has been upheld.

The formation of a long-term record is variably affected by inhibitors of Na/K ATPase, depending on the learning task. Long-term retention (24 hr) is blocked by cycloheximide in all tasks in which it was used. Long-term retention in the one-trial passive-avoidance task is prevented by inhibition of amino acid transport into brain cells and by colchicine, known to block intracellular transport.

HYPOTHESIS

The whole theory can now be put together as a suggested outline of the way in which events encoded in a spatiotemporal pattern of nerve impulses can be laid down in a structural form that can be read out as nerve impulses (Fig. 1). Nerve cells that are made to fire rapidly during a learning experience lose potassium and accumulate sodium. This has little effect on their ability to carry impulses, but sets off a relatively long-lasting recovery process in which sodium is pumped out of cells and potassium in. Because of the asymmetry of ion exchange, this leads to an equally long-lasting change in membrane potential, a hyperpolarisation that, in theory at least, could alter the signal-carrying function of nerve networks of which the cells form a part. Accompanying this, and linked in some way, is an acceleration of amino

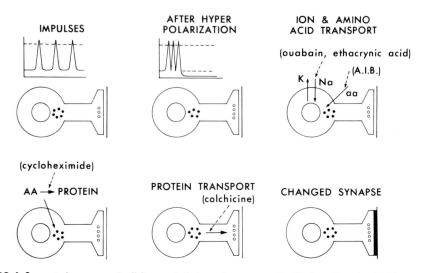

FIG. 1. Suggested sequence of cellular events that may be necessary for the formation of a short-term and a long-term stable memory. Further explanation in the text.

acid transport that is linked, in its turn, with increased synthesis of a particular protein or proteins. Protein is then transported to the synapses of the neuron, either to pre- or postsynaptic elements where it becomes incorporated in the transmission mechanisms to increase or perhaps decrease the efficacy of synaptic transmission. This structural change, in contrast to the ion movements, is very long-lasting and now independent of the ongoing activity of the nervous system. Patterns of impulses that resemble those on which the short-term change was based are nevertheless rerouted preferentially by alterations in the efficacy of synapses on the changed pathways.

There may be biochemical analogy to this process in the transformation of lymphocytes in the immune response. This is known to involve an early influx of K^+ and Ca^{2+} ions that, after an hour or so, triggers off RNA, protein, and then DNA synthesis (1,7), which may also be blocked by the early application of ouabain. There is evidence from biochemical studies of brains exposed to new experiences that there is an early and transient increase in RNA and protein synthesis, the events of which are comparable, with the exception of cell division, to the initial events in lymphocyte transformation, and there are numerous associated changes in cyclic nucleotides and amino acid uptake and so on. A consolidation period in redirecting nerve cell metabolism in memory may be necessary because the size and shape of nerve cells, even those involved in memory, require a comparatively long-time for products of new RNA to be inserted into their sites of action in the cell membrane. In lymphocyte transformation, a time lag of hours between the triggering ionic events and subsequent mitosis is of little concern. In nerve cells that direct behaviour, it would be disastrous and has led to a double system of memory retention with an ion-dependent storage process immediately interpretable to the impulse code bridging the gap.

This theory is deliberately sketchy with regard to anatomical details, because there is not enough known of this. It makes no distinction among the various kinds of conditioning, avoids other behavioural problems altogether, like the relevance of reinforcement, and makes no attempt to incorporate all the biochemical correlates of learning. It is quite specific about some of the biochemical events that may be needed to get information from a functional impulse code into the structure of the brain and out again into the impulse code. As such it is easily testable, and maybe it is useful as a framework in which the many other known physiological and biochemical concomitants of learning can be considered.

REFERENCES

1. Allwood, A., Asherson, G. L., Davey, M. J., and Goodford, P. J. (1971): The early uptake of radioactive calcium by human lymphocytes treated with phytohaemagglutinin. *Immunology,* 21:509–516.
1a. Bell, G. A., and Hambley, J. (1978): *In preparation.*
1b. Cherkin, A. (1969): Kinetics of memory consolidation: Role of amnesic treatment parameters. *Proc. Natl. Acad. Sci. USA,* 63:1094–1101.
2. Cronly-Dillon, J. R., Carden, D., and Birks, C. (1974): The possible involvement of brain microtubules in memory fixation. *J. Exp. Biol.,* 61:443–454.
3. Gibbs, M. E., and Mark, R. F. (1973): *Inhibition of Memory Formation,* Plenum Press, New York.
4. Gibbs, M. E., and Ng, K. T. (1976): Memory formation: A new three-phase model. *Neurosci. Lett.,* 2:165–169.
5. Gibbs, M. E., Jeffrey, P. L., Austin, L., and Mark, R. F. (1973): Separate biochemical actions of inhibitors of short- and long-term memory. *Pharmacol. Biochem. Behav.,* 1:693–701.
6. Gibbs, M. E., Robertson, S., and Hambley, J. (1977): Amino acid uptake required for long-term memory formation. *Neurosci. Lett.,* 4:293–297.
7. Hesketh, T. R., Smith, G. A., Houslay, M. D., Warren, G. B., and Metcalfe, J. C. (1977): Is an early calcium flux necessary to stimulate lymphocytes? *Nature,* 267: 490–494.
8. Mark, R. F., and Watts, M. E. (1971): Drug inhibition of memory formation in chickens. I. Long-term memory. *Proc. R. Soc. Lond. [Biol.],* 178:439–454.
8a. Martin, G., Bellingham, W., and Mark, R. (1978): *In preparation.*
9. Rogers, L. J., Oettinger, R., Szer, J., and Mark, R. F. (1977): Separate chemical inhibitors of long-term and short-term memory: Contrasting effects of cycloheximide, ouabain and ethacrynic acid on various learning tasks in chickens. *Proc. R. Soc. Lond. [Biol.],* 196:171–195.
10. Watts, M. E., and Mark, R. F. (1971): Drug inhibition of memory formation in chickens. II. Short-term memory. *Proc. R. Soc. Lond. [Biol.],* 178:455–464.

Brain Mechanisms in Memory and Learning:
From the Single Neuron to Man,
edited by M. A. B. Brazier.
Raven Press, New York © 1979.

Physiological and Pharmacological Dissection of the Main Factors in the Acquisition and Retention of Shuttle Behaviour

Ivan Izquierdo* and Elaine Elisabetsky*

Disciplina de Neurofisiologia, Departamento de Biofísica e Fisiologia, Escola Paulista de Medicina, 04023 São Paulo, SP, Brasil

Learning and memory cannot be measured directly and have to be inferred from the observation of animal behaviour (27,42). Therefore, the main problem in learning research is to decide, when observing a particular behaviour, how much of it depends on associative (i.e., true learning) factors and how much results merely from nonassociative effects of the stimuli being used (2,3,5,16,26). In addition, it is important to establish, among associative factors, the relative weight of stimulus–stimulus (Pavlovian) and of response–reinforcement (instrumental) interactions (26,29,48). It is obvious that if these questions are left unanswered, it will be impossible to show that the effect of any independent variable (drugs, age, lesions, etc.) on any given behaviour is due to an influence on learning or on other concomitant processes, and it will also be impossible to know if any accompanying physiological activity (unit firing, slow potentials, biochemical changes) is a correlate of learning or of nonassociative factors.

The present chapter reviews recent data from this laboratory that provide tentative answers to these questions for at least one particular class of learned behaviours, namely, the development of shuttle behaviour responses (SBs) to acoustic stimuli in rats placed in a shuttle-box.

NONASSOCIATIVE VERSUS ASSOCIATIVE EFFECTS OF FOOTSHOCKS IN THE DEVELOPMENT OF SBs

The response repertoire of rats to a brief acoustic stimulus, such as a 5-sec tone or buzzer, is quite limited. Normally it involves a startle reaction, followed by an orienting response (lateral or upward movement of the head, with or without pricking of the ears, sniffing and/or rearing), and then by a

---

* *Present address:* Departamento de Bioquímica, Instituto de Biociencias, Federal University of Rio Grande do Sul, 90000 Porto Alegre, RS, Brazil.

freezing reaction. If the buzzer is repeatedly presented alone, other responses, such as running, jumping, or shuttling, are exceedingly rare (0.04% of all responses in a 50-trial session, ref. 26). If footshocks are randomly interspersed among the buzzers, without any specific temporal relation to them or any contingency on responses, shuttle, jumping, and squealing responses to the buzzer appear in at least 10% of the trials (23,24,26). These are the natural responses to footshocks in this species (45). If the footshocks are paired to the buzzers on every trial and omitted every time that the animals make an SB (avoidance contingency), the incidence of SBs increases to 30 to 70% (13–15,26,29,33,35,36). The former, or "random mode" test, may

TABLE 1. *Effect of drug treatments on SB performance of rats in pseudoconditioning and two-way avoidance tests in a shuttle-box*

Treatment	Dose (mg/kg)	Pseudo-conditioning	Two-way avoidance	References
Tyramine	5	+	−	24, 26
Epinephrine	0.5	−	−	36
Guanethidine	5	−	−	36
Eserine	0.1–0.2	−	+	24, see 31
Nicotine	0.2	0	+	14, see 31
Atropine[a]	2	0	−	14, see 31
Methylatropine[a]	2–5	0	−	14, 25, 31
Hexamethonium	5	0	0	15, 24
Amphetamine[b]	1	+	+	13, 24
Caffeine	30	+	+	23
Strychnine	1	0	+	23
Metrazol	10	+	+	23
Picrotoxin	1.25	0	+	23
Atro.[a] + Amphet.[b]	2 + 1	++	++	14
Hexamet. + Amphet.[b]	5 + 1	++	++	24
Me. Atro[a] + Amphet.[b]	5 + 1	++	+	15, 23
Hexamet. + Nicotine	5 + 0.2	0 or +	0	23
Atro.[a] + Nicotine	2 + 0.2	0	0 or −	14, see 31
Phenobarbital	40	−	0	23, 35
Amobarbital	10	−	0	23
Meprobamate	100	−	0	23
Diazepam	5	−	+	23, 26
Chlorpromazine	2	−	−	23
Reserpine[c]	2	−	−	23
Haloperidol	0.5	0	−	31
Diphenylhydantoin	80	0	−	23, 33
Cannabidiol	3.5	0	−	23, 33
Trimethadione	200	+	0	23,35
LSD-25	0.075	+	+	26
LSD-25	0.3	+	0	26
Dibenamine	10	0	0	23, 26
LSD + Dibenamine	0.075 + 10	++	−	26
LSD + Dibenamine	0.3 + 10	++	−	26

+, Increase; ++, potentiation; 0, no effect; −, decrease.
[a] Given 1 hr before.
[b] Expressed as d-amphetamine sulfate.
[c] Given 24 hr before.

be considered a pseudoconditioning situation (17,23,24,26,36,46), and the other test is a typical two-way avoidance paradigm (16,17,26,29).

The starting point of our investigations was the repeated finding that the pharmacology (23,24,26) and the neurochemical correlates (17,22,25,46) of SB performance were very different in the two situations, in spite of the fact that the animals, the apparatus, and the nature, number, and distribution over time of the stimuli (23,24) were the same in both. In fact, of 33 different drug treatments investigated in the two tests up to 1975, 15 had different effects on SB responding in the two, five had opposite effects, and only 13 influenced SB performance in the same direction in both tests (Table 1). With regard to biochemical variables, pseudoconditioning was accompanied by an increase of hippocampal acid ribonuclease activity and by a concomitant fall of total hippocampal RNA concentration, which were followed by a late "rebound" increase of nucleoside incorporation into nuclear RNA. Two-way avoidance, instead, was accompanied by a primary increase of precursor incorporation into RNA, with an increase of total hippocampal RNA concentration, and no change of ribonuclease activity (17,22,25,27).

Since rats normally do not perform SBs unless they also receive footshocks, the occurrence of SBs in the pseudoconditioning situation may be attributed to a nonassociative effect of the shocks (2,3,5,16), which is expressed precisely by the development of SBs and may be defined as a "drive" state (D) (26,29). Now, it is known that each footshock leaves an effect that can be measured by proactive changes of behaviour (3) and that lasts for several minutes. Since the intensity, number, and distribution over time of shocks were the same in the two tests (23,24,26), it may, therefore, be considered that there is a similar "amount" of shock-induced D in both (26,31). However, in addition to D, in the two-way avoidance paradigm there is a stimulus–stimulus relationship that may be defined as "pairing" (P) and there is an avoidance contingency (C). In principle, then, the various pharmacological and biochemical differences observed between the two tests cannot be ascribed to the D factor, but to the presence of the other two factors, P and C, in the avoidance paradigm.

D, DP, DC, AND DPC TESTS

At this point it became necessary to define D, P, and C in some simple and useful way. P was operationally defined as a constant temporal relation between the buzzers (or tones) and the shocks (28,29). In most of our experiments, this relation was one of contiguity (8,10,23,24,26,28–32,50,51). C was defined as the main avoidance contingency by which each SB cancelled the next scheduled shock (5,27–29,48). D was defined as a state of the animal brought about by the mere presence of footshocks in the experimental situation (3,26,28).

Certainly, P and C, as defined above, do not exhaust all possible forms of stimulus–stimulus and response–reinforcement interactions, respectively. Visual or olfactory cues may play a role in addition to the acoustic (tone or buzzer) or algogenic (shocks) stimulation used in the various tests (38,41). Buzzer termination, subtle position changes, alterations of muscular tonus, etc., may play instrumental roles in addition to the main avoidance contingency (7,16,26,27,29). Even D may be viewed as a complex of various nonassociative factors, of which the one resulting in the development of SBs may be just one (3). However, the above operational definitions of D, P, and C proved to be useful, and, as will be seen, there was no need to resort to any other minor, more vague, hypothetical, or ill-defined supplementary factors in order to adequately explain rat shuttle behaviour (see the following three sections).

Two tests were devised in which P and C acted separately from each other —the DP and the DC tests (28–31). The DP test is a classic or Pavlovian conditioning paradigm, in which buzzers (or tones) and shocks are paired on all trials, irrespective of whatever responses may be made during the buzzer. The DC test is a situation in which the buzzer (or tone)–shock interval is varied at random, so that it is not predictable by the animal on any trial, and there is no pairing in the sense defined above; however, in the DC test, each SB cancels the next scheduled shock (avoidance contingency). The random procedure described in the preceding section, which we have so far called pseudoconditioning, was rebaptized the "D test." The typical two-way avoidance situation, in which the stimuli are paired on every trial but shocks are omitted when there is an SB on that trial, was renamed the "DPC test."

Typically, in all tests, 50 5-sec buzzers or tones are delivered at randomly variable 10- to 40-sec intervals, and shocks are 60 Hz, 1.5 mA, and scrambled. The buzzer–shock intervals vary randomly between 5 and 30 to 35 sec in the D and DC tests, and the two stimuli are contiguous or they overlap in DP and DPC. The total duration of a D, DP, DC, or DPC session is between 15 and 30 min.

PHARMACOLOGICAL DISSECTION OF D FROM P FROM C

Our first aim was to investigate, on the DP and DC situations, drug treatments that had previously been investigated on D and DPC and that were found to have had opposite effects on SB behaviour in these two tests (Table 1) (28,29). The drugs chosen for these first studies were tyramine, lysergic acid diethylamine (LSD), dibenamine, LSD + dibenamine, diazepam, diphenylhydantoin, cannabidiol, and phenobarbital. Their effect on D and DPC is shown in Table 1. Their effect on DP and DC is shown in Table 2.

It can be seen in Table 2 that some of the treatments had a similar qualitative effect on D and DP; others, instead, affected DP and DPC in the same direction, and D in an opposite way; in other cases, the effect on DC and DPC was similar and different from the one on D and DP; etc. For the eight

TABLE 2. Effect of drug treatments on SB performance of rats in a Pavlovian conditioning situation (DP) and in an avoidance test without stimulus pairing (DC) in a shuttle-box

Treatment	Dose (mg/kg)	DP	DC	Reference
Tyramine	5	0	—	29
LSD-25	0.3	+	0	29
Dibenamine	10	0	0	29
LSD-25 + dibenamine	0.3 + 10	+	—	29
Diazepam	5	+	+	29
Cannabidiol	3.5	—	0	28
Diphenylhydantoin	80	—	0	28
Phenobarbital	40	0	0	28

For the effect of these same treatments on D and DPC, see Table 1.
+, Increase; ++, potentiation; 0, no effect; —, decrease.

drug treatments shown in Table 2, the pharmacological "profile" of each of the four tests—D, DP, DC, and DPC—was different. In consequence, each of the three factors—D, P, and C—may be considered to have a pharmacological, and therefore presumably a physiological, substrate of its own. The depressant effect of tyramine, or of LSD + dibenamine, on DPC may be explained by an influence predominantly on the C factor. The action of cannabidiol or of diphenylhydantoin on DPC may be due to an influence predominantly on the P factor, etc.

The drug studies summarized in Table 2 (28,29), however, allowed for very few conclusions about the physiological mechanisms of D, P, and C. With the exception of tyramine, known to act by releasing norepinephrine from sympathetic nerve endings (44), and of dibenamine, a well-known alpha-receptor antagonist, the mode of action of the other compounds is quite obscure (26,28,29). Furthermore, the effect of these agents on D and DPC, on one hand, and on DP and DPC, on the other, was studied in different laboratories and on different batches of rats, and so any direct quantitative comparison is precluded.

Therefore, we set out to study other pharmacological agents whose influence on neurohumoral processes is better understood—nicotine and eserine, which enhance the operation of central and peripheral cholinergic systems; the muscarine receptor blockers atropine (with both a central and a peripheral action) and methylatropine (which acts only at the periphery); clonidine, an agonist, and phenoxybenzamine, an antagonist, at central and peripheral norepinephrine receptors; and apomorphine, a stimulant, and haloperidol, a blocker, at central dopamine receptors (31). Each of these drugs, and appropriate combinations thereof, was studied on the four tests—D, DP, DC, and DPC—in a homogeneous population of rats. Results are summarized in Fig. 1.

The only compound in this series that had an effect on the D test was eserine, a depressant. Its influence was counteracted by atropine and methyl-

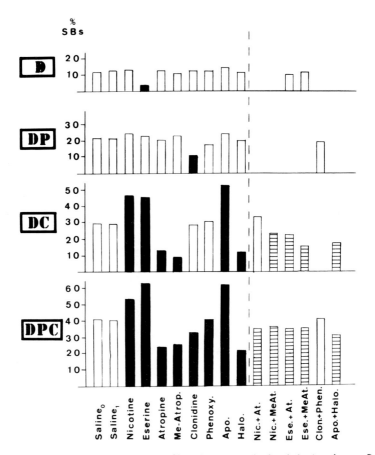

FIG. 1. Effect of several drug treatments on rat SB performance in the four behavioural tests—D, DP, DC, and DPC (50 trial sessions; each block represents the mean % SBs per session). All drugs were given 7 min before the tests, with the exception of atropine and methylatropine, which were given 1 hr before. The doses used were: nicotine, 0.2 mg/kg; eserine, 0.1 mg/kg; atropine, 2 mg/kg; methylatropine, 5 mg/kg; clonidine, 0.1 mg/kg; phenoxybenzamine, 10 mg/kg; apomorphine, 0.5 mg/kg; haloperidol, 0.5 mg/kg. All injections were i.p. in a volume of 1 ml/kg; all drugs were dissolved in saline. The black blocks indicate significant differences from the white blocks at 1% level in a Duncan multiple range test. Striped blocks indicate significant differences at 1 or 5% level from the values obtained with each of the two drugs separately. Each group consists of eight animals (31). Saline₀: saline given 7 min before the first trial of each test; Saline₁: saline given 1 hr before.

atropine, which were ineffective on their own. Therefore, there is presumably a nontonic, peripheral cholinergic inhibitory influence on operation of the D factor. This influence is opposite in sign to that of the sympathetic system, which may be stimulated by tyramine or amphetamine (24,26,36) the effects of which are, in turn, antagonized by the alpha-blockers, yohimbine, and dibenamine (24).

In the DP test, SB performance was depressed by clonidine, which was antagonized by phenoxybenzamine. Since tyramine has no effect on this test (see Table 2, and ref. 29), it seems logical to ascribe this effect of clonidine to stimulation of a central noradrenergic system, the operation of which would inhibit that of the P factor (31). Such systems are now well known to exist, and their possible influence on behaviour has been commented on by Gray et al. (18).

SB performance in the DC test was enhanced by nicotine, eserine, and apomorphine and depressed by atropine, methylatropine, and haloperidol. The effect of the two cholinergic stimulants was antagonized by the two cholinergic blockers, and the effect of apomorphine was antagonized by haloperidol. Therefore, there seems to be both a peripheral cholinergic and a central dopaminergic influence on the C factor. Both are stimulant influences, and it may be noted that the cholinergic one is opposite in sign and

TABLE 3. *Values for the D factor, for P (DP − D), for C (DC − D), for calculated DPC performance [D +* $P + C = D + (DP − D) + (DC − D)]$, *and for real or experimentally determined DPC performance in 30 different groups of rats submitted to various experimental conditions*

Rat group (ref. no.)	D	P	C	DPC_{calc}	DPC_{real}
Untreated adult (30)	7.8	14.9	21.5	44.2	43.3
Untreated weanling (30)	9.7	12.1	0	21.8	21.0
Saline 7 min before (31)	11.5	11.0	17.8	40.3	40.5
Saline 1 hr before (31)	12.3	9.0	16.0	37.3	40.3
Nicotine (0.2 mg/kg) (31)	12.5	11.5	33.5	57.5	52.5
Eserine (0.1 mg/kg) (31)	3.3	19.0	41.5	63.8	61.8
Atropine (2 mg/kg) (31)	11.8	8.2	0.2	20.2	23.3
Me-atropine (5 mg/kg) (31)	10.3	12.2	−2.3	20.2	24.3
Clonidine (0.1 mg/kg) (31)	12.0	−1.7	16.3	26.6	32.5
PhenoxybenzNH₂ (10 mg/kg) (31)	12.0	6.3	18.5	36.8	40.3
Apomorphine (0.5 mg/kg) (31)	14.0	10.0	38.0	62.0	61.5
Haloperidol (0.5 mg/kg) (31)	11.5	8.5	−0.2	19.8	21.0
Hippocampal cannula (10)	11.3	14.5	16.0	41.8	43.5
Neocortical cannula (10)	9.7	17.3	22.3	49.3	44.0
Hippo. spread. depression (10)	36.2	2.0	16.1	54.3	54.3
Neocx. spread. depression (10)	9.4	20.9	21.6	51.9	46.3
Untreated adult (8)	10.9	12.0	14.9	37.8	36.6
Sham-operated (8)	11.5	14.5	12.1	38.1	38.6
CA1-CA2 hippo. lesion (8)	36.9	0.4	14.7	52.0	53.8
Untreated adult (51)	9.5	13.1	18.5	41.1	40.7
Sham-operated (51)	9.8	13.7	19.8	43.3	41.5
Amygdala-pyriform lesion (51)	28.6	10.7	20.3	59.6	62.0
Untreated adult (50)	12.2	12.9	15.0	40.1	41.0
Sham-operated (50)	10.0	16.0	17.6	43.6	38.8
Vent. caudate lesion (50)	10.4	5.2	0.1	15.7	20.6
Icteric Gunn rats (37)	9.6	12.4	2.4	24.4	23.6
Nonicteric Gunn rats (37)	9.3	1.0	1.5	11.8	14.6
Normal Long Evans (37)	9.6	9.5	12.7	31.8	32.2
Normal adult Wistar male[a]	11.0	15.8	19.7	45.5	45.4
Normal adult Wistar female[a]	12.5	13.3	19.3	45.1	45.0

Seven to 44 animals per group.

[a] Taken from the diverse untreated adult groups described in refs. 8, 32, 50, and 51. In all cases, DPC_{calc} fell within one standard deviation from DPC_{real} (see text).

From Figs. 1 to 3.

somewhat different (*viz.,* the effect of nicotine and of the two blocking agents in this test) from the one on the D factor.

In the DPC situation, performance was affected by each of these treatments in a manner both qualitatively (Fig. 1) and quantitatively (see Table 3 and section entitled Apparent Additive Property of D, P, and C) predictable from the effect that each treatment had on the other three tests (31).

MATURATIONAL AND OTHER INFLUENCES ON D, P, AND C

Immature rats are known to perform poorly in various learning situations (see 1,34). We studied the behaviour of 20-day-old and of adult Wistar rats on the D, DP, DC, and DPC tests (30). No difference in SB performance was found between the two groups in the D (young, 9.7%; adult, 7.8% SBs) and in the DP tests (young, 21.8%; adult, 22.7% SBs). However, 20-day-old animals made fewer responses than adults both in the DC test (9.7% against 29.3%) and in the DPC situation (21.0% against 43.3%). Furthermore, in the younger group, performance in the DP and DPC tests was about the same, suggesting that all of it could be due to operation of factors D and P alone. This certainly was not the case in the adult group, in which animals made many more responses in the DPC situation than in DP. Therefore, it was concluded that in the rat, at the age of 20 days, factors D and P are already present, whereas C is not yet developed (30). These observations are in agreement with others that suggest immature rats are less able than adults to learn instrumental, but not classic, conditioned behaviours (34).

Gunn rats are a hooded variety of Wistar rats obtained by inbreeding (19), in which homozygous animals develop congenital nonhemolytic unconjugated hyperbilirubinemia due to a very low activity of liver uridine 5′-diphosphate (UDP)-glucuronosyltransferase (9,49). The heterozygous offspring present this enzymatic defect to a lesser extent and are not jaundiced (40). The icteric syndrome in the homozygous Gunn rat is accompanied by severe and widespread brain damage (6,53), believed to result from bilirubin binding to brain proteins (20), including probably mitochondrial and other enzymes (47).

One of us (I.I.), while recently visiting Robert Zand's laboratory at the University of Michigan Institute of Science and Technology, studied SB behaviour in icteric and nonicteric Gunn rats and compared it with that of normal hooded animals. Homozygous (icteric) Gunn rats behaved as if they were immature Wistar rats; their performance in the D and DP tests was normal, in the DPC test it was as in DP, and in the DC situation it was as that in the D test. In sum, icteric Gunn rats behaved as if they lacked the C factor. Their heterozygous (nonicteric) littermates, on the other hand, behaved as if, in addition, they also lacked the P factor; their performance in all four tests was about the same (DPC = DC = DP = D = 10 to 14% SBs over 50 trials). This difference between icteric and nonicteric Gunn rats might be due to a higher tendency of the latter to freeze (3,37) in situations that require stimulus–stimulus associations; heterozygous Gunn rats also had a higher latency to enter the dark side of a step-through passive-avoidance apparatus (43) on their first exposure to it than homozygous Gunn or normal hooded animals. Whatever the explanation for these behavioural defects in the two Gunn groups, it seems clear that they were unrelated to bilirubin levels and to brain damage, for these are absent in the heterozygous population. In consequence, it must be concluded that additional genetic defects developed in this strain by inbreeding, and a cautionary note should be made with regard to behavioural experiments carried out in animals that are inbred for many generations for nonbehavioural reasons (37).

No sex differences in performance were observed in normal Wistar rats in any of the four tests—D, DP, DC and DPC (Table 3 and section entitled Apparent Additive Property of D, P, and C) contrary to some previous data by other authors in DPC or DPC-like situations (see ref. 4). We have no explanation for this discrepancy. Possibly, slight variations in the experimental procedures or differences in the strain of rats used account for it.

SPREADING DEPRESSION AND LESION STUDIES

Neocortical spreading depression (10) or lesions (cf. the sham-operated groups of Figs. 2, 3, and 4) had no influence on D, DP, DC, or DPC performance, suggesting that the neocortex as a whole plays no important role in the operation of the D, P, and C factors during SB acquisition. This conclusion applies particularly to the spreading depression experiments, in which electroencephalogram recording showed that it extended to all of the neocortex within a few minutes (10).

On the other hand, hippocampal spreading depression (10) or hippocampal lesions (8) had very pronounced effects. They increased SB responding in all four tests (a fact that had previously long been known for the DPC situation, see refs. 1,27). The increase, however, was more marked in those tests that did not involve the P factor, namely, D and DC. Performance in the DP test was not significantly different from that in the D paradigm in hippocampal animals, and that in the DPC test was not different from the one in the DC situation. The simplest explanation for these findings is that the hippocampus (particularly the subareas affected by the lesions, CA1 and CA2, ref. 8) normally plays an inhibitory role in the operation of the D factor and a facilitatory role in that of P (8,10). This interpretation fits nicely both with the hypotheses that attribute to the hippocampus a role in behavioural inhibition (1,11,12) and with those that consider it crucial to the processing of stimulus–stimulus-related information (12,22,25,27,52) (Fig. 2).

Electrolytic lesions of the area of the anterior amygdala and pyriform cortex increased SB performance to about the same extent in all four tests (Fig. 3). In consequence, these lesions may be considered to release D from

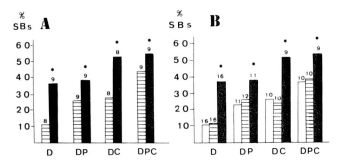

FIG. 2. A: Effect of hippocampal spreading depression *(black blocks)* on SB performance of rats in the four tests—D, DP, DC, and DPC. Control animals *(striped blocks)* had cannulae implanted in this structure. Asterisks indicate significant differences at 1% level in a t-test. Number of animals shown in each block. B: Same, for rats with electrolytic lesions placed in areas CA1–CA2 of their dorsal hippocampus *(black blocks)*. Striped blocks are sham-operated animals, and white blocks are intact controls. Asterisks indicate significant differences at 1% level in a Duncan test between the hippocampal group and the two control groups. Number of animals shown in each block (8,10).

an inhibitory influence, without affecting the operation of either P or C (51).

Lesions of the ventral part of the caudate nucleus had no effect on SB performance in the D test, but depressed it very markedly in the other three situations, DP, DC, and DPC (Fig. 3). It seems likely, therefore, that the ventral part of the caudate nucleus is important for the normal operation both of P and C and relatively unimportant for that of D (50).

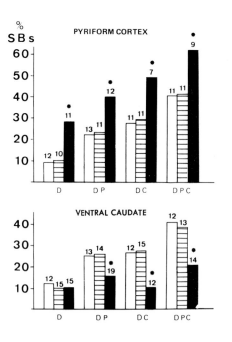

FIG. 3. Above: Effect of lesions of the anterior amygdala–pyriform cortex region *(black blocks)* on SB performance in the D, DP, DC and DPC tests. Striped blocks correspond to sham-operated animals and white blocks to intact controls. Asterisks indicate significant differences at 1% in Duncan test between lesioned animals and both control groups. Number of animals shown in each block. Below: Same for electrolytic lesions placed in the ventral caudate nucleus (50,51).

APPARENT ADDITIVE PROPERTY OF D, P, AND C

It is obvious from the data enumerated in the preceding three sections that the three factors we defined operationally as D, P, and C are separate and that they are the main factors in the elicitation of SBs in the situations we called D, DP, DC, and DPC. Other possible stimulus–stimulus and response–reinforcement relations, such as were briefly discussed in the second section, are clearly of lesser importance (29,31).

These conclusions pose several questions. Do D, P, and C interact with each other up to any significant extent or do they operate independently? Conceding that they are the main factors in shuttle avoidance, what is their relative importance compared with that of the other minor, more vague, or ill-defined factors mentioned above? In a DPC situation where the three are present, do they act convergently every time there is a response, or are, instead, some responses due to one factor alone and others to the other two factors?

If D, P, and C really were the three main factors in the development of SBs in each of the four tests and if they acted independently of each other, then SB performance in a DP test should result from D + P, performance in a DC test should result from D + C, and performance in a DPC paradigm should be, for any given homogeneous rat population, equal to

$$D + P + C = D + (DP - D) + (DC - D) = DP + DC - D.$$

Table 3, composed of data from all the papers from this laboratory in which the four tests—D, DP, DC, and DPC—were carried out in homogeneous rat populations (as defined by strain, age, and treatment if any), shows that this is the case in all of the 30 groups in which the simple equation DPC = DP + DC − D was applied. This was so in spite of the wide variety of treatments used in the various papers. Therefore, the three factors behave as if they were the *only* really important factors in shuttle behaviour (*all* shuttling to the buzzer or tone in the DPC test may be explained by D + P + C, and, in addition, DP = D + P, and DC = D+ C), and there is no need to resort to any other minor or ill-defined stimulus–stimulus or response–reinforcement interaction to explain this behaviour. D, P, and C act as if they were additive in all four tests. This result responds to the first two questions raised earlier on in this section.

As to the third question, that of whether D, P, and C converge in order to elicit each response or whether some SBs are due to one and some to another factor, there is no direct answer. There is, however, a simple way to provide a clear, if indirect, answer, illustrated by the analysis of Fig. 4 (which is a considerable extension of a previous similar analysis, ref. 31).

Figure 4 comprises data from 480 adult control animals, all of the Wistar strain, and all tested in the same shuttle-box in our laboratory in São Paulo.

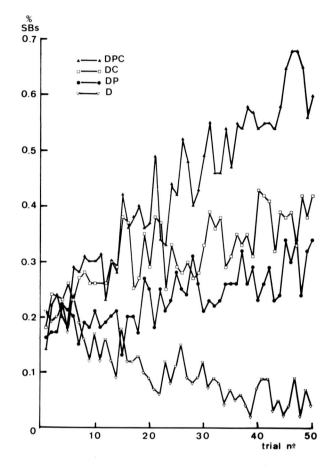

FIG. 4. Mean SB performance (*ordinates*) on each of the 50 trials (*abscissa*) of D, DP, DC, and DPC tests. One hundred and twenty intact or saline-treated animals per test. See text.

One hundred and twenty animals were examined in each of the four behavioural paradigms—D, DP, DC, and DPC. These animals include intact and saline-treated controls described in several previous papers (8,26,28–32, 50,51) as well as some additional untreated rats. Their performance in each test was examined trial by trial over the 50 trials of each of the test situations.

From trials 1 to 6, there was no difference in SB performance between any of the four tests. Therefore, it is likely that in all of them, the only factor active during the first six trials was the D factor. On trials 7 and 8, SB performance in the two tests that included the C factor—DC and DPC—became significantly higher (1% level in a Duncan multiple range test) than that of the other two tests and remained so until the end of the sessions. In consequence, the C factor seems to enter into operation at trials 7 to 8 and to stay on until the end, in the DC and DPC situations. On trials 19 and 20 and then from trial 22 on, performance in the DP test became higher than that in the D test, and from trial 24 on, performance in the DPC paradigm became higher than that in DC (again, at a 1% level in a Duncan multiple range test). Therefore, P appears to enter in operation in the DP and DPC situations from trials 19 to 24 on. In all points (i.e., on every trial), $DP + DC - D = D + (DP - D) + (DC - D)$ gave a value that fell within one standard deviation from the experimentally obtained DPC figure (Fig. 5; standard deviations are not illustrated in the figure for the sake of clarity).

Over the 50 trials, the surface occupied by D in Fig. 4, plus that occupied by DP minus D, plus that occupied by DC minus D, gave a value within 1% of the surface occupied by DPC.

In consequence, Fig. 4 may be interpreted as showing that in a DPC session, the first factor to enter into play is D, the second one, at about the seventh or eighth trial, is C, and the last one, around the 20th trial, is P. This

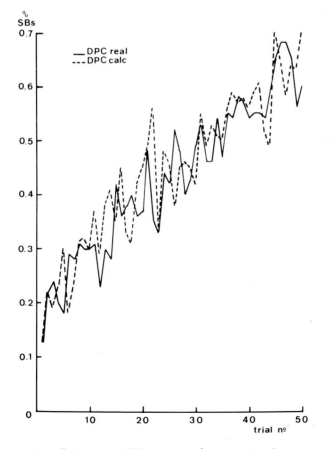

FIG. 5. Real or experimentally determined DPC performance (same as in Fig. 4) and theoretical or calculated DPC performance $[D + (DP - D) + (DC - D) = D + P + C]$ for the animals of Fig. 4.

conclusion agrees with that of a previous paper (31) in which a similar analysis was applied to data from a much lower number of rats (N = 16 per test). In that paper, however, the conclusion was considerably strengthened by the finding that several drugs (those of Fig. 1 and section entitled Pharmacological Dissection of D from P from C) that acted separately on D, P, and C started to act on the various tests precisely on the block of five trials in which the respective factor initiated its own independent operation.

Now, even if the data from Table 3 and Figs. 4 and 5 show quite unequivocally the additive property of D, P, and C, this property may result from a more complex phenomenon than simple outright addition.

As was mentioned in the first section, shuttling is not a natural component of a rat's response repertoire to a tone or a buzzer (26,37). In order to shuttle, in fact, these animals must overcome their more natural tendency to freeze (3,7). In fact, shuttle avoidance is commonly viewed as a typical example of a conflict between the tendency to shuttle and the tendency to refrain from doing so (7,31,37). In none of the four tests would this be more obvious than in DP, in which the animals get shocked even when they shuttle. It is, in fact, quite frequently observed that rats in this test make a good start toward the midline mark, or the hurdle or the hole, if there is one, and then freeze right in front of it instead of shuttling past it. It is also quite common to find, in all tests, that following one or more clear-cut SBs, rats respond to the next buzzer with freezing, without even making an orienting response. Therefore, D, P, and C may be viewed as "antifreezing" factors (3,37), which tend to resolve, each on its own, the conflict between "freezing and fleeing" (7) in favor of the latter. Possibly P is the factor with the strongest antifreezing power, inasmuch as it has to fight against circumstances that presumably act much in favour of the tendency to freeze (37). The apparent additive property of D, P, and C, therefore, may just be a felicitous coincidence, observed in all the groups so far examined in the four tests (Table 3), by which the antifreezing power of the three factors equilibrated in such a way as to yield an actual sum in all cases.

LONG-TERM MEMORY OF DP AND DC LEARNING (32)

Memories lasting for 1 day or more are considered long-term, and those lasting only for a few minutes or hours are called short-term (42,43).

D is known to leave no long-term memory whatever, and animals submitted to the D test perform in a DPC situation carried out a few days later as if they were naive (34). DPC, on the other hand, leaves good memory traces. If an animal is trained on DPC on one day and retested in the same paradigm 1 to 7 days later, it makes many more SBs on the retest than on the first test. This has been observed in several species, including the rat, and the increased performance in the retest session is quite commonly used as a measure of long-term memory of multitrial learning experiments (13,14,26, 36,39,42,43).

Since DP and DC are apparently independent forms of learning and since D, P, and C apparently add to give DPC performance, it was of interest to find out whether previous DP or DC training would leave any detectable long-term memory traces that could influence DPC performance in a retest session carried out 1 or 7 days later. Figure 6 shows that they did.

This led to an additional question. Is DP and DC memory stored separately, or would learning in DP affect performance in a DC retest and vice versa? Rats were trained on either DP or DC on one day (day 0) and retested on either the same or the other test 1 or 7 days later. In total there were,

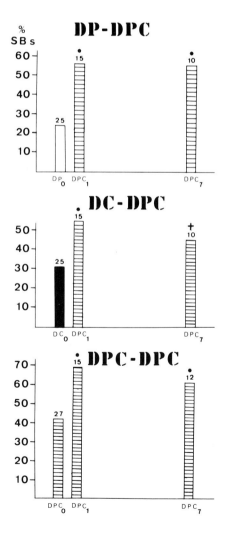

FIG. 6. SB performance in training sessions (DP$_0$, DC$_0$, DPC$_0$) and in retest sessions carried out 1 or 7 days later in the DPC paradigm (DPC$_1$ and DPC$_7$). Asterisks indicate significant differences at 1 or 5% level in a Duncan multiple range test from the DPC$_0$ group; the cross indicates a significant difference from all other DPC$_1$ or DPC$_7$ groups. Number of animals in each group shown in each block.

therefore, eight groups: DP_0–DP_1, DP_0–DP_7, DC_0–DC_1, DC_0–DC_7, DP_0–DC_1, DP_0–DC_7, DC_0–DP_1, and DC_0–DP_7. Results appear in Fig. 7.

It can be seen that DP training left memory traces that influenced retrieval in the same test 1 or 7 days later. DP_0–DP_1 memory was the same as DP_0–DP_7, so there was no build-up and no decay of DP–DP memory between days 1 and 7. Rats trained in a DC paradigm showed better retention when retested in the same situation on day 1 than on day 7, showing that DC–DC

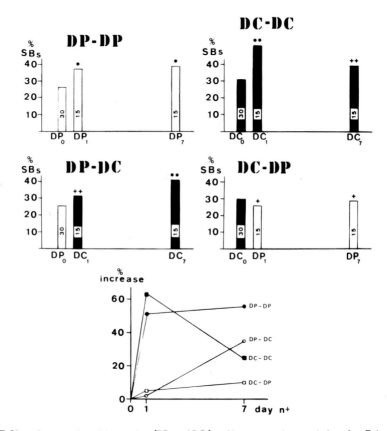

FIG. 7. SB performance in training sessions (DP_0 and DC_0) and in retest sessions carried out 1 or 7 days later in the same or in the other test (DP_1, DP_7, DC_1, DC_7). In the DP–DP groups, asterisks show significant differences at 1% level in a Duncan test from performance in the training session (DP_0). In the DC–DC groups, double asterisk indicates significant difference from performance in the DC_0 training session, and the double cross indicates a significant difference from the DC_1 block in that group. In the DP–DC groups, the double cross on the DC_1 block indicates that it was not significantly different at a 10% level from any of the DC_0 groups, and the double asterisk shows that the DC_7 block was different at a 1% level from all DC_0 groups. In the DC–DP group, the crosses indicate that DP_1 and DP_7 were not different at a 10% level from any of the DP_0 groups. The number of animals per group and per block is shown in each block. The lower graph illustrates performance in the retest sessions of each of the four groups (DP–DP, DP–DC, DC–DC, and DC–DP), expressed as % of increase over the corresponding training day levels (DP_0 or DC_0) (*ordinates*), on retest days 1 and 7. Note that DP–DP memory is stable between days 1 and 7; DP–DC memory builds up between day 1 and day 7; DC–DC memory decays between day 1 and day 7; and DC–DP memory was unmeasurable. See text.

memory was different from DP–DP in that it suffered decay between days 1 and 7. When rats were trained on DP and retested on DC, they made no more responses in the DC retest on day 1 than would a naive animal submitted to DC; however, when the retest was on day 7, performance was considerably higher. Therefore, DP training leaves memory traces that affect retrieval in a DC mode, but this DP–DC memory builds up between days 1 and 7, unlike the other two forms of memory mentioned above. Training in DC did not influence DP performance either on day 1 or on day 7, so there was no evidence for a DC–DP memory "channel."

These data pointed to the existence of three different forms of long-term memory for SBs, which may be called memory "channels"—DP–DP, DC–DC, and DP–DC. Each of these channels was different from the others in the time course of build-up and of decay of the memory traces (or of the animals' capacity to retrieve). If the physiological substrates of the three memory channels are indeed different from each other, then there must be some demonstrable pharmacological differences between them. Among the various drugs that are well known to influence memory processes (42,43), both d-amphetamine (13,27,42) and metrazol (42,43) have repeatedly been found to enhance retention of a wide number of tasks when given shortly after the initial training session (posttrial treatment, refs. 14,15,39,42,43). We trained rats on either DP or DC and gave them, immediately after the last trial, an i.p. injection of d-amphetamine sulfate (1 mg/kg) or of metrazol (10 mg/kg). Control animals received an equal volume of saline (1

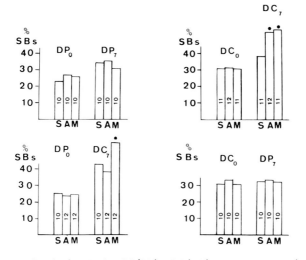

FIG. 8. SB performance in animals trained on DP (DP$_0$) or DC (DC$_0$) and retested on DP (DP$_7$) or DC (DC$_7$), 7 days later. These animals received an i.p. injection of saline (S), d-amphetamine, 1 mg/kg (A), or metrazol, 10 mg/Kg (M), immediately after the last trial of the training sessions. Asterisks indicate significant differences (1 or 5% level in a Duncan test) between A or M and S in the retest session. Note that DP$_0$–DP$_7$ memory is unaffected by A or M, DP$_0$–DC$_7$ memory is enhanced by M but not by A, and DC$_0$–DC$_7$ memory is enhanced both by A and by M. See text.

ml/kg). The animals were retested 7 days later on either the same or the other test (DP_0–DP_7, DC_0–DC_7, DP_0–DC_7, and DC_0–DP_7). Results appear in Fig. 8.

It can be seen that the DP–DP channel was insensitive to both drugs. The DC–DC channel was sensitive to metrazol, but not to amphetamine; metrazol prevented the decay normally seen in untreated (Fig. 7) or in saline-treated animals. The DP–DC channel was sensitive to both amphetamine and metrazol, which enhanced performance in the retest session relative to the levels of the saline group. Therefore, and in addition to their different time course of build-up and decay, the three channels each had a pharmacology of its own. In consequence, the three channels—DP–DP, DP–DC, and DC–DC —must be considered to involve distinct processes and probably to have each a physiological substrate of its own, a problem that is currently under investigation in our laboratory.

The concept of three different long-term memory channels, derived from the experiments detailed in this section, is a major departure from the idea implicit in most current memory "theories" (for reviews see 42,43) that long-term memory is a single entity or process. Although none of these theories spells this idea out in detail, all of them recognize it implicitly (32). There are some data in the literature, however, that also suggest the existence of more than one long-term memory channel. Hine and Paolino (21) observed that posttrial electroconvulsive shock disrupts consolidation of passive-avoidance behaviour, but not that of a concomitantly acquired cardioaccelerator response. H. Bruce Ferguson and his group (*personal communication*), at the Department of Psychology of Carleton University in Ottawa, found that under certain conditions passive-avoidance learning may affect subsequent active-avoidance learning and vice versa.

It may be noted in Fig. 8 that animals trained in DC and retested in DP 7 days later (DC_0–DP_7 group) made more responses in this DP_7 retest than naive animals submitted to DP (all DP_0 groups) or than the DC_0–DP_7 rats of Fig. 7. This increase was slightly below the 5% significance level in a Duncan multiple range test (32) and, therefore, does not support any conclusion about the eventual existence of a fourth, DC–DP, channel. However, there might be conditions in which that channel could be shown to operate, and we would prefer to consider it, for the time being, as a theoretical channel, whose existence has not so far been proved, rather than a nonexistent entity. It should be pointed out that if the DC–DC channel had been investigated only on day 7 (that is, in DC_0–DC_7 groups), it would also have been ruled out as nonexistent unless animals with posttrial metrazol injections had been examined (Fig. 8).

CONCLUSIONS

SBs are acquired by rats through the operation of three separate factors that may be called D, P, and C. Drugs and other variables affect shuttle behaviour differently as a result of their independent influence on one or the other factor. The operation of D is enhanced by pharmacological stimulation of the sympathetic system and depressed by that of the parasympathetic system. In addition, D is subject to tonic inhibitory influences from areas CA1 to CA2 of the hippocampus and from the region of the anterior amygdala and pyriform cortex. Operation of the P factor seems to depend on the integrity of the hippocampus and of at least the ventral portion of the caudate nucleus, and, in addition, is amenable to depressant influences of centrally acting noradrenergic drugs. The C factor appears later in life than the other two. It is absent in both homo- and heterozygous Gunn rats, and it seems to require a normal central dopaminergic system and is enhanced by stimulation of that system. It is also enhanced by pharmacological stimulation of the parasympathetic system. In a typical two-way avoidance or DPC session, the first few responses are due to operation of the D factor, the second factor to enter into action is C, and the last one is P, the influence of C and P superimposing on that of D, which gradually declines along the session. D, P, and C behave at all times as if they were additive, so that SB performance on every trial of a DPC session results from D + P + C. Shuttle learning, therefore, be it classic (DP) or instrumental (DC and DPC), is due to the concurrent operation of three distinct systems, definable both operationally and physiologically. If there are additional factors in such learning, they obviously play a minor role.

SBs acquired through a DP mode (classic or Pavlovian conditioning) or through a DC mode (instrumental conditioning without stimulus pairing) are stored in three separate long-term memory systems or channels: DP–DP, DP–DC, and DC–DC. Each of these channels has a different time course for build-up and decay and a different sensitivity to drugs.

ACKNOWLEDGMENTS

The data on which this review is based, as well as the previously unpublished data (see section on the Apparent Additive Property of D, P, and C and section on Long-term Memory of DP and DC Learning) were supported by grants and fellowships from the Fundação de Amparo à Pesquisa do Estado de São Paulo (FAPESP), from the Conselho Nacional de Desenvolvimento Científico e Tecnológico (CNPq), and from Financiadora de Projetos (FINEP), all from Brazil. We express our gratitude to Drs. G. Bignami (Rome) and H. Anisman (Ottawa) without whose valuable ideas, expressed both in their published papers and in personal communications, the development of the concepts of the present article would not have been possible. We also thank Drs. E. A. Cavalheiro, D. O. de Souza, and R. A. Schutz for their many valuable comments and suggestions expressed in our daily contact at the laboratory.

ADDENDUM

After this chapter was written, some experiments were made on the long-term memory of DP and DC learning that substantially add to, and partially modify, the results shown in Fig. 8 and commented on in the section Long-term Memory of DP and DC Learning, as well as in the conclusions.

A group of animals received an i.p. injection of nicotine (0.2 mg/kg) immediately after DP or DC training and were retested, either on DP or on DC, 7 days later. Nicotine had no effect on the DP–DP, DP–DC, and DC–DC channels, but it "unclogged" the normally "dormant" DC–DP channel (rats made an average of 46.9% SBs on the DP_7 retest session of the DC_0–DP_7 group as opposed to controls who made 33.2%; $N = 14$ and 13, respectively). Therefore, there are four instead of just three memory channels in the rat brain, of which DC–DP is normally nonoperative, but can be "awakened" by posttrial nicotine (32).

REFERENCES

1. Altman, J., Brunner, R. L., and Bayer, S. A. (1973): The hippocampus and behavioral maturation. *Behav. Biol.,* 8:557–596.
2. Anisman, H. (1975): Time dependent variations in aversively motivated behaviors: Non-associative effects of cholinergic and catecholaminergic drugs. *Psychol. Rev.,* 82:359–385.
3. Anisman, H., and Waller, T. G. (1973): Effects of inescapable shock on subsequent avoidance performance: Role of response repertoire changes. *Behav. Biol.,* 9:331–355.
4. Archer, J. (1975): Rodent sex differences in emotional and related behavior. *Behav. Biol.,* 14:451–479.
5. Bignami, G. (1976): Nonassociative explanations of behavioral changes induced by central cholinergic drugs. *Acta Neurobiol. Exp. (Warsz),* 36:5–90.
6. Blanc, W. A. (1961): Kernicterus in Gunn's strain of rats. In: *Kernicterus,* edited by A. Sass-Kortsák, pp. 150–152. Toronto Univ. Press, Toronto.
7. Bolles, R. C. (1970): Species-specific defense reactions and avoidance learning. *Psychol. Rev.,* 71:32–48.
8. Calderazzo Filho, L. S., Moschovakis, A., and Izquierdo, I. (1977): Effect of hippocampal lesions on rat shuttle responses in four different behavioral tests. *Physiol. Behav.,* 18. (*In press.*)
9. Carbone, J. V., and Grodsky, G. M. (1957): Constitutional hyperbilirubinemia in the rat. *Proc. Soc. Exp. Biol. Med.,* 94:461–463.
10. Cavalheiro, E. A., and Izquierdo, I. (1977): The effect of hippocampal and of neocortical spreading depression on rat shuttle behavior in four different experimental paradigms. *Physiol. Behav.,* 18. (*In press.*)
11. Douglas, R. J. (1967): The hippocampus and behavior. *Psychol. Bull.,* 67:416–422.
12. Douglas, R. J. (1972): Pavlovian conditioning and the brain. In: *Inhibition and Learning,* edited by R. A. Boakes and M. S. Halliday, pp. 529–553. Academic Press, New York.
13. Evangelista, A. M., and Izquierdo, I. (1971): The effect of pre- and post-trial amphetamine injections on avoidance responses of rats. *Psychopharmacologia,* 20: 42–47.
14. Evangelista, A. M., and Izquierdo, I. (1972): Effects of atropine on avoidance conditioning: Interaction with nicotine and comparison with N-methylatropine. *Psychopharmacologia,* 27:241–248.
15. Evangelista, A. M., Gattoni, R. C., and Izquierdo, I. (1970): Effect of amphetamine, nicotine, and hexamethonium on performance of a conditioned response during acquisition and retention trials. *Pharmacology,* 3:91–96.
16. Frontali, M., Amorico, L., Acetis, L., and Bignami, G. (1976): A pharmacological analysis of processes underlying differential responding: A review and further

experiments with scopolamine, amphetamine, lysergic acid diethylamide (LSD-25), clordiazepoxide, physostigmine, and chlorpromazine. *Behav. Biol.*, 18:1–74.

17. Gattoni, R. C., and Izquierdo, I. (1974): The effect of conditioning and pseudo-conditioning on hippocampal and neocortical RNA. *Behav. Biol.*, 12:67–80.

18. Gray, J. A., McNaughton, N., James, D. T. D., and Kelly, P. H. (1975): Effect of minor tranquillisers on hippocampal θ rhythm mimicked by depletion of fore-brain noradrenaline. *Nature*, 258:424–425.

19. Gunn, C. K. (1944): Hereditary acholuric jaundice in the rat. *Can. Med. Assoc. J.*, 50:230–237.

20. Gurba, P. E., and Zand, R. (1974): Bilirubin binding to myelin basic protein, histones and its inhibition *in vitro* of cerebellar protein synthesis. *Biochem. Biophys. Res. Commun.*, 58:1142–1147.

21. Hine, B., and Paolino, R. M. (1970): Retrograde amnesia: Production of skeletal but not cardiac response gradients by electroconvulsive shock. *Science*, 169:1224–1226.

22. Izquierdo, I. (1972): Hippocampal physiology: Experiments on regulation of its electrical activity, on the mechanism of seizures, and on a hypothesis of learning. *Behav. Biol.*, 7:669–698.

23. Izquierdo, I. (1974): Effect on pseudoconditioning of drugs with known central nervous activity. *Psychopharmacologia*, 38:259–266.

24. Izquierdo, I. (1974): Possible peripheral adrenergic and cholinergic mechanisms in pseudoconditioning. *Psychopharmacologia*, 35:189–193.

25. Izquierdo, I. (1974): Regulation of information processing in the hippocampus by K^+ release and $(K^+)_0$ accumulation. In: *Neurohumoral Coding of Brain Function*, edited by R. D. Myers and R. R. Drucker-Colin, pp. 151–166. Plenum Press, New York.

26. Izquierdo, I. (1975): Relations between orienting, conditioned and pseudocondi-tioned responses in a shuttle-box—a pharmacological analysis by means of LSD and dibenamine. *Behav. Biol.*, 15:193–205.

27. Izquierdo, I. (1975): The hippocampus and learning. *Prog. Neurobiol.*, 5:37–75.

28. Izquierdo, I. (1976): Stimulus pairing and the response-reinforcement contingency as separate factors in the elicitation of shuttle responses: The effect of anti-convulsant drugs. *Ciência e Cult. (São Paulo)*, 28:1334–1336.

29. Izquierdo, I. (1976): A pharmacological separation of buzzer-shock pairing and of the shuttle-shock contingency as factors in the elicitation of shuttle responses to a buzzer in rats. *Behav. Biol.*, 18:75–87.

30. Izquierdo, I., and Cavalheiro, E. A. (1976): The influence of stimulus pairing and of the shuttle-shock contingency in the performance of shuttle responses to a buzzer by weanling rats. *Behav. Biol.*, 17:119–122.

31. Izquierdo, I., and Cavalheiro, E. A. (1976): Three main factors in rat shuttle be-havior: Their pharmacology and sequential entry in operation during a two-way avoidance session. *Psychopharmacology*, 49:145–157.

32. Izquierdo, I., and Elisabetsky, E. (1978): Four memory channels in the rat brain. *Psychopharmacology*, 57:215–222.

33. Izquierdo, I., and Nasello, A. G. (1973): Effects of cannabidiol and of diphenyl-hydantoin on the hippocampus and on learning. *Psychopharmacologia*, 31:167–175.

34. Izquierdo, I., Salzano, F., Thomé, F., and Thaddeu, R. C. (1975): Shuttle con-ditioning and pseudoconditioning in weanling and in adult rats. *Behav. Biol.*, 14:461–466.

35. Izquierdo, I., Tannhauser, M., and Tannhauser, S. (1973): On the relation be-tween hippocampal K^+ release and learning: A negative result with trimethadione and phenobarbital. *Ciência e Cult. (São Paulo)*, 25:1163–1165.

36. Izquierdo, I., and Thaddeu, R. C. (1975): The effect of adrenaline, tyramine and guanethidine on two-way avoidance conditioning and on pseudoconditioning. *Psy-chopharmacologia*, 43:85–91.

37. Izquierdo, I., and Zand, R. (1978): Behavioural observations in Gunn rats. *Psycho-pharmacology*, 57:155–162.

38. King, M. G., Pfister, H. P., and DiGiusto, E. I. (1975): Differential preference for

and activation by the odoriferous compartment of a shuttlebox in fear-conditioned and naive rats. *Behav. Biol.,* 13:175–181.

39. Lauzi Gozzani, J., and Izquierdo, I. (1976): Possible peripheral adrenergic and central dopaminergic influences in memory consolidation. *Psychopharmacology,* 49:109–112.

40. Marniemi, J., Vainio, H., and Parkki, M. (1975): Drug conjugation in Gunn rats: Reduced UDP-glucuronosyl transferase and UDP-glucosyl transferase activities with increased glycine-N-acyl transferase activity. *Pharmacology,* 13:492–501.

41. McAllister, W. R., and McAllister, D. E. (1971): Behavioral measurement of conditioned fear. In: *Aversive Conditioning and Learning,* edited by F. R. Brush, pp. 105–179. Academic Press, New York.

42. McGaugh, J. L. (1973): Drug facilitation of learning and memory. *Annu. Rev. Pharmacol.,* 13:229–241.

43. McGaugh, J. L., and Herz, M. J. (1972): *Memory Consolidation.* Albion, San Francisco.

44. Muscholl, E. (1966): Indirectly acting sympathomimetic amines. *Pharmacol. Rev.,* 18:551–559.

45. Myer, J. S. (1971): Some effects of noncontingent aversive stimulation. In: *Aversive Conditioning and Learning,* edited by F. R. Brush, pp. 469–536. Academic Press, New York.

46. Nasello, A. G., and Izquierdo, I. (1969): Effect of learning and of drugs on the ribonucleic acid concentration of brain structures of the rat. *Exp. Neurol.,* 23:521–528.

47. Noir, B. A., Boveris, A., Garaza Pereira, A. M., and Stoppani, A. O. M. (1972): Bilirubin: A multi-site inhibitor of mitochondrial respiration. *FEBS Lett.,* 27:270–274.

48. Rescorla, R. A., and Solomon, R. L. (1967): Two process learning theory: Relationships between Pavlovian and instrumental learning. *Psychol. Rev.,* 74:151–182.

49. Schmid, R., Axelrod, J., Hammaker, L., and Swarm, R. (1958): Congenital jaundice in rats due to a defect in glucuronide formation. *J. Clin. Invest.,* 37:1123–1130.

50. Schutz, R. A., and Izquierdo, I. (1977): Efeito de lesões no núcleo caudato sôbre comportamento aversivo em ratos. *Ciência e Cult.* (*São Paulo*), 29. (*In press.*)

51. Schutz, R. A., Nasello, A. G., and Izquierdo, I. (1978): Effect of lesions of the anterior amygdala-pyriform cortex region on rat shuttle behavior in four different experimental paradigms. *Ciência e Cult.* (*São Paulo*), 30:595–599.

52. Solomon, P. R. (1977): Role of the hippocampus in blocking and conditioning inhibition of the rabbit's nictitating membrane response. *J. Comp. Physiol. Psychol.,* 91:407–417.

53. Tamaki, Y., Semba, R., and Tooyama, S. (1977): Cerebellar hypoplasia and motor development in congenitally jaundiced Gunn rats. *Physiol. Behav.,* 18:255–259.

Brain Mechanisms in Memory and Learning:
From the Single Neuron to Man,
edited by M. A. B. Brazier.
Raven Press, New York © 1979.

Role of Monoamines in Mediating the Action of Hormones on Learning and Memory

Gyula Telegdy and Gábor L. Kovács

Institute of Pathophysiology, University Medical School, Szeged, Hungary

The effects of hypophyseal proteohormones and carbohydrate-active steroids on central nervous function in humans and laboratory animals have long been known. Adrenocorticotrophic hormone (ACTH) and ACTH fragments are able to modify the mental functions in healthy subjects (43) and may cause psychotic reactions (21,62) and alter the electrical activity of the brain (14,16). In animal studies ACTH and ACTH fragments influence the conditioned reflex activity by delaying the extinction of an avoidance (4,6,37) and of an approach task (19,20). The antiamnestic action of this peptide has also been observed (41,42).

Vasopressin also delayed the extinction of an active-avoidance reflex (8) and improved the memory in one passive-avoidance test (1,11). Rats with hereditary hypothalamic diabetes insipidus (Brattleboro strain), on the other hand, were inferior in acquiring a two-way active-avoidance reflex and exhibited a severe memory deficit that could be restored by vasopressin administration (5,10,57). These data led to the hypothesis that vasopressin is involved in the physiological control of memory processes (12). This supposition was further substantiated by the observation that not only pharmacologically high doses but also physiological doses influenced higher nervous activity, the extinction of an active-avoidance reflex (44,45), and self-stimulation in rats (49).

In spite of the fact that the action of ACTH on behaviour is independent of the adrenal gland, the ACTH 4–10 heptapeptide residue is as active on higher nervous activity as the whole peptide and has no endocrine effect. Many data have accumulated indicating that the carbohydrate-active steroids of the adrenal cortex may influence conditioned reflexes. On avoidance extinction, the effect of corticosteroids is opposite that of ACTH or vasopressin. Corticosterone, dexamethasone, or cortisone treatment during the extinction period leads to facilitation of the extinction of a conditioned-avoidance reflex (3,7,9,13,28,53).

Although a significant amount of evidence exists about the action of these hormones on various behavioural patterns both in humans and in laboratory animals, the biochemical mechanism by which these hormones modulate central nervous function is poorly understood.

In the present chapter, evidence is presented on the involvement of cerebral monoaminergic mechanisms in the actions of different hormones, such as vasopressin, oxytocin, ACTH, and corticosterone, on certain types of behavioural patterns—learning and memory.

EFFECTS OF PEPTIDE HORMONES ON BRAIN MONOAMINES AND ON ACTIVE- AND PASSIVE-AVOIDANCE BEHAVIOUR

Effect of Vasopressin on Monoamine Metabolism in the Brain, and on Active- and Passive-Avoidance Behaviour

Following a single intraperitoneal injection of lysine-8-vasopressin (Sandoz, 300 mU/kg) (Fig. 1), the norepinephrine (NE), dopamine (DA), and serotonin (5-HT) contents were measured in various discrete brain regions according to the method of Shellenberger and Gordon (50). The plasma corticosterone level was estimated according to the method of Zenker and Bernstein (64).

Lysine-8-vasopressin, administered 10 min prior to the killing of the animals, had no effect on the NE contents of the hypothalamus, septum, striatum, or mesencephalon. The DA contents decreased significantly ($p < 0.05$) in all brain areas investigated. The plasma corticosterone content was increased by vasopressin administration ($p < 0.01$).

In order to clarify the mechanism of action of vasopressin on the DA and NE metabolisms (Fig. 2), the turnover rates of these monoamines were measured by the method of Nagatsu et al. (40), using 250 mg/kg alpha-methyl-p-tyrosine (α-MT) as a depletor of catecholamine contents. The rats were injected with the hormone together with α-MT treatment, and the NE and DA contents were measured 4 hr later.

Following vasopressin treatment, the DA turnover was increased in the septum and striatum, but that of NE was increased only in the hypothalamus.

Under similar experimental conditions, vasopressin had no effect on the 5-HT content of the brain areas mentioned above.

Since vasopressin influenced the contents and turnovers of brain catecholamines, it seemed worthwhile to reinvestigate the mechanism of action of vasopressin on avoidance behaviour in order to establish whether the changes caused in the catecholamine metabolism are relevant in the behavioural action of the posterior pituitary hormone.

The acquisition and extinction of an active-avoidance reflex was studied in the bench-jumping apparatus described in an earlier paper (54). Briefly, the animal was trained in the experimental box with 10 conditioning trials per day, with a light signal as the conditioned stimulus, followed by electric shocks (1.0 mA) delivered through the feet of the animal. In order to avoid

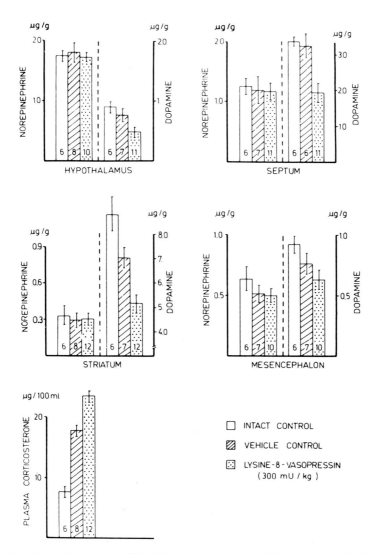

FIG. 1. Effect of lysine-8-vasopressin (300 mU/kg) on norepinephrine (NE) and dopamine (DA) content of different brain areas as well as on plasma corticosterone.

the electric shocks, the animal could jump onto a bench on the wall of the box. The learning and the extinction of this reflex was studied. During the extinction period, no reinforcement was given.

Vasopressin had no marked action on the acquisition of the conditioned-avoidance reflex (Fig. 3). α-MT (80 mg/kg, 4 hr prior to conditioning), which inhibits the synthesis of the catecholamines (38,51), significantly ($p < 0.05$) reduced the learning of the conditioned-avoidance reflex; (the treatment also significantly reduced the DA and NE contents in all brain

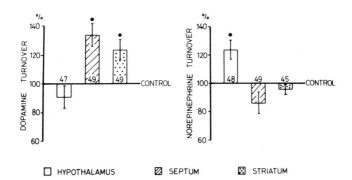

☐ HYPOTHALAMUS   ▨ SEPTUM   ▧ STRIATUM

FIG. 2. Effect of lysine-8-vasopressin (300 mU/kg) on NE and DA turnover in the hypothalamus, septum, and striatum.

regions investigated). Vasopressin, however, in a dose of 300 mU/kg 10 min prior to the conditioning was able to counteract the effect of α-MT on the learning and thus compensate the learning deficiency elicited by the administration of α-MT ($p < 0.05$ versus α-MT, not significant versus control).

Lysine-8-vasopressin delayed the extinction ($p < 0.01$), and hence the effect was the same as described earlier (Fig. 4) (8,44,45). α-MT facilitated the extinction of the active-avoidance reflex ($p < 0.05$); however, when given in combination with vasopressin, the hormone was not able to compensate the facilitatory action of α-MT on the extinction (not significant versus α-MT).

The effect of lysine-8-vasopressin on passive-avoidance behaviour was studied as described by Fibiger et al. (17) and Kovács et al. (34). The animals were placed on the grid floor of a bench-jumping-conditioning apparatus and were trained to jump onto the bench. Current (1.0 mA) was applied through the grid until the rats jumped onto the bench, and the total time to reach criterion (remaining on bench for 180 sec) was measured. This time was termed the "step-on latency." After having met this criterion, the rats were immediately removed from the apparatus; 24 hr later each animal was

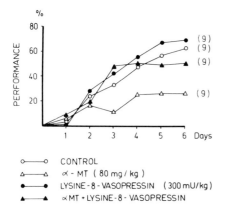

FIG. 3. Effect of vasopressin and α-MT on acquisition of active-avoidance reflex. (Number in brackets represents the animal used.)

○——○   CONTROL
△——△   α - MT (80 mg / kg)
●——●   LYSINE - 8 - VASOPRESSIN   (300 mU/kg)
▲——▲   αMT + LYSINE - 8 - VASOPRESSIN

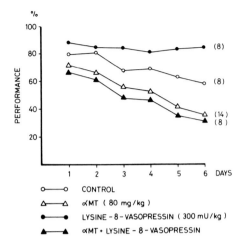

FIG. 4. Effect of vasopressin and α-MT on extinction of active-avoidance reflex.

again placed on the bench and the latency to step-down ("step-down latency") was measured to a maximum of 180 sec. On both days prior to the behavioural session, the animals were treated with 80 mg/kg α-MT 3 hr before or with 300 mU/kg lysine vasopressin 10 min before the session. The drugs were given alone or in combination with each other and were injected intraperitoneally in a volume of 0.1 ml/100 g. For statistical treatment of data, analysis of variance was used.

Although neither vasopressin or α-MT had any action on the step-on latency, vasopressin considerably lengthened ($p < 0.01$) the step-down latency (Fig. 5). α-MT treatment alone had no effect on the step-down la-

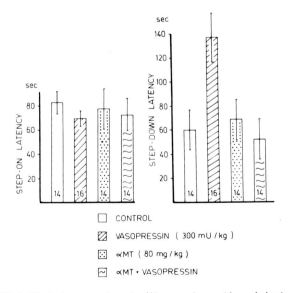

FIG. 5. Effect of vasopressin and α-MT on passive-avoidance behavior.

tency, but when given in combination with vasopressin, was able to prevent the action of vasopressin ($p < 0.01$ versus vasopressin).

Our data support the previous findings of other investigators showing that vasopressin influences the central nervous processes mainly by changing memory consolidation and retrieval processes (5,8,12,57). The action is probably mediated by the facilitated catecholamine metabolism mainly of a dopaminergic nature. However, in certain brain areas, NE might also be involved in the mediation of the effect of memory (extinction, passive-avoidance test) processes. It seems that the effect of vasopressin on the learning rate—in animals with a lowered catecholamine level (α-MT-treated rats)—is mediated either by the activation of the partially inhibited catecholaminergic system or by some other mechanism.

Effect of Oxytocin on Monoamine Metabolism and on Active- and Passive-Avoidance Behaviour

Oxytocin (300 mU/kg, i.p.), given 10 min before the animals were killed, decreased the NE contents in the hypothalamus, septum, and striatum ($p < 0.05$), whereas it did not affect the DA contents of the same regions (Fig. 6).

The same dose of oxytocin increased the 5-HT content in the hypothalamus ($p < 0.05$ versus the injected control group) and decreased the 5-HT content in the septum ($p < 0.05$) (Fig. 7). It was ineffective in the striatum and in the mesencephalon.

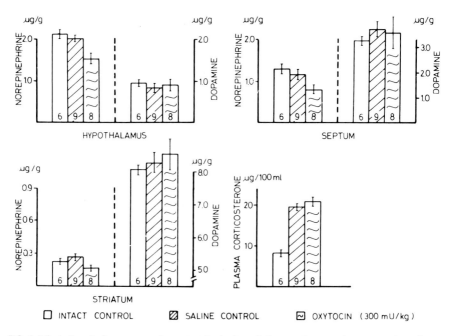

FIG. 6. Effect of oxytocin on monoamine content in the hypothalamus striatum and septum, and on plasma corticosterone striatum.

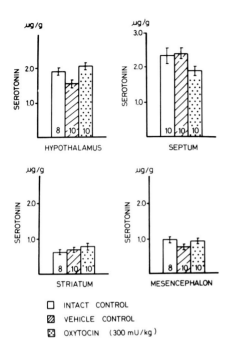

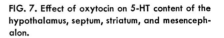

FIG. 7. Effect of oxytocin on 5-HT content of the hypothalamus, septum, striatum, and mesencephalon.

Oxytocin treatment increased the DA turnover in the hypothalamus ($p <$ 0.05) and decreased that of DA and of NE in the striatum ($p < 0.05$) (Fig. 8).

Oxytocin had no effect on the acquisition of an active-avoidance reflex and was unable to counteract the learning deficit caused by α-MT (Fig. 9).

In a dose of 30 mU/kg, oxytocin showed a facilitatory action ($p < 0.05$) on extinction of the active-avoidance reflex (Fig. 10).

In a passive-avoidance situation, oxytocin was ineffective regarding the step-on latency, but significantly ($p < 0.05$) shortened the step-down latency (Fig. 11).

The present data clearly showed an antagonistic effect for oxytocin to

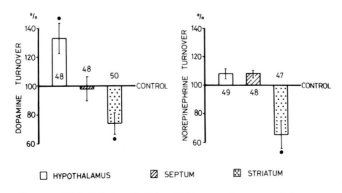

FIG. 8. Effect of oxytocin (300 mU/kg) on the DA and NE turnover in the hypothalamus, septum, and striatum.

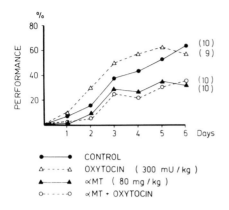

FIG. 9. Effect of oxytocin and α-MT on acquisition of the active-avoidance reflex.

vasopressin, which had already been suggested by electrophysiological findings (46,47) and behavioural studies (44,45,48,49). It seems that behind this electrophysiological and behavioural antagonism the brain's neurotransmitter metabolism is also different following oxytocin or vasopressin treatment. Oxytocin increased the DA turnover in the hypothalamus and decreased the turnovers of both catecholamines in the striatum.

Effect of ACTH on Monoamine Metabolism in the Brain and on Active and Passive Avoidance Behaviour

ACTH (2.0 IU/animal, Exacthin, Richter), given i.p. 30 min prior to the animals' being killed, had no effect on the NE contents of the hypothalamus, striatum, and mesencephalon, but significantly increased the DA level

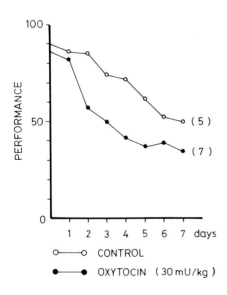

FIG. 10. Effect of oxytocin on extinction of active-avoidance reflex.

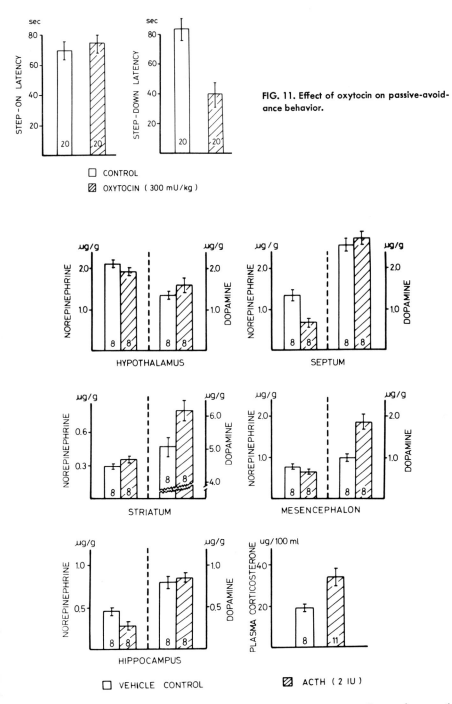

FIG. 11. Effect of oxytocin on passive-avoidance behavior.

FIG. 12. Effect of ACTH (2.0 IU) on NE and DA content of different brain areas as well as on plasma corticosterone.

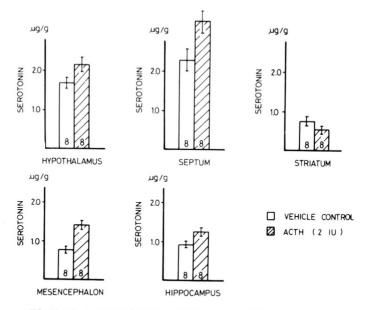

FIG. 13. Effect of ACTH (2.0 IU) on 5-HT content of different brain areas.

in the striatum and mesencephalon ($p < 0.05$) and decreased the NE levels in the septum and dorsal hippocampus ($p < 0.05$) (Fig. 12).

ACTH, in the same dose and under identical conditions, increased the 5-HT levels in the hypothalamus, septum, mesencephalon, and hippocampus ($p < 0.05$) (Fig. 13).

Following adrenalectomy, however, ACTH had no action on the NE contents in any of the brain areas studied (Fig. 14). The DA content of the hypothalamus decreased ($p < 0.05$), whereas in the striatum a further DA increase could be observed ($p < 0.01$).

After adrenalectomy, ACTH had no action on the 5-HT contents of the hypothalamus or mesencephalon (Fig. 15).

The effect of ACTH and ACTH fragments on behaviour has already been well documented by different laboratories. ACTH delays the extinction of an active-avoidance reflex, influences the approach behaviour and sexually motivated behaviour, improves the passive-avoidance behaviour by an antiamnestic action, and increases the maintenance of the reflex activity in an avoidance situation (2,4,6,19,20,25,37,39,42).

The mode of action of ACTH does not seem to be related to the cerebral serotoninergic system, since adrenalectomy eliminated its effect on the brain 5-HT content (56); on the other hand, the behavioural action became more clear in adrenalectomized rats (4). Our data support the findings of other investigators (9,15,22,35,36,59–61) that the brain catecholaminergic system might be responsible for the central nervous action of ACTH. This view was

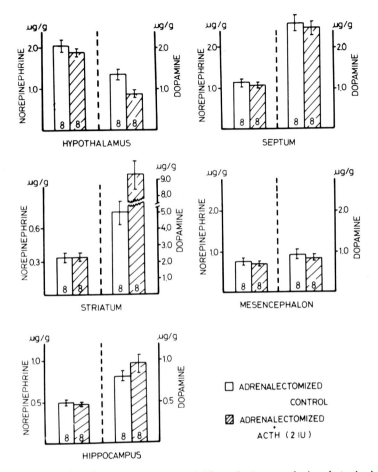

FIG. 14. Effect of ACTH (2.0 IU) on NE and DA content of different brain areas of adrenalectomized animals.

further corroborated by the recent study of Wiegant et al. (63), who showed that local injection of a dopaminergic receptor blocker into the substantia nigra prevented some behavioural effects of ACTH.

EFFECT OF CORTICOSTERONE ON BRAIN MONOAMINES AND ON ACTIVE- AND PASSIVE-AVOIDANCE BEHAVIOUR

The effects of two doses of corticosterone (1.0 and 10.0 mg/kg), given i.p. 30 min prior to the killing of the animals, were tested on the 5-HT contents of the hypothalamus and mesencephalon (Fig. 16). One mg/kg increased the 5-HT contents ($p < 0.05$) of the hypothalamus and mesencephalon, whereas 10.0 mg/kg decreased ($p < 0.05$) them. The plasma corticosterone level increased with the increase in the dose of corticosterone

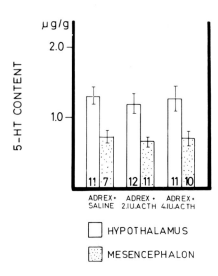

FIG. 15. Effect of ACTH on 5-HT content in the hypothalamus and mesencephalon after adrenalectomy.

administered ($p < 0.001$). The 5-HT contents of other brain regions (parietal cortex, frontal cortex, hippocampus) did not change following the corticosterone treatment (27,52).

The 5-HT turnover was studied according to the method of Tozer et al. (56) and calculated by means of linear regression as described by Finney (18) (Fig. 17). The 5-HT turnovers in the hypothalamus and mesencephalon increased after 1.0 mg/kg corticosterone ($p < 0.05$), whereas they decreased after 10.0 mg/kg corticosterone.

Administration of DL-p-chlorophenylalamine (PCPA), an inhibitor of tryptophan hydroxylase (23), in a dose of 300 mg/kg i.p., given 48 hr prior to the killing of the animals, decreased the 5-HT levels in the hypothalamus and mesencephalon ($p < 0.01$) and prevented the rise of 5-HT caused by 1.0 mg/kg corticosterone ($p < 0.01$) (Fig. 18). The plasma corticosterone level increased to the same magnitude in PCPA-pretreated and in nonpretreated animals.

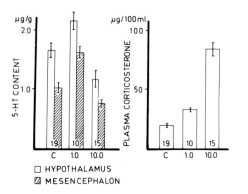

FIG. 16. Effect of 1.0 and 10.0 mg/kg corticosterone on 5-HT content of the hypothalamus and mesencephalon and on plasma corticosterone.

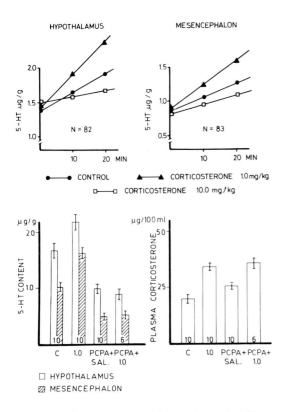

FIG. 17. Effect of 1.0 and 10.0 mg/kg corticosterone on 5-HT turnover (0 to 30 min) in the hypothalamus and mesencephalon.

FIG. 18. Effect of 1.0 mg/kg corticosterone on 5-HT content of the hypothalamus and mesencephalon after PCPA treatment.

Nialamide, a monoamine oxidase inhibitor, was injected i.p. in a dose of 125 mg/kg 4 hr prior to the animals' being killed (Fig. 19). This treatment increased ($p < 0.001$) the 5-HT content of the hypothalamus and the mesencephalon. In combination with nialamide, corticosterone in a dose of 10.0 mg/kg did not decrease the 5-HT content, in contrast to 10.0 mg/kg corti-

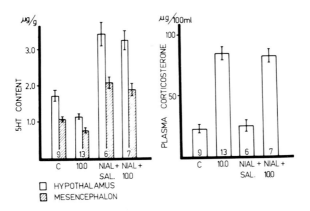

FIG. 19. Effect of 10.0 mg/kg corticosterone on 5-HT content of the hypothalamus and mesencephalon after nialamide treatment.

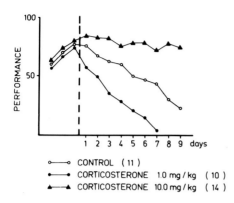

FIG. 20. Effect of 1.0 and 10.0 mg/kg corticosterone on extinction of active-avoidance reflex.

costerone alone. The plasma corticosterone level increased after administration of 10.0 mg/kg corticosterone either combined with nialamide or without nialamide.

Corticosterone had a dose-dependent dual action on the extinction of the active-avoidance reflex similar to that of the hypothalamic and mesencephalic 5-HT contents.

One milligram per kilogram corticosterone facilitated ($p < 0.05$), whereas 10.0 mg/kg delayed, the extinction ($p < 0.01$) (Fig. 20).

The facilitatory action of 1.0 mg/kg corticosterone on the extinction was prevented by PCPA ($p < 0.05$) given every other day (Fig. 21). PCPA itself caused a slight delay ($p < 0.05$) in the extinction.

Corticosterone given in 10.0 mg/kg delayed the extinction of the active-avoidance reflex ($p < 0.01$) (Fig. 22). In combination with nialamide, the extinction was facilitated ($p < 0.05$), as in animals treated with nialamide alone.

The effects of these two doses of corticosteroids were tested on the passive-avoidance behaviour. The method has been described in detail in earlier

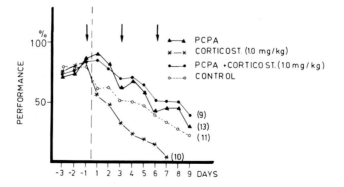

FIG. 21. Effect of 1.0 mg/kg corticosterone on extinction of active-avoidance reflex in PCPA-pretreated animals.

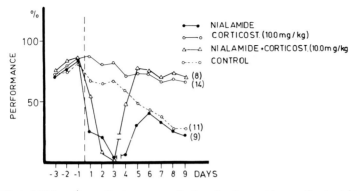

FIG. 22. Effect of 10.0 mg/kg corticosterone on extinction of active-avoidance reflex in nialamide-pre-treated animals.

papers (26,32). Briefly, the avoidance behaviour was investigated in water-deprived animals by placing the animals in a box divided into two compartments, a dark and a light one. The dark compartment contained a drinking tube. The animal had learned to drink in the dark compartment for 4 days. On the fifth day of training the animal received an electric shock through the drinking tube. The number of drinking attempts was counted; on day 6 the time to return to the drinking tube was measured, and this was termed the "passive-avoidance latency."

One milligram per kilogram corticosterone decreased ($p < 0.05$) the number of drinking attempts, whereas 10.0 mg/kg corticosterone increased it ($p < 0.01$) (Fig. 23). The passive-avoidance latency lengthened ($p < 0.05$) after 1.0 mg/kg, whereas it shortened after 10.0 mg/kg corticosterone ($p < 0.05$).

In the same passive-avoidance situation, PCPA treatment counteracted ($p < 0.05$) the effects of 1.0 mg/kg corticosterone on the drinking attempts and on the avoidance latency (Fig. 24).

Nialamide antagonized the effects of 10.0 mg/kg corticosterone on the drinking attempts and the avoidance latency ($p < 0.01$) (Fig. 25).

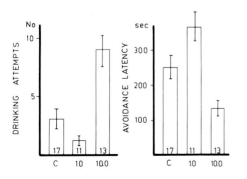

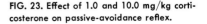

FIG. 23. Effect of 1.0 and 10.0 mg/kg corticosterone on passive-avoidance reflex.

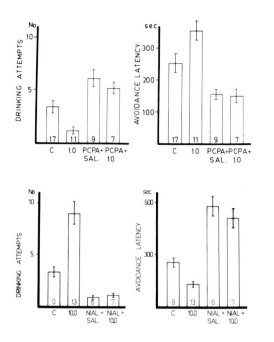

FIG. 24. Effect of 1.0 mg/kg corticosterone on passive-avoidance reflex in PCPA-pretreated animals.

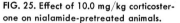

FIG. 25. Effect of 10.0 mg/kg corticosterone on nialamide-pretreated animals.

The effects of corticosterone on different patterns of avoidance behaviour (active and passive) are related to the changes caused in the central nervous serotoninergic metabolism by the hormone treatment. One milligram per kilogram corticosterone increased the hypothalamic and mesencephalic 5-HT levels and turnovers, facilitated the avoidance extinction, and improved the fear-versus-thirst-motivated passive-avoidance behaviour. Increasing the serotoninergic activity by monoamine oxidase inhibitors (28,30,31,55) or by electrical stimulation of the serotoninergic perikarya at the mesencephalic level (raphe stimulation) (24) caused identical or similar behavioural effects. Ten milligram per kilogram corticosterone decreased the hypothalamic and mesencephalic 5-HT levels and turnovers, delayed the extinction of the avoidance reflex, and impaired the passive-avoidance behaviour. Similar behavioural changes were observed following PCPA administration (30,55), by blockade of the serotoninergic receptors (24,25,33), or by lesion of the raphe system (31).

This conception was further corroborated by the observation that, when the 5-HT metabolism was influenced by drugs interfering with the transmitter metabolism, the behavioural action of corticosterone could also be modified.

CONCLUSION

The information presented indicates that the effects of anterior and posterior pituitary hormones and of adrenocortical steroids on certain behavioural patterns might be mediated by different mechanisms (catecholaminergic and indoleaminergic) in various brain structures.

ACKNOWLEDGMENT

This work has been supported by the Scientific Research Council, Ministry of Health, Hungary (4–08–0302–03–0/T).

REFERENCES

1. Ader, R., and de Wied, D. (1972): Effects of lysine vasopressin on passive avoidance learning. *Psychon. Sci.,* 29:46–48.
2. Bohus, B., Hendrickx, H. H. L., Van Kolfschoten, A. A., and Krediet, T. G. (1975): Effect of ACTH$^{4-10}$ on copulatory and sexually motivated approach behavior in the male rat. In: *Sexual Behavior: Pharmacology and Biochemistry,* edited by M. Sandler, and G. L. Gessa, pp. 269–275. Raven Press, New York.
3. Bohus, B., and Lissák, K. (1968): Adrenocortical hormones and avoidance behaviour of rats. *Int. J. Neuropharm.,* 7:301–306.
4. Bohus, B., Nyakas, C., and Endröczi, E. (1968): Effects of adrenocorticotrophic hormone on avoidance behaviour of intact and adrenalectomized rats. *Int. J. Neuropharm.,* 7:307–314.
5. Bohus, G., Van Wimersma Greidanus, Tj. B., and de Wied, D. (1975): Behavioral and endocrine responses of rats with hereditary hypothalamic diabetes insipidus (Brattleboro strain). *Physiol. Behav.,* 14:609–615.
6. de Wied, D. (1966): Inhibitory effect of ACTH and related peptides on extinction of conditioned avoidance behavior. *Proc. Soc. Exp. Biol. Med.,* 122:28–32.
7. de Wied, D. (1967): Opposite effects of ACTH and glucocorticosteroids on extinction of conditioned avoidance behavior. In: *Proc. Second Int. Congr. Hormonal Steroids, Excerpta Medica Int. Congr. Ser.* No. 132, edited by L. Martini, F. Fraschini, and M. Motta, pp. 945–951. Excerpta Medica, Amsterdam.
8. de Wied, D., and Bohus, B. (1966): Long term and short term effect on retention of a conditioned avoidance response in rats by treatment with long acting pitressin or α-MSH. *Nature,* 212:1484–1486.
9. de Wied, D., Bohus, B., and Greven, H. M. (1968): Influence of pituitary and adrenocortical hormones on conditioned avoidance behavior in rats. In: *Endocrinology and Human Behavior,* edited by R. P. Michael, pp. 188–199. Oxford Univ. Press, Oxford.
10. de Wied, D., Bohus, B., and Van Wimersma Greidanus, Tj. B. (1975): Memory deficit in rats with hereditary diabetes insipidus. *Brain Res.,* 85:152–156.
11. de Wied, D., Bohus, B., and Van Wimersma Greidanus, Tj. B. (1976): The significance of vasopressin for pituitary ACTH release in conditioned emotional situations. In: *Cellular and Molecular Bases of Neuroendocrine Processes,* edited by E. Endröczi, pp. 547–553. Akadémiai Kiadó, Budapest.
12. de Wied, D., Bohus, B., Gispen, W. H., Urban, I., and Van Wimersma Greidanus, Tj. B. (1975): Pituitary peptides on motivational, learning and memory processes. In: *CNS and Behavioural Pharmacology, Vol. 3., Proc. Sixth Int. Congr. Pharmacology,* edited by M. Airaksinen, pp. 19–30. Finnish Pharmacological Society, Helsinki.
13. Endröczi, E. (1972): *Limbic System, Learning and Pituitary-Adrenal Function.* Akadémiai Kiadó, Budapest.
14. Endröczi, E., and Fekete, T. (1971): Thalami-cortical synchronization, habituation and hormone action. *Recent Developments of Neurobiology in Hungary. Vol. III,* edited by K. Lissák, pp. 115–131. Akadémiai Kiadó, Budapest.
15. Endröczi, E., Hraschek, A., Nyakas, C., and Szabó, G. (1976): Brain catechol-

amines and pituitary-adrenal function. In: *Cellular and Molecular Bases of Neuroendocrine Processes,* edited by E. Endröczi, pp. 607–618. Akadémiai Kiadó, Budapest.

16. Endröczi, E., Lissák, K., Fekete, T., and de Wied, D. (1970): Effects of ACTH on EEG habituation in human subjects. In: *Pituitary, Adrenal and the Brain, Progress in Brain Research, Vol. 32,* edited by D. de Wied and J. A. W. M. Weijnen, pp. 254–263. Elsevier, Amsterdam.

17. Fibiger, H. C., Robert, D. C. S. and Price, M. T. C. (1975): The role of telencephalic noradrenaline in learning and memory. In: *6-Hydroxydopamine as a Denervation Tool in Catecholamine Research. Chemical Tools in Catecholamine Research, Vol. 1,* edited by G. Jonsson, T. Malmfors, and C. Sachs, pp. 349–356. Elsevier, Amsterdam.

18. Finney, D. J. (editor) (1964): *Statistical Methods in Biological Assay.* Griffin, London.

19. Gray, J. A., Mayes, A. R., and Wilson, M. (1971): A barbiturate-like effect of adrenocorticotropic hormone on the partial reinforcement acquisition and extinction effects. *Neuropharmacology,* 10:223–230.

20. Guth, S., Levine, S., and Seward, J. P. (1971): Appetitive acquisition and extinction effects with exogenous ACTH. *Physiol. Behav.,* 7:195–200.

21. Hoffer, P. F. A., and Glaser, H. G. (1950): Effect of pituitary adrenocorticotrophic hormone (ACTH) therapy. Electroencephalographic and neuropsychiatric changes of fifteen patients. *JAMA,* 143:620–629.

22. Hökfelt, T., and Fuxe, K. (1972): On the morphology and the neuroendocrine role of hypothalamic catecholamine neurons. In: *Brain-Endocrine Interaction. Median Eminence: Structure and Function,* (International Symposium, Munich, 1971) edited by K. M. Knigge, D. E. Scott, and A. Weindl, pp. 181–223. Karger, Basel.

23. Koe, B. K., and Weissman, A. (1966): P-Chlorophenylalanine a specific depletor of brain serotonin. *J. Pharmacol. Exp. Ther.,* 154:499–516.

24. Kovács, G. L., and Telegdy, G. (1976): Inhibitory effect of midbrain raphe stimulation on the maintenance of an active avoidance reflex. *Pharmacol. Biochem. Behav.,* 5:709–711.

25. Kovács, G. L., and Telegdy, G. (1977): Indoleamines and behaviour. The possible role of serotoninergic mechanisms in the pituitary-adrenocortical hormone-induced behavioural action. In: *Recent Development of Neurobiology in Hungary,* edited by K. Lissák. Akadémiai Kiadó, Budapest. (*In press.*)

26. Kovács, G. L., Gajári, I., Telegdy, G., and Lissák, K. (1977): Effect of melatonin and pinealectomy on avoidance and exploratory activity in the rat. *Physiol. Behav.,* 13:349–355.

27. Kovács, G. L., Kishonti, J., Lissák, K., and Telegdy, G. (1976): Dose-dependent dual effect of corticosterone on cerebral 5-hydroxytryptamine metabolism. *Neurochemical Res.,* 2:311–322.

28. Kovács, G. L., Telegdy, G., and Lissák, K. (1975): The role of monoamines in avoidance behavior in rats. *Brain Res.,* 85:198–199.

29. Kovács, G. L., Telegdy, G., and Lissák, K. (1977): Possible role of serotonin in corticosterone-induced behavioural action. *VIth Int. Congr. Pharmacology,* Helsinki (Abstr. No. 376). Pergamon Press., Oxford-New York.

30. Kovács, G. L., Telegdy, G., and Lissák, K. (1975): The effect of drug-induced changes of brain monoamines on avoidance behaviour and open-field activity. *Acta Physiol. Acad. Sci. Hung.,* 26:331–339.

31. Kovács, G. L., Telegdy, G., and Lissák, K. (1976): 5-Hydroxytryptamine and the mediation of pituitary-adrenocortical hormones in the extinction of active avoidance behaviour. *Psychoneuroendocrinology,* 1:219–230.

32. Kovács, G. L., Telegdy, G., and Lissák, K. (1977): Dose-dependent action of corticosteroids on brain serotonin content and on passive avoidance behavior. *Horm. Behav.,* 8:155–165.

33. Kovács, G. L., Telegdy, G., and Lissák, K. (1977): The effect of stress on avoidance behaviour and on brain serotonin metabolism in rats. In: *Proc. Acad. Sci. GDR,* edited by H. J. Matthies. (*In press.*)

34. Kovács, G. L., Vécsei, L., Szabó, G., and Telegdy, G. (1977): The involvement of

catecholaminergic mechanisms in the behavioural action of vasopressin. *Neurosci. Lett.,* 5:337–366.
35. Leonard, B. L. (1974): The effect of two synthetic ACTH analogues on the metabolism of biogenic amines in the rat brain. *Arch. Int. Pharmacodyn. Ther.,* 207:242–253.
36. Leonard, B. E., Ramaekers, F., and Rigter, H. (1975): Effects of adrenocorticotrophin-(4–10)-heptapeptide on changes in brain monoamine metabolism associated with retrograde amnesia in the rat. *Biochem. Soc. Trans.,* 3:113–115.
37. Levine, S., and Jones, L. E. (1965): Adrenocorticotrophic hormone (ACTH) and passive avoidance learning. *J. Comp. Physiol. Psychol.,* 59:357–360.
38. Levitt, M., Spector, S., Sjoerdsma, A., and Udenfriend, S. (1965): Elucidation of the rate limiting step in norepinephrine biosynthesis in the perfused guinea pig heart. *J. Pharmacol. Exp. Ther.,* 148:1–8.
39. Lissák, K., Kovács, G. L., and Telegdy, G. (1977): Involvement of serotoninergic system in mediation of corticosteroid action on avoidance behaviour. (In Russian.) In: *Novoe o Gormonah i Mehanisme ih Dejstvijah,* edited by M. F. Gulij, R. E. Kaveckij, P. G. Kostuk, K. P. Zak, and R. C. Filatova, pp. 180–192. Naukova Dumka, Kiev.
40. Nagatsu, J., Levitt, M., and Udenfriend, S. (1964): Tyrosine hydroxylase. *J. Biol. Chem.,* 239:2910–2917.
41. Rigter, H., and Van Riezen, H. (1975): Anti-amnestic effect of ACTH₄₋₁₀: Its independence of the nature of the amnestic agent and the behavioral test. *Physiol. Behav.,* 14:563–566.
42. Rigter H., Van Riezen, J., and de Wied, D. (1974): The effects of ACTH- and vasopressin-analogues on CO₂-induced retrograde amnesia in rats. *Physiol. Behav.,* 13:381–388.
43. Sandman, C. A., George, J. M., Nolan, J. D., Van Riezen, H., and Kastin, A. J. (1975): Enhancement of attention in man with ACTH/MSH 4–10. *Physiol. Behav.,* 15:427–431.
44. Schulz, H., Kovács, G. L., and Telegdy, G. (1974): Effect of physiological doses of vasopressin and oxytocin on avoidance and exploratory behaviour in rats. *Acta Physiol. Acad. Sci. Hung.,* 45:211–215.
45. Schulz, H., Kovács, G. L., and Telegdy, G. (1976): The effect of vasopressin and oxytocin on avoidance behaviour in rats. In: *Cellular and Molecular Bases of Neuroendocrine Processes,* edited by E. Endroczi, pp. 555–564. Akadémiai Kiadó, Budapest.
46. Schulz, H., Unger, H., and Schwarzberg, H. (1973): Einfluss von intraventrikulär applizierter Glutaminsäure und Oxytocin auf die Impulsentladungsrate hypothalamischer Neuronengebiete. *Acta Biol. Med. Ger.,* 30:197–202.
47. Schulz, H., Unger, H., Schwarzberg, H., Pommrich, G., and Stolze, R. (1971): Neuronenaktivität hypothalamischer Kerngebiete non Kaninchen nach intraventrikulärer Applikation von Vasopressin und Oxytocin. *Experientia,* 27:1482.
48. Schwarzberg, H., and Unger, H. (1970): Anderung der Reaktionszeit von Ratten nach Applikation von Vasopressin, Oxytocin und Na-thiglykolat. *Acta Biol. Med. Ger.,* 24:507–516.
49. Schwarzberg, H., Hartman, G., Kovács, G. L., and Telegdy, G. (1976): The effect of intraventricular administration of oxytocin and vasopressin on self-stimulation in rats. *Acta Physiol. Acad. Sci. Hung.,* 47:127–131.
50. Shellenberger, M. K., and Gordon, J. H. (1971): A rapid simplified procedure for simultaneous assay of norepinephrine, dopamine, and 5-hydroxytryptamine from discrete brain areas. *Anal. Biochem.,* 39:356–372.
51. Spector, S., Sjoerdsma, A., and Udenfriend, S. (1965): Blockade of endogenous norepinephrine synthesis by alpha-meth-tyrosine, an inhibitor of tyrosine hydroxylase. *J. Pharmacol. Exp. Ther.,* 147:86–102.
52. Telegdy, G., and Vermes, I. (1975): Effect of adrenocortical hormones on activity of the serotoninergic system in limbic structures in rats. *Neuroendocrinology,* 18: 16–26.
53. Telegdy, G., Kovács, G. L., and Lissák, K. (1975): Role of serotonin in corticosterone-induced behavioural action. *Acta Endocrinol. [Suppl.] (Kbh),* 199:188.

54. Telegdy, G., Hadnagy, J., and Lissák, K. (1968): The effect of gonads on conditioned avoidance behaviour of rats. *Acta Physiol. Acad. Sci. Hung.,* 33:439–446.
55. Telegdy, G., Vermes, I., and Kovács, G. L. (1966): Effect of drug-induced changes of brain monoamines on neuroendocrine and behavioral processes. In: *Symp. Pharmacology of Catecholaminergic and Serotoninergic Mechanisms, Vol. 3,* edited by J. Knoll, pp. 101–105. Akadémiai Kiadó, Budapest.
56. Tozer, T. N., Neff, N. H., and Brodie, B. B. (1966): Application of steady-state kinetics to the synthesis rate and turnover time of serotonin in the brain of normal and reserpine-treated rats. *J. Pharmacol. Exp. Ther.,* 153:177–182.
57. Van Wimersma Greidanus, Tj. B., Bohus, B., and de Wied (1975): The role of vasopressin in memory processes. In: *Hormones, Homeostasis and the Brain, Progress in Brain Research, Vol. 42,* edited by W. H. Gispen, Tj. B. Van Wimersma Greidanus, B. Bohus, and D. de Wied, pp. 135–141. Elsevier, Amsterdam.
58. Vermes, I., Telegdy, G., and Lissák, K. (1973): Correlation between hypothalamic serotonin content and adrenal function during acute stress: Effect of adrenal corticosteroids on hypothalamic serotonin content. *Acta Physiol. Acad. Sci. Hung.,* 43:33–42.
59. Versteeg, D. H. G. (1973): Effect of two ACTH-analogs on noradrenaline metabolism in rat brain. *Brain Res.,* 49:483–485.
60. Versteeg, D. H. G., and Wurtman, R. J. (1975): Effect of $ACTH_{4-10}$ on the rate of synthesis of (H^3) catecholamines in the brains of intact, hypophysectomized and adrenalectomized rats. *Brain Res.,* 93:552–557.
61. Versteeg, D. H. G., Gispen, W. H., Schotman, P., Witter, A., and de Wied, D. (1972): Hypophysectomy and rat brain metabolism: Effects of synthetic ACTH analogs. *Adv. Biochem. Psychopharmacol.,* 6:219–239.
62. Wayne, H. L. (1954): Convulsive seizures complicating cortisone and ACTH therapy: Clinical and electroencephalographic observations. *J. Clin. Endocrinol. Metab.,* 14:1039–1045.
63. Wiegant, V. M., Cools, A. R., and Gispen, W. H. (1977): ACTH-induced excessive grooming involves brain dopamine. *Eur. J. Pharmacol.,* 41:343–346.
64. Zenker, N., and Bernstein, E. (1958): The estimation of small amounts of corticosterone in rat plasma. *J. Biol. Chem.,* 231:695–701.

Brain Mechanisms in Memory and Learning:
From the Single Neuron to Man,
edited by M. A. B. Brazier.
Raven Press, New York © 1979.

Action of Hyoscine on Verbal Learning in Man: Evidence for a Cholinergic Link in the Transition from Primary to Secondary Memory?

T. J. Crow

Division of Psychiatry, Clinical Research Centre, Northwick Park Hospital, Harrow, London HA1 3UJ, England

The possible selectivity of action of hyoscine (scopolamine) on memory processes was first suggested by clinical observation. Patients premedicated with hyoscine have increased difficulty in estimating postoperative duration of consciousness (7) and are more often unable to recall information presented before anaesthesia than patients premedicated with atropine (6). Pandit and Dundee (10) found partial or complete amnesia for the details of the preoperative period in 14% of patients premedicated with hyoscine, 0.4 mg, and 24% of patients receiving diazepam, 10 mg, combined with hyoscine, 0.4 mg.

These learning deficits have been validated in experimental studies. Safer and Allen (13) found registration of new information (assessed as immediate recall) to be only mildly impaired following hyoscine, 10 μg/kg, whereas after a 20-sec delay, there was gross impairment of recall. A comparison (3) of hyoscine (scopolamine) with methscopolamine, which does not enter the CNS, established deficits of memory storage and cognitive nonmemory tasks following 1 mg of hyoscine but no deficit of immediate memory. The pattern of cognitive and memory defects following hyoscine resembled that seen in a group of aged subjects. Other experiments (4,12) have established that the effects of hyoscine are primarily on the acquisition of new information rather than its retrieval from a memory store.

The following two experiments were conducted to validate the selectivity of hyoscine on human learning processes and to attempt to determine the point at which the drug exerts its effect, using the free-recall learning test devised by Glanzer and Cunitz (5). In this test, the subjects were presented with lists of 10 words, at a rate of one word/3 sec, and were asked to recall these words in any order, either immediately after presentation (immediate recall) or after approximately 60 sec of an interpolated task (delayed recall). When tested in this way, subjects recall the later words in the immediate recall condition much more frequently than the earlier words (the "recency effect"), but there is no preferential recall of later words in the delayed recall condition. It is, therefore, suggested (5) that the recency effect reflects the operation of a short-term memory mechanism and that this can be separated from the longer-term memory processes that are seen in the findings on the earlier part of the immediate recall and in the delayed-recall condition. In the 60-sec delay before recall in the latter condition, subjects were presented with random letter sequences at a rate of one letter/sec and were asked to record alphabetical sequences (e.g., ab, st, mn, etc). This task (the scanning task) had two functions—to prevent rehearsal and to provide a measure of information-processing ability with a minimal learning component.

EXPERIMENT 1 (1)

Twelve subjects (aged 19 to 23 years) were submitted to a battery of tests on three occasions, receiving on each occasion either hyoscine, 0.4 mg, atropine, 0.6 mg, or sodium chloride injection, 1 ml, in a balanced design. As well as the free-recall and scanning tasks referred to above, they were also required to complete a simple number-colour association learning task.

The results (Table 1) demonstrate significant deficits on each of the learning tasks (immediate and delayed recall and number-colour association) following hyoscine but not atropine, but no significant deficits following either drug on the information-processing (scanning) task. An analysis of results with respect to order of presentation of words within the 10-word lists (Fig. 1) reveals that there is little effect of hyoscine on that part of the curve attributed to short-term memory (the recency effect) but that the amnestic influence of the drug is seen on the earlier part of the immediate-recall curve, and uniformly on the delayed-recall curve.

The results, therefore, confirm the selectivity of hyoscine for learning processes and suggest that this action is on the transition from short- to long-term memory, or on retrieval from long-term memory, and not on short-term acquisition or retrieval processes. The relative ineffectiveness of atropine in these experiments is consistent with the lower incidence of amnesia following

TABLE 1. *Effects of saline, hyoscine, and atropine on human learning*

	Immediate recall	Delayed recall	Number-colour associations	Scanning task
Maximum score	50	50	7	25
	Mean correct responses $\pm$ 1 SEM			
Saline (1 ml)	27.9 $\pm$ 1.6	14.3 $\pm$ 1.3	7 $\pm$ 0	22.3 $\pm$ 1.2
Hyoscine (0.4 mg)	24.0 $\pm$ 1.3[a]	10.2 $\pm$ 1.3[b]	5.9 $\pm$ 0.5[a]	20.5 $\pm$ 1.1
Atropine (0.6 mg)	25.9 $\pm$ 1.3	14.1 $\pm$ 1.7	6.9 $\pm$ 0.1	20.3 $\pm$ 1.2

[a] $0.05 > p > 0.01$.
[b] $0.001 > p$ vs saline.

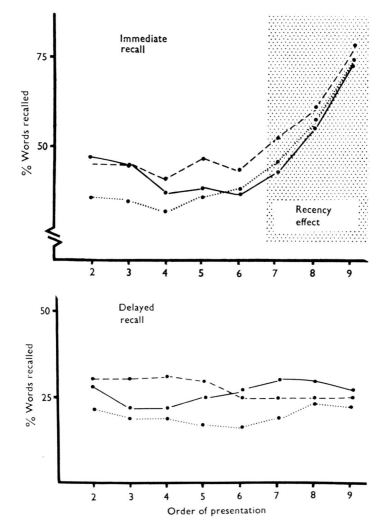

FIG. 1. An analysis of the free-recall test results by order of presentation of words within the 10-word list (running totals, averaged over three positions-at-a-time). – – – –, Saline; ———, atropine, 0.6 mg; . . . ., hyoscine, 0.4 mg (experiment 1).

atropine as premedication (6) and may merely reflect the fact that central effects are generally seen at higher dose levels of atropine than of hyoscine (8).

EXPERIMENT 2 (2)

To determine whether the effects of hyoscine on learning are specific to this drug, the effects of hyoscine on free-recall learning were compared with those of amylobarbitone, diazepam, and chlorpromazine, as representatives of other classes of depressant compound. Drugs were administered 5 min

TABLE 2. Specificity of drug effects on human learning

	Maximum score	Saline	Chlorpromazine (12.5 or 25 mg)	Amylobarbitone (125 mg)	Diazepam (5 mg)	Hyoscine (0.4 mg)
Verbal learning						
Immediate recall	50	32.0 ± 1.2	[a]25.3 ± 1.8	28.6 ± 2.2	27.9 ± 2.0	27.9 ± 2.5
Delayed recall	50	16.1 ± 2.0	[a]8.6 ± 1.3	15.3 ± 2.9	14.0 ± 2.6	[b]10.6 ± 1.4
Scanning task	25	22.4 ± 1.6	[a]16.4 ± 1.4	[b]17.9 ± 1.3	20.4 ± 1.9	22.0 ± 1.5

[a] $p < 0.01$ for comparison with scores after saline.
[b] $p < 0.02$ for comparison with scores after saline.

before testing began, and the subjects (eight medical students aged between 19 and 23 years) recorded their pulse rates at fixed points in the test schedule. Subjective side effects and pulse observations suggested that the initial dose of chlorpromazine (25 mg) was exerting significant hypotensive effects and the dose was reduced to 12.5 mg after the first two sessions.

Even with the reduction the effects of chlorpromazine on test performance were substantial and not confined to the learning task (Table 2). By contrast, the effects of diazepam (5 mg) were insignificant. There was, however, an interesting contrast between amylobarbitone (125 mg) and hyoscine, (0.4 mg) in that the former drug significantly impaired performance on the scanning task without significantly impairing free-recall learning, whereas hyoscine did not affect scanning task performance, but significantly impaired delayed-recall learning. This contrast is particularly apparent when the effects of these two drugs are examined on the order of presentation curves in immediate and delayed recall (Figs. 2 and 3).

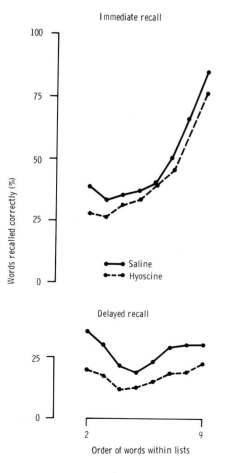

FIG. 2. Analysis of the free-recall test results by order of presentation of words within the 10-word list for hyoscine, 0.4 mg (experiment 2).

The results, therefore, confirm those of experiment 1 concerning the selectivity of the action of hyoscine on learning processes and suggest that this action is not shared by some other types of central depressant. There is some evidence (e.g., 11) that diazepam exerts amnesic effects similar to those seen following hyoscine. Since only one dose (5 mg) was used in the present study, it cannot be excluded that a similar pattern of impairments would be seen after a higher dose of diazepam. It is also possible that a smaller dose of chlorpromazine would exert lesser effects on information processing than on learning, although this seems unlikely in view of the finding of Mirsky and Kornetsky (9) on the selectivity of action of chlorpromazine on vigilance task performance. The differential actions of hyoscine and amylobarbitone have, however, been established by the results of experiment 2, and it is apparent that the amnesic effects of the former drug cannot be explained as being secondary to sedation. On the contrary, it appears that hyoscine exerts specific effects on learning processes.

The findings suggest that hyoscine impairs the transition from short-term

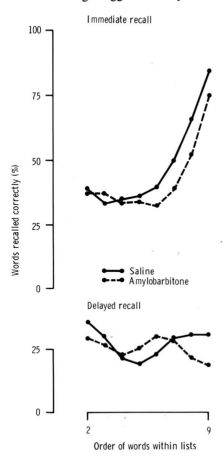

FIG. 3. Analysis of the free-recall test results by order of presentation of words within the 10-word list for amylobarbitone, 125 mg (experiment 2).

(or primary) memory (i.e., a store with a life of approximately 6 to 8 sec) to a longer-term store. An action on retrieval from long-term storage could also explain the present findings. However, this interpretation is rendered less plausible by the findings of Ghoneim and Mewalt (4) and Petersen (12), who both found that retrieval processes were much less affected by hyoscine than was the process of acquisition.

SUMMARY

The centrally acting anticholinergic agent hyoscine (scopolamine) exerts a selective effect on learning processes in man. When examined in a free-recall learning situation, this action occurs on long-term rather than short-term memory processes and can be dissociated from any sedative properties the drug may have. Hyoscine may impair the transition from short- to long-term memory storage, and therefore it is suggested there is a cholinergic link in this process.

REFERENCES

1. Crow, T. J., and Grove-White, I. G. (1973): An analysis of the learning deficit following hyoscine administration to man. *Br. J. Pharmacol.,* 49:322–327.
2. Crow, T. J., Grove-White, I. G., and Ross, D. G. (1976): The specificity of the action of hyoscine on human learning. *Br. J. Clin. Pharmacol.,* 2:367–368P.
3. Drachman, D. A., and Leavitt, J. (1974): Human memory and the cholinergic system. A relationship to ageing? *Arch. Neurol.,* 30:113–121.
4. Ghoneim, M. M., and Mewalt, S. P. (1975): Effects of diazepam and scopolamine on storage, retrieval and organisational processes in memory. *Psychopharmacologia,* 44:257–262.
5. Glanzer, M., and Cunitz, A. R. (1966): Two storage mechanisms in free recall. *J. Verb. Learn. Verb. Behav.,* 5:351–360.
6. Hardy, T. K., and Wakely, D. (1962): The amnesic properties of hyoscine and atropine in pre-anaesthetic medication. *Anaesthesia,* 17:331–336.
7. Lambrechts, W., and Parkhouse, J. (1961): Pre-operative amnesia. *Br. J. Anaesth.,* 33:397–404.
8. Longo, V. G. (1966): Behavioural and electroencephalographic effects of atropine and related compounds. *Pharmacol. Rev.,* 18:965–996.
9. Mirsky, A. F., and Kornetsky, C. (1964): On the dissimilar effects of drugs on the digit symbol substitution and continuous performance tests. *Psychopharmacologia,* 5:161–177.
10. Pandit, S. K., and Dundee, J. W. (1970): Pre-operative amnesia. *Anaesthesia,* 25:493–499.
11. Pandit, S. K., Dundee, J. W., and Keilty, S. R. (1971): Amnesia studies with intravenous premedication. *Anaesthesia,* 26:421–428.
12. Petersen, R. C. (1977): Scopolamine induced learning failures in man. *Psychopharmacology,* 52:283–289.
13. Safer, D. J., and Allen, R. P. (1971): The central effects of scopolamine in man. *Biol. Psychiatry,* 3:347–355.

Brain Mechanisms in Memory and Learning:
From the Single Neuron to Man,
edited by M. A. B. Brazier.
Raven Press, New York © 1979.

Hypoxia-Induced Retrograde Amnesia

H. Flohr

University of Bremen, 2800 Bremen 33, Federal Republic of Germany

Hypoxia is regarded as an effective amnestic agent. This fact is claimed to be an essential indication of the correctness of the so-called *consolidation hypothesis.* An examination of the data available at present on hypoxia-induced retrograde amnesia shows, however, that these suppositions are controversial:

1. It has not been established beyond doubt whether short periods of hypoxia of the central nervous system (CNS) really cause retrograde amnesia.

2. If this—as it appears from several investigations—is the case, it remains uncertain which of the presently discussed interpretations of the phenomenon of retrograde amnesia are possible on the basis of the actual findings.

It is possible that there is a close connection between both questions. An examination of the relevant publications shows that the number of investigations where positive amnestic effects are described is nearly the same as of those investigations where no amnesia could be observed. Positive results were obtained by Hayes (24), Ransmeier and Gerard (45), Thompson and Pryer (53), Thompson (52), Ledwith (28), Galluscio and Young (19), Giurgea et al. (21), Sara (46,47), Sara and Lefevre (48,49), Giurgea (20), D'Andrea and Kesner (11), David-Remacle (12), Anderson and Robichaud (2), and Flohr et al. (17), whereas Bryant and Thompson (7), Nielson et al. (38,39), Baldwin and Soltysik (3–5), Taber and Banuazizi (51), Vacher et al. (54), and Cherkin (10) arrived at negative results. The reasons for these differences are not clear. Both positive and negative results were found in different species as well as in very different models of learning. Hypoxic conditions have been produced by such techniques as chest compression (24), altitude simulation (52,53), cerebral ischemia (3–5,39), or exposure to $O_2:N_2$ mixtures with subnormal oxygen content (2,10,17,18). It seems impossible that all negative results can be attributed to insufficient cellular hypoxia in the CNS. In some investigations (3–5), this was thoroughly checked. Possibly the environmental conditions of training and treatment or the training–treatment interval chosen in the different investigations can explain some of these discrepancies.

In the explanation of the phenomenon retrograde amnesia, there are two groups of hypotheses that play a role at present. Since the publication of Duncan's study (15) on the retroactive effects of electroshock on learning, the *consolidation hypothesis,* as formulated by Müller and Pilzecker (37), has played an important part in most theories about the nature of the engram. It says that the information to be stored is retained in different stores and is transferred in a time-dependent process from one or more labile transitory traces to a permanent and stable one (33,34). This supposition is supported by psychological experience and by numerous observations that the storing process, as long as labile phases are existent, can be modified (i.e., inhibited or enhanced) by experimental procedures that modify neuronal activity in some way. Retrograde amnesia is explained as a partial or total disruption of the consolidation process.

The so-called *retrieval hypothesis,* on the other hand, supposes that the actual fixation process is of relatively short duration, leading to a stable structure in fractions of a second. It is suggested that it is not the fixation process that is disturbed by amnestic treatments, but rather retrieval processes, i.e., processes through which the stored information is read out and gains influence over subsequent behaviour. There exist several modifications of this hypothesis, e.g., those proposed by Weiskrantz (55), Nielson (39), and Miller and Springer (35).

Both theories lead to different predictions on the characteristics of retrograde amnesia. These predictions concern the permanence of the amnesia, the time dependence of the effects of amnestic treatments, and the influence of pre- or posttraining situations or manipulations on the degree of amnesia (9,34,35).

The differing consequences of these two theories of retrograde amnesia have so far been discussed mostly with reference to amnesia induced by electroconvulsive shock (ECS). With a few exceptions (12,46,47), the results obtained with other amnestic agents including hypoxia have hardly played a part in this discussion. This is, however, problematic. A crucial point in the discussion of the consolidation hypothesis and its alternatives is the definition of the expressions "stable" and "labile." In the typical amnesia experiment, these terms are defined only operationally by the amnestic agent (22). Which physicochemical or physiological characteristics of the storage process are actually recognized and hence the real meaning of "stable" and "labile" remains vague. This is especially true for ECS, which has numerous direct and indirect, immediate and delayed, effects on neuronal activity that may be different in different experimental situations. With hypoxia as an amnestic agent, however, it seems possible to define certain —admittedly very general—*physical* characteristics of the engram. Information storage in the CNS thermodynamically means the formation of time-independent states of low entropy. In principle, in the CNS, two such states are possible: (a) a *steady state,* the existence of which is dependent on a permanent supply of free energy and (b) *metastable states,* which are surrounded by high-activation energy barriers and can persist without a continuous flow of free energy. These different states differ from each other in their energy requirements and hence in their dependence on cerebral energy metabolism. Information kept in a steady-state type of trace should be erased by a short interruption of energy supply; metastable traces should survive this. Experimentally induced cerebral hypoxia should, therefore, help to identify the nature of the trace (or traces) from a thermodynamic point of view and to check predictions and conjectures deduced from the multitrace theories and their alternatives sketched above on the nature of retrograde amnesia.

This chapter gives a review of some recent experimental studies on hypoxia as an amnestic agent and examines the results under this aspect.

TIME DEPENDENCE OF HYPOXIC EFFECTS

The basic assumption of the consolidation hypothesis is that the permanent trace emerges gradually from a labile one. The source of amnesia is the disruption of this process. Since the degree of consolidation is a function of time, it follows that the amnesic effects depend on the time interval between training and treatment; memory is most vulnerable immediately after the information input, but becomes resistant to the same interference after some period of time. In the interval between these two phases, a gradient in the amnestic effects is to be expected with an increase in memory failure as the interval between information input and the administration of the amnestic agent decreases (25,33,37).

The "impaired retrieval" hypothesis of retrograde amnesia proceeds from the idea that the information is stored in physicochemical changes that have a metastable character within very short periods, e.g., in fractions of seconds (29–31,35,36). This would mean that the consolidation is completed before a sufficient degree of cellular hypoxia in the CNS can be produced by the various techniques. In this case hypoxia can remain ineffective. In fact, a number of investigators, as shown, arrive at negative results of this kind. The conditions under which they were obtained deserve special consideration. The negative results often were obtained with very brief training–treatment intervals, whereas it seems that most of the positive results were obtained after relatively long training–treatment intervals. In the careful investigations of Baldwin and Soltysik (3–5), it was shown that an experimental cerebral ischemia starting directly after training, lasting about 1.5 min, and resulting in a reversible cessation of the cortical and subcortical electroencephalogram did not prevent the acquisition of a classic conditioned response in goats. The authors came to the conclusion that the results preclude a longer labile phase and that "a consolidation of the learning had occurred in less than 65 seconds after each learning trial." Vacher et al., (54) working with a one-trial avoidance task, were not able to produce an amnesia with a controlled hypoxia beginning directly after the training. Similarly to Baldwin and Soltysik, they arrived at the conclusion that it is impossible to produce cellular hypoxia of the brain with sufficient rapidity to interfere with consolidation processes. In some investigations with positive results, the training–treatment intervals were relatively long, e.g., in those of Ledwith (28) and Giurgea et al. (21), where treatment began after a multitrial learning procedure, of Ransmeier and Gerard (45), where hypoxia was administered "some minutes" after the training, and of Hayes (24), where the interval was 1 hr. In the decompression technique used by Thompson and Pryer (53), the final value was reached in about 104 sec. In a study of Sara and Lefevre (48), both immediate and delayed hypoxia were effective, but the retention deficit was more pronounced in the latter technique. Flohr et al. (17,18) found that exposure to 8% O_2 immediately after a one-trial avoidance test did not result in a significant retrograde amnesia, whereas exposure after training–treatment intervals of 10 to 30 min did result in a marked amnesia. Very similar results were observed by Anderson and Robichaud (2) in the albino (but not in the hooded) rat.

Figure 1A and B show the results of an attempt to determine the influence of the training–treatment interval.

The investigations were carried out on 1,700 albino mice. The animals were, at the time of the experiments, 3 months old. They were kept in groups of 20 and taken to the laboratory 3 to 4 days before the experiments began.

The animals were trained on a one-trial passive-avoidance task, according to Madsen and McGaugh (32). The apparatus consisted of a perspex box (49 × 27.5 × 26 cm) in the centre of which was a platform (5.5 × 3.5 cm), the height of which was adjustable from 17 to 2.5 cm above the floor of the cage. The floor consisted of a shock grid that was connected to a Lehigh Valley solid-state shocker with scrambler.

The animals were placed on the raised platform that, after approximately 2 sec, was slowly lowered to a height of 2.5 cm above the grid. If the animal left the platform, a footshock (1 mA) could be given. Animals who did not move off within 10 sec were removed from the apparatus and discarded. Animals stepping off within the criterion time after receiving a footshock were removed and either returned to their home cages or subjected to treatment as described below. A retention test was run after 24 hr.

The animals were divided into six groups. The animals of group 1 received a footshock but no subsequent treatment (FSNT). The animals of group 4 received no footshock and no treatment (NFSNT). The animals of the group 2 (FSH) were subjected to periods of 5 min of hypoxia (8% O_2 in N_2) at different time intervals (0, 5, 10, 15, 30, 45, 60, 75, 210, and 420 min). The exposure to the hypoxic gas mixture was carried out in small perspex cages. The waiting time between footshock and treatment in these

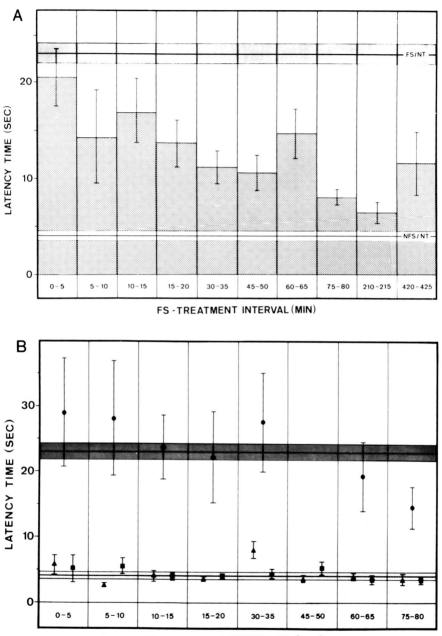

FIG. 1. Influence of training–treatment interval on hypoxia-induced retrograde amnesia. A: Mean retest latencies (and standard error) for animals subjected to hypoxia (8% O$_2$ in N$_2$) after training at different intervals (group 2). The upper and lower horizontal lines indicate latencies (and standard error) of control groups 1 and 4. B: Mean retest latencies for the control groups 3 (●), 6 (▲), and 5 (■). The horizontal lines indicate the values of groups 1 and 4.

groups was spent in cages similar to the home cages. After the treatment the animals were returned to their home cages. The animals of group 3 were subjected to exactly the same procedure, but the exposure was conducted with room air (FS AIR). The animals of group 5 received no footshock, but were subsequently treated by hypoxia at the same intervals as in group 2

TABLE 1. *Treatment of the experimental groups*

Group	N^a	Procedure	Training–treatment interval (min)	Training– retention test interval (hr)
1.	513	FSNT		24
2.1	37	FSH (8% O_2 in N_2; 5 min)	0	24
2.2	27	FSH	5	24
2.3	39	FSH	10	24
2.4	45	FSH	15	24
2.5	30	FSH	30	24
2.6	36	FSH	45	24
2.7	80	FSH	60	24
2.8	70	FSH	75	24
2.9	35	FSH	210	24
2.10	34	FSH	420	24
3.1	20	FS AIR (room air, 5 min)	0	24
3.2	10	FS AIR	5	24
3.3	23	FS AIR	10	24
3.4	14	FS AIR	15	24
3.5	16	FS AIR	30	24
3.6	21	FS AIR	60	24
3.7	32	FS AIR	75	24
4	62	NFS NT		24
5.1	34	NFSH (8% O_2 in N_2; 5 min)	0	24
5.2	34	NFSH	5	24
5.3	25	NFSH	10	24
5.4	74	NFSH	15	24
5.5	35	NFSH	30	24
5.6	39	NFSH	45	24
5.7	23	NFSH	60	24
5.8	33	NFSH	75	24
6.1	16	NFS AIR (room air, 5 min)	0	24
6.2	38	NFS AIR	5	24
6.3	23	NFS AIR	10	24
6.4	34	NFS AIR	15	24
6.5	62	NFS AIR	30	24
6.6	35	NFS AIR	45	24
6.7	20	NFS AIR	60	24
6.8	31	NFS AIR	75	24

^{a}N, number of animals tested.

(NFSH). The animals of group 6 received no footshock and were subsequently exposed to room air (NFS AIR) at the same intervals as in group 4.

Table 1 summarizes the treatment of the experimental groups.

As shown in Fig. 1A and B, hypoxia of 8% O_2 in N_2 for 5 min, which in itself has no aversive effect, causes considerable retention deficits if the exposure is carried out between 5 and 420 min after training. The difference of the latency times of the experimental and the corresponding control groups is significant in all cases (Wilcoxon test, 56,57). If the exposure is carried out immediately after training, no significant amnesia is to be observed.

The observed amnesia is not complete, i.e., the retention latencies of the amnestic groups are higher than those of the control groups. Within the vulnerable period of 5 to 420 min, there is no significant gradient in the amnestic effect of hypoxia; the retention deficit is independent of the training–treatment interval. As the training–retention test interval was constant (24 hr) in all experiments, it follows that the amnestic effect is also independent of the treatment–retention test interval.

If the degree of hypoxia is intensified, no principal change in the results is observed. The results, summarized in Fig. 2, were carried out in the same way as the experiments described above, with one exception, that the animals were exposed to 5.5% O_2 in N_2. The period of exposure was also 5 min in all experiments. It is of special interest that under the stronger hypoxia there is no significant amnesia with immediate exposure.

Figure 3 summarizes some experiments on the question whether the hy-

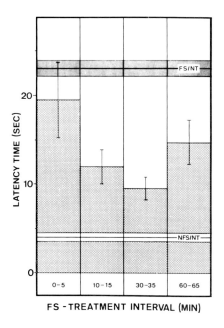

FIG. 2. Effect of severe hypoxia. Mice were trained on a one-trial avoidance task and subjected to hypoxia (5.5% O_2 in N_2) at training–treatment intervals of O (N = 35), 10 (N = 37), 30 (N = 40), and 60 (N = 80) min. The exposure time was 5 min. Retention was tested 24 hr after training.

poxia used in the investigations can produce an anterograde amnesia. In these experiments, hypoxia was administered 30 and 60 min before the training, which was the same as in the experiments described above. A retention test was run 24 hr after the training. As can be seen, no significant proactive effect of hypoxia is provable.

One essential conclusion of these findings seems to be that hypoxia is indeed an amnestic agent with retroactive but not proactive effects. With respect to its effectiveness, two phases are to be differentiated—an initial phase, occupying a period of 5 min after the information input during which hypoxia is ineffective, and a relatively long phase, lasting (at least) 7 hr during which hypoxia causes a retrograde amnesia. In this phase the effect is, however, not graded. Intensifying the degree of hypoxia does not alter the results.

As mentioned above, the finding of an initial hypoxia-resistant phase is possibly compatible with earlier findings, in which hypoxia immediately following the information input did not cause amnesia. It is also in substantial agreement with the results of Anderson and Robichaud (2). These authors compared the effects of ECS and hypoxia administered after one-trial passive-avoidance learning in two strains of rats. In the hooded rat, hypoxia was effective in producing retrograde amnesia when administered up to 40 min after training. In the albino rat, however, it was effective only when administered between 20 and 30 min after training.

It can be concluded from these results that metastable states can be reached in relatively short periods of time. For the vulnerable period thereafter, two explanations are possible: (a) the trace is again transformed into a labile one and (b) the observed amnesia is not caused by interference with a consolidation process.

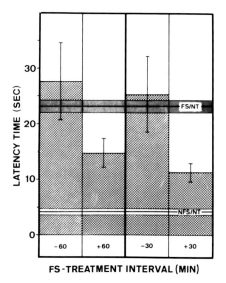

FIG. 3. Anterograde effects of hypoxia. Hypoxia (8% O_2 in N_2) was administered 30 and 60 min before (−) and after (+) a one-trial avoidance (step down) task. Exposure time was 5 min. The latencies were tested 24 hr after training. There is no significant anterograde effect.

PERMANENCE OF HYPOXIA-INDUCED RETROGRADE AMNESIA

A critical issue in the interpretation of retrograde amnesia concerns the permanence of the memory loss caused by the amnestic treatments. According to the conventional formulation of the consolidation hypothesis, amnesia should be permanent. A recovery would rather support the retrieval position (31,41,44,58). Figure 4 shows the results of an experiment in which the training–retention test interval was varied systematically. The animals received a single trial, as described above, and an exposure to hypoxia (8% O_2 in N_2) 10 min after training. With independent groups, retention tests were run after 45, 60, 210, and 360 min, 24 and 48 hr, and 1 and 4 weeks. There was no significant difference in the latencies between these groups. The same is valid for the control groups (footshock-no treatment and no footshock-no treatment).

This means that hypoxia-induced retrograde amnesia seems to be stable for weeks. A spontaneous change in the retention deficit was not observable in this experiment. These results are not fully in accordance with those of Sara (47), who found that the retention deficit depended on the interval between treatment and retention test. In experiments with rats, amnesia was observed after 6 and 24 hr but not after 1 and 3 hr. Clinical evidence, however, (16,43,50) shows that hypoxia-induced amnesia can recover spontaneously like traumatic amnesia. Sara (46) observed in experimental hypoxia- (and ECS-) induced retrograde amnesia that a recovery is possible. A single reexposure to the training environment for 3 min, given 30 min before the retention test, was sufficient to produce recovery. The recovery through reexposure in the training situation could not be prevented by a

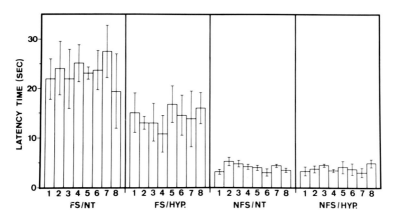

FIG. 4. Permanence of hypoxia-induced retrograde amnesia. Mice were given a single trial in a step-down avoidance task and treated as indicated. Independent groups (1–8) were given retention tests after 45, 60, 210, and 360 min, 24 and 48 hr, and 1 and 4 weeks. FS/NT, footshock, no treatment; FS/HYP, footshock, hypoxia (8% O_2 in N_2; training–treatment interval 10 min); NFS/NT, no footshock, no treatment; NFS/HYP, no footshock, hypoxia (8% O_2 in N_2; training–treatment interval 10 min).

second hypoxia (of the same duration and intensity as the first) given immediately after the reexposure. This result is not in accordance with the classic consolidation concept. It also contradicts the assumption that hypoxia acts by producing changes in brain state and that this explains the observed recovery, since the recovery could be seen immediately after the memory loss was evidenced. As a possible explanation, Sara (46) proposes "that hypoxia does not prevent the acquisition of elements of the learning situation, but that it prevents a subsequent organization into existing functional systems."

Gold and King (22), King and Glaser (27), and Haycock et al. (23), however, argued that a recovery from amnesia does not necessarily contradict the consolidation concept if it occurs in animals with partial amnesia. In fact, in our studies it seems as if hypoxia causes only incomplete amnesias in most experiments. The present findings do not, therefore, reveal unequivocal evidence against the consolidation hypothesis.

MODIFICATION OF HYPOXIA-PRODUCED RETROGRADE AMNESIA

Of equal importance in the discussion of the consolidation concept is the observation that amnesia can be modified by physiological and environmental events, occurring before treatment and during the retention interval. This was shown for ECS-induced amnesia, which can be modified by numerous pre- and posttraining experiences, e.g., drugs (13), reexposure to the training apparatus (1), or alteration of the sensory environment (8,42). According to a recent investigation by Sara and Lefevre (49), the same is true for hypoxia-induced retrograde amnesia. The effect seems to be highly restricted to the experimental condition. In these experiments, rats were given a single familiarization session before they were trained in a one-trial passive-avoidance task and then submitted to hypoxia (3.5% O_2 for 10 min, exposure beginning immediately after training). Another group received the same training and the same treatment but no prior familiarization session. The results indicate that familiarization is a necessary condition for hypoxia to produce a retrograde amnesia. David-Remacle (12), working on rats with a similar passive-avoidance task, found that a placebo treatment by a single oral injection of distilled water, 35 min before training, protected the rats from amnesia, which was present in the noninjected control group. Hypoxia in these experiments was induced by compression of the thorax, beginning immediately after training and continuing for 60 sec.

Sara, Lefevre, and David-Remacle conclude from their results that the consolidation concept cannot explain these findings. They advance another concept "that the memory trace of an event depends not only on (consolidation) time, but also on prior and subsequent experience. New information is not fixated in isolation, but is integrated into a pre-established long-term memory of past experience which never consolidates but evolves by continuous dynamic reorganization" (12).

Perhaps the explanation for the results on the effects of repeated hypoxic treatments, shown in Fig. 5, is similar to the proposed one. If the combination footshock-hypoxic treatment, as applied in experiment 1, is repeated after 24, 48, and 72 hr, the effect of hypoxia on the memory formation disappears. From the curves in Fig. 5, it is recognizable that after three trials there is no difference between the retention times of hypoxia-treated groups and untreated groups. This is valid for all training–treatment intervals tested. In a multitrial learning process, hypoxia does not produce amnesia. It simply slows down the achievement of the maximum value of memory strength. Starting with the first repetition of the footshock-hypoxic-treatment combination, the learning curves are as steep as, or steeper than, those of the untreated groups at corresponding points. The results are consistent with those observed by Ledwith (28). In this investigation rats were trained on the ac-

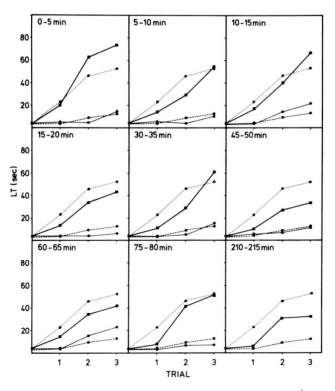

FIG. 5. Effect of repeated hypoxia on learning. Mice were given repeated training/treatment combinations in a step-down avoidance task. Procedure and N of the different experimental groups are those summarized in Table 1. ● .... ●, Group 1; ■——■, group 2, training–treatment intervals as indicated, exposure 5 min; ●- - - -●, group 4; ●——●, group 5, training–treatment intervals as indicated.

quisition of shuttle avoidance under different levels of oxygen concentration between 9 and 21%. Initially the performance was poorer at 9%. With repeated testing, the differences between this group and the normoxic controls disappeared. Similar observations have repeatedly been made for ECS-induced amnesia (6,26,40).

It follows that either the organism adapts to oxygen lack, the fixation processes in subsequent trials are different from those taking place in the first trial, or the amnesic effects of hypoxia cannot be explained as a disruption of the fixation process. The first two possibilities appear to be the least likely.

CONCLUSIONS

According to the above, it seems certain that hypoxia is an amnestic agent, in that it leads to a retention deficit in a one-trial avoidance task. The amnesia is not complete with tolerable degrees of hypoxia. It is time dependent; the application of hypoxia before and immediately after training does not produce amnesia. However, if administered 5 to 420 min after training, significant amnesia results. In this phase, the effect is not graded, i.e., there is no correlation between the retention deficit and the training–treatment interval. Although a spontaneous recovery was not observed, hypoxia-induced retrograde amnesia is not necessarily permanent and can be modified by pre- and posttraining experiences. If applied repeatedly in multitrial situations, the amnestic effect disappears.

It is unlikely that the observed effects can be explained as side effects on posttreatment behaviour that were mistakenly interpreted as evidence of memory impairment, e.g., effects on the development of fear or a conditioned emotional response. The fact that hypoxia itself does not alter activity and has no proactive effects on retention as well as the observed dependence of the effects on the training–treatment and training–retention test intervals do not support this view.

The results do not support the classic consolidation concept. Thermodynamically, there is no labile phase. The engram gains the characteristics of a metastable state within a few seconds. To this degree, a necessary condition of the so-called retrieval hypothesis is confirmed. This period is followed by a relatively long phase in which "memory strength" depends on cerebral energy metabolism. However, there is no evidence that the amnestic effects observed in this phase are due to an interference with a consolidation process.

Different retrieval hypotheses have been formulated that permit predictions with different degrees of precision. Common to all models is the assumption that the observed behavioural deficit after amnestic treatment is a failure to read out information from long-term storage. According to Nielson (39) and De Vietti and Larson (14), the amnestic treatment produces changes in "brain state" that persist up to 72 hr and prevent retrieval. The assumptions of Weiskrantz (55) are similar in their consequences. He proposed that retrieval is possible if the signal underlying memory is sufficiently strong to exceed the background level or noise of ongoing brain activity. Amnestic treatments decrease the signal-to-noise ratio by elevating the background noise level.

The predictions of these hypotheses are similar (9,34). For example, amnesia should be temporal and spontaneous recovery should be observable. The amnestic effect of treatment should decrease with increasing training–treatment intervals and increase with decreasing treatment–retention test intervals; amnestic agents should have anterograde effects and these should persist as long as retrograde amnesia persists. Hypoxia-induced amnesia does not have these properties.

From this, it is obvious that hypoxia-induced retrograde amnesia cannot be explained by the current concepts. Neither the consolidation hypothesis nor "state-dependency" nor "signal-to-noise" interpretations seem to be plausible for the experimental data available at present.

REFERENCES

1. Adams, H. E. (1966): Extinction of the effect of a single ECS. *Psychon. Sci.,* 5:295–296.
2. Anderson, J. E., and Robichaud, R. C. (1975): Retrograde amnesia induced by hypoxia and electroconvulsive shock in two rat strains. *Physiol. Behav.,* 14:81–84.
3. Baldwin, B. A., and Soltysik, S. S. (1965): Acquisition of classical conditioned defensive responses in goats subjected to cerebral ischemia. *Nature,* 206:1011–1013.
4. Baldwin, B. A., and Soltysik, S. S. (1966): The effect of cerebral ischemia, resulting in loss of EEG on the acquisition of conditioned reflexes in goats. *Brain Res.,* 2:71–84.
5. Baldwin, B. A., and Soltysik, S. S. (1969): The effect of cerebral ischemia or intracarotid injection of methohexitone on short term memory in goats. *Brain Res.,* 16:105–120.
6. Benowitz, L., and Magnus, J. G. (1973): Memory storage processes following one-trial aversive conditioning in the chick. *Behav. Biol.,* 8:367–380.
7. Bryant, I. H., and Thompson, R. (1958): The effect of anoxia on the acquisition of a discrimination habit. *J. Comp. Physiol. Psychol.,* 51:202–204.
8. Calhoun, K. S., Prewet, M. J., Peters, R. D., and Adams, H. E. (1975): Factors in the modification by isolation of electroconvulsive shock-produced retrograde amnesia in the rat. *J. Comp. Physiol. Psychol.,* 85:373–377.
9. Cherkin, A. (1970): Retrograde amnesia: Impaired memory consolidation or impaired retrieval? *Commun. Behav. Biol.,* 5:183–190.
10. Cherkin, A. (1971): Memory consolidation in the chick. *Commun. Behav. Biol.,* 5:325–330.
11. D'Andrea, I. A., and Kesner, R. P. (1973): The effects of ECS and hypoxia on information retrieval. *Physiol. Behav.,* 11:747–752.
12. David-Remacle, M. (1973): Attenuation of anoxia-induced retrograde amnesia in rats by a pretraining placebo injection. *Physiol. Behav.,* 10:693–696.
13. Davis, I. W., Thomas, R. K., and Adams, M. E. (1971): Interactions of scopolamine and physostigmine with ECS and one trial learning. *Physiol. Behav.,* 6:210–222.
14. DeVietti, T. L., and Larson, R. C. (1971): ECS effects: Evidence supporting state dependent learning in rats. *J. Comp. Physiol. Psychol.,* 74:407–415.
15. Duncan, C. P. (1949): The retroactive effects of shock on learning. *J. Comp. Physiol. Psychol.,* 42:32–34.

16. Fisher, C. M., and Adams, R. (1964): Transient global amnesia. *Acta Neurol. Scand.,* 40 (Suppl. 9):7–83.
17. Flohr, H., Hoelscher, H., and Trockel, C. (1979): Cerebral energy metabolism and memory. *Proc. Third Eur. Mtg. Cybernetics and Systems Research* (Vienna, April 1976). (*In press.*)
18. Flohr, H., Hoelscher, H., Trockel, C., and Mielke, M. (1976): Effect of hypercapnia on hypoxia-induced retrograde amnesia. *Arzneim. Forsch.,* 26:1243–1244.
19. Galluscio, E. H., and Young, A. G. (1970): Hypoxia and retrograde amnesia. *Psychon. Sci.,* 18:17–18.
20. Giurgea, C. (1972): Vers une pharmacologie de l'activité integrative du cerveau. Tentative du concept nootrope en psychopharmacologie. *Actualités Pharmacologiques,* 25:115–156.
21. Giurgea, C., Lefevre, D., Lescrinier, C., and David-Remacle, M. (1971): Pharmacological protection against hypoxia induced amnesia in rats. *Psychopharmacologia,* 20:160–168.
22. Gold, P. E., and King, R. A. (1974): Retrograde amnesia: Storage failure versus retrieval failure. *Psychol. Rev.,* 81:465–469.
23. Haycock, J. W., Gold, P. E., Macri, J., and McGaugh, J. L. (1973): Noncontingent footshock "attenuation" of retrograde amnesia: A generalization effect. *Physiol. Behav.,* 11:99–102.
24. Hayes, K. I. (1953): Anoxia and convulsive amnesia in rats. *J. Comp. Physiol. Psychol.,* 46:216–217.
25. Hebb, D. O. (1949): *The Organization of Behavior.* Wiley, New York.
26. Kesner, R. P., and McDonough, J. H., Jr. (1970): Diminished amnestic effect of a second electroconvulsive seizure. *Exp. Neurol.,* 27:527–533.
27. King, R. A., and Glaser, R. L. (1970): Duration of electroshock-induced retrograde amnesia in rats. *Physiol. Behav.,* 5:335–340.
28. Ledwith, F. (1967): The effects of hypoxia on shuttle avoidance in the rat. *Psychon. Sci.,* 8:203–204.
29. Lewis, D. J. (1969): Sources of experimental amnesia. *Psychol. Rev.,* 76:461–472.
30. Lewis, D. J., Miller, R. R., and Misanin, J. R. (1968): Control of retrograde amnesia. *J. Comp. Physiol. Psychol.,* 66:48–51.
31. Lewis, D. J., Misanin, J. R., and Miller, R. R. (1968): Recovery of memory following amnesia. *Nature,* 220:704–705.
32. Madsen, M. C., and McGaugh, J. L. (1961): The effect of ECS on one-trial avoidance learning. *J. Comp. Physiol. Psychol.,* 54:522–523.
33. McGaugh, J. L. (1966): Time-dependent processes in memory storage. *Science,* 156:408–410.
34. McGaugh, J. L., and Dawson, R. G. (1971): Modification of memory storage processes. In: *Animal Memory,* edited by W. K. Honig and P. M. R. Jones, pp. 215–242. Academic Press, New York, London.
35. Miller, R. J., and Springer, A. D. (1973): Amnesia, consolidation and retrieval. *Psychol. Rev.,* 80:69–79.
36. Miller, R. J., Misanin, J. R., and Lewis, D. J. (1969): Amnesia as a function of events during the learning ECS interval. *J. Comp. Physiol. Psychol.,* 67:145–148.
37. Müller, G. E., und Pilzecker, H. (1900): Experimentelle Beiträge zur Lehre vom Gedächtnis. *Z. Psychol.,* 1:1–288.
38. Nielson, H. C., Zimmermann, J. M., and Colliver, J. C. (1963): Effect of complete arrest of cerebral circulation on learning and retention in dogs. *J. Comp. Physiol. Psychol.,* 56:974–978.
39. Nielson, H. C. (1968): Evidence that electroconvulsive shock alters memory retrieval rather than memory consolidation. *Exp. Neurol.,* 20:3–20.
40. Nachmann, M., and Meinecke, R. O. (1969): Lack of retrograde amnesia effects of repeated electroconvulsive shock and carbon dioxide treatments. *J. Comp. Physiol. Psychol.,* 68:631–696.
41. Pagano, R. R., Bush, D. F., Martin, G., and Hunt, E. B. (1969): Duration of retrograde amnesia as a function of electroconvulsive shock intensity. *Physiol. Behav.,* 4:19–21.
42. Peters, R. D., Calhoun, K. S., and Adams, H. E. (1973): Modification by environ-

mental conditions of retrograde amnesia produced by ECS. *Physiol. Behav.,* 11:889–892.
43. Posner, C., and Ziegler, D. (1960): Temporary amnesia as a manifestation of cerebrovascular insufficiency. *Trans. Am. Neurol. Assoc.,* 85:221–223.
44. Quartermain, D., McEwen, B. S., and Azmita, E. C. (1970): Amnesia produced by electroconvulsive shock or cycloheximide: Conditions for recovery. *Science,* 169: 683–686.
45. Ransmeier, R. E., and Gerard, R. M. (1954): Effects of temperature, convulsion and metabolic factors on rodent memory and EEG. *Am. J. Physiol.,* 179:663–664.
46. Sara, S. J. (1973): Recovery from hypoxia and ECS-induced amnesia after a single exposure to training environment. *Physiol. Behav.,* 10:85–89.
47. Sara, S. J. (1974): Delayed development of amnestic behavior after hypoxia. *Physiol. Behav.,* 13:693–696.
48. Sara, S. J., and Lefevre, D. (1972): Hypoxia-induced amnesia in one-trial learning and pharmacological protection by piracetam. *Psychopharmacologia,* 25:32–40.
49. Sara, S. J., and Lefevre, D. (1973): Reexamination of role of familiarization in retrograde amnesia in the rat. *J. Comp. Physiol. Psychol.,* 84:361–364.
50. Shuttleworth, E. C., and Wise, G. R. (1973): Transient global amnesia due to arterial embolism. *Arch. Neurol.,* 29:340–341.
51. Taber, R. A., and Banuazizi, A. (1966): CO_2-induced retrograde amnesia in a one trial learning situation. *Psychopharmacologia,* 9:382–391.
52. Thompson, R. (1957): The comparative effects of ECS and anoxia on memory. *J. Comp. Physiol. Psychol.,* 50:397–400.
53. Thompson, R., and Pryer, R. S. (1956): The effect of anoxia on the retention of a discrimination habit. *J. Comp. Physiol. Psychol.,* 49:297–300.
54. Vacher, I. M., King, A., and Miller, A. T. (1968): Failure of hypoxia to produce retrograde amnesia. *J. Comp. Physiol. Psychol.,* 66:179–181.
55. Weiskrantz, L. (1966): Experimental studies of amnesia. In: *Amnesia,* edited by C. M. W. Whitty and O. L. Zangwill, pp. 1–35. Butterworths, London and Washington, D.C.
56. Wilcoxon, F. (1945): Individual comparison by ranking methods. *Biometrics,* 1:80–83.
57. Wlcoxon, F. (1947): Probability tables for individual comparisons by ranking methods. *Biometrics,* 3:119–122.
58. Zinkin, S., and Miller, H. J. (1967): Recovery of memory after amnesia induced by electroconvulsive shock. *Science,* 155:102–104.

Brain Mechanisms in Memory and Learning:
From the Single Neuron to Man,
edited by M. A. B. Brazier.
Raven Press, New York © 1979.

Recovery from Retrograde Amnesia: A Behavioral Analysis

Allen M. Schneider

Department of Psychology, Swarthmore College, Swarthmore, Pennsylvania 19081

Memory researchers recognize two kinds of memory loss, each reflecting a different underlying problem: recoverable (temporary) losses are retrieval related (that is, are caused by the inability to get access to information); nonrecoverable (permanent) losses are storage related (caused by an inability to encode information). However, the line between recoverable and nonrecoverable losses is not a sharp one. As the methods for studying memory have become more precise, researchers have found that memory losses once thought to be nonrecoverable and, therefore, storage related, are in fact recoverable and, therefore, retrieval related.

There is much to be drawn both experimentally and clinically from the methodological advances in research on memory. And yet, there is a crucial element to this research that I find disconcerting. My quarrel is not with the premise that memory losses that seem to be storage related might well turn out to be, at closer examination, retrieval related; rather it is with the methodology presently being used to establish this distinction. Not all methodological advances have equal value. The reminder procedure, in many experiments an extremely useful tool for studying memory, has been used inappropriately. Thus, although I agree with the goal of the current storage-retrieval studies and the general direction that they are taking, I disagree with one of the means by which this research is being carried out. In this chapter, I critically evaluate the reminder procedure and suggest a new way of using it to address storage-retrieval problems. A brief review of the concepts and data from which this new procedure derived serves as an introduction to the supporting research.

DISTINGUISHING BETWEEN STORAGE AND RETRIEVAL PROCESSES

Retention depends on storage—the process by which learned information endures over time and retrieval, the process by which learned information is accessed during recall. This is one of the few propositions on which most

researchers on memory agree: our evidence comes not only from the laboratory, but from everyday experience such as the common memory block. Unable to recall a familiar event, we often give up; later, for no apparent reason,
the missing memory suddenly returns. Since we had no opportunity between
the time of the block and the time of recall to reacquire the information, it
seems reasonable to conclude that it was present (i.e., in storage) all along
but the ability to get access to it (i.e., retrieval) was not.

We do not know exactly what controls retrieval; it probably involves a
combination of neural and environmental factors. Penfield's (14) electrical
stimulation of the temporal lobes in humans and Deutsch's (5) chemical
stimulation of the hippocampus in rats are well-known instances in which
manipulation of neural factors has facilitated retrieval of forgotten information. Environmental factors include both internal and external stimuli. Overton's (13) work with drugs and Tulving's (21) cue-dependent forgetting experiments show how stimulus change between the time of training and the
time of testing impairs retrieval.

The telling feature in all of these cases, indeed the feature that marks them
as retrieval-related problems, is that memories eventually return. There are
instances, however, in which memories may be permanently lost, and no
amount of jogging will bring them back. It is convenient to describe this
condition as a disruption of storage. This should be done with great caution.
Lack of experimental success in demonstrating recovery of retention does not
foreclose the possibility that recovery will occur in unforeseen circumstances.
Absence of evidence, as the saying goes, is not evidence of absence. Recovery
is always possible, and, therefore, any conclusion about disruption of storage
must always be subject to change.

As we learn more and more about memory processing, we begin to discover
that what at one time were considered "storage failures" are actually "retrieval failures." For example, consider recent work involving analysis of
memory loss in brain-damaged humans (23). Typically, the victims find it
difficult, if not impossible, to remember newly learned information. Since the
patients show no signs of recovering lost memories, it seems natural to conclude that the patients are suffering from storage disruption. Recent work by
Warrington and Weiskrantz (23) questions this conclusion. They report that
memory loss in brain-damaged patients is not as intractable as originally
thought. They found that a patient's memory for pictures or words improved
significantly when they prompted the patient during the recall test, using
fragments of the pictures or words. Apparently the problem with the patients
is not that they are unable to store information, but that they are unable to
retrieve it without help.

Although this type of experiment leads to progress in refining the diagnosis
of certain clinical disorders, it also undermines our confidence in present
interpretations of data about memory loss. As an instance, consider retrograde amnesia; of all the types of memory loss that have come under in-

vestigation, this is the one that has received the most attention. Victims of neural trauma (e.g., concussion) are able to recall old, long-term memories, but fail to recall recent, short-term memories (17). Further investigations with these subjects reveal that the amnesia tends to shrink with passage of time and that the lost memories tend to return. But not all memories recover; the memory of those events that occur immediately before the trauma (i.e., the most recent memories) appear to be permanently lost. These observations led researchers to draw two conclusions regarding neural trauma and its impact on memory. First, because the loss of recent memory appears to be permanent, neural trauma presumably disrupts storage of recent memory. Second, because recent memory appears to be more vulnerable to interference than long-term memory, neural trauma presumably disrupts a process that mediates the transformation from the vulnerable to the resistant state, a process known as memory consolidation (7,10).

Follow-up studies using rats and mice, with electroconvulsive shock (ECS) as the source of the neural trauma, confirmed the observations made in humans and, thus, added further support to the two conclusions (4). Specifically, studies of lower animals showed that ECS delivered after training disrupted short-term but not long-term memory, and the disruptive effect on short-term memory appeared to be permanent; that is, retention did not recover with passage of time alone (3,8,10).

Recent work with amnesic patients suggests the need for a change in our view of memory consolidation (20,22). The use of more sensitive questionnaires as tools for probing past memories has shown that amnesic patients experience no more impairment on recall of recent memories than on recall of long-term memories. This work is an example of how increased precision of measurement, resulting in a significant increase in the quantity of available data, instead of merely completing our collection of facts, may require us to reclassify them. Although the evidence does not yet support a refutation of consolidation theory, these data certainly suggest that the differences between short- and long-term memory have been overestimated.

The conclusion that neural trauma disrupts storage of recent memory may also need rethinking. Is the loss of retention that follows neural trauma really a permanent one? Suppose we observe a loss of retention for which passage of time is the only factor influencing recovery. Suppose further that recovery does not occur. If we classify this loss as permanent, we fail to take into account an important alternative: there may be a variety of retrieval problems, some of which will not respond to passage of time alone. In other words, the mere fact that memory loss does not respond to passage of time alone does not permit the inference that the loss is permanent or that it is storage related. It may be that passage of time alone alleviates only certain types of retrieval problems. The loss of short-term memory may be a retrieval problem not yet observed or imagined, and not a storage problem at all.

Now, if the loss of short-term memory is caused by retrieval problems similar to those seen by Warrington and Weiskrantz (23) in their brain-damaged patients, a reminder procedure modeled on their work should produce recovery in a variety of controlled situations. The hypothesis seems simple enough to test; the necessary controls could be achieved by using rats in a laboratory.

A study by Quartermain et al. (15) provides one of the more complete accounts of the reminder procedure used with rats. They trained rats by punishing them with footshock for stepping from a lighted to a darkened compartment. They, then, subjected the rats to ECS 1 sec later and tested them for retention the next day. As expected, they found retention disrupted. They, then, gave the rats a reminder shock (a footshock outside the training apparatus), tested them the next day, and found retention restored. To make certain that the reminder shock was the reason for the recovery, they repeated the procedure in control animals, omitting the reminder shock. Finding no retention on the second test trial, they concluded that reminder shock did restore retention. They found, on further analysis, that the first test trial was as important as the reminder shock in restoring retention. When they omitted the test trial, retention did not recover.

What do these data indicate about the state of memory following neural trauma? Should we abandon the notion that storage is disrupted and in its place substitute the notion that retrieval is disrupted? Should we go a step further and conclude that memory storage of the avoidance response was present all the time, that ECS blocked its retrieval, and that the reminder cues (test trial and reminder shock) undid the block? Finally, should we conclude that we now have an animal model of the reminder effect seen by Warrington and Weiskrantz in brain-damaged humans?

I think not. In my opinion, no conclusions can be drawn from these reminder data with respect to disruption of storage or retrieval. I base this view on the following observations.

One of the first lessons that animal work teaches us is: Do not trust behavior. What animals do in a retention test and what they actually retain are often entirely different. It is true that animals receiving reminder cues perform well on later retention tests, but this does not necessarily mean that they remember information acquired during the original training. It is possible that they perform well because they remember information acquired during the reminder manipulations.

My view is that the reminder cues (i.e., the test trial and reminder shock) themselves constitute a learning experience and produce retention, not because they bring back suppressed memories, but because they produce acquisition of new memories (18,19). New memories simply replace old memories; the resulting behavior does not tell us about storage or retrieval. We must not, however, dismiss the possibility that neural trauma disrupts retrieval. It may indeed; but the reminder shock effect is not evidence.

The remainder of this chapter is devoted to two issues. One is a methodological issue. In considering this problem I present data that question the validity of the conclusions drawn from experiments using the reminder procedure in lower animals and suggest an alternate way of discerning between storage and retrieval problems. The other is a more substantive issue; it regards the state of memory itself following neural trauma. I present data suggesting that neural trauma (produced by ECS) disrupts both a storage and a retrieval process.

REMINDER PROCEDURE AS A LEARNING EXPERIENCE

My interpretation of the reminder effect and its relation to learning can be stated in terms of the following set of theoretical assumptions:

1. During passive-avoidance training, when the animal steps from the lit to dark compartment and is punished, we assume that the animal learns *two* types of behavior: (a) the association of fear with cues in the dark compartment; and (b) the avoidance of the stepthrough response.

2. Instead of ECS affecting retention of fear behavior in the dark, we assume that it disrupts retention of the avoidance behavior.

3. ECS disrupts retention of the avoidance behavior by disrupting two memories—the memory of the avoidance response and the memory of the motivation to perform the avoidance response.

4. The disrupted memories are restored by a combination of the test trial and the reminder shock; in each case the restorative process involves relearning.

The rat relearns the avoidance response as follows: placed in the lighted compartment during the first test trial, the rat steps into the dark, having forgotten (traumatized by ECS) the punishment (footshock) previously administered. Once in the dark, the animal behaves *as if* frightened; for instance, Hine and Paolino (9) observed a change in heart rate, indicating that the rat experiences a fear response to the dark. I take this fear to act as punishment in producing relearning of the avoidance response.

Now, removed from the test apparatus, the animal is given a reminder shock. This shock is presumed to produce learned fear that generalizes to the test apparatus. This fear, in turn, provides the motivation to perform the avoidance response. Consequently, when returned to the apparatus on the second test trial, the rat "remembers" not to step into the dark.

In summary, learning according to this theory, plays two roles in the reminder effect. During the test trial, it produces memory of the avoidance response. During the reminder shock, it produces memory of the motivation to perform the avoidance response. If either memory is disrupted, retention is disrupted.

To test the theory, we conducted six experiments. The sequence of experiments was as follows:

Replication of the reminder effect
Strength of conditioning and the reminder effect
Reminder effect as a learning experience
Reminder shock as a motivator
Test trial as a memory source
Recovery of retention: a component-memory analysis

The first five experiments constitute an analysis of the methodological issue: Does the reminder procedure act as a learning experience? The sixth experiment used the data of the first five together with a new application of the reminder procedure to differentiate the particular memories (avoidance and motivation) as they are affected by ECS.

In each experiment the subjects were male rats of the Long-Evans strain weighing 225 to 275 g; the training apparatus was a standard passive-avoidance two-compartment box. Statistical analysis in all experiments consisted of a Mann-Whitney U test for between-group comparisons and a Wilcoxon-Matched Sign test for within-subject comparisons. Each test was two-tailed, and each statistically significant result has a p value of less than 0.05.

Experiment 1: A Replication of the Reminder Effect

This experiment repeated the standard reminder shock procedure in order to assess the importance of the test trial and reminder shock in restoring retention. The procedure was as follows: on day 1, the animals received an habituation trial in which they stepped from a lit to dark compartment. On day 2, the animals received passive-avoidance training in which they were punished with footshock (1.6 mA, 2 sec) for stepping from the lit to dark compartment; ECS (35 to 50 mA, 0.3 sec) was delivered through ear snaps 1 sec after training. On day 3, the animals were divided into six groups and were given different test trial-reminder shock procedures. On day 4, the animals were given a retention test in which they stepped from the lit to dark compartment, but did not receive punishing footshock. Retention was seen as increasing, as stepthrough latencies increased. If an animal refrained from making a stepthrough response within 300 sec, the test trial was terminated. Two control groups, one given training but no ECS (group 1) and one given ECS but no training (group 2), received a single test trial plus reminder shock on day 3 and a test trial on day 4.

Table 1 shows that we replicated the basic reminder shock effect. Animals (group 3) receiving a single test trial followed 1 hr later by reminder shock (1.6 mA, 2 sec) on day 3, recovered retention to the level of the trained control (group 1) on day 4. We also confirmed that both the single test trial and reminder shock are necessary for recovery. Animals not given both manipulations, but instead given either the test trial alone (group 4) or the reminder shock alone (group 5) or neither the test trial nor the reminder shock (group 6), showed no signs of recovery on day 4.

TABLE 1. *Median stepthrough latencies (sec) on the retention-test trial(s) for the groups in experiments 1, 2, and 3*

Expt.	Group	Treatment	T_1(sec)	T_2(sec)
1	1	Tr, NECS, T_1-RS	300	300
	2	NTr, ECS, T_1-RS	12	15
	3	Tr, ECS, T_1-RS	7	300
	4	Tr, ECS, T_1-NRS	5	8
	5	Tr, ECS, NT_1-RS	—	18
	6	Tr, ECS, NT_1-NRS	—	16
2	7	Tr*, ECS, NT_1-RS	—	300
	8	Tr*, ECS, T_1-RS	58	300
3	9	Tr, ECS, T_1(ext)-RS	11	16
	10	Tr, ECS, T_1-RS(ext)	14	20

Each group contained eight animals.

Tr, training with moderate footshock; NTr, no training; Tr*, training with intense footshock; NECS, no ECS; RS, reminder shock; NRS, no reminder shock; RS(ext), reminder shock followed by extinction: T_1(ext), test trial$_1$ followed by extinction; T_1, test$_1$ on day 3; NT_1, no test$_1$; T_2, test$_2$ on day 4.

Experiment 2: The Relation Between Strength of Conditioning and the Reminder Effect

It should be noted that although our data and those of Quartermain et al. (15) agree that both the test trial and reminder shock are necessary to produce recovery, data recently reported by Miller and Springer (11) suggest that the test trial is expendable and that reminder shock alone is sufficient to produce recovery. In an attempt to account for these different results, we repeated two groups—the reminder shock alone (group 7) and the test trial and reminder shock (group 8)—with one major change: we increased the intensity and the duration of footshock during training (from 1.6 mA, 2 sec to 2 mA, 10 sec) to match that used by Miller and Springer.

It can be seen from Table 1 that the increase in footshock intensity during training had two effects. It produced recovery in the reminder shock alone group (T_2 in group 7), a result consistent with that of Miller and Springer (11). And, equally important, it increased the strength of retention that survived the disruptive effects of ECS (T_1 in group 8). Apparently, the extent to which the test trial is involved in recovery depends on the strength of retention following ECS. As retention increases (in this case caused by the increased footshock during training), the need for the test trial decreases. On the other hand, the data have no bearing on the issue of whether the test trial serves as a learning trial.

Experiment 3: The Reminder Effect as a Learning Experience

It is clear that with moderate footshock intensity (1.6 mA, 2 sec) during training, both the test trial and reminder shock are necessary to restore retention. Using these training parameters, we examined the extent to which the test trial and reminder shock restore retention by producing learning. Table 1 presents data from two groups (group 9 and 10) that received manipulations designed to extinguish the learning properties of either the test trial or the reminder shock. We reasoned that if learning produced recovery, then extinction should prevent it.

We gave both groups the standard reminder shock procedure; that is, we gave both groups habituation on day 1, training and convulsion on day 2, a test trial and reminder shock on day 3, and a test trial on day 4. In order to extinguish the learning properties of the first test trial, we confined one group (group 9) to the dark compartment for 30 min after their stepthrough response on the test trial. To extinguish the learning properties of the reminder shock, we confined the other group (group 10) to the reminder apparatus for 30 min after reminder shock. In each case, the confinement manipulation was effective in preventing recovery. Neither group recovered retention to the level of the trained control group.

The results are clear; the test trial and reminder shock produce recovery as long as we preserve their conditioned aversive properties. The implications are also clear; the test trial and reminder shock restore retention by producing learning.

Given that learning is the process by which the test trial and reminder shock restore retention, the question remains, How is learning involved? According to my theory, learning plays two roles; during the test trial it produces the avoidance response, and during the reminder shock, it produces the motivation to perform the avoidance response. The next two experiments test these assumptions.

Experiment 4: Reminder Shock as a Motivator

To examine the motivational properties of reminder shock, we studied the effect of reminder shock on unlearned avoidance behavior. Our reasoning was based on the generally accepted principle that motivation has a strengthening effect on *existing* behavior, whether the behavior is learned or unlearned (1). Therefore, if reminder shock produces motivation that generalizes to the testing apparatus, not only should it strengthen learned behavior in that apparatus, an effect that presumably occurs when it produces recovery of retention, but also it should strengthen unlearned avoidance behavior. That reminder shock has the potential to enhance virtually any avoidance behavior, learned or unlearned, as long as there exists an inclination toward that behavior to begin with, cannot be overemphasized. It is this feature that identifies the effect of reminder shock as motivational in nature. And it is this feature that distinguishes this interpretation from that of others (2,6).

In deference to the earlier work, it should be noted that not all researchers (15) were oblivious to the possibility that the success of reminder shock in restoring retention depends on its acting as a learning experience. The possibility was dismissed, however, when it was found that after giving reminder shock to both amnesic and naive animals, only the amnesic animals benefited from the shock and showed retention of the passive-avoidance response. I agree that absence of retention in naive animals clearly indicates that reminder shock does not produce learning of a passive-avoidance response. I disagree, however, with the conclusion that reminder shock does not produce learning at all. Maintaining, as I do, that reminder shock produces learned motivation and thereby strengthens only *existing* avoidance behavior, I would *not* expect the reminder shock to help naive animals unless I tested the naive animals on retention of inherent (unlearned) avoidance behavior. This experiment examines this hypothesis.

The procedure was as follows: we chose as the unlearned behavior the tendency of naive rats to avoid illumination in the two-compartment training apparatus. To measure the inherent avoidance behavior, we placed animals (group 1) in the dark compartment and measured the time that it took them to step into the lit compartment. We measured the behavior twice, once before reminder shock to confirm that an aversion to light existed and once after shock to determine if the aversion was strengthened. Two control groups were included. In one case, the animals (group 2) were given the two test trials, but were not given reminder shock. In the other case, the animals (group 3) were given the two test trials and reminder shock, except, instead of stepping from a dark to lit compartment, they stepped from a dark to dark compartment on each trial. The test trials were given on successive days, and reminder shock was given 1 hr after the first test trial.

It can be seen from Table 2 that naive animals do have an inherent aversion to light. Measurements taken before shock (trial 1) indicate that animals (group 1 and group 2) that step from a dark to lit compartment step slower than animals (group 3) that step from a dark to dark compartment. It can also be seen from Table 2 that reminder shock acts as a motivator and strengthens the inherent aversion to light. Measurements taken after shock (trial 2) indicate that animals (group 1) that step from the dark to lit com-

TABLE 2. Median stepthrough latencies on the retention-test trial(s) for the groups in experiment 4

Group	Treatment	T_1(sec)	T_2(sec)
1	DL,RS	38	300
2	DL,NRS	51	63
3	DD,RS	9	13
4	DL,RS(ext)	33	41

Each group contained eight animals.

DL, dark in one compartment, light in the other; DD, dark in both compartments; RS, reminder shock; NRS, no reminder shock; RS(ext), reminder shock followed by extinction; T_1, test 1; T_2, test 2.

partment increase their avoidance of light, stepping even more slowly than they did before shock. On the other hand, animals in neither of the control groups showed a significant increase in avoidance behavior from the first to second trial. Thus, it does appear that for reminder shock to strengthen unlearned avoidance behavior, reminder shock must be given in conjunction with an inherent aversion.

Finally, Table 2 presents data that show that learning is the process by which reminder shock strengthens the aversion to light. Animals (group 4) that were not only allowed to step from a dark to lit compartment on each of the test trials, but also confined to the reminder apparatus for 30 min after they were given shock (a procedure designed to produce extinction) showed no significant change in avoidance behavior from the first to second trial.

The data indicate that the effectiveness of reminder shock in strengthening retention of unlearned avoidance behavior depends on two factors: (a) the learning properties of reminder shock must be preserved, and (b) a tendency toward avoidance behavior must exist before reminder shock is given. We can take these data as evidence that reminder shock produces learned motivation.

Experiment 5: The Test Trial as the Source of the Recovered Memory

It should be emphasized that the motivation data (experiment 4) are not at variance with the traditional view of retrieval. Retrieval is defined as the process by which memory is accessed during recall, and the data simply implicate motivation as one of the mechanisms by which accessing takes place. On the other hand, it is an entirely different matter when we raise questions regarding the source of the memory that recovers following reminder shock. It is here that the theories disagree. According to the retrieval theory, the memory that recovers is the original memory acquired during training (12). I suggest, instead, that the memory that recovers is a new memory, one acquired during testing (19).

Because it may seem contradictory to assume that a test trial can serve as a learning trial, I risk belaboring the point and describe again the behavior that supports this assumption. Consider an animal that is given training and ECS on day 1 and a test trial and reminder shock on day 2. During the test trial, the animal steps from the light to the dark, clearly indicating that ECS disrupted the avoidance behavior. However, once in the dark, the animal shows autonomic signs of fear (9). I take this fear to act as punishment in producing learning of the avoidance behavior. According to the learning theory, it is this new avoidance response, not one acquired during the training trial, that recovers following the test trial and reminder shock.

To distinguish between the retrieval and learning theories, we conducted an experiment to determine whether the memory that recovers following reminder shock was acquired during training or during testing. Any experiment employing reminder shock faces a built-in obstacle: the memory that recovers following reminder shock could come from either the training trial or the first test trial. To resolve this problem, we used a training procedure in which the animals could *not* acquire a memory of the passive-avoidance response and a testing procedure in which they *could* acquire a memory of the passive-avoidance response. We then tested whether retention of the passive-avoidance response recovered after reminder shock. If it did, we could conclude that the test trial, not the training trial, is the source of the recovered response.

Exploratory work in our laboratory (18) indicated that we could accomplish both aims—that is, prevent avoidance learning during the training trial and produce avoidance learning during the first test trial—by making a single change in the conventional training procedure. Instead of allowing animals to step from the lit to dark compartment during training, we placed the animals directly in the dark compartment and gave them footshock. We found that by eliminating the stepthrough response in this way, we prevented the animals from learning a passive-avoidance response during training. And we also found that by administering footshock directly in the dark compartment, we could produce acquisition of a passive-avoidance response during a subsequent test trial. Specifically, the footshock in the dark compartment apparently produced conditioned fear of the dark that, together with the stepthrough response during the subsequent test trial, was sufficient to produce acquisition of avoidance behavior.

Having prepared animals this way, we administered the standard reminder shock procedure, that is, we gave animals ECS 1 sec after training and reminder shock 1 hr after the first test trial. Consistent with the learning theory prediction, we found that the animals showed recovery of the passive-avoidance response. Thus we concluded that the test trial, not the training trial, is the source of the recovered response.

Conclusion

Knowing that recovery of retention occurs because the test trial and reminder shock produce learning (i.e., produce memories of avoidance behavior and motivation, respectively), what can we now conclude about the nature of the ECS disruption? Does the disruption involve storage or retrieval? As I noted earlier, we can draw no conclusions regarding the nature of the disruption. ECS may disrupt storage, in which case acquisition of new memories is the only way that retention can be produced; or, ECS may disrupt retrieval, in which case acquisition of new memories is simply an alternative way that retention can be produced.

REMINDER PROCEDURE AS A COMPONENT MEMORY ANALYSIS

The results from the preceding experiments indicate that the retrieval explanation of the reminder effect is inappropriate, and support an alternative explanation based on the view that the reminder procedure produces new learning. The failure of previous work to recognize this alternative probably stems from a narrow and, in my opinion, inadequate view of the retention process *per se*. To measure retention behaviorally is not to measure the effect of a single memory, but to measure the combined effect of a number of different component memories. Retention of behavior as simple as the passive-avoidance response requires the coalescence of at least two memories—a response memory and a motivation memory. For example, during a retention test of the passive-avoidance response, a rat that is missing a motivation memory is behaviorally indistinguishable from a rat missing a response memory or, for that matter, from a rat missing both a response and a motivation memory. Thus, individual memories cannot be identified or studied simply by observing avoidance behavior during a retention test. We need a way to analyse the avoidance behavior into its component memories. The reminder procedure, considered in a new light, fulfills this need.

By indicating the conditions necessary to restore retention, the reminder procedure reveals the memories that must have initially been disrupted. If the test trial and the reminder shock are both necessary to restore retention, then two memories—a response memory and a motivation memory—must have been disrupted. If, on the other hand, only one condition is necessary to restore retention, then only one memory need have been disrupted.

Once we established that the reminder procedure could be used to identify the individual memories disrupted by neural trauma, it seemed natural to take the next step and examine whether the disruptive effects were permanent. To accomplish this we determined whether or not the memories would recover with passage of time alone. In light of the existing studies, this may seem like a duplication of effort. Indeed there is a plethora of data indicating that retention of the passive-avoidance response does not recover with passage of time alone (3,8). But, as we have been saying all along, we are not concerned with retention of the passive-avoidance response *per se;* we are concerned with the individual memories (i.e., the response memory and the motivation memory) that interact to produce retention of the passive-avoidance response. It is possible that one of these memories will recover even though retention of the passive-avoidance response does not recover.

Experiment 6: Recovery of Retention: A Component-Memory Analysis

To test this hypothesis, we repeated the standard reminder experiment (experiment 1) with a crucial difference. Instead of giving the reminder conditions the day after training–ECS, we gave the reminder conditions 2 weeks after training–ECS. As before, the reminder conditions consisted of four different procedures—a test trial alone, a reminder shock alone, both a test trial and a reminder shock, and no treatment. Each procedure was given to a different group of animals, and a final test trial was given the next day.

We know from our earlier work (experiment 1) that when the reminder

TABLE 3. Median stepthrough latencies on the retention-test trial(s) for the groups in experiment 6

Group	Treatment	T_1(sec)	T_2(sec)
1	Tr,NECS T_1-RS	300	300
2	Tr,ECS NT_1-NRS	—	18
3	Tr,ECS T_1-RS	12	251
4	Tr,ECS NT_1-RS	—	218
5	Tr,ECS T_1-NRS	15	23

Each group contained eight animals.

Tr, training; NECS, no ECS; T_1, test$_1$ on day 15; T_2, test$_2$ on day 16; NT_1, no test$_1$; RS, reminder shock; NRS, no reminder shock.

conditions are given the day after training–ECS, none of the conditions produces recovery except the combination of reminder shock and test trial. The results presented in Table 3 indicate that this is not the case after a 2-week period. Reminder shock no longer had to be given in combination with a test trial to produce recovery; rather it needed only to be given in conjunction with passage of time (group 4).

These results support the view that one of the two memories disrupted by ECS, the response memory, recovers with passage of time alone. Specifically, given that recovery of retention of the passive-avoidance response depends on two memories, a response memory and a motivation memory, and given that reminder shock restores one of the memories, the motivation memory, it seems reasonable to conclude that the other memory, the response memory, must be restored by the passage of time.

On the other hand, as the data from Table 3 indicate, recovery does *not* occur when the *test-trial-alone* condition (group 5) is given after a 2-week period. Apparently, in this case, passage of time alone is not sufficient to restore the motivation memory. Therefore, even though the test trial restores the response memory, retention does not recover.

These results also support the view that the nature of the disruption of the two memories is different. The loss of the response memory, because it is temporary, may be taken as a retrieval failure; the loss of the motivation memory, because it appears to be permanent, may be taken as a storage failure. Here, as I urged earlier, we must exercise caution.

In summary, three basic conclusions derive from these data. I offer each at a different level of confidence.

The first, and safest, conclusion is that the passage of time significantly increases the effectiveness of the reminder-shock-alone condition.

The second, a more speculative conclusion, is that the response memory, not the motivation memory, recovers with passage of time. This conclusion rests on a persuasive but as yet insufficiently tested assumption: that the reminder shock and test trial produce motivation and response memories, respectively.

The third, and most speculative, conclusion is that loss of motivation memory is a storage failure, loss of response memory, a retrieval failure. I am diffident in offering this conclusion because it rests on two assumptions, neither of which I am completely confident in making: first, that motivation and response memories differentially recover; and second, that differential recovery indicates the class of disruption, storage or retrieval.

SUMMARY AND CONCLUSION

I have argued that the reminder procedure does not bring back retention of seemingly lost memories, but rather produces acquisition of new memories. Reviewing the literature and recounting some supportive experiments, we saw that the two conditions that constitute the reminder procedure, a test trial and a reminder shock, produce acquisition of avoidance behavior and motivation, respectively. On this basis I suggested that the reminder procedure is not a valid means of distinguishing between disruption of storage and retrieval and proposed an alternative approach to the problem of making this distinction. This alternative consisted of combining features of the reminder procedure (that is, reminder shock alone or test trial alone) with passage of time. Here we saw that the effect of ECS on retention varied with individual memories; ECS disrupts retrieval of the avoidance memory and it appears to disrupt storage of the motivation memory. These data suggest a method for isolating individual memories. This isolation is the key feature of my experiments.

Memory researchers cannot blindly enter the nervous system and piece together even a rough picture of the neural substrates of memory. They need behavioral coordinates by which to guide their neural search. Storage, retrieval, consolidation, information content—these are some of the behavioral features of memory processing for which we seek corresponding neural functions and structures. Data from both human and animal experiments suggest that information content of individual memories is the most important behavioral feature of these processes (16). How particular memories are organized in the nervous system, how they are retrieved, stored, and consolidated—all these may ultimately be seen to depend on their content, but direct ties between information content and neural structures remain elusive.

Analysis of particular memories, a fairly straightforward procedure in research with humans, poses special problems in research with lower animals. We know particular memories by their content; this content is manifested by humans in language, the cognitive content of which provides a basis for a kind of detailed inference unavailable from the nonverbal behavior of animals. Without language, lower animals express memories crudely; individual memories go unheeded until a full complement produces behavior.

Animal researchers can observe this behavior. They know that this behavior issues from a complex of memories. They can classify the types of memory in the behavior. In our example of the passive-avoidance response, for instance, they know that the avoidance behavior is composed of a response memory and a motivation memory. They induce amnesia in the rat, and the rat no longer exhibits the avoidance behavior. Researchers do not know which of the component memories has been disrupted. To find out, they reinstate one of the known components; when they see the behavior again, they know the other was there. In this way they identify the content of individual memories.

To recognize that retention is a blend of different memories is not the same as to study that blend. The reminder procedure, when uncoupled from its persuasive, although misleading, analogy with human behavior, provides a useful tool for analysis of the blend's constituent parts. It would be presumptuous to argue that these data and the behavioral implications I have outlined in this chapter should be taken as more than a first step in the understanding of a relationship between information content of particular memories and the complex structure of the nervous system. Nonetheless, I am confident that a method of deciphering the content of memories, this or some other, will prove indispensable in understanding the neural basis of memory.

ACKNOWLEDGMENTS

The research from our laboratory reported here was supported by NSF Grant GB 35205 and a faculty research grant from Swarthmore College. The secretarial skills of Ms. Dorothea Beebe and the critical comments of my students Glen Rosen, Paula Durlach, and Karen Strier added immeasurably to the preparation of this chapter. Particular thanks go to my colleague Lee Devin for invaluable, painstaking criticism of an earlier draft.

REFERENCES

1. Bolles, R. C. (1975): *Theory of Motivation.* Harper & Row, New York.
2. Cherkin, A. (1969): Kinetics of memory consolidation: Role of amnesic treatment parameters. *Proc. Natl. Acad. Sci. USA,* 63:1094–1101.
3. Chevalier, J. A. (1965): Permanence of amnesia after a single posttrial electroconvulsive seizure. *J. Comp. Physiol. Psychol.,* 59:125–127.
4. Chorover, S. L., and Schiller, P. H. (1965): Short-term retrograde amnesia in rats. *J. Comp. Physiol. Psychol.,* 59:73–78.
5. Deutsch, J. A. (1971): The cholinergic synapse and the site of memory. *Science,* 174:788–794.
6. Gold, P. E., Haycock, J. W., Macri, J., and McGaugh, J. L. (1973): An explanation of the reminder effect: A case for retrograde amnesia. *Science,* 180:1199–1201.
7. Hebb, D. O. (1949): *The Organization of Behavior.* Wiley, New York.
8. Herz, M. J., and Peeke, H. V. S. (1968): ECS-produced retrograde amnesia: Permanence vs. recovery over repeated testing. *Physiol. Behav.,* 3:517–521.
9. Hine, B., and Paolino, R. M. (1970): Retrograde amnesia: Production of skeletal but not cardiac response gradients by electroconvulsive shock. *Science,* 169:1224–1226.

10. McGaugh, J. L. (1966): Time-dependent processes in memory storage. *Science,* 153:1351–1358.
11. Miller, R. R., and Springer, A. D. (1972): Induced recovery of memory in rats following electroconvulsive shock. *Physiol. Behav.,* 8:645–651.
12. Miller, R. R., and Springer, A. D. (1973): Amnesia, consolidation, and retrieval. *Psychol. Rev.,* 80:69–79.
13. Overton, D. A. (1964): State dependent or "dissociated" learning produced with pentobarbital. *J. Comp. Physiol. Psychol.,* 57:3–12.
14. Penfield, W., and Roberts, L. (1959): *Speech and Brain Mechanisms.* Princeton Univ. Press, Princeton.
15. Quartermain, D., McEwen, B., and Azmitia, E. (1972): Recovery of memory following amnesia in the rat and the mouse. *J. Comp. Physiol. Psychol.,* 79: 360–379.
16. Rozin, P. (1976): The psychobiological approach to human memory. In: *Neural Mechanisms of Learning and Memory,* edited by M. R. Rosenzweig and E. L. Bennett, pp. 3–48. MIT Press, Cambridge.
17. Russell, W. R., and Nathan, P. W. (1946): Traumatic amnesia. *Brain,* 69:280–300.
18. Schneider, A. M. (1975): Two faces of memory consolidation: Storage of instrumental and classical conditioning. In: *Short-term Memory,* edited by D. Deutsch and J. A. Deutsch, pp. 339–354. Academic Press, New York.
19. Schneider, A. M., Tyler, J., and Jinich, D. (1974): Recovery from retrograde amnesia: A learning process. *Science,* 184:87–88.
20. Squire, L. R. (1974): Amnesia for remote events following electroconvulsive therapy. *Behav. Biol.,* 12:119–125.
21. Tulving, E. (1974): Cue-dependent forgetting. *Am. Sci.,* 62:74–82.
22. Warrington, E. K., and Sanders, H. T. (1971): The fate of old memories. *Q. J. Exp. Psychol.,* 23:432–442.
23. Warrington, E. K., and Weiskrantz, L. (1968): A new method of testing long-term retention with special reference to amnesic patients. *Nature,* 217:972–974.

STUDIES IN MAN

Brain Mechanisms in Memory and Learning:
From the Single Neuron to Man,
edited by M. A. B. Brazier.
Raven Press, New York © 1979.

Bioelectrical Expression of Long-Term Memory Activation and Its Possible Mechanisms

N. P. Bechtereva

Institute for Experimental Medicine,
Academy of Medical Sciences of the USSR, Leningrad, USSR

Recordings from electrodes implanted in deep brain structures for diagnostic or therapeutic purposes have revealed patterns of neuronal discharge peculiar to the response of the patient to verbal tests. Clear differentiation has been made between the discharge pattern evoked by the necessity to draw on long-term memory and that seen when the test word is semantically unfamiliar and cannot be matched to anything in storage.

The problem of memory is a subject for continuing research in physiology, biochemistry, molecular biology, biophysics, genetics, and cybernetics. The experience of these investigations has shown that sufficiently significant solutions are only possible on the basis of an integrative approach. The advantages of the integrative approach, however, do not exclude separate analytical stages of the problem and aspects of its investigation, different as they are in relative importance.

The physiological study of memory is based on investigation of those changes that occur in the brain during memorizing (learning); of the dynamics of trace phenomena and of the process of readout from long-term memory; and of the formation of cerebral signals, which either control verbal responses or play the part of the operative memory units.

Recording and study of the dynamics of the physiological changes occurring in different phases of memory are quite possible, because the process of memorizing during learning usually does not happen instantaneously, although phenomena of the imprinting type (instant memorizing) are plausible as has been shown in literature and observed by us (12,18,43,44,46) during electrical stimulation of the brain. And imprinting can be observed not only at the earliest stages of ontogenesis but also later.

It is evidently most advantageous biologically for the organism to have various forms of memory. Most important for preservation of the species is genetic memory, which unfolds during ontogenesis and into which the individually acquired memory brings only adaptive corrections. For realization of activities most important for preservation of an individual as the species representative and in which separate components are unpredictable, the mechanism of instant memory—imprinting—is used. And finally, all other kinds of activity determining the life of an individual in a changing environment, and particularly the life of a human being in the social milieu, are based on more or less rapidly, but not instantly, formed memory. The speed of formation in this case, even though associated with genetic features is much more the function of the objective or subjective significance of an element and, therefore, of the development of motivational mechanisms; hence, in a general way, it is a function of the brain's functional background.

The biological advantage of this kind of memorizing in the course of learning is, apparently, not only the possibility of selection, of filtration of the incoming information, but also of its order and the juxtaposition of different semantic fields with all the respective consequences of hierarchy of the subsequent associative search.

Genetically, a human being has perfect premises for the psychoneural memory realized during learning and in the course of individual socially enriched development. In the course of learning, the long-term psychoneural memory base is formed simultaneously with its usage in the form of readout, of transfer from the long-term memory into the operative one.

The connection between mental operations and memory processes is unbreakable. Separation of studies of mental processes proper from the memory process as such is always to a considerable extent artificial, and involves placing emphasis on the studies rather than in their essence. Indeed, the simplest mental conclusions are unthinkable without activation of a corresponding long-term memory base of verbal and nonverbal orders. In the course of these processes, not only does replenishment of the memory base occur continuously, but the transformation of associations and of their heirarchy occurs as well.

The data obtained from singling out, describing, and deciphering the cerebral coding of words and of intellectual-mnestic processes (7,8,16,17) proved to be essential for the understanding of the whole range of neuropsychology and neurolinguistics, including the physiology of analyzing systems, artificial intelligence, and a number of other lines of research. These data proved to be most important for the complex approach to the problem of memory.

Our studies were based on recording and analysis of impulse activity in neuronal populations of different subcortical structures within the thalamus, striopallidal system, upper portions of the brainstem, and some cortical areas in patients whose treatment and/or diagnosis were performed with the aid of implanted electrodes. The electrodes were made of 98% gold, 50 to 100 μm in diameter, and were covered up to the 1 mm tip with a neutral plastic phtoroplast-2 and gathered into bundles in such a way that each successive electrode terminated 3 to 5 mm above the preceding one. The impulse activity of neuronal populations was recorded on tape and analyzed with the

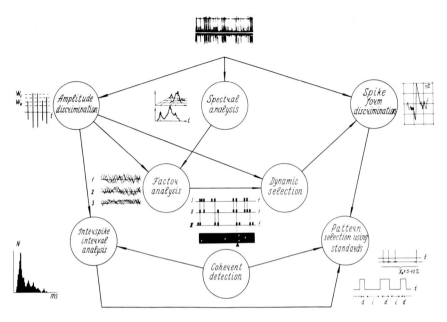

FIG. 1. Block-scheme of the methods for analysis of the impulse activity.

aid of analog and digital computers (Didac 4000, M-6000, Minsk-32) by special programs. Discrimination of the impulse activity was made by the frequency and structure of the impulse trains, by amplitude and form of impulses, and by the interrelationships between neurons and groups of neurons. From this primary analysis, specific patterns associated with the input signal were singled out and, on this basis, the following standard search for their analogs in the impulse activity was performed; the elementary components of these patterns were studied and used later for the further standard search (Fig. 1) (22,25). The impulse activity was studied during presentation of familiar and unfamiliar words, word-like signals, verbal short-term memory tests, and tests for generalization and mental conclusions. Different aspects of the method have been reported in more detail elsewhere (14,16,25,26, 28,40).

EFFECT OF THE LONG-TERM MEMORY BASE ON BIOELECTRIC PATTERNS

In the course of investigation into the neurophysiological correlates of words, it has been shown that, on perception of words, a pattern is being formed in the impulse activity of neuronal populations that is characterized by changes in the frequency and structure of the impulse trains; in the form of neuronal firing; by change of the interaction between neurons and groups of neurons both within neuronal populations and between distant populations (6,7,9,11).

In psychological tests, when words with semantic similarity were used, this pattern revealed a correlation of the newly presented signal with a certain associative field previously formed in the long-term memory of the individual.

Following the full pattern in the short-term memory verbal tests, a compressed pattern occurred in the impulse activity while retaining the basic elements of the full pattern. The time of occurrence and the dynamics of this compressed pattern depended on the subject's degree of familiarity with the words, for this determined the bioelectric expression of interaction between the initially occurring pattern and the long-term memory (16,17,22,23).

Analysis of the changing bioelectric patterns that occurred in tests for short-term memory, generalization, and mental conclusions revealed the compressed pattern to be functionally significant. One illustration of its functional significance is its role in the subject's verbal response. In the short-term memory tests, during the phase of retention in memory, it is possible to detect, in the impulse activity, different ratios between the full and the compressed patterns, depending on the contents of the task (presentation of familiar or unfamiliar words or word-like signals). And at the moment of the subject's verbal response, the full pattern of the impulse activity reappears as a copy of the initial one—in other words, the controlling pattern (7,10, 15,17). The ratio of the full controlling pattern to the compressed one during the short-term verbal memory tests is determined by the initial task given to the subject.

The effect of the trace existing in the long-term memory on the dynamics (i.e., changing of the pattern of the impulse activity of neuronal populations) can be brought out by varying the contents of the short-term memory test. After presentation of words seldom or frequently encountered in speech, or word-like signals, these may be correctly or wrongly reproduced verbally on the request, "Please, repeat!" Neurophysiologically, however, after perception of familiar words, there is a rapid disappearance of the developed full pattern of impulse activity, followed by a brief occurrence of the compressed patterns. Only at the moment of verbal response is there "reconstruction" of the full pattern similar to, although not identical with, the initial one. In contrast, during retention in memory of an unfamiliar word, the pattern appearing at the moment of its perception retains its form until the subject's verbal response. Evidently, preservation of the pattern in this latter case is associated with the necessity to remember the presented signals. However, the identity of tasks in both the first (familiar) and the second (unfamiliar) variants of the short-term memory test, differing only in the character of presented signals and in impulse changes, suggests that both phenomena are influenced by the long-term memory base. The disappearance of pattern on presentation of familiar words occurs as a result of recognition of the signal, whereas stability of the pattern on presentation of unfamiliar words and word-like signals is associated with the absence of inhibiting influences from the long-term memory base, for the new signal is not recognized subjectively. The stability of the bioelectric pattern optimizes conditions for the formation of a new long-term memory base.

The dependence of neurodynamic phenomena that occurs in the retention-in-memory phase, on the long-term memory base, and the character of this dependence are corroborated by the evidence that the second impulse pattern switches over to the first after the subject learns the meaning of previously unfamiliar words. After formation of this new base in long-term memory, the pattern appearing at the moment of perception of the word rapidly disappears from the impulse activity (i.e., it is inhibited on recognition of the now familiar word).

The compressed pattern is not always strictly the same but undergoes various neurodynamic transformations depending on the phase and character of the test and is neurophysiologically displayed, primarily, in the dynamics of correlation of the pattern's different elements and in the relative degree of their prominence (7,15,22,24,27). A long and tedious stretch of work lies ahead for determining exactly what the different variants of the compressed pattern are as juxtaposed with the word's elements: phoneme, syllables, morpheme, etc. In the physiology of mental activity, in neuropsychology and structural linguistics, the comparative study of the full and compressed patterns may help to answer the question: How, in the interaction with long-term memory, is the storage of new information absorbed, making possible its complete reconstruction? The data on the full and compressed patterns of the coding of words also make it possible to study the neurophysiological mechanisms of so-called inner speech, the phenomena used by the subject for transition from thought to verbal utterance (48).

BIOELECTRIC EXPRESSION OF LONG-TERM MEMORY ACTIVATION

The findings in coding of intellectual-mnestic processes indicate the presence in deep brain structures of information-specific links of the system for maintenance of mental activity. Traditional views of the science of the human brain explained the neurophysiological phenomena occurring in subcortical structures as the reflection of events at the cortical level. Thus, for instance, it was assumed that wherever the specific bioelectric code pattern appeared, the brain cortex was the address of the long-term memory (5). More recently, however, neuropsychology has accumulated an increasing amount of data on the significance of subcortical structures for long-term memory processes (35). The study of mnestic processes during electrical stimulation of subcortical structures makes it possible to reveal various structure-dependent activities for different types of memory (45). Further investigation into the neurophysiology of mental activity also makes one revise the idea of the exclusively cortical storage of the long-term memory and suggests the necessity to correct the hypothesis of spatial relationships between the intellectual processes and their basis, the long-term memory. The point lies, primarily, in neurophysiological differences of the pattern-code of words and its components in different subcortical structures and, therefore, in distribution of coding.

Following the discovery and description of the pattern-code of words, an analysis of its elementary components was carried out. The analysis showed that the code's elementary components reflect the activity of the successive firing of two, three, four, and more neurons of a single neuronal population with stable intervals between firings (8,22,27,37).

Study of these elementary components confirmed the hypothesis advanced in 1971 (4), namely, that a mutually complementing activity of the links in the system for maintenance of mental activity and of the distributed coding of verbal signals is the basis for intellectual-mnestic activity. Actual expression of this principle was the presence of different group sequences of firings in different links of the system. Only infrequently were the firing sequences very similar. The full cerebral pattern-code of a word is an envelope of the pattern-codes in different links of the system, the number of which seems to be rather great, particularly considering the presence in this system of flexible links (4,13).

The pattern-code, individual in each neuronal population, and the vast number of links in the system seem to create in every subject an individually unrepeatable cerebral code for a word. This is in formal agreement with psychological data on individual psychological variations in different subjects. As has been shown, however, the "kaleidoscope" of group sequences of firings in a neuronal population consists of code elementary sequences and in the patterns of the same word in different neuronal populations. In a single neuronal population, on successive presentation of words with elements of semantic similarity, very similar sequences of intervals are revealed (Fig. 2). These data give reason to study the hypothesis that elementary code-forming sequences of firings can aid in revealing a species similarity in the cerebral codes of words and intellectual-mnestic processes and in finding the species characteristics of the verbal signals reflected in the human brain. Naturally, hard work lies ahead for the accumulation, analysis, and systematization of elementary code patterns in order to check this assumption.

The results of the standard search showed that the vast number of links in the system did not lead to devaluation of the informational significance of each single link or of a single bioelectric pattern-code or code sequence. Using not only the general distributive pattern of a single population as the pattern-standard, but also the elementary group sequence of neuronal firings in cerebral subcortical structures, it is possible to detect pattern-codes in the impulse activity and to observe recognition of the test word by their elements (Fig. 3). Reconstruction (recognition) of a word by the pattern-code or by

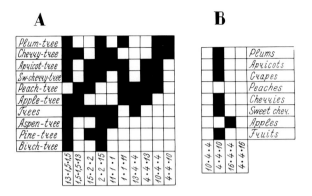

A **B**

FIG. 2. Matrix representation of a set of verbally specific group sequences of the pattern-code's interimpulse intervals singled out from the impulse activity of a neuronal population within the center median during utterance of words connected to each other by their sense. Horizontal line at the bottom, the averaged values of the group sequences of interimpulse intervals; vertical line, a series of verbal signals; black squares, certain code elements are present in the IA during a given verbal signal; white squares, code elements are absent.

its elements corroborates the proposal that these patterns are indeed codes. These data from subcortical recordings are also of importance for the problem of memory. They suggest revision of earlier ideas about the location of information storage in long-term memory, of the location of so-called engrams (matrices) of memory. The distribution of code in subcortical neuronal populations with the significance of its elements identified suggests a dis-

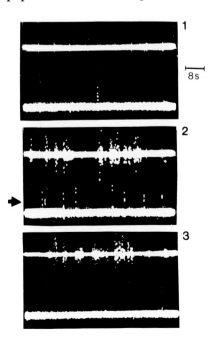

8 s

FIG. 3. The results of search in the impulse activity for the sequences of interimpulse intervals on a real time scale by a corresponding standard $(2-2-15 \pm 10\%$ msec). 1: Analysis of spontaneous activity (80 sec). 2: Analysis of activity during reproduction of the semantic field "trees." 3: The same for the verbal signals related to the semantic fields "flowers" and "rivers." Top (in each case): Phonogram. Bottom: Moments of the code elements singling out.

tributed character of the long-term verbal memory matrices and of the significance of subcortical elements.

What other findings, obtained in the course of studying the neurophysiological basis of intellectual-mnestic processes, confirm the role of subcortical structures in the long-term verbal memory?

Bundzen et al. (24–26), when studying neuronal firing during short-term memory tests with presentation of frequent and rare familiar words and meaningless sounds, showed neuronal firing stabilized in form, in subcortical structures of the human brain that was dependent on the degree of familiarity with the word and, therefore, on the long-term memory base (16,23). This stabilization was brief on presentation and reproduction of a frequent familiar word, lasted longer on presentation of rare familiar words, and persisted during the whole retention-in-memory phase, developing a tendency toward spatial spreading (over a population of neurons). It is highly probable that this phenomenon reflects a certain state of neuronal membranes (30,34,36, 41,47) supposedly related to those processes that underlie the activation of the long-term memory base. Discovery of these phenomena in the subcortical structures increases the probability of cortical-subcortical storage of the long-term memory matrices.

Analysis of the code elementary units (in the form of group-firing sequences with fixed intervals), in studies of recordings made during tests for generalization, gave new and more detailed data on the representation in the impulse activity of the process of long-term memory activation. Following the first presented word, a great number of group-firing sequences with three or four intervals appear repeatedly. This phenomenon is regarded as a neurophysiological expression of activation of the search for association. This change in the impulse activity becomes less obvious when the subject perceives that two or three words belong to the same semantic field; a complex block then appears comprising the group-firing sequences characteristic for the already presented words and the new firing sequences (Fig. 4). Later, this complex block was found to be the element of a generalizing word's pattern-code (22), and it could be an initial reflection of the probability for generalization by the minimum of word-elements of the semantic field.

In this case, from the standpoint of the memory problem, the appearance of the complex block is a bioelectric expression of the moment that long-term memory is being activated. A schematic presentation of this process is sketched in Fig. 4. Comparison of the initially occurring complex block with the pattern-code of a generalizing word emphasizes that, initially, not the complete cerebral reflection of a well-formed generalization appears but, rather, one of the stages of the process; this could be a phase of the probability decision-making concerning the semantic field, or a decision about the presence of semantic similarity in the presented words. Study was made of this question by comparing the appearance, after two or three words, of complex patterns included later in the controlling pattern of the

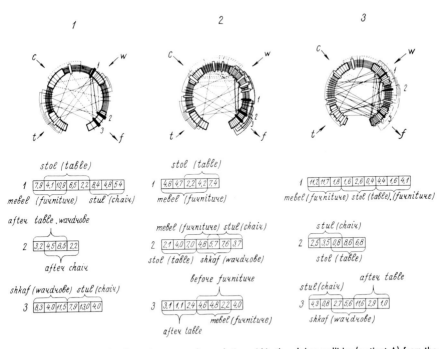

FIG. 4. Structure of impulse flow of a neuronal population within the globus pallidus (patient A) from the viewpoint of distribution of reappearing group sequences of firing. Top: Order of presenting the words and the subject's response (the time axis, in the form of an arch). Presentation of words marked with white sections of the arch outlined with solid line. Intervals between words are emphasized with hatching arches of different radii. The radially directed squares crossing the arch correspond to the sequences repeatedly reproduced and to complex blocks of elementary components of the patterns. The radially directed lines crossing the arch designate the singled out group sequences of firing. Solid lines connect the group sequences occurring during and after presentation of the word "table" with the loci of their reproduction; the hatched and undulate lines do the same for the words "chair" and "wardrobe," respectively. Bottom (1–3): Structure of the complex blocks presented as blackened squares. Each interimpulse interval has a corresponding square with the interval duration in msec inside. Near the parentheses containing the group sequences that constitute a block, it is shown where else, except the given block, this sequence is reproduced. t, table; c, chair; w, wardrobe; f, furniture.

generalizing idea. Naturally, if the given pattern is a signal associated only with the generalization process, if it is a reflection of recognition of semantic similarity, it should be highly similar in both cases. The possibility of the subject responding with a generalizing idea to presentation of only two or three words connected by semantic similarity suggests that a complex pattern such as that in Fig. 4 is, most probably, a representative pattern-code of the word "mabel" (in English, "furniture"); however, it cannot be fully excluded that the pattern is also associated here with a particular case of similarity recognition.

In the example in Fig. 4 of the formation of a generalization pattern-code, the importance of the bioelectric component of cerebral code pattern is once more emphasized. The word, "mebel" ("furniture") itself was absent from the test. Only semantically related words were used (stul, chair, etc.) but its pattern appears as the result of activation of the corresponding matrix present in the long-term memory. Thus, it turns out that the bioelectric representation of the activation of this long-term memory matrix comprises the elements of words belonging to the same semantic field. The pattern-code of a generalizing word reproduces separate elementary code patterns of words in combination with its own additional specific pattern. Neurophysiologically, this means that the generalization is not a single sampling and summation of significant elements but it introduces a new feature.

The bioelectric result of activation of the associative fields of long-term memory proved decipherable by analysis (on the basis of distributive pattern-standard; Fig. 5) of records of impulse activity obtained during tests for mental decision making.

Presentation of a visual image (the first item of the associative search) followed by a given verbal request (the second item outlining and limiting the associative search) led to the appearance in the impulse activity of a whole series of pattern-codes for those words that share a semantic connection with the test word and are also related to the response and limited by the verbal request (Fig. 6) (7,8,24).

These kinds of studies could add to the psychological data by presenting objective evidence about the character of the associative search during intellectual-mnestic activity. Continuation of these studies should further the

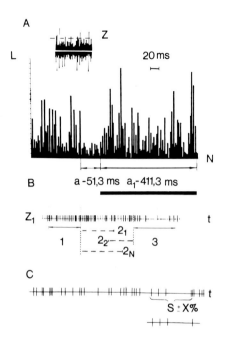

FIG. 5. Selection of the substandards of distributive patterns for optimal computer search. The top of the figure shows an epoch of the impulse activity with the amplitude section Z. A: Analogous representation of durations digitizing for successive interimpulse intervals at the amplitude section (0.7 of the maximal amplitude) of the impulse activity (Didac-4000). Abscissa: successive interimpulse intervals (N). Ordinate: duration of the intervals (L) (the epoch of intervals quanting 20 msec). The horizontal square beneath the abscissa marks the moment of utterance of the word "summer" by the subject, the epoch "a_1." The epoch "a" is the aggregate of intervals prior to utterance of the word "summer." B: Choice of the substandards for the following selection from the impulse flows. "Z_1" is a formed flow of neuronal discharges singled out at the amplitude section of the impulse activity; the vertical hatched lines delineate the time of perception of verbal signal (pattern 1), the interval between the perception, and the utterance of the verbal signal (pattern 2_1–2_N), and the time of utterance of the verbal signal (pattern 3). C: Search for the S standard with admittance $\pm \times \%$ in the successive series of interimpulse intervals.

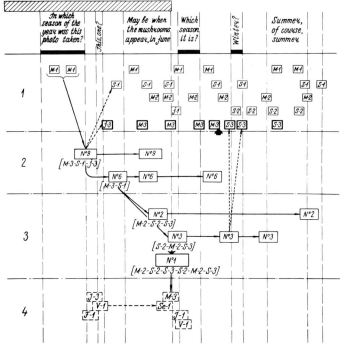

FIG. 6. Top: Picture presented as a test to the subject. Bottom: Results of the search for standard distributive patterns of verbal signals and their transformation in the course of mental conclusion in response to the question, "In which season of the year was this photo taken?" The hatched square represents the time of presentation of the picture. The impulse activity was recorded from the area of center median in patient A. 1. Results of direct selection of the impulse activity's standard patterns of three substandards singled out during processing of the words "mushroom" (1–1,2,3), "summer" (L–1,2,3), and "June" (1,2,3). 2. Results of selection of the "hybrid" patterns formed as the result of temporal occlusion of the code forms. Code block No. 6 includes the substandards "mushroom-3" and "summer-1." Code block No. 9 includes the substandards "mushroom-3," "summer-1," "June-1," and "July-3." 3. Results of selection of the "overlapping" patterns. Code block No. 3 includes the substandards "summer-2," "mushroom-2," "summer-3," the code block No. 1, "mushroom-2," "summer-2," and "summer-3." Code block No. 1 is the overlapping of the code blocks Nos. 2 and 3. 4. Results of selection of the impulse activity's standard patterns by the substandards singled out from the impulse activity during presentation of the test, retention in memory, and verbal response, which are the subjective signs of the result of mental conclusion: "June," "vegetables," "fruit," "sea," and "rest." Arrows show the temporal sequence of the code block's formation. The other designations are identical to the fragments 1 to 3 of this figure.

elucidation of the transfer from the potential form into the active one, from the long-term memory into the operative one, when a decision is made.

Studies of this kind are also promising for understanding the neuro-physiological basis of the complicated disorders of mental functions. The first results of these studies have already made an important contribution to the problem of memory. As in the short-term memory tests, both the full and the compressed patterns were found. In the full form, pattern-codes associated with verbalization of the test and with the response were present. The vast majority of pattern-codes for other words had the compressed form. There were also complex patterns combining the compressed form with incomplete codes for various words. We examined these data to evaluate the neurodynamics of intellectual-mnestic activity (10,15,23).

From the standpoint of the memory problem, one has to assume at least that a greater portion of verbal memory exists in this economical, com-pressed form and, probably, also as a combined complex. The appearance of the released pattern-codes in the form of controlling signals and com-parison of these data of pattern-codes of words in the short-term memory tests suggest that the signal that emerges and the mechanism of its emergence are most closely related to recognition of the signal and to verbalization of the response. The release of a pattern as well as its compression cannot proceed without participation of the information-specific long-term memory. One cannot exclude, however, that some other less specific cerebral mech-anisms may take part in the mechanism of release. Are not these factors the emotionally active or emotionally neutral activating influences, the sig-nificance of which, for memory mechanisms, although acknowledged, is far from being fully understood?

HYPOTHETICAL MECHANISMS FOR ORGANIZATION OF INTERACTION BETWEEN THE BIOELECTRIC AND THE STRUCTURAL COMPONENTS OF MEMORY

One of the major problems is the question: How, and by what mechanisms, does the rapid involvement of a multitude of links occur in the system for maintenance of mental activity? What about synaptic delay and is this al-ways the same? Is it possible that a pace-maker mechanism exists?

Neurophysiological study emphasizes the difference of mental activity from other kinds of activity in complexity and in cerebral organization. We have already mentioned the relatively greater role of the flexible links in the system maintaining mental, as compared with other, activities. It is necessary to bear in mind in this case the considerably greater role of the specific neurodynamics in a structure as compared with the specifics of the structure itself and of its functional state. The electrical stimulation of different cerebral regions is known to elicit different motor, visceral, and emotional effects. Varying the parameters of the current alters the character of the result (19). Stimulation evoked different kinds of nonspecific effects in mental activity. One exception seems to be the phenomena in epileptic patients cited by Penfield and Jasper (38,39)—the reproduction of coherent pictures from past experience. These phenomena should be regarded, however, as evidence of the reinforcement of block memory in the abnormal epileptic brain, rather than imposing the mental activity. Considering the possibility of word reconstruction from the elements of its pattern, the significance of ontogenetically formed neurodynamics, with its peculiar dependence on the long-term memory base, really acquires first-rate importance. (To say in a figurative manner, the "talk" between structures proves to be no less important for mental activity than the activity of the structure itself.)

Assuming this importance of the neurodynamics as the cerebral basis for mental activity, it should be admitted that if a pace-maker is involved, the latter must differ in principle from the rigid structure-bound formations and must instead be a dynamic constellation of structures springing up under the influence of inner or environmental factors, verbal request included. Concrete significance of a pace-maker mechanism can and must differ according to the character of the activity. Thus, for instance, its primary role in tasks for generalization involves providing the conditions for a wide associative search resolved, apparently, with the aid of nonspecific activating (synchronizing) (32,33) influences. The recognition of the belonging of two or three words (phenomena) to a common semantic (associative) field determines the direction of the subsequent associative search and its limitation (i.e., inhibition of excessive search).

If the activity is repeated, facilitation of the formation of the pace-maker occurs owing to constant activation of a corresponding matrix in the long-term memory. If the activity changes, the dynamic pace-maker changes as well. The role of this pace-maker involves, primarily, controlling the organization and reorganization of the system for maintenance of mental activity, with proper activation or limitation of the long-term memory associative fields as is appropriate for the situation. This hypothetical dynamic pace-maker would not exclude the presence of the "comparing apparatus" (Anokhin's "acceptor," ref. 3) that is, most likely, one of the phases of the pace-maker development.

There is neurophysiological evidence (35) that deep regions of the frontal lobes maintain the selectivity of memory along with deep regions of the temporal lobes (21). One can assume that these brain regions take part in the constellation of structures constituting the dynamic pace-maker. The pace-maker mechanism includes both the specific and nonspecific elements, the specific brain regions being those to which a stimulus launching the developing activity is addressed.

The novelty of such ideas about the organization of mental activity rests on the idea of a pace-maker appearing as the result of events occurring in the inner milieu and in the environment (including the social one) to form a dynamic constellation of structures, the pace-maker not being rigidly bound to any one structure.

The dynamic (i.e., movable) character of the pace-maker's organization is extremely advantageous for the vast variety of mental processes. Were there multiple pace-makers, each located within its own specific structure, their number would have to be astronomical.

Development of mental activity is possible only if it is based on the principle of dynamic controlling apparatuses, the number and form of which are not limited to a brain region. The phasic development and reorganization of dynamic pace-makers either determine the logic of mental processes or are the neurophysiological mechanism of this logic, thus preventing a chaos of associations, and a chaos in mental activity.

Transmission of a coded excitation proceeds from pace-maker to other links of the system for maintenance of mental activity through synapses between neurons that take part in the formation of elementary code sequences where their synaptic delays can play the role of a quantifying factor. However, even the presence of pace-maker mechanism and the vast amount of intracerebral connections cannot, apparently, secure a rapidly enough and (what is especially important) a practically simultaneous involvement of the *whole* system needed for a complex mental activity.

An alternative is suggested: Either the pace-maker apparatus proves able to transmit signals to all significant links of the system simultaneously, by creation of the conditions for optimal spread of excitation or, between the numerous links of the system, yet another form of connection exists. The former assumption is supported by the studies and theoretical view of Livanov (32) concerning the synchronizing role of nonspecific intracerebral influences providing optimization of conditions for interaction. The latter assumption, however, should also be studied in relation to the data obtained by Kvassov (31), Rusinov (42), Golikov (29), Adey (1,2), Bogoch (20), and others.

When the specific features of mental activity and its cerebral maintenance are borne in mind, it seems plausible that its spatial-temporal relationships are realized in the brain by interaction between different forms of information transmission.

A growing number of studies are aimed at the problem of memory. Regardless of whether memory is considered to be a single process or whether the processes of short- and long-term memory differ from each other, the great majority of investigators are unanimous that comprehending the neurophysiology of memory is impossible without knowledge of its structural-biochemical mechanisms. More complete data of this nature need to be obtained by studying the neurophysiological basis of mental activity because of the particular significance of specific neurodynamics in cerebral structures required.

REFERENCES

1. Adey, W. R. (1970): Spontaneous electrical brain rhythms accompanying learned responses. In: *The Neurosciences,* edited by F. O. Schmitt, pp. 224–243. Rockefeller University, New York.
*2. Adey, W. R. (1977): The models of cerebral cell membranes as the substratum for information storage. *Fiziol. Tcheloveka,* 3, 5:774–788.
*3. Anokhin, P. K. (1968): *Biology and Neurophysiology of Conditioned Reflex.* Meditzina, Moscow. (In English: Pergamon Press, Oxford, New York, 1974.)
*4. Bechtereva, N. P. (1971): *Neurophysiological Aspects of Mental Activity in Man.* Meditzina, Leningrad.
*5. Bechtereva, N. P. (1974): *Neurophysiological Aspects of Mental Activity in Man,* 2nd. ed. revised and completed. Meditzina, Leningrad.
6. Bechtereva, N. P. (1974): Neurophysiological mechanisms of mental activity in man. In: *Proc. Int. Union of Physiol. Sci., 26th Int. Congr., New Delhi, Vol. X: 18–19.* Thomson Press, India.
*7. Bechtereva, N. P. (1975): The neurophysiological code of simplest mental processes in humans. *Vestn. AN SSSR,* 11:84–91.
*8. Bechtereva, N. P. (1975): Particular and general mechanisms for cerebral maintenance of mental activity and the prospects of the problem. *Fiziol. Tcheloveka,* 1, 1:6–17.
9. Bechtereva, N. P. (1976): Neurophysiological particular and general mechanisms of the cerebral maintenance of mental activity in man, and prospects of the problem. In: *Mechanisms in Transmission of Signals for Conscious Behaviour,* edited by T. Desiraju, pp. 323–344. Elsevier, Amsterdam.
*10. Bechtereva, N. P. (1976): Coded by nature, deciphered by man. *Nauka i zhizn,* 9:79–83.
*11. Bechtereva, N. P., and Bundzen, P. V. (1974): On neurophysiological coding of mental phenomena in man. *Totus Homo,* 5:68–78.
*12. Bechtereva, N. P., and Smirnov, V. M. (1975): Cerebral organization of emotions in humans. *Vestn. AMN SSSR,* 8:8–19.
*13. Bechtereva, N. P., Bondartshuk, A. N., Smirnov, V. M., and Trohatchev, A. I. (1967): *Physiology and Pathophysiology of Human Deep Brain Structures.* Meditzina, Moscow-Leningrad.
*14. Bechtereva, N. P., Bundzen, P. V., and Gogolitsyn, Yu. L. (1977): *Cerebral Codes of Mental Activity.* Nauka (Science), Leningrad.
*15. Bechtereva, N. P., Bundzen, P. V., Gogolitsyn, Yu. L., Kaplunovsky, A. S., and Malyshev, V. N. (1975): Organizational principles of the neural code of in- dividual-mental activity. *Fiziol. Tcheloveka,* 1, 1:44–58.
*16. Bechtereva, N. P., Bundzen, P. V., Keidel, W. D., and David, E. E. (1973): The principles of organization of the structure of spatial-temporal code of the short- term verbal memory. *Fiziol. Zh. SSSR,* 59, 12:1785–1802.
*17. Bechtereva, N. P., Bundzen, P. V., Matveev, Yu. K., and Kaplunovsky, A. S. (1971): Functional reorganization of activity in neuronal populations of the human brain in short-term memory. *Fiziol. Zh. SSSR,* 57, 12:1745–1761.
*18. Bechtereva, N. P., Gratchev, K. V., Orlova, A. N., and Yatsuk, S. L. (1963): Usage of multiple electrodes implanted into the human deep brain structures, for therapy in hyperkineses. *Zh. Nevropatol. Psikhiatr.,* 1:3–8.
*19. Bechtereva, N. P., Moiseeva, N. I., Orlova, A. N., and Smirnov, V. M. (1964): Some data on neurophysiology and functions of subcortical structures of the human brain. In: *Proc. X Natl. Congr. Physiologists,* pp. 124–125. Nauka, Mos- cow-Leningrad.
20. Bogoch, S. (1973): Glycoproteins and brain circuitry: The signpost theory in normal memory function, and in the regressive states of brain tumours and the psychoses. In: *Biological Diagnosis of Brain Disorders: The Future of the Brain Sciences,* edited by S. Bogoch, pp. 123–137. Spectrum, New York.

* In Russian.

*21. Brazier, M. A. B. (1962): Long-persisting electrical traces in the brain of man and their possible relationship to higher nervous activity. In: *Electroencephalographic Investigation of Higher Nervous Activity,* edited by G. D. Smirnov, pp. 341–353. Academy of Medical Science of the USSR, Moscow. (In English: *EEG Journal,* Suppl. 13:347–358, 1960.)

*22. Bundzen, P. V. (1976): Further analysis of code maintenance of cerebral informational-controlling functions. *Fiziol. Tcheloveka,* 2, 2:39–49.

23. Bundzen, P. V. (1976): Analysis of informational-controlling functions of the long-term memory engrams. In: *Mechanisms of Memory Modulation,* edited by N. P. Bechtereva, pp. 35–38. Nauka (Science), Leningrad.

24. Bundzen, P. V. (1977): Analysis of structural-systemic organization of informational coding. *Fiziol. Tcheloveka,* 3, 3:404–414.

*25. Bundzen, P. V., Gogolitsyn, Yu. L., David, E. E., Kaplunovsky, A. S., and Perepelkin, P. D. (1973): The structural-systemic approach to analysis of the processes of functional reorganization in neuronal populations. *Fiziol. Zh. SSSR,* 59, 12:1803–1810.

*26. Bundzen, P. V., Malyshev, V. N., and Perepelkin, P. D. (1975): Standard discrimination of the multi-unit activity and selection of code patterns from the standpoint of systemic-structural approach. *Fiziol. Tcheloveka,* 1, 6:1064–1069.

*27. Gogolitsyn, Yu. L. (1976): Some neurophysiological correlates of the process of word sense generalization. *Fiziol. Tcheloveka,* 2, 3:425–432.

*28. Gogolitsyn, Yu. L., and Perepelkin, P. D. (1975): Construction of similarity matrices for factor representations of temporal-spatial organization of neuronal ensembles. *Fiziol. Tcheloveka,* 1, 5:916–919.

*29. Golikov, N. V. (1970): The problem of local and spreading excitation in the modern neurophysiology. In: *The Mechanisms of Local Response and Spreading Excitation,* pp. 5–12. Nauka (Science), Leningrad.

*30. Khodorov, B. I. (1969): *The Problem of Excitability.* Meditzina, Leningrad.

*31. Kvassov, D. G. (1957): Conduction, inhibition, and stability. *Fibiol. Zh. SSSR,* 43, 8:744–752.

*32. Livanov, M. N. (1975): Neuronal mechanisms of memory. *Uspekhi Fiziol. Nauk,* 6, 3:66–89.

*33. Livanov, M. N., and Raeva, S. N. (1976): Microelectrode study of neuronal mechanisms of voluntary mnestic activity in humans. In: *Mechanisms of Memory Modulation,* edited by N. P. Bechtereva, pp. 14–24. Nauka (Science), Leningrad.

34. Llinás, R. (1974): The role of dendritic impulses in neuronal integration. In: *Mechanisms of Uniting Neurons in a Neural Center,* pp. 12–21. Academy of Medical Science of the USSR, Leningrad.

*35. Luria, A. R. (1976): *Neuropsychology of Memory,* Part II. Pedagogika, Moscow.

36. Machek, J., and Pavlik, V. (1973): Averaged extracellular field potentials of spontaneously firing brain neurons influenced by pentylenetrazole. *Activ. Nerv. Sup. (Praha),* 15, 3:172–174.

*37. Malyshev, V. N. (1977): Differentiation of code elements of the verbal signals constituting semantic fields. *Fiziol. Tcheloveka,* 3, 1:37–43.

38. Penfield, W. (1958): The role of the temporal cortex in recall of past. Experience and interpretation of the present. In: *Ciba Foundation Symposium on Neurological Basis of Behaviour,* edited by G. Wolstenholme and C. O'Connor, pp. 149–172. London.

39. Penfield, W., and Jasper, H. (1954): *Epilepsy and the Functional Anatomy of the Brain.* Little, Brown, Boston.

*40. Perepelkin, P. D. (1977): Selection of interval patterns of the multi-unit activity on the real time scale. *Fiziol. Tcheloveka,* 3, 3:553–556.

41. Rosenthal, F. (1967): A dendritic component in extracellular records from single cortical pyramidal tract neurons. *J. Neurophysiol.,* 30, 4:753–768.

*42. Rusinov, V. S. (1969): *The Dominanta.* Meditzina, Moscow. (In English: *The Dominant Focus,* edited by R. W. Doty. Consultants Bureau, New York, 1973.)

43. Sem-Jacobsen, C. W. (1968): *Depth-Electrographic Studies of the Human Brain and Behaviour.* Charles C. Thomas, Springfield, Ill.

*44. Smirnov, V. M. (1970): Neuropsychology and the problems of studying the deep structures of the human brain. *Vestn. AMN SSSR,* 1:35–42.
*45. Smirnov, V. M. (1976): Electric stimulation of the human brain and the mechanisms of long-term memory. In: *Mechanisms of Memory Modulation,* edited by N. P. Bechtereva, pp. 120–125. Nauka (Science), Leningrad.
*46. Smirnov, V. M. (1976): *Stereotaxic Neurology,* Meditzina, Leningrad.
*47. Vislobokov, A. I. (1974): Forms of the intracellular action potentials of body of the mollusk identified giant neurons. *Fiziol. Zh. SSSR,* 60, 1:42–47.
*48. Vygotsky, L. S. (1934): *Thought and Language.* Moscow. [In English: (Vygotsky, L. S.) edited and translated by E. Haufman and G. Vakar. MIT Press, Cambridge, 1962.]

Brain Mechanisms in Memory and Learning:
From the Single Neuron to Man,
edited by M. A. B. Brazier.
Raven Press, New York © 1979.

Relationship Between Paradoxical Sleep and Memory Processes

Vincent Bloch, Elizabeth Hennevin, and Pierre Leconte

Université de Paris-Sud, and Département de Psychophysiologie, Laboratoire de Physiologie Nerveuse, Centre National de la Recherche Scientifique, 91190 Gif-sur-Yvette, France

The idea is now widely accepted that the memory trace is not built up instantaneously and that the sensory encoding of information is followed by a perseveration of brain activity that is indispensable for the storage of this information. It is assumed that this perseveration is based on bioelectrical events that are the condition for the establishment of permanent structural changes. A first critical period is known as the phase of memory "consolidation," but it would be better named the early phase of "information processing" because the word "consolidation" implies some sort of a priming mechanism acting on an already established trace (2,3). Many data suggest that processing is not completed at the end of this phase and that dynamic processes can be reinstalled either when brain activation favors them (4) or when a pertinent signal triggers the readout of the trace (29). For instance, after the perturbation of the consolidation phase, McGaugh (37) was able to reactivate the trace by injection of excitatory drugs. Moreover, after spontaneous forgetting, the delivery of a "reminder" reactivates the memory trace and reintroduces a period of susceptibility during which this trace can be either perturbed by an amnesic agent (15) or facilitated by a stimulating agent (20). So, dynamic processes involved during the so-called consolidation period or during retrieval seem to be sustained by brain activation. It has been demonstrated that mild electrical stimulation of the reticular activating system increases retention when it is delivered during the first 90 sec after the learning trials (5,6,12). It has also recently been shown that such stimulation enhances memory retrieval when it is delivered just after the presentation of a reminder (16).

In this chapter, we discuss data that suggest that processing mechanisms following learning are spontaneously reinstalled during paradoxical sleep (PS), the main characteristic of which is brain activation. The beneficial effect of sleep on the retention of information acquired during wakefulness has been demonstrated many times in man since the first Jenkins and Dallenbach study (28). Recently it has been demonstrated (1) that memory traces established shortly before sleep onset are not simply insulated from interference during the sleep period, and such a study suggests that sleep plays an active role in memory mechanisms. When PS was discovered, such an "active" hypothesis was reinforced because of the considerable brain activity recorded during this phase, pointing to the existence of an active functional process. In addition, the sensory isolation during this sleep would suggest that any processing during this phase must involve information that has been previously registered during wakefulness.

To test the hypothesis of relations between PS and memory processes, two experimental procedures have been used. One consists of studying the effects of postlearning PS deprivation on memory; convincing evidence shows that even short PS deprivation, imposed immediately after acquisition, impairs memory (22,31).

The second method consists of studying the effect of learning on characteristics of subsequent PS. Lucero (36) was the first investigator to publish data showing an augmentation of PS following maze learning, and since 1969, we have accumulated in our laboratory considerable evidence showing that a great variety of learning tasks produce, in rats and mice as well as in cats, an increase in the amount of PS during the period of spontaneous sleep following the training period. Other investigators have also observed this PS-augmentation phenomenon after learning in mice (19,47,48) and even in human babies (41).

PARADOXICAL SLEEP AUGMENTATION AFTER LEARNING

The general procedure was to record, in all animals, the activity of the cortex and the hippocampus and the electromyogram; the durations of wakefulness, slow-wave sleep (SWS), and PS were measured through a computer. In order to have stable references of sleep characteristics, rats were kept in their recording cages 3 weeks before the experiments, and they were daily handled and familiarized with the recording cables. For 3 days before the experiment, a recording period of 2 or 3 hr was taken, always at the same time of the day for each animal. Afterward, learning schedules were programmed in order to record subsequent free-sleep periods at the same time of the day as the reference recordings. If animals had to be fed or provided with water for learning, reference recordings were taken after the same amount of food or water delivery.

Paradoxical Sleep Increases in Rats After Positively as Well as Negatively Reinforced Learning Tasks

An active-avoidance conditioning with massed or distributed practice was followed in the subsequent 3-hr period by important PS-duration increases (25,32,34).

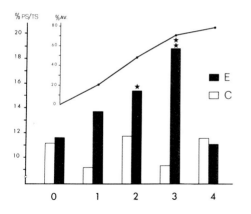

FIG. 1. PS augmentation after avoidance learning. Ratio of PS to total sleep (% PS/TS) during a 3-hr recording period after each daily block of 15 trials in avoidance conditioning. Column marked 0 shows the PS/TS ratio before learning. The learning curve for group E is shown above the histograms. Note the increase in PS ratio in relation to the level of learning and the return to the prelearning level when the learning "plateau" is reached. Level of significance: *, between $p < 0.05$ and $p < 0.02$; **, between $p < 0.01$ and $p < 0.001$. Black columns, conditioning, group E; white columns, pseudoconditioning, group C (Modified from Leconte et al., ref. 34.)

In the distributed practice experiment (one 15-trial session each day), experimental rats underwent shuttle-box–avoidance conditioning during 4 days. A yoked control group was tested for the effects of shock and tone stimulations. The control rats showed no significant change in PS ratio at any time during the experiment. By contrast, in the experimental group, there were significant increases in the PS ratio after the second (30% increase) and third (62% increase) conditioning sessions. On the fourth day, when performance reached the asymptote, PS ratio returned to the reference level (see Fig. 1). Each PS ratio increase was due to a PS duration increase, SWS duration not showing any change (see Fig. 2). This PS-duration increase appeared to be a function of an increase of the number of PS, whereas the average duration of each phase remained invariable.

The acquisition of Skinnerian conditioning was also followed by PS-duration increases (26). Rats were placed daily in a Skinner box where, for 6 min, they could receive water by pressing a bar. Immediately after each learning

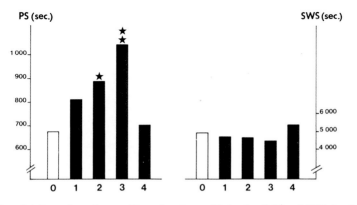

FIG. 2. Effect of daily sessions of an avoidance learning on PS duration (left) and SWS duration (right) during 3-hr recording period. Note the absence of modification of the SWS duration. See Fig. 1 for the learning curve. Level of significance: *, between $p < 0.05$ and $p < 0.02$; **, between $p < 0.01$ and $p < 0.001$. White columns (0), reference levels.

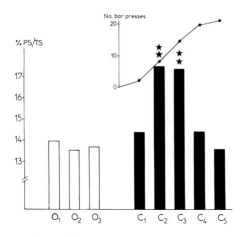

FIG. 3. PS augmentation after Skinnerian conditioning. Ratio of PS to total sleep (% PS/TS) during a 3-hr recording period after each daily session of 6 min of a Skinnerian learning. The learning curve is shown above the histograms. Note the return to reference level after the fourth and fifth sessions. Level of significance: **, between $p < 0.01$ and $p < 0.001$. White columns, PS ratio before learning (3 consecutive days); black columns, PS ratio after each learning session. (Modified from Hennevin et al., ref. 26.)

session, sleep phases were measured during a 3-hr recording period. With respect to the prelearning reference level, we observed a significant PS ratio increase after the second (27% increase) and third (26% increase) learning sessions and a return to reference level in the fourth and fifth sessions (see Fig. 3). These PS-ratio increases appeared to be a function of increases in the PS duration without any modification of SWS.

Similarly, the acquisition of a maze learning task was followed by increases in PS-duration (7). In a linear maze formed from a series of T units, condensed milk was placed in the goal box as the reward. The learning problem consisted of a right-left-right-left alternation. Rats were given only one learning trial each day. With respect to the prelearning reference level, we observed, in the 2 hr following each learning trial, no modification in SWS but

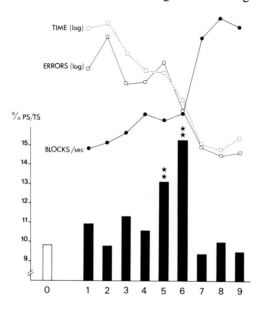

FIG. 4. Effect of maze learning on subsequent PS ratio (% PS/TS). Columns show the PS ratio during the daily 2-hr recording periods. The learning (three parameters) is shown above the columns. Level of significance: **, between $p < 0.01$ and $p < 0.001$. White column, PS ratio before learning (reference level); black columns, PS ratio after each daily trial of maze learning. (Modified from Hennevin and Leconte, ref 24.)

a significant increase of PS duration after the fifth (34% increase) and sixth (56% increase) trials (see Fig. 4).

In our experiments PS augmentation appears to begin almost immediately, counting either from the latency of sleep onset or from the latency of the first PS phase. This characteristic is a relative phenomenon since we have found (33) that we could artificially delay sleep onset by 90 min without altering the PS-augmentation effect or producing a learning deficit (see Fig. 5). But, by delaying sleep onset for 3 hr, the acquisition of learning was impaired and PS augmentation was not observed (see Fig. 5). Regarding the useful duration of PS augmentation, we observed (35) that a period of 90 min of free sleep following each learning session was sufficient for good retention to occur, but a period of only 30 min of free sleep—during which PS increase was not observed—did not allow the learned attribute to be established. Sixty minutes of free sleep—with PS increases—only slightly disturbed the learning curve (see Fig. 6). Therefore, the period immediately following learning, during which time the integrity of sleep seems necessary, is, in rats, between 60 and 90 min.

This result confirms the data of PS-deprivation experiments showing that a

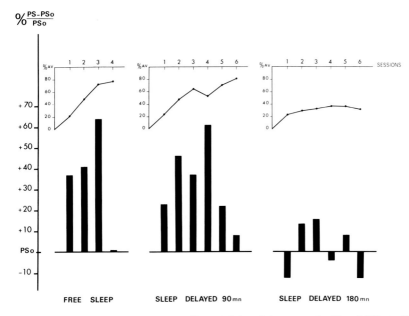

FIG. 5. PS increase after avoidance learning; effects of delay of sleep onset for 90 and 180 min. Three groups of animals were studied. This figure shows the relative PS variations during 2 hr of recording after each daily block of 15 trials for each group. Sleep delays were produced by total sleep deprivation. PS_0 is the PS duration obtained before conditioning in the same conditions of sleep deprivation. The avoidance-response learning curve of each group is shown above the columns. Note that if sleep onset is delayed for 180 min after each conditioning session, learning is impaired and no PS increase can be observed. By contrast, retarding sleep onset for 90 min does not affect conditioning or the subsequent increase of PS. AV, avoidance. (From Leconte and Hennevin, ref. 33.)

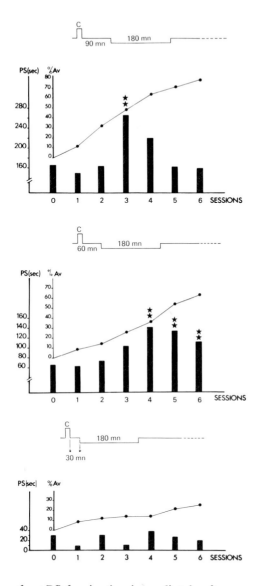

FIG. 6. PS increase after avoidance learning; effects of sleep limitation to 30, 60, and 90 min. Three groups of animals were studied. This figure shows the variations of PS duration for each group during the free-sleep period following each daily block of 15 trials. After each period of free sleep, the animal was kept awake for 3 hr. Column 0 presents the reference level of PS duration obtained before conditioning in the same conditions (i.e., period of free sleep following which the animal was kept awake for 3 hr). Above the columns are shown the learning curve and experimental design of each group. Note that a period of 90 min of free sleep immediately following each conditioning session is sufficient for good retention to occur. Whereas a period of only 30 min free sleep does not allow conditioning to be established; limitation to 60 min of free sleep only slightly disturbs the learning curve. Level of significance: **, between $p < 0.01$ and $p < 0.001$. C, conditioning; AV, avoidance. (Modified from Leconte et al., ref. 35.)

short PS deprivation immediately after an acquisition session impairs memory in rats; if this same deprivation is delayed after learning for 2 or 3 hr, memory is not impaired (21,42–45).

So, it would appear that one of the essential elements for memory fixation is the presence of PS in sufficient quantity, occurring quickly after learning.

Paradoxical Sleep Augmentation in Cats

PS augmentation after learning has been also shown in our laboratory in cats by Lecas (30) and Maho (38).

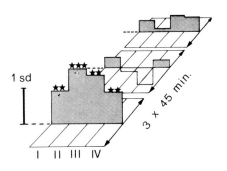

FIG. 7. Three-dimensional representation of changes in cumulative PS duration at the four successive steps of learning in cats (roman numbers at bottom front). Step II corresponds to the largest improvement of performance; step IV corresponds to the "plateau" of the learning curve. Shifts are plotted as differences from control means. On the Z axis are drawn the three histograms related to the first three 45 min of sleep. Amplitude scale is one standard deviation of the control distribution. Note the highest increase of PS at step II and no further increase of PS after the first 45-min period. Level of significance: **, $p < 0.01$; ***, $p < 0.001$. (From Lecas, ref. 30.)

In the Lecas study, within the control situation, the animals were passively provided with milk before going to sleep. Within the learning situation, they were given 25 trials of training (about 1 min per trial) during which they had to lick the small reward cup during a 5-sec tone. When this response was given, a photocell actuated the distributor and milk was delivered. It took cats from 2 to 6 days to reach the learning criterion (90% success in the same session). In both control and learning situations, the maximum liquid intake (25 ml) was far less than the quantity necessary for the satiation of the animals. Results showed a PS-duration augmentation after every step of learning and especially after the second step corresponding to the largest improvement of performance (see Fig. 7). A discrepancy between cats and rodents appears from these data since PS changes resulted from an increase of PS-episode duration rather than from an augmentation of the number of PS phases. Nevertheless, as in rats, the PS increase appeared during the first 45 min after learning; afterward, no further augmentation was observed.

In the Maho study, a PS augmentation was observed after trials of an active-avoidance conditioning, with a maximum occurring before the stabilization of performance.

RELATION BETWEEN PARADOXICAL SLEEP INCREASES AND ACQUISITION PROCESSES

The central problem raised by the results discussed above is whether PS increases are truly related to memory mechanisms or are dependent on factors associated with the experimental conditions imposed on the animal. Among the factors that could be followed by sleep modifications are the handling of animals, a new situation producing fear or exploration, the motor activity implied by learning, stimulations by conditioned stimulus, the effect of reinforcement (negative or positive), and even the sleep deprivation produced by the time spent in learning. But, our results show that none of these factors account for PS increase. Indeed, the reference recordings were made after handling, after placing the animals in experimental cages for the same time as for acquisition periods, and—in the case of positive-reinforcement learnings—after feeding or drinking the same quantity as during acquisition sessions.

On the other hand, it is not the duration of the acquisition period that is the important factor for triggering PS augmentation. For instance, in maze learning, only one trial lasting about 10 sec was followed by PS augmentation.

Last, the following results give evidence that PS increases are truly related to acquisition:

1. PS augmentation is correlated with learning achievement.

First, we have already seen that pseudoconditioned rats, yoked to animals trained to an avoidance learning, did not present any change in subsequent PS.

Moreover, when animals are unable to learn the task, they do not present any PS increase. Indeed, animals trained during 90 min to avoid an electric footshock in a shuttle-box without success, did not show subsequent PS augmentation (34). We have found the same results with a Skinnerian conditioning (see Fig. 8). The same result has also been obtained by Paul and Dittrichova (41) in human infants. These observations may be related to data in the literature showing the existence of a positive correlation between acquisition ability and spontaneous PS amount in animals (11,40), and in man (8–10,17,18,46).

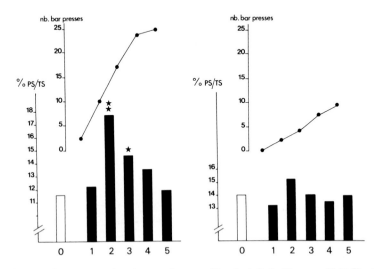

FIG. 8. Effect of a Skinnerian conditioning on subsequent PS ratio. Left: Fast learners. Right: Slow learners. The learning curve is shown above the columns. Note the absence of PS increase in the slow learners group. Level of significance: *, between $p < 0.05$ and $p < 0.02$; **, between $p < 0.01$ and $p < 0.001$. *White columns,* PS ratio reference level (mean of three recordings; the daily recording periods lasted 2 hr); *black columns,* PS ratio obtained for the 2 hr following each daily learning session of 6 min.

In addition, simple tasks like escape learning do not produce **PS** augmentation (22). Similarly, Pearlman et al. (21,42,44,45) show that only complex tasks are impaired by **PS** deprivation.

2. PS augmentation is correlated with critical stages of learning.

We have already observed that **PS** augmentation appears at some definite place in the course of learning. The greatest **PS** increase always occurs at an acquisition stage between the first training sessions and the stabilization of performance.

Such a result has been corroborated with an avoidance-learning task using a very distributed practice (one daily session of only six trials) where **PS** duration increases appeared neither after the first sessions of acquisition nor when the performance reached the asymptote, but appeared in the middle of acquisition (between 25 and 36%) (22).

The same observations have been made for maze learning done with only one trial a day (24). In this experiment, one peak of **PS** augmentation followed the fifth (34% increase) and sixth (56% increase) trials; before and after this step of acquisition, no change in **PS** could be observed. It must be pointed out that the day following the **PS** increase a large improvement of the performances could be observed (see Fig. 4).

We hypothesize that these peaks of **PS** increase are linked to a critical period of acquisition and are a manifestation of high-level central nervous system activity necessary for information processing. Moreover, the existence of such a critical period revealed by **PS** augmentations seems confirmed by the study of variations of some peripheral and central indices of arousal. So, in our laboratory, Maho has shown that a maximum of central (cortical arousals) and peripheral (heart rate and respiratory changes) activation characterizes the stage of acquisition just preceding the asymptote of the learning curve in an avoidance task. In the same manner, Lecas (J. C. Lecas, *unpublished data*) shows, in cats, the existence of a peak of reticular and hippocampal multiunitary activation when there is a maximum increase in correct responses in a reaction time task.

Finally, we have seen that, in all cases, **PS** duration returns to its normal value when the learning task has been mastered. However, if then the animals are facing a new situation that starts again a learning activity, **PS** augmentation reappears immediately. That could be seen when animals were retrained in the same maze but with a new configuration of gates (24). It was also observed when a complication of an active-avoidance conditioning was given by introducing a stimulus differentiation (31). In Fig. 9, it can be seen that the introduction of a 250 Hz S^- to be discriminated from the 1,000 Hz S^+ provokes an augmentation (40%) of **PS**, which had previously returned to its reference level.

Is PS augmentation a reflection of memorizing mechanisms or a delayed consequence of acquisition activity?

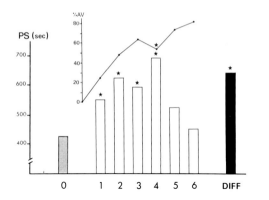

FIG. 9. Paradoxical sleep increase after a complication of the learning task. Level of significance: *, between $p < 0.05$ and $p < 0.02$; **, between $p < 0.01$ and $p < 0.001$. 0, reference PS duration; 1 to 6, PS duration during a 3-hr recording period after each daily session of avoidance conditioning (the learning curve is shown above the columns); DIFF, differentiation experiment with the presentation of two tones, one being the CS (note the immediate increase of PS, which had returned to the reference level at the end of the preceding learning). (Modified from Bloch ref. 4.)

Although we start from the hypothesis that PS modifications reflect information processing actually reinstalled during this state, it is also possible that PS augmentation is a delayed consequence of the waking brain activity previously implicated in registration of information. In other words, PS augmentation could be associated with a restoration process, and it could be assumed that the amount of PS increases is a function of neural material utilized during wakefulness in the acquisition process (49). And today there is a good deal of evidence that PS is a time when it is possible for certain synthetic processes in the brain to be increased above waking level (39). In the present state of our knowledge, it is difficult to settle the questions raised by the two alternative hypotheses. But we now present two different experiments that seem to support the idea that PS augmentation reflects memory mechanisms that are taking place at the time of this phase of sleep rather than after-effects of the waking learning activity.

The first experiment has been conducted in collaboration between our group (Hennevin and Leconte) and B. Cardo's group (Destrade and Soumireu-Mourat). This experiment relates to the so-called reminiscence phenomenon that is a time-dependant improvement of performance appearing after an incomplete learning session (13,27). The authors have shown in mice submitted to three daily 15-min sessions in an operant continuous reinforcement-conditioning procedure that PS increases between the first and second learning sessions (14). In this period of time, the maximum improvement also occurs. Moreover, there is a striking parallel between the time course of PS increase and the time-dependant establishment of reminiscence phenomenon, both phenomenon being maximal between the third and sixth hr following conditioning sessions. Thus, we can see that the mechanisms of maturation of the trace that lead to a subsequent increase of the level of performance are taking place in the same period when the phenomenon of PS augmentation occurs.

The second set of experiments shows an interdependence between the

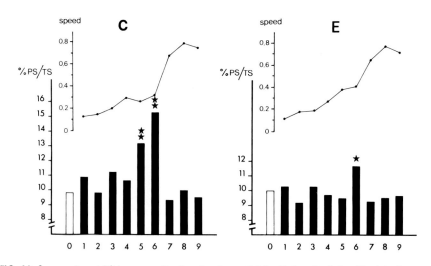

FIG. 10. Suppression of PS increase after learning by posttrial reticular stimulation. The learning curve (speed) of each group is shown above the columns. Note the almost total suppression of PS increase in group E. Level of significance: *, between $p < 0.05$ and $p < 0.02$; **, between $p < 0.01$ and $p < 0.001$. C, control group, with no reticular stimulation; E, experimental group that received the posttrial reticular stimulation; *white columns,* reference PS ratio of each group; *black columns,* PS ratio of each group during a 2-hr recording period following each daily trial in a maze learning task. (Modified from Bloch et al., ref. 7.)

mechanisms implicated during the so-called consolidation phase and those responsible for subsequent PS augmentation, suggesting that both phenomena are successive manifestations of a process that can be periodically reactivated.

Posttrial reticular stimulation suppresses subsequent PS augmentation. In a maze learning experiment with one trial a day, two groups of rats were compared. The first group received a posttrial 5 μA reticular stimulation (6); the other group had no stimulation. Then the animals of both groups were returned to their home cages after each trial, and the sleep phases were monitored for 2 hr. The records were compared with the reference values obtained previously under the same conditions (reward consumption followed by stimulation or no stimulation). The nonstimulation group showed the PS-augmentation phenomenon after the fifth and sixth trials just before the asymptote of the learning curve. But, in the stimulated group, in which performance was slightly enhanced by reticular stimulation, there was no PS augmentation (with the exception of a small increase the sixth day) (see Fig. 10).

Thereafter, both groups were trained in a new task involving another configuration of gates in the maze with no reticular stimulation after the trials. In these conditions PS augmentation was present after the second trial for both groups with the same amplitude (7). Thus, it was, in fact, reticular stimulation that in the first experiment prevented the PS augmentation phe-

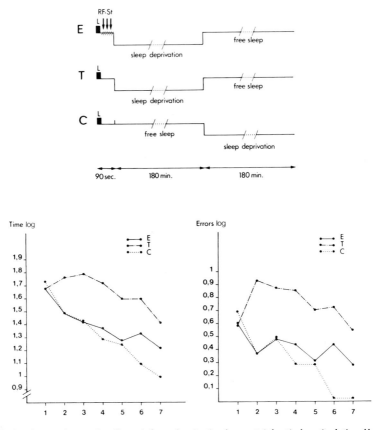

FIG. 11. Annulment of amnesic effect of sleep deprivation by posttrial reticular stimulation. Upper: Experimental procedure. Group E received a 90-sec reticular stimulation after each daily trial, then was deprived of total sleep for 3 hr. Group T did not receive the stimulation, but was deprived of total sleep for 3 hr. Group C did not receive the stimulation, could sleep freely during 3 hr, and then was deprived of total sleep during 3 hr. Lower: Learning curves for the three groups [*left:* running time (log); *right:* number of errors (log); *abcissa:* each daily maze learning trial.] Group C and T were significantly different from second and seventh trials. Group E and T differed significantly from second and seventh trials. Groups E and T differed significantly from second to fifth trials. Groups E and C showed no significant difference throughout the experiment. (From Bloch et al., ref. 7.)

nomenon. It must be pointed out that reticular stimulation alone produced in our experimental conditions no modification of PS in the subsequent sleep episodes.

Reticular stimulation annuls the amnesic effect of sleep deprivation. In the same maze learning situation with one trial a day, a posttrial 3-hr sleep deprivation impaired acquisition. But, a reticular stimulation between the trial and the sleep deprivation annulled the amnesic effect of sleep deprivation (see Fig. 11).

So, it seems that some need of arousal for processing new information has been fulfilled by reticular stimulation immediately after registration, and that a PS supplementary period is no longer necessary in subsequent sleep. The present data also reinforce the idea that information processing is triggered after registration and continues during sleep in the periods when the necessary brain activation normally occurs.

REFERENCES

1. Benson, K., and Feinberg, I. (1977): The beneficial effect of sleep in an extended Jenkins and Dallenbach paradigm. *Psychophysiology,* 14(4):375–384.
2. Bloch, V. (1970): Facts and hypotheses concerning memory consolidation processes. *Brain Res.,* 24:561–575.
3. Bloch, V. (1973): L'activité cérébrale et la fixation mnésique. *Arch. Ital. Biol.,* 3:577–590.
4. Bloch, V. (1976): Brain activation and memory consolidation. In: *Neural Mechanisms of Learning and Memory,* edited by M. R. Rosenzweig and E. L. Bennett, pp. 583–590. MIT Press, Cambridge.
5. Bloch, V., Denti, A., and Schmaltz, G. (1966): Effets de la stimulation réticulaire sur la phase de consolidation de la trace mnésique. *J. Physiol. (Paris),* 58:469–470.
6. Bloch, V., Deweer, B., and Hennevin, E. (1970): Suppression de l'amnésie rétrograde et consolidation d'un apprentissage à essai unique par stimulation réticulaire. *Physiol. Behav.,* 5:1235–1241.
7. Bloch, V., Hennevin, E., and Leconte, P. (1977): Interaction between post-trial reticular stimulation and subsequent paradoxical sleep in memory consolidation processes. In: *Neurobiology of Sleep and Memory,* edited by R. R. Drucker-Colin and J. L. McGaugh, pp. 255–272. Academic Press, New York.
8. Castaldo, V. (1969): Down's syndrome: A study of sleep patterns related to level of mental retardation. *Am. J. Ment. Defic.,* 74:187.
9. Castaldo, V. (1972): Effects of a training program on the REM sleep of mentally retarded. *Psychophysiology,* 9:140.
10. Castaldo, V., and Krinicki, V. (1973): Sleep pattern and intelligence in functional mental retardation. *J. Ment. Defic. Res.,* 17:231–235.
11. Delacour, J., and Brenot, J. (1975): Sleep patterns and avoidance conditioning in the rat. *Physiol. Behav.,* 14:329–335.
12. Denti, A., McGaugh, J. L., Landfield, P., and Shinkman, P. (1970): Facilitation of learning with post-trial stimulation of the reticular formation. *Physiol. Behav.,* 5: 659–662.
13. Destrade, C., and Cardo, B. (1974): Effects of post-trial hippocampal stimulation on time-dependent improvement of performance in mice. *Brain Res.,* 78:447–454.
14. Destrade, C., Hennevin, E., Leconte, P., and Soumireu-Mourat, B. (1978): Relationship between paradoxical sleep and time-dependent improvement of performance in Balb/c mice. *Neurosci. Lett.,* 7:239–244.
15. De Vietti, T. L., and Holliday, J. L. (1972): Retrograde amnesia produced by electroconvulsive shock after reactivation of a consolidation memory trace. *Psychonomic. Sci.,* 29:137–138.
16. De Vietti, T. L., Conger, G. L., and Kirkpatrick, B. R. (1977): Comparison of the enhancement gradients of retention obtained with stimulation of the mesencephalic reticular formation after training or memory reactivation. *Physiol. Behav.,* 19:549–554.
17. Feinberg, I. (1968): The ontogenesis of human sleep and the relationship of sleep variables to intellectual function in the aged. *Compr. Psychiatry,* 9:138–147.
18. Feinberg, I., Braun, M., and Shulman, E. (1969): EEG sleep patterns in mental retardation. *Electroenceph. Clin. Neurophysiol.,* 27:128–141.
19. Fishbein, W., Kastaniotis, C., and Chattman, D. (1974): Paradoxical sleep: Prolonged augmentation following learning. *Brain Res.,* 79:61–75.
20. Gordon, W. C., and Spear, N. E. (1973): The effects of strychnine on recently

acquired and reactivated passive avoidance memories. *Physiol. Behav.,* 10:1071–1075.

21. Greenberg, R., and Pearlman, C. (1974): Cutting the REM nerve: An approach to the adaptative role of REM sleep. *Perspect. Biol. Med.,* 17:513–521.
22. Hennevin, E. (1976): Relation Entre le Sommeil Paradoxal et les Processus d'Acquisition. Approche des Mécanismes Mis en Jeu. Thèse, Doctorat ès-Sciences, Université Paris XI.
23. Hennevin, E., and Leconte, P. (1971): La fonction du sommeil paradoxal:Faits et hypothèses. *Année Psychol.,* 2:489–519.
24. Hennevin, E., and Leconte, P. (1977): Etude des relations entre le sommeil paradoxal et les processus d'acquisition. *Physiol. Behav.,* 18:307–319.
25. Hennevin, E., Leconte, P., and Bloch, V. (1971): Effet du niveau d'acquisition sur l'augmentation de la durée de sommeil paradoxal consécutive à un conditionnement d'évitement chez le rat. *C. R. Acad. Sci. (Paris),* 273:2595–2598.
26. Hennevin, E., Leconte, P., and Bloch, V. (1974): Augmentation du sommeil paradoxal provoquée par l'acquisition, l'extinction et la réacquisition d'un apprentissage à renforcement positif. *Brain Res.,* 70:43–54.
27. Jaffard, R., Destrade, C., Soumireu-Mourat, B., and Cardo, B. (1974): Time-dependent improvement of performance on appetitive tasks in mice. *Behav. Biol.,* 11:89–100.
28. Jenkins, J., and Dallenbach, K. (1924): Obliviscence during sleep and waking. *Am. J. Psychol.,* 35:605.
29. John, E. R. (1972): Switchboard versus statistical theories of learning and memory. *Science,* 177:850–864.
30. Lecas, J. C. (1976): Changes in paradoxical sleep accompanying instrumental learning in cat. *Neurosci. Lett.,* 3:349–355.
31. Leconte, P. (1975): Mise en Evidence du Rôle de la Phase Paradoxale du Sommeil dans les Processus de Mémorisation. Thèse, Doctorat ès-Sciences, Université de Paris XI.
32. Leconte, P., and Hennevin, E. (1971): Augmentation de la durée de sommeil paradoxal consécutive à un apprentissage chez le rat. *C.R. Acad. Sci. (Paris),* 273:86–88.
33. Leconte, P., and Hennevin, E. (1973): Caractéristiques temporelles de l'augmentation de sommeil paradoxal consécutif à l'apprentissage chez la rat. Physiol. Behav., 11:677–686.
34. Leconte, P., Hennevin, E., and Bloch, V. (1973): Analyse des effets d'un apprentissage et de son niveau d'acquisition sur le sommeil paradoxal consécutif. *Brain Res.,* 49:367–379.
35. Leconte, P., Hennevin, E., and Bloch, V. (1974): Duration of paradoxical sleep necessary for the acquisition of conditioned avoidance in the rat. *Physiol. Behav.,* 13:675–681.
36. Lucero, M. (1970): Lengthening of REM sleep duration consecutive to learning in the rat. *Brain Res.,* 20:319–322.
37. McGaugh, J. L. (1968): A multi-trace view of memory storage. (Presented at the "International Symposium on Recent Advances in Learning and Retention" in Rome, 1967.) In: *Recent Advances on Learning and Retention,* edited by D. Bovet, F. Nitti, and A. Oliverio, pp. 13–24. Academia Nazionale Dei Lincei, Rome.
38. Maho, C. (1977): Concomitants physiologiques de l'apprentissage et sommeil paradoxal consécutif chez le chat. *Physiol. Behav.,* 18:431–438.
39. Oswald, I., and Adam, K. (1976): Studies in human sleep. *Acta Neurobiol. Exp. (Warsz),* 36:463–473.
40. Pagel, J., Pegram, V., Vaughn, S., Donaldson, P., and Bridgers, W. (1973): The relationship of REM sleep with learning and memory in mice. *Behav. Biol.,* 9:383–388.
41. Paul, K., and Dittrichova, J. (1975): Sleep patterns following learning in infants. In: *Sleep 1974,* edited by P. Levin and U. Koella, pp. 388–390, *Proc. 2nd Eur. Congr. Sleep Research,* Rome. Karger, New York.
42. Pearlman, C., and Becker, M. (1973): Brief posttrial REM sleep deprivation impairs discrimination learning in rats. *Physiol. Psychol.,* 1:373–376.

43. Pearlman, C., and Becker, M. (1974): REM sleep deprivation impairs serial reversal and probability maximizing in rats. *Physiol. Psychol.*, 2:509–212.
44. Pearlman, C., and Becker, M. (1974): REM sleep deprivation impairs bar press acquisition in rats. *Physiol. Behav.*, 13:813–817.
45. Pearlman, C. A., and Greenberg, R. (1973): Posttrial REM sleep: A critical period for consolidation of shuttlebox avoidance. *Anim. Learn. Behav.*, 1:49–51.
46. Petre-Quadens, O., and Jouvet, M. (1966): Paradoxical sleep and dreaming in the mentally retarded. *J. Neurol. Sci.*, 3:608–612.
47. Smith, C. F., Kitahama, K., Valatx, J. L., and Jouvet, M. (1972): Sommeil paradoxal et apprentissage chez deux souches consanguines de souris. *C.R. Acad. Sci. (Paris)*, 275:1283–1286.
48. Smith, C., Kitahama, K., Valatx, J. L., and Jouvet, M. (1974): Increased paradoxical sleep in mice during acquisition of a shock avoidance task. *Brain Res.*, 77:221–230.
49. Stern, W., and Morgane, P. (1974): Theoretical view of REM sleep function: Maintenance of catecholamine systems in the central nervous system. *Behav. Biol.*, 11:1–32.

Brain Mechanisms in Memory and Learning:
From the Single Neuron to Man,
edited by M. A. B. Brazier.
Raven Press, New York © 1979.

Visual Input and the Motor System in Man

Manik Shahani

Everest Chemical Industries, Institute of Electrophysiology for Fundamental and
Applied Research, Parel, Bombay-400 012, India

That visual input should have an obvious influence on the motor behaviour of man and animals is almost taken for granted, but there are few neurophysiological studies of this subject. In cat, the tectal and tegmental influences on forelimb and hindlimb motor neurones were reported by Anderson et al. in 1972 (2). In 1973, Shahani (4) demonstrated the influence of visual input on the alpha neuronal pool in spasticity in man, by the simple experiments started in his laboratory in 1971.

In order to study the influence of the visual input on the motor system of man, the following experiments were carried out in normal and abnormal men (patients with pathophysiology) with and without visual input (blindfolding).

EXPERIMENTAL RESULTS

Performance of Learned Voluntary Movements

Patients with hemiplegia were asked to perform simple learned movements, such as picking up a glass of water, tearing paper with both hands, etc., while electromyographic (EMG) activity was picked up from the axial and proximal muscles of the upper extremities (upper fibres of trapezius, pectoralis major, latissimus dorsi, and middle fibres of deltoid). EMG activity was generally more on the affected side of hemiplegia. However, on blindfolding, this was reduced quite significantly although the patients were able to carry out the given task adequately (Table 1).

Minimal Isometric Contraction

Normal subjects were asked to hold a lightweight empty plastic container (of 35 mm film roll) between the thumb and index finger. A concentric needle electrode was introduced in the abductor pollicis muscle, and the rate of firing of a single motor unit was calculated for 10 consecutive sec. Invariably the rate of motor unit firing fell significantly when the same task was performed

TABLE 1. *Visual input and learned movements in patients with upper motor neurone lesions*

Activity	Results
1. Tearing paper with both hands	Significant decrease in the EMG activity was noticed on closing both eyes in proximal and axial muscles (trapezius) bilaterally in a patient having hemiplegia.
2. Drinking a glass of water (affected side)	Slight reduction was seen, on closing both eyes, in the EMG activity of proximal muscles like pectoralis major and latissimus dorsi. Almost no change was seen in the axial muscle (trapezius).
3. Picking up blocks (affected side)	Reduction in activity was noticed, on closing both eyes, on the affected side in both axial and proximal muscles. Interestingly, EMG increased in the axial muscle (trapezius) of the unaffected side on shutting the eyes.
4. Tearing paper with both hands	EMG activity was recorded by proximal and axial muscles only on the affected side, and there was no activity on the unaffected side even though the activity is carried out by both hands.

with the visual input cut (by blindfolding for 2 min) (Fig. 1). When attempts were made to cut or partially eliminate other sensory inputs, like group IA, and tactile sensations either singly or in combinations, a reduction in firing rate of the motor unit was observed, although not to the same extent as when the visual input was cut.

Monosynaptic and Polysynaptic Reflexes

'H' reflex was studied by averaging out the signal every 10 sec with eyes open and with eyes blindfolded for 2 min. These studies were carried out at or near threshold stimulation. When visual input was cut off, the peak-to-peak amplitude of the averaged 'H' response was significantly reduced (Table 2) (Fig. 2).

Polysynaptic reflexes were carried out in the form of withdrawal reflexes by recording from tibialis anterior muscle on stimulation of the sole of the foot, from biceps femoris muscle on stimulation of the sural nerve, and from

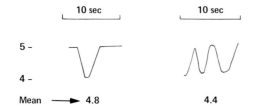

FIG. 1. Rate of motor unit firing.

TABLE 2. *Visual input and monosynaptic and polysynaptic reflexes*

'H' reflex (normal subject)	Threshold stimuli	Significant reduction in the amplitude of 'H' response on blindfolding. Latency remains unaffected.
'H' reflex (normal subject)	Suprathreshold stimuli	Behaviour of 'H' response not consistent on blindfolding as seen at threshold stimuli.
Withdrawal reflex	Threshold stimuli	Marked reduction of peak-to-peak voltage (early or first component) on blindfolding. Reduction of duration and amplitude of early or second component seen on blind-folding; also increase in the latency of second component.

orbicularis oculi muscle on stimulation of supraorbital nerve. When subjects were blindfolded for 2 min, the late component showed changes in latency (slight increase), duration (slight decrease), and amplitude (significant decrease). These changes are similar to those observed by other workers in subjects in sleep (3) (Table 2).

'M' Response

Median nerves of the normal subjects were stimulated at or about threshold stimuli, and the direct muscle response called the 'M' response (1) was picked up with a concentric needle electrode from abductor pollicis brevis muscle. The averaged 'M' response on blindfolding for 2 min was always smaller and occasionally also had a slightly increased latency (Table 3 and Fig. 3).

The evidence obtained from all these experiments strongly suggests that visual input exerts an important influence on the motor neurones. It is difficult to say how this is brought about. There are many possibilities, although one of the most important pathways is likely to be connected with the reticulospinal system, which is considered to be a sort of integrating system for

 BLINDFOLDED

 EYES OPEN

FIG. 2. 'H' reflex: normal subject.

100 μV

10 msec

TABLE 3. *Visual input and 'M' response—median nerve*

Subject	Eyes open			Blindfolded			Eyes open		
	Lat.	Dur.	Ampl.	Lat.	Dur.	Ampl.	Lat.	Dur.	Ampl.
U.J.	8.8	10.6	70	9.0	9.25	15.0	9.0	10.2	105
V.F.	6.0	15.0	5.5	—	—	—	6.0	15.0	6
S.U.	9.5	12.7	20	9.5	11.5	17.5	9.7	11.2	20
S.P.	9.7	10.7	20	9.7	8.7	12.5	9.7	8.5	25
I.K.	10.1	10.1	115	12.7	3.7	10.0	10.0	10.7	80
Average percentage decrease					42.2	62.97			

Lat., latency; Dur., duration; Ampl., amplitude.

various sensory inputs. Corticospinal and tectospinal tracts can also be implicated. The cerebellum may have a part to play, climbing fibres bringing in the influence of visual input.

Reduction in motor activity (as seen by EMG recording) and reduced rate of motor unit firing suggest that learned simple voluntary acts can be performed with less cost of energy when sensory inputs are absent. However, it seems plausible to suggest that this redundancy to which sensory inputs contribute, may be providing a safety margin for any need for a sudden change in programme.

Changes in reflex studies, especially the withdrawal reflexes on blindfolding for 2 min, are quite compatible with those observed in sleep, thus strongly implicating visual input with sleep. It may be understood, however, that all the subjects in the study were quite alert and not drowsy, as the experiment demanded eyes open and then blindfolded at intervals of every 2 min.

That changes in the amplitude of 'M' response on cutting off of visual input have a significant influence on central excitability is an observation with great implications. It seems that the changes in the excitability of a parent neurone are reflected all along its axon; whether this could be as a result of fast axonal transport or some other mechanism that brings about changes in ionic balance is difficult to determine at this stage.

 EYES OPEN

BLINDFOLDED

EYES OPEN

100 μV

5 msec

FIG. 3. *Visual input and 'M' response.*

REFERENCES

1. Adrian, E. D., and Bronk, D. W. (1929): The discharge of impulses in motor nerve fibres. Part II. The frequency of discharge in reflex and voluntary contractions. *J. Physiol. (Lond.)*, 67:119–151.
2. Anderson, M. E., Yoshida, M., and Wilson, V. J. (1972): Tectal and tegmental influences on cat forelimb and hindlimb motoneurones. *J. Neurophysiol.*, 35:462–470.
3. Shahani, B. (1968): Effects on human reflexes with a double component. *J. Neurol. Neurosurg. Psychiatry*, 31:575–579.
4. Shahani, M. (1973): Visual input and alpha pool in spasticity. *J. Postgrad. Med.*, 19:139–144.

Brain Mechanisms in Memory and Learning:
From the Single Neuron to Man,
edited by M. A. B. Brazier.
Raven Press, New York © 1979.

General and Specific Handicap
in Cognitive Development

N. O'Connor

Medical Research Council, Developmental Psychology Unit, London, WC1H 0AN, England

The nature of the learning process is seen by psychologists today from two apparently incompatible points of view—the Skinnerian and the Chomskian. One sees learning as a piecemeal elaboration on a house-building programme with the reflex as the brick. The other provides the architect-designed conceptual plan of the building that, like Leibniz's monads, contains within the infant offspring the growth potential that determines the ultimate realisation of the completed edifice. One way of interpreting this latter view is to describe it as a schema in which input and output are, in part, independent. In a modified but similar approach, one could say that miniprogrammes within the same overall plan may follow different lines of development.

The first approach described above—the Skinnerian—is clearly Pavlovian in origin and logically irreconcilable with the second. They are not, however, ontogenetically irreconcilable. Pavlov regarded conditioning as a method of influencing the first signalling system. He believed that it gave an appropriate account of the acquisition of skills, but that it was inadequate in explaining speech. His reason for believing this was the peculiar "generalising" quality of speech, whereby a single communication can have widespread and frequent application in the behaviour of a listener. A useful illustration is Luria's (11) example of the instruction: "Always press the button when the red light appears." A subnormal person cannot accept this instruction for more than one occasion without having to have it reinforced, any more than a dog can learn to salivate to a novel signal without many repetitions and associated rewards. A normal adult can, however, readily obey such a command without any difficulty. What, therefore, accounts for this peculiar character of the secondary signalling system? Is it the inborn quality of the words themselves that retain a "general" significance without reinforcement? Alternatively, is it a quality of the mind of the adult human being that for some reason can learn by words faster than by any other means, in fact, in one trial?

Following these observations, we might say that the nature of the ontogeny of learning has reached a critical stage at the point when the existence of verbal ability makes a difference in the permanence of an encoded signal.

Clearly, if language has such a significant effect on coding strategy in this instance, it may have other significant effects also. If language has the power to change the way in which encoding occurs in memory, it may also affect other aspects of the recall of events. Some, like Piaget (20), dispute this, saying that language simply expresses the more mature thinking of developing children. This might be described as Piaget's original view, and some aspects of Chomsky's (2) attitude to the ambiguous sentence might bear a similar interpretation. However, in the example I have given, the power to use language, or to use words, as an encoding medium enables us to regard words as conveyors of thoughts or self-instructions that would not otherwise be available to the hearer.

This example, of course, does not permit us to say that language is learned in a different manner than, say, the image coding in which a preverbal child solves a form board type of task. It does show, however, that this sort of operation may follow different rules of processing. The evidence that phonology and syntax may be acquired by a developmental process only partly dependent on input and, therefore, only in part conditioned, lies in the mass of work now available concerning the child's acquisition of speech and the infant's acquisition of phonology. This work could be represented by the studies of Jakobson (8) and Lenneberg (10) with the babbling of normal, deaf, and subnormal children and by the work of Smith (22) in isolating the rules of the acquisition of phonology in his own child. Essentially, Lenneberg demonstrated that the acquisition of babbling occurs quite independently of input as shown by the deaf children of deaf parents who, nonetheless, babble normally. Smith (22) demonstrated that his son set himself an adult model of speech and, even so, was unable to detect his own production errors, i.e., he could not detect their difference from the adult model he appeared to be following. Clearly, the imputation is that more than simple imitation is involved in this process, and input and output in learning are only occasionally associated or associated in a complex fashion.

I would like to develop this point concerning the apparent independence of speech input and output by referring to some work in the Medical Research Council Developmental Psychology Unit. This is the work of Dodd (4). Dodd has followed Smith's and Lenneberg's studies and made an analysis of the development of phonology in normal, deaf, and severely subnormal children, both Down's syndrome and undifferentiated. She has found in a number of studies that the normal children manifest, in their acquisition of phonology, most of the phenomena of distortions of production shown by Smith's son, but, in addition, she has demonstrated that these occur also in subnormal and in deaf children. This happens despite the fact that input in these two instances may be handicapped. Thus, although there may be deficiencies in input in the deaf, many of the rules of normal output will be followed as they will also be followed in the subnormal child, according to mental age in the latter case and according, perhaps, to hearing age or degree of deafness in the former. Of course, the deaf face certain additional hazards. Some sounds such as velars are made invisibly in the throat by pulling back the tip of the tongue. Not only are these sounds not heard by the deaf, they also do not contain a lip-reading component and cannot be interpreted except phonically. This additional hazard can be represented by the output sequences in Table 1. So, although children cannot produce what they do not hear unless there is another source of input, they do not by any means always produce what they do hear. As shown in the table, presumably normal and subnormal children can hear the "SKL" input perfectly well, but only gradually reproduce it correctly.

This relative independence of input and output in the normal and subnormal, so far as phonology is concerned, has been demonstrated for psycholinguistics in many studies including those of Lackner (9) and Cromer (3). Most of these studies show that children do not produce compound, complex, or passive sentences until they are ready to do so, even though they may hear such sentences every day.

Turning to a visual input, we find a different state of affairs. As far as can be assessed, the position with the infant's perception of space, colour, and simple form is entirely different. Differentiation of distance, colour, size, and quite soon shape as well as accurate response to these dimensions occur at a very early age. It may be the case, therefore, that in considering the ontogeny of learning, we should take careful account of these two kinds of development —visual-spatial, on the one hand, and auditory-verbal, on the other, represented, as one knows, primarily in the right and left hemispheres, respectively. At the beginning, I said that there were two views of learning—conditioning as seen by Skinner (21) and the acquisition of hierarchically organised propositions as seen by Chomsky (2). Pavlov (19) thought learning in animals was by the former (primary) signalling system, in man by the latter secondary system. Piaget, however, took the view that language, like other kinds of sensory motor learning, was on first acquisition, only a minimal advance on nonverbal symbolising. In his view, unlike that of Vygotsky (23), language or speech did not represent a new and liberating technique, transforming the thinking and categorising capacity of man, but only became of use to man when he virtually was a man, i.e., at adolescence. At this stage, it has a cultural significance in passing on information. However, children cannot

TABLE 1. *Input and output of consonants in deaf and hearing children*

Normal age or subnormal mental age	Input	Normal output	Subnormal output (IQ 50)	Deaf output
18 months	SKL	K	K 36 months	L
27 months	SKL	SK	SK 54 months	?
36 months	SKL	SKL	SKL 72 months	SL

learn what they are not ready to learn, even with language. This view, strangely enough, would not be contradicted by psycholinguistic theory as expounded by Lenneberg (10) or Lackner (9), who discussed the language of subnormals.

This leaves us with a problem. If symbolic generalisation is not dependent on speech or language, at least when first language develops in young children, what is the basis for the kind of generalisation characteristic of adult behaviour? Although Luria (11) is not entirely correct in his assumption that subnormals cannot generalise, as work by O'Connor and Hermelin (13) and Bryant (1) has shown, we still do not know exactly why or how generalisation occurs, or on what basis. However, it would seem that in Piaget's work on prelinguistic thought, there is some basis for assuming that Piaget may be right about the slow growth of adult forms of speech and language.

So the problem of how generalisation first occurs remains a problem. It cannot be attributed to language apparently, although the evidence against language is neither strong nor weak. It must, therefore, be a function of a different kind, but as yet, we have not unravelled this knot. What we have to go on, so far as human cognitive ontogeny is concerned, is a well-developed series of studies by Piaget of a biological character that shows that children acquire their first knowledge by experience without language and only later test this knowledge in a linguistic form. For the right-handed human, therefore, early thinking and problem solving will be either image- or kinaesthesia-based and the dominant hemisphere, at this point, might be the right.

The theme I have developed above is quite consistent with the major trend in developmental psychology, but, interestingly, would fit both Skinner and Chomsky, allowing infant language to the former and a comprehensive generalised secondary signalling system to the latter. If the subnormal is of a low mental age, his use of language might be expected to be primitive or stimulus-response in type, rather than hierarchically organised, thus explaining Luria's example.

The situation I have tried to develop suggests that cognitive ontogeny is marked by the successive acquisition of, first, visual-spatial and, second, auditory-verbal schemata. It also suggests that first speech is mechanically and not hierarchically integrated and therefore has a more "conditioned" than insightful character. Such views, I have suggested, make it possible to reconcile Skinner (21) and Chomsky (2) via Pavlov (19). At the same time, the suggestion does no violence to Piaget's (20) views. Overall, however, we are still unable to explain generalisation.

What could we learn about the truth or falsity of such speculations from an analysis of cortical or sensory dysfunction? In a recent series of experiments involving the blind, the deaf, the subnormal, and the autistic, we (17) have explored the effect of such specific and general handicaps in the development of memory functions. The purpose of this series of studies was to compare the consequences of overall central nervous lesions, such as those occurring in severe subnormality, with the consequence of specific restrictions of sensory input, such as congenital deafness and blindness unaccompanied by intellectual deficiency.

One reason for making such an approach to the subject was because the current analysis of the cognitive behaviour of subnormals makes the unverified assumption that subnormality can be the consequence of a break in a consecutive information-processing chain. Such a chain is supposed to begin with sensory input and proceed via short- and long-term memory coding to output. This view has led to progress in the field of the psychology of subnormality, but despite the fact that it is a promising approach in so far as it might tend to explain the dynamics of subnormality of intellect, it is almost certainly wrong. Even if a defect in speed of input as that demonstrated by O'Connor and Hermelin (14) should occur, or of short-term memory (5) or attention (24), such specific deficits might occur in the presence, or the absence, of other handicaps. Thus they might not be isolated causes of subnormality, although, given the consecutive interdependent model of information processing, they could be. Rather they would seem to be the accessory events associated with other similar events. In other words, each and all of these defects could occur together and could be as much the consequences of, or associates of, subnormality of intellect as its causes. Thus we believe that subnormality could not necessarily be considered a consequence of specific defects of input, although such defects do occur in subnormality.

However, the example of specific coding differences we have just illustrated could be significant in developing different approaches to categorization and consequently to that important aspect of learning known as generalisation. If, as we have shown, some subnormals do not encode verbally, they may lack that aspect of verbal encoding that Pavlov apparently considered characteristic of speech, its tendency to convey a timeless general character concerning the things it represents. Nothing Piaget has written about prelinguistic development would gainsay such a suggestion. Similarly, the cognitive backwardness of the deaf must be taken into account in considering specific defects.

Many advantages have been claimed for the verbal form of encoding stimuli, and in the Developmental Psychology Unit, we have explored some of the characteristics of this method. However, one aspect of verbal descriptions we have not investigated is the tendency children have to use a word in an overgeneralised way. One aspect of a nonauditory stimulus tends to be its specificity. I can quote one of our experiments as an example. Deaf and blind children and normal and subnormal controls for each group were asked to judge the duration of a rotary tactile probe placed against the palm of the hand (15). All subjects acquired the capacity to discriminate durations of 6 and 2 sec at the mental age of 8 years, and all subjects, except the deaf, could verbalise the principle of solution. Despite this success in acquisition and even in verbalisation, no one group successfully transferred this skill to another appropriate modality. So, for example, the deaf failed to show any saving in learning a visual form of the same task, the blind failing similarly with sound, and the control groups with both.

This experiment and its results could be interpreted in one of two ways. It could be accepted as evidence of failure to transfer a conditional response across modalities irrespective of verbal description, at this relatively primitive level of verbalisation. Alternatively, it could be seen as a failure of transfer across modalities of a relatively advanced dimension like time, which unlike space, takes some years to acquire and which young children have to learn even though they show considerable competence with spatially organised sensory input. It could be additively interpreted both ways.

By describing another experiment, I can illustrate the point further. Language does not always serve as the encoding medium for stimuli, especially, for example, in those subjects deprived of language. In earlier remarks, we discussed the function of specific deficits as a possible explanation for general subnormality and rejected it in any simple form. The experiment I describe now illustrates a more subtle approach to this problem. A phenomenon that occurs in all subjects given a visual presentation of digits can be illustrated in a figure. If subjects are shown three digits visually in succession, but in such a way that successive and spatial orders are incongruent, and are then asked ambiguously which is the middle one, they give as an answer the spatial middle. However, if presented with the same series auditorily, they select the sequentially middle one. Normal, subnormal, deaf, and blind subjects give the same kinds of answers.

An example from another aspect of this experiment illustrates how words may function in subnormals of different verbal capacities. O'Connor and Hermelin (16) carried out an experiment with the deaf that asked them to recall three (or more) digits (or letters) presented visually in an order that was random as compared with the visual left-to-right reading order. In this case the deaf, unlike the normal hearing controls, always recalled digits in their presented left-to-right, and not in their sequential, first-to-last order. Subnormal results were bimodal. About 60% of the subjects responded as if deaf, 40% as if hearing. The division of the two groups were explained by results from another experiment. Miklausic (12) collected two groups of severely subnormal adults, one of which recalled the series sequentially and one spatially. The former group had a significantly higher verbal IQ than the latter with a cut off point at IQ 65. Both groups could hear and speak, but the sequential group could apparently code linguistically, whereas the other,

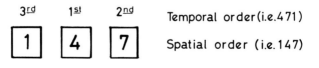

FIG. 1. Coding of order in an ambiguous visual presentation of digits.

we assumed, coded visually (18). The capacity to encode verbally was also probably deficient in the autistic children in this experiment, who all behaved like the deaf and all had low verbal IQs (see Fig. 1).

Our explanation of this set of results is in terms of the verbal encoding that appears to characterise older children and adults. They give themselves verbal descriptions of stimuli they see or hear, especially if a language description already exists. So, in the case of a string of numerals, nothing is easier for us than to verbally encode them as they occur. If, however, we lack verbal facility, either because we are deaf or because we lack access to a useful vocabulary because of low verbal mental age, we may revert to a less advanced encoding medium, i.e., either a visual-iconic or a motor, representational code.

We established this phenomenon more soundly by the use of a recognition procedure with young children. Roman or Arabic letters were shown to children in an incongruent (random) presentation, and after the display, they were asked to recognise the order of three letters they had seen from a matrix containing the three possible arrangements of these letters, i.e., random, sequential, or spatial, i.e., left to right. Children aged 6, 8, and 10 all gave a high proportion of sequential responses to the roman and a high proportion of spatial responses to the Arabic letters.

Another instance of the possible association many authors have assumed to exist between language or speech and the appreciation of temporal sequence is an experiment concerned with sequence matching. In this study, deaf, blind, normal, and subnormal children were required to decide whether two successive sequences of stimuli were the same or different. The stimuli were either light or sound flashes. We predicted (7) that sequences that were spatially characterised would be better remembered when they were lights and sequences that were temporally characterised would be better remembered when they were sounds.

A temporally characterised series was one in which successive stimuli differed in duration, like Morse code, and were emitted from one source only. A spatially characterised series was one in which sequences consisted of stimuli of equal duration, but emitted from two sources. Such a series, whether of lights or sounds, could then be, for example, such a one as left, left, right, left, right. Subjects were required to listen to or watch two successive sequences and then decide whether they were the same or different. Sequences were of 500 msec with 50 msec or a regular 300-msec duration with interstimulus intervals of 150 msec. Auditory sequences did, in fact, yield more correct comparisons when temporally, and visual sequences when spatially, emitted. Once again the evidence suggests that there is an elective concordance of temporal and auditory, or auditory-verbal, mnemonic encoding.

I have thought it less necessary to present many examples of the tendency to encode spatially organised material visually, but we do have a number of experiments that show this tendency. One case will have to serve in a short presentation. We (6) arranged a series of four spots on a card in front of seated subjects and placed the first and second fingers of each hand on the spots. The digits thus ran away from the body across the desk in the midline. Subjects were taught to respond to a tactile stimulus to the fingers with a word associated with the finger touched. When a criterion of successful responses had been achieved, the hands were switched and the task continued.

There were two conditions, a sighted and a blind. In the former, those who could see responded always in the same way, naming the spots and not the fingers. In the blind, or blindfolded condition, subjects after hand reversal named the fingers and not the spots, reversing the order as the hands were reversed. The lesson of this particular experiment is that vision carried a predetermined spatial schema that disappeared in its absence despite years of visual experience. On the other hand, other spatial experiments have demonstrated to us that certain phenomena, such as shape or form, can be just as well tactually perceived as they can visually. Obviously, spatial dimensions vary in their modality-specificity.

What can be concluded concerning the ontogeny of learning from this brief exposition of some of our recent experiments? The most obvious conclusion is that the effect of specific damage can, in many cases, be general, as the last described 'dots' experiment showed. In this sense specific damage resembles general defect in its consequences, being developmental and regressive rather than deviant. Second, despite Piaget's impressive evidence concerning the states of development from proprioceptive to iconic and auditory-verbal symbolic, it does seem as if the use of temporal ordering and successiveness is language dependent or speech dependent. Finally, language development in children, although only in its use for self-instruction or motor control, seems to go through two stages, a (Skinnerian) conditioning and a more hierarchically ordered (Chomskian) stage.

Children who are unable to draw on sensory experiences from an appropriate modality are obliged to adopt alternative encoding strategies in some circumstances, usually less appropriate ones. This can occur either because such a modality source is not available, as with the deaf or blind, or because, in the case of subnormal or autistic children, it is inaccessible. What appears to be meant by "less appropriate" in these cases can therefore be interpreted as developmentally prior.

The organisation of stimuli appears to depend on the modality to which the stimuli are presented, and some stimuli can only be processed in one modality. With other stimuli, however, our experiments show that they tend to be translated into a "more appropriate" modality. When this cannot be done, for the reasons given, alternative symbolic codes are employed. All the evidence we have from our Unit work, therefore, whether of our own work or that of Dodd or of Cromer, points to the existence of developmental types of cognitive ontogeny, even in cases of specific defects such as blindness and deafness. It points also, independently, to a relatively advanced development of spatial-immediate, as opposed to temporal-successive, forms of stimulus scanning and encoding. To some degree we could infer from these facts that temporal sequential judgments are language dependent as our experiments seem to show, although this conclusion remains to be verified.

ACKNOWLEDGMENT

This research is entirely supported by the Medical Research Council.

REFERENCES

1. Bryant, P. E. (1967): Verbal labelling and learning strategies in normal and severely subnormal children. *Q. J. Exp. Psychol.*, 19:155–161.
2. Chomsky, N. A. (1959): A review of B. F. Skinner's *Verbal Behaviour. Language*, 35:26–58.
3. Cromer, R. F. (1975): Are subnormals linguistic adults? In: *Language, Cognitive Deficits, and Retardation*, edited by N. O'Connor, pp. 169–183. Butterworths, London.
4. Dodd, B. (1975): Children's understanding of their own phonological forms. *Q. J. Exp. Psychol.*, 27:165–172.
5. Ellis, N. R. (1963): The stimulus trace and behavioural inadequacy. In: *Handbook of Mental Deficiency*, edited by N. R. Ellis, pp. 134–158. McGraw Hill, New York.
6. Hermelin, B., and O'Connor, N. (1971): Spatial coding in normal, autistic and blind children. *Percept. Mot. Skills*, 33:127–132.
7. Hermelin, B., and O'Connor, N. (1978): Light and sound sequences from one and from two sources. (*In preparation.*)
8. Jakobson, R. (1941): *Child Language Aphasic and Phonological Universals.* (Translated by A. R. Keiter in 1968.) Morton, The Hague.
9. Lackner, J. R. (1968): A developmental study of language behaviour in retarded children. *Neuropsychologica*, 6:301–320.
10. Lenneberg, E. H. (1976): *Biological Foundation of Language.* Wiley, New York.
11. Luria, A. R. (1961): *The Role of Speech in the Regulation of Normal and Abnormal Behaviour*, edited by J. Tizard. Pergamon Press, London.
12. Miklausic, K. (1976): The Spatial or Temporal Organisation of Short-Term Memory in the Severely Subnormal. Dissertation, University College, London.
13. O'Connor, N., and Hermelin, B. (1959). Some effects of word learning in imbeciles. *Lang. Speech*, 2:63–71.
14. O'Connor, N., and Hermelin, B. (1965): Input restriction and immediate memory decay in normal and subnormal children. *Q. J. Exp. Psychol.*, XVII:323–328.
15. O'Connor, N., and Hermelin, B. (1971): Inter- and intra-modal transfer in children with modality specific and general handicaps. *Br. J. Soc. Clin. Psychol.*, 10:346–354.
16. O'Connor, N., and Hermelin, B. (1973): The spatial and temporal organization of short-term memory. *Q. J. Exp. Psychol.*, 25:335–343.
17. O'Connor, N., and Hermelin, B. (1978): *Seeing and Hearing and Space and Time.* Academic Press, London. (*In press.*)
18. Paivio, A., and Csapo, K. (1972): *Picture Superiority in Free Recall. Imagery or Dual Coding.* Research Bulletin, No. 243, Univ. of Western Ontario.
19. Pavlov, I. P. (1927): *Conditioned Reflexes.* Clarendon Press, Oxford.
20. Piaget, J. (1956): *Le Language et la Pensée chez L'enfant.* Delachaux et Niestlé, Neuchâtel.
21. Skinner, B. F. (1957): *Verbal Behaviour.* Appleton, New York.
22. Smith, N. (1973): *The Acquisition of Phonology.* Cambridge Univ. Press, London.
23. Vygotsky, L. S. (1962): *Thought and Language.* MIT Press and Wiley, New York.
24. Zeaman, D., and House, B. J. (1963): The role of attention in retardate discrimination learning. In: *Handbook of Mental Deficiency*, edited by N. R. Ellis, pp. 159–223. McGraw-Hill, New York.

Brain Mechanisms in Memory and Learning:
From the Single Neuron to Man,
edited by M. A. B. Brazier.
Raven Press, New York © 1979.

Ontogeny of Learning in Man

Reuven Feuerstein

Hadassah-Wizo-Canada Research Institute, Beit Hakerem, Jerusalem 96308, Israel;
Bar Ilan University, Ramat Gan, Israel

The problem of the differential capacity of individuals to become affected by experiences of a formal or informal nature is a crucial one for both theoretical and applied aspects of psychology and is certainly a question to be addressed within the framework of this volume. The International Brain Research Organization is the framework that may be best equipped with the knowledge, instruments, and methodology necessary for the solution of the problem of differential returns of learning, characteristic for different organisms.

Studies in sensory or social deprivation, or both, studies using anatomical techniques, are essential for determining those characteristics of the organism that are necessary for its generalized or more specific capacity to become modified, i.e., to learn from its exposure to stimuli. The relationship between brain and behavior, the cognitive and affective behavior of the organism, has proved to be a two-way transaction, with the brain being affected by, no less than affecting, behavior. The changes occurring on various levels in the brain following exposure to stimulation have been well documented and their meaning stressed.

My presentation attempts to outline a theory of the ontogeny of human learning by which differential levels of cognitive development are attributed to the differential learning capacity of a given organism, and the etiology of these differences is suggested. The problem is, to what extent can one look for the neurophysiological substrata of such differences as the direct function of this particular etiology?

Learning is defined as the generation *of* or change *in* the structure of activities of the organism following the exposure to stimuli or active involvement of the organism in experiencing them, or both. This definition distinguishes between those changes produced by learning and those incurred by the organism as a result of growth or the unfolding of innately determined responses. Furthermore, in order to consider the emergence of a new behavior or the change of an existing behavior as a product of a learning process, a certain degree of stability and permanence should be attributed to it, as well as a certain degree of resistance to the effects of forgetting, fatigue, and other transient adverse conditions of the organism.

In the present framework, learning as a construct is considered to have serious advantages over other constructs such as intelligence or capacities concerned with cognitive behavior. This is so since learning involves a dynamic view of the organism and a concern with the processes rather than with the static, fixed immutable characteristics inferred from and inherent in the constructs "intelligence" or "capacities."

And yet, learning is not always accepted as reflecting, determining, or being determined by the intelligence of the organism. There are theories that make a sharp distinction between the two. The relationship between intelligence and learning has become obscured often to the extent that the two are seen as different and, to a certain extent, even opposing conditions of the organism. A "learned behavior" is not considered an intelligent act since it does not involve the transformations and adaptations characteristic of intelligence. This attitude is reflected in the way intelligence is assessed, in the use of static measures of spontaneous response to tasks assumed to present the same degree of novelty to all of the examinees.

Furthermore, this approach is reflected in the very limited interest conventional psychometric approaches, based on theories of intelligence that adhere to a static concept, have in the phenomena of change and its determinants.

By the same token these theoretical and applied approaches show very limited interest, if any, in the antecedents of intelligent behavior and the differential impact these antecedents have on the current manifest level of functioning of the individual, as disclosed in the results he or she obtains.

It seems to us, therefore, that the importance of the concept of learning, as compared with the construct of intelligence, should be stressed, and its differential development is the subject of our presentation.

Changes produced by learning vary in amplitude, generalizability, rapidity with which they are achieved, and finally, their permanence and stability. Variations are specific to different species, but differ also within each species, along a great variety of parameters of the organism. Different rates of learning may prove to be the most appropriate explanation for the variations in the efficiency of the organism to respond to situations that require the emergence of or a change in behavior in order to adapt to them.

Viewed as such, learning is considered an important constituent of intelligence even when not equated with it. Consider, for instance, the following definition of intelligence: intelligence is the capacity of an organism to use previously acquired principles, skills, and strategies for its adaptation to new situations. The emphasis in this definition, as contrasted with others, is on the *capacity to use previous experience,* which, to a certain degree, resembles the capacity to learn, and also, at a certain point, the propensity of the organism to learn how to learn.

In attempting to grasp the structural difference between individuals who vary in their manifest level of cognitive functioning, we have defined the low achiever, the dysfunctional individual variously described as disadvantaged or economically, socially, and/or culturally deprived, in the following way: The cognitive structure of the culturally deprived, low-functioning individual is characterized by his low degree of modifiability, i.e., learning through direct exposure to stimuli (1). The definition represents an attempt to define the disadvantaged by a structural determinant, capable of explaining the great diversity of behavior dysfunctions observable in both academic activities and life at large. It does not use concepts, such as capacities, that infer immutable states of the organism, as is done often by theoreticians relying on hereditary models. This definition describes, rather, a condition of the organism that makes it inefficient in its use of stimuli impinging on it and therefore affected only in a limited way in the direction necessary for further adaptation.

Furthermore, this definition does not blame the immediate environment for not providing the organism with the stimuli necessary for its growth, as certain theorists in deprivational studies have done. The individual, in this definition, may live in conditions abundant in stimuli. The fact that he is affected only a little by them has to do with the specific conditions of the organism, rather than by the quality and quantity of the stimuli to which the organism is directly exposed. Limited modifiability is often reflected in an episodic grasp of reality that turns the registered stimuli or the experienced event into an isolated, unique phenomenon with little relationship between it and its precedents and/or what will follow it. This episodic grasp of reality explains the small value an experienced event has in preparing the organism for better adaptation to future events.

Deficiencies in the prerequisites of proper cognitive functioning are observable in the three stages of the mental act—input, elaboration, and output —with a preponderance in the two peripheral stages—input and output (4). The peripheral deficiencies play a heavier role in the ineffectiveness of the organism to become modified through direct exposure to experiences, but also show greater resistance to interventional strategies. Blurred perception, unsystematic sweeping exploration, lack of need for precision, inappropriate use of temporal and spatial dimensions as attributes of experienced stimuli and events, lack of perception and projection of sequences in the data gathered by the organism, lack of spontaneous comparative behavior, and lack of need for logical evidence or summative behavior—all these hamper and impair the organism in becoming affected by its interaction with the environment in the direction of a higher level of efficiency in new situations.

All these deficiencies are responsible for the character of immediacy the world takes on and for the delimitations of the organism who experiences the world only in the dimensions of here and now.

The syndrome of low modifiability is the direct determinant of the failure of the organism to cope with a world that requires behaviors and strategies transcending by far those emerging and developing from the biological nature of the individual. One of the most interesting aspects of this syndrome is the relative ease by which it is changed and remediated under specific conditions of training. Our clinical experience, as well as our experimentally derived data, provide us with ample support for our contention that many of those who function on the level of moderate retardation are accessible to meaningful redevelopment, not only in those areas directly affected by training, but also precisely in what we have defined as their cognitive structure, responsible for the low level of modifiability. There is improvement in many of the deficient functions determining the low level of modifiability, especially those in the central area of elaboration of thought processes. The relatively great resistance of deficient functions in the peripheral stages, as compared to the more central elaborative stage, is more task-specific and/or related to a specific modality of presentation to which the individual is exposed.

This structural change is best observed in our assessment of retarded performers with the Learning Potential Assessment Device (LPAD). The LPAD attempts to produce an index of modifiability of the individual by varying the quality and quantity of investment necessary to reach a criterion behavior, rather than by measuring the constituted presence of a behavior in the repertoire of the individual. It is during these sessions that we often observe dramatic changes with the emergence of previously nonexistent behaviors, following investment geared to producing them. Furthermore, once established, these behaviors prove to be efficient in the adaptation of the organism to progressively new situations.

This accessibility to change of the syndrome of low modifiability poses a serious question to the hereditary, organic, or even the neurophysiological substrata of this syndrome. All these hypothesized etiological determinants of retarded performance imply either total immutability of the condition or, at best, only partial remediation. In many cases, prolonged and tedious investments are required as a contrast to the efficiency of the above-mentioned training system, which produces the change in a relatively brief and controlled period.

In what follows, we present an outline of a theory of cognitive development that may account for the modifiability of the organism. This theory is based on the assumption that the human organism is an open system, whose level of functioning depends on specific events impinging on him at various stages of his development.

The modifiability of the living organism is produced by two distinct modalities or interactions between the organism and the environment. The first modality is through direct exposure to stimuli. Each such exposure produces a change in the organism, as discernible from the changes in the behavior of the organism when it is confronted again with the same stimuli. Direct exposure affects the organism and its structure of behavior throughout its life, with the amplitude and extent of change related to the novelty, the intensity, and the meaning of the stimuli. Direct exposure to stimuli is certainly the most pervasive source for changes brought about in the organism. It includes those developments produced through interaction with the environment described in the stimulus–response (S–R) processes. Even the change to stimulus–organism–response (S–O–R) introduced by Piaget (10) into the S–R formula, which introduces the organism and its active involvement in experiencing the stimuli and determining the nature of the R, conceives of the development through the modality of direct exposure.

The interaction described by Piaget between the organism and the world is a pure exposure to objects, which remain objects even if they are human. Thus, the modality of change, i.e., learning, through direct exposure to stimuli is certainly a powerful tool for the development of the organism, especially through the dynamics of assimilation and accommodation, which determine the enlargement of biologically determined schemata at the basis of the development of intelligence, according to the Piagetian school.

Piaget's theory represents a monocotyledonic structure, in that it considers that each behavior acquired throughout life stems directly from innate roots of behavior, such as the schemata with which the newborn is equipped at birth. It is this structure of the theory of Piaget that enables him to speak of stages of development and the fixed immutable succession of these stages, to a very large extent, as the succession of the leaves in a monocotyledon plant. No later stage of development can precede an earlier one, and there can be no acceleration of the development of a later stage prior to an earlier one or before reaching certain biological conditions that enable the next stage to appear.

From this discussion and description of Piaget's theory, it becomes obvious that learning plays only a very limited role in the development of specific schemata unless the biological conditions do exist; then, very often, learning is not necessary beyond the direct exposure to stimuli and the active involvement of the experiencing organism.

However, the sole use of the direct-exposure modality, even when it takes into account constitutional variations of the organism, will never explain differential cognitive development, horizontal decallage, and—what is even more important—the fact that so few people in our world attain the higher levels of functioning described by Piaget as formal operations. Were formal operations really the sole epiphenomena of biologically determined developments and interaction between these maturational processes and direct exposure to stimuli, we would have to witness a much greater frequency of these behaviors in the normal population.

It is, therefore, necessary that we consider a second modality by which the organism develops and becomes modified, i.e., learns. This modality we defined as Mediated Learning Experience (MLE) (5). Here the stimuli impinging on the organism are transformed before they enter into the system by another organism that interposes itself between the sources of stimuli and the organism receiving them. It is this interposing individual who mediates the world to the child by transforming the stimuli—selecting stimuli; scheduling them; framing and locating them in time and space; grouping certain stimuli or segregating others; providing certain stimuli with specific meanings as compared with others; providing opportunities for recurrent appearances; bringing together objects and events that are separate and discrete in terms of temporal and spatial dimensions; reevoking events and reinforcing the appearance of some stimuli; rejecting or deferring the appearance of others; and through this, providing the organism with modalities of selecting, focusing, and grouping objects and events. What is even more important, the mediating individual enables the child to extend his activities over dimensions of reality that are not in his immediate reach either temporally or spatially. It is MLE that orients the child toward encoding and decoding of reality and toward establishing networks of relationships among the discrete and disparate stimuli, objects, and events.

MLE is considered in this framework to be the determinant of the proper use of direct exposure to stimuli. The more an organism has been subjected to adequate levels of mediation, the greater is its capacity to learn, i.e., to become modified, through direct exposure to stimuli. An organism whose development is based only on direct exposure, such as described by theoreticians who invoke the S–R or S–O–R model of Piaget, has a limited range of learning capacity and a limited degree of modifiability through direct exposure. Its use of stimuli is limited to the immediacy of their meaning, and an episodic grasp of reality is the modality of registering stimuli whenever the more relational abstract encoding system has not been established by MLE.

In the animal world, the modality of direct exposure is the most preponderant since very limited amounts of MLE are possible between the generations. However, in the human organism, MLE is a constituent part of the developmental process without which only a limited part of development could be explained.

MLE can be divided into two broad categories. The first has to do with the process of transmission of information, values, and attitudes, the presence of which in the repertoire of human behavior is inconceivable were they not transmitted by the initiated generation. The whole past of humanity—its achievements, its crystallized forms of communication, its elaborate system of mastery of skills, and its instruments—are transmitted to the new generation *in toto*. It would take an individual the whole prehistory and history of humanity if he were to have to construct them on his own. There are clearly regions of life totally inaccessible if they are not transmitted to the individual.

But this is only a part of the mediation process and, to a certain extent, not even the most important one. This is so because transmission of information is always culturo- and ethnospecific. Not all the history of humanity is transmitted to the same degree to each person across variations in his culture. The specific content of this transmission varies widely across humanity, affecting each person differentially.

The other category of MLE relates to the more molecular elements that produce in the growing organism dispositions, attitudes, and approaches to the world and to the self and make the individual sensitive to stimuli, enabling him to use them to become modified through his encounter with them. MLE is produced mainly through the manipulation of the mediator who uses the stimuli in such a way as to produce changes in the receiving child, the effects of which will transcend his immediate needs. In other words, in scheduling the appearance of certain stimuli and events, the aim of the mother is not merely to solve a current problem. Her intention is to produce a change whose effects are anticipated for longer periods in the life of the child. In establishing a given order in which certain events in the life of the child occur, relationships between events are established; these produce anticipations in the child and, later, lead to insights into the meaning of the established order.

These various activities have an effect on the organism that can best be described as a disposition to perceive the events as linked to each other and to orient the search not for the objects of perception, but rather for the relationships existing between them.

MLE covers a wide range of interactions between the learning organism and the world mediated to it. It starts with interactions on a perverbal level in the earliest stages of life, in which the use of metalinguistic modalities of interaction as well as manipulative motor type of communication is pervasive; it extends to higher levels of mental processes, such as the mediation of abstract thinking principles, both cognitive and moral, and elements of emotional experience.

However, MLE, as a basic process enhancing the capacity of the individual to become modified through direct exposure, is not contingent on modality or language of mediation, nor on the content by help of which mediation processes take place. As such, MLE can be perceived as a universally determining factor inasmuch as no matter what the language of mediation or its content, an individual subjected to MLE will be sensitive to learning experiences presented to him, formally or informally, as direct exposure to stimuli.

Thus anthropologists have often defined processes of cultural transmission and learning experiences that were totally devoid of verbal communication, with the teacher demonstrating behaviors in front of the learner who observed the various acts, without any labeling, instruction, or explanation. Furthermore, in many instances, during these periods of observation, the observer-learner was not allowed to manipulate the objects by himself or to act in imitation of the behavior of the mediator. At the end of the period, however, the observer proved able to perform in a most efficient way the behavior mediated to him. Many descriptions point to the great increment in the capacity of such individuals to continue to learn novel and more complicated behavior. What MLE has produced here is a capacity to learn, to focus not only on objects but also on transformations and the succession of events producing them and to perceive a relationship between an end-product and the means used to attain it. These learned elements affect the organism's capacity to use reality, perceived and experienced, in an efficient way. They have acquired what Harlow (6) terms "learning sets."

MLE implies a certain degree of awareness on the part of the mediator of the meaning of his intervention for the development, growth, and adaptation of the child who is the subject of mediation. The intentionality of the act eventually produces in the child a growing awareness of the goals of the mediational process, its meaning in terms of the past of the mediator as the source of the goals and in terms of the patterns of behavior the mediator attempts to project into the future by mediating them to the new generation. Even though this awareness varies from individual to individual, it always reflects an intentionality pertaining to the collective representations of the enlarged family or of the larger socioethnic group.

It is this intentionality that not only makes the mediator do things for the child, or even with the child, but also makes him act so as to draw the attention and to arouse the vigilance of the child to a given event, helping the child focus on it or repeating it in front of the child until it has penetrated the system. It is also this intentionality and this need to project oneself, one's past into the future, that makes the mediator enlarge the perceptual areas of the child into temporal and spatial dimensions not directly accessible to his experience. By doing so, a whole world opens up to the child. The cognitive activities of the child transcend the immediate world of the here and now, and he forges for himself the keys to open new worlds for his exploration. Thus, representational thinking, internalized manipulation, and relational behavior using sources of information for generation of new data—all these are not the outcome of direct exposure to stimuli, neither in the sense of S–R nor even in the sense of S–O–R; they are rather the products of MLE offered to the child in a great variety of ways, modalities, languages of presentation, and contents of interaction with the world.

One of the great observations of all who attempt to analyze the interaction between the mother and the young child is that the naive, unsophisticated mother does exactly what theoreticians find necessary for the proper growth of the child. Theoreticians do not always isolate the most important ingredient of these behaviors affecting the development of cognitive processes. For many years, the psychoanalytic model has proposed that the warmth and emotional, affectionate ties of the mother with her child are responsible for the proper development of the child's cognitive processes. On the other hand, the proponents of sensory stimulation have considered the exposure to stimuli, and their quantity and quality, the determinant factors in the development of the child.

Yarrow (12) and Wolf (11) have attempted to refine the concepts of the environment and through systematic studies point to those dimensions in the environment directly responsible for certain specific differences in the development of individuals. However, all these theoreticians have used the first modality we described—direct exposure to stimuli—as the most important determinant for differential cognitive development.

The theory of MLE does not negate the role of direct exposure. However, it considers it an insufficient modality for growth and development whenever the organism has to accede to higher orders of cognitive behavior.

Viewed as such, MLE represents the proximal etiological determinant for differential cognitive behavior. In considering a variety of etiological determinants for differential cognitive behavior, such as genetic disorders, adverse conditions affecting the brain's growth and development, poverty, emotional disorders of the parents, emotional problems of the child, and other possible environmental conditions of the organism, one cannot attribute to them the power of causality for low cognitive functioning, since—as is well known—they do not necessarily and invariably determine a specific outcome. There is a great deal of variation in the levels of functioning among individuals suffering from the same genetic disorder, and we do not yet know the extent of variations that could be produced by help of specific intervention.

We cannot, therefore, perceive these determinants but as distal etiological factors. In order to bring about the specific outcome of mental retardation and retarded performance, the intervention of a second set of determinants—those of proximal etiology—are needed because only if the proximal are triggered by the distal factor is a specific outcome produced (see Fig. 1).

Among other possible factors, we consider MLE the proximal determinant for retarded performance. Lack of MLE can be produced by two broad categories of factors. The first has to do with the condition of the organism itself—neurological, physiological, or emotional states that make the organism more or less impenetrable to attempts at mediation by the caregiving environment. The barriers established by the condition of the organism itself may be transient and limited to a specific phase of development in the maturation of the organism, or they may be permanent. In certain cases, they can be bypassed using a different modality of mediation more effective for the specific organism and its difficulties. In other cases, barriers need variations in the intensity and duration of the exposure to the mediating investment in order to penetrate the system and to produce in the organism those tools necessary for increasing its modifiability.

If barriers are not bypassed, MLE does not occur. The determinant that has established the barrier, such as genetic disorder or other conditions of the organism, can be considered only a distal determinant because it only indirectly produces the ill effect by disabling the organism in its use of regular modalities of mediation, thereby depriving it of the necessary tools for the development of learning abilities.

The second category that reduces the occurrence of MLE in a more or less severe way includes environmental determinants. The poor, socially and culturally disadvantaged families do not always provide the growing child with

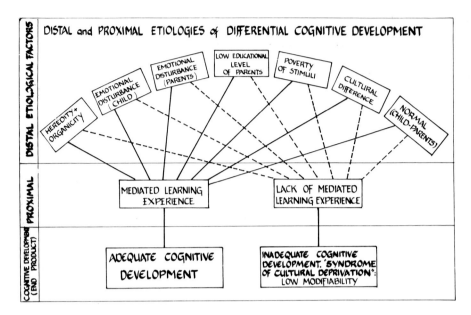

FIG. 1.

MLE—whether because of a lack of physical and mental resources or because of a lack of need to transmit, to provide the child with anything that transcends his immediate biological needs, is not known.

In such instances, the interaction between the mother and the child is limited to the immediate, to the here and now. There is a shrinkage in the experienced world to the horizontal dimension of the immediate with very limited concern, if any, with the vertical axis that crosses the present and bridges between the past and the future of an individual or a group.

Many of those who become alienated from their own culture for any number of reasons, especially because of social disorganization, manifest this attitude toward their progeny and do not provide them with any, or with only a very limited amount, of MLE. Other environmentally determined factors giving rise to lack of MLE are emotional disturbance on the part of the parent toward all or one specific child.

The effects of the lack of MLE, as described above, are highly reversible. Clinical studies, follow-up studies, and experimental research using phase-specific substitutes for MLE as the intervening variable have firmly established the possibility of reversibility in those individuals suffering from the syndrome of low modifiability. During the last 20 years these phase-specific substitutes for MLE have become constituted into various methods, one of which is an intervention program called "Instrumental Enrichment" (2), that have proved their efficacy in changing the structure of the cognitive behavior of the individual, a change that manifests itself in the increased capacity of the organism to use formal and informal encounters with sources of stimulation and learning for increasing the effects of this encounter on the organism.

Divergent effects of this intervention program (3), as observed in a follow-up study on the subjects of Instrumental Enrichment intervention, manifested themselves in an important increment in the effects of the program with time elapsed since intervention. These results bring evidence for the hypothesis that what is produced by MLE and its phase-specific substitutes is not an increase in information, or in specific skills, but rather in the cognitive structure of the organism and its disposition to become modified through direct exposure to stimuli. This result raises the problem we address here: To what extent can one find neurophysiological and neurochemical substrata of the processes elicited by MLE and its phase-specific substitute, Instrumental Enrichment?

The fact that we observe meaningful changes in the cognitive behavior of individuals even after limited investment may point to the necessity for the search for the ill effects of the lack of MLE in the deficiencies of attitudes, orientation, modalities of focusing, and attending that are characteristic of the retarded performing individual.

One must, however, also consider the more lasting effects of intensive investment on the neural structure of the brain. Our findings do not confirm the Hebbian hypothesis (7) of critical periods of development beyond which no meaningful changes are expected because of the neural substrata of the produced deficit. Konrad and Melzack (9), in their interpretation of the effects of sensory and social deprivation, describe the inefficiency of the sensorially and/or socially deprived organism to respond properly to the new situation as the result of the novelty enhancement of the new situation on the naive organism. They, too, confirm the high level of reversibility observed in the deprived organism following training and experience. However, in the human organism, exposure to sensorial stimulation, as Hebb (7), and following him, Hunt (8) have proposed, cannot determine the full development of learning capacity. To this end, we suggest MLE as the necessary determinant for cognitive modifiability.

ACKNOWLEDGMENTS

The author expresses his gratitude to the Hadassah-Wizo of Canada Organization, Besner Foundation, and Deitcher Center for their generous support of the work carried out at the Hadassah-Wizo of Canada Organization Research Institute that made this contribution possible. Appreciation is also expressed to Martin Hamburger, M. B. Hoffman, David Krasilowski, A. Harry Passow, Y. Rand, and A. J. Tannenbaum for their critical remarks and their contribution to the development of the theory of Mediated Learning Experience.

REFERENCES

1. Feuerstein, R. (1970): A dynamic approach to the causation, prevention and alleviation of retarded performance. In: *Social-Cultural Aspects of Mental Retardation,* edited by H. C. Haywood, pp. 341–377. Appleton, New York.
2. Feuerstein, R. (1969): *The Instrumental Enrichment Method: An Outline of Theory and Technique.* Hadassah-Wizo of Canada Research Institute, Jerusalem.
3. Feuerstein, R. (1977): *Studies in Cognitive Modifiability. Instrumental Enrichment: Redevelopment of Cognitive Functions of Retarded Early Adolescents.* Hadassah-Wizo of Canada Research Institute, Jerusalem.
4. Feuerstein, R., and Krasilowsky, D. (1972): Interventional strategies for the significant modification of cognitive functioning in the disadvantaged adolescent. *J. Am. Acad. Child Psychiatry,* 11:572–581.
5. Feuerstein, R., and Rand, Y. (1974): Mediated learning experiences: An outline of the proximal etiology for differential development of cognitive functions. *Int. Understanding,* 9/10:7–37.
6. Harlow, H. F. (1949): The formation of learning sets. *Psychol. Rev.,* 56:51–65.
7. Hebb, D. D. (1949): *The Organization of Behavior.* Wiley, New York and London.
8. Hunt, J. McV. (1961): *Intelligence and Experience.* Ronald, New York.
9. Konrad, K., and Melzack, R. (1975): Novelty-enhancement effects associated with early sensory-social isolation. In: *The Developmental Neuropsychology of Sensory Deprivation,* edited by A. H. Riesen, pp. 253–276. Academic Press, New York.
10. Piaget, J. (1969): *Six Psychological Studies.* Univ. of London Press, London; Random House, New York.
11. Wolf, R. (1974): The Identification and Measurement of Environmental Process Variables Related to Intelligence. Doctoral Dissertation, University of Chicago Press, Chicago.
12. Yarrow, Leon J. (1972): Mother-infant interaction and development in infancy. *Child Dev.,* 43:31–41.

CONCLUDING COMMENTS

Brain Mechanisms in Memory and Learning:
From the Single Neuron to Man,
edited by M. A. B. Brazier.
Raven Press, New York © 1979.

Concluding Comments

Richard Mark

Department of Behavioural Biology, Research School of Biological Science, Australian National University, Canberra, Australia

Due to both the efforts of Dr. M. A. B. Brazier and the ideals of the International Brain Research Organization, this is a true international volume. The diversity of topics covered in the chapters is as great as that of the nations represented, so much so that it would be almost impossible for one person to summarize and evaluate them.

The studies presented range from memory in the setting of the child guidance clinic, through some human and animal neurophysiology, to details of neuronal biochemistry. With apologies to people whose interests in memory lie elsewhere, I concentrate here on those experiments directed at finding out the physical basis of memory formation.

After reviewing the chapters, I find, not surprisingly, no common thread to connect them, and memory is seen to have many meanings in different contexts. The common thread is absent because we have almost no idea of how any nervous system retains impressions for more than a few seconds. One might argue that the diversity of behaviour that requires some temporal carryover of information is so great that a common thread is unlikely to exist and that a search for one is a result of semantic confusion. On the other hand, the similarities in the design of all nervous systems and the ubiquity of signalling mechanisms suggest that there may be a common way in which nerve networks can store impressions. Optimists feel that we may be just on the brink of a discovery that could bring as much unity to memory research as the discovery of impulse coding by Adrian (1) brought to the understanding of the representation of sensory experience. In the absence of such illumination those researchers who are drawn to the problem have to decide what to do in the meantime.

Several of the chapters presented do not deal with memory as such, but present theoretical views, sometimes with experimental backing, of mechanisms that could possibly be used in brains to store information. There has been a lot of imaginative thought about this, and there is a bewildering variety of possible mechanisms, only some of which are represented in this volume. None of these proposed mechanisms has any use unless it can be tested for an action on memory, and this is when the trouble starts. The main obstacle to be surmounted is in the behavioural expression of memory. When using animals, one is forced to rely on the observation of behavioural change to reveal stored information. This means that the information is unobservable until the brain goes through the read-out process, and any physical correlates of the registration of information are indistinguishable from those associated with the new behavioural response built on the new store. This applies to one-trial learning as well as to that requiring multiple trials. The learning experience has to be so strong or so suitably meshed with the animal's normal behaviour that the linked motor response is instantly available. Bureš and Burešová (*this volume*), in describing their work on learned food-avoidance, point out that novel flavours not paired with a nauseating injection are not lost to the animal, even though in classic terms no unconditioned response occurs, but pass into the animal's memory as safe food. This is shown by reduced neophobia on subsequent presentations. It means that, as far as such learning tasks are concerned, there can be no control experiments. No known behavioural situation can prohibit an animal from making memories. Conversely, we cannot affirm that a behavioural situation can be designed that will reveal any memory.

Yet on the biochemical level, control experiments appear to work, which is something to give great cause for alarm. The excellent work of the group from Magdeburg led by Matthies (*this volume*) is a very clear example. Autoradiographic evidence of increased incorporation of labeled uridine is found in rats that learn a shock-motivated task. Those that are shocked, but not allowed to escape, show no more incorporation than those that are simply handled. It is inconceivable that the shocked controls learn nothing extra. They most certainly learn they are in an unpleasant situation from which they cannot escape. The biochemical correlates so convincingly demonstrated are then the correlates of a successful behavioural strategy built on some very strong motivating stimuli, but can have nothing to do with the registration of the motivating shocks or of the setting in which they occur.

Since learning, in common language, refers to the acquisition of information, rather than to the elaboration of behaviour patterns founded on the information, it seems to follow that the biochemical processes of the acquisition are too subtle to be detected by present techniques. If the changes really depended on memory, differences should appear between the passive and active control groups as well as between shocked controls and experimental animals.

The physiological and biochemical mechanisms by which behavioural change comes about are, of course, as interesting as those by which new information is registered. It would be, at this stage, a great mistake to equate such mechanisms with memory as it is usually understood in human terms.

The changes in the central nervous system must be more like those needed to learn to play the violin than those needed to associate a name with a face.

There continues to be a great deal of mystification of memory, brought on to some degree by the behavioural techniques of strong stimuli in confined situations that are usually used to study it. A moment's introspection or a short period of watching one's animals shows memory of one kind or another to be a constant process that can never be dissociated from mechanisms of perception or from the performance of motor acts. The very great methodological problems that confront the attempt to dissect even a simple avoidance response into motivation and response components constitute another warning. Schneider (*this volume*) succeeds in showing that this division leads to a better explanation of the effects of reminder shock than that it really does remind, but he then reminds us that to identify such components is not to study them. Further behavioural analysis conceivably could introduce further components, each contributing more or less to the observed behaviour, the apparent clarity of which is really an artefact of the confined situation and of an arbitrary latency limit.

The feeling that there are multiple mechanisms for behavioural change, which are differentially highlighted by different techniques, is exemplified in the experiments described by Llinás and Walton (*this volume*). They present results of a direct test of a very elaborate theory of learning in the cerebellar cortex by questioning whether the cortex is essential for motor learning at all. And, in their situation of recovery from motor asymmetry produced by vestibular lesions, it is not. This is not proof that the cerebellum is of no use in normal motor learning, a view that Llinás favours, but it does emphasize that theories of the kind put forward for the cerebellar cortex are unlikely to be more than special cases of a much more widely spread and perhaps anatomically less identifiable mechanism. It is Lashley's conclusion once again that in the presence of brain damage, the animal uses any strategy that is left to it to achieve its end.

The same might be said of pharmacological damage. The use of chemical inhibitors of various kinds or of agonists of suspected transmitter agents has given very little evidence that a particular biochemical reaction is absolutely essential for the formation of memory. I like to think that the various inhibitors used by my collaborators (Mark, *this volume*) come closer to revealing essential actions, but even the problem of whether inhibitors of protein synthesis produce amnesia by blocking registration or deranging recall is not quite settled. There is no knowing whether information in a chemically disordered brain is processed as in a normal one with only a critical step deleted. One would expect some kind of behavioural cascade effect whereby block of one avenue would lead the animal to throw its resources toward other behavioural strategies that were still working. The only time this could not occur is when the blocked mechanism was completely fundamental to the registration process such that all other strategies were equally closed. We tentatively make this claim for the involvement of Na/K ATPase in the initiation of memory in chickens and for the membrane transport of amino acids for the later stable registration of memory.

Such a claim is naturally not made for many other chemical treatments that can be shown to change behaviour based on memory. McGaugh and his colleagues (*this volume*) demonstrate very complete understanding of the techniques that have been used by them and others to establish the time dependency of memory storage processes. Experiments are done with the maximum of care and systematic variation of doses of the chemical agents, the behavioural situation, and the timing of events. This work has shown that both electrical stimulation of the amygdala and adrenocorticotropic hormone administration can either enhance or impair memory-based behaviour. The effects of playing off doses of norepinephrine, inhibitors of its synthesis, and levels of footshock are also detailed and the arguments about central-versus-peripheral actions considered in full. Nevertheless, their conclusions can only be that their treatments "modulate" the neuronal processes underlying memory, which is a valid conclusion from their results but does not help very much in the construction of a precise hypothesis of how the modulation works.

Careful work by de Wied and others (*this volume*) is subject to the same criticism. There is no doubt of the effects being obtained, but the questions of mechanisms of action and even whether a mechanism basic to memory is being effected or behavioural expression is at fault cannot be fully answered. Some of the behavioural and pharmacological complexities of this kind of current research are discussed in Miller et al. (3). One might question also whether an experiment designed to check if a function can be modulated by some chemical treatment is based on a firm enough hypothesis to give a lead to the mechanisms involved. The theory must be sufficiently predictive to say, in a new situation, which way the modulation should go and preferably how far.

The use of any chemical treatment of the brain raises also the question of cascade effects in biochemical terms. Any chemical interference with a series of linked control systems as complex as a cell is bound to produce a whole set of chemical changes in addition to the prime action of the agonist or antagonist in use. Cycloheximide, for example, blocks ribosomal protein synthesis but not breakdown, leading to sudden increases in free amino acids, some of which may be transmitters and may set off disturbances quite remote from the inhibition of protein synthesis (2). One could trace out many similar metabolic sequels for anything one might think of adding to the brain.

So, if behavioural methods are too crude, biochemical correlations are not sensitive enough, and the use of inhibitors not suited to make inferences of cause and effect, is the study of the physical basis of memory still possible? There are precedents in other biochemical research that do hold out some hope. The main problem is still that of behaviour. Even the simplest learned behaviour of whole animals is too complicated a matter to be used as a straight pharmacological assay, and yet memory in the biological laboratory is a behavioural matter. One solution, therefore, is to find a measure of memory that is not behavioural. This is not an outrageous suggestion. The study of the operation of the genetic code suddenly became much clearer when the end-point of the assay was not a whole organism, some macroscopic character of an organism, but a protein and, best of all, an enzyme (4). The assay of genetic operation then came down to the same language of molecules as the genetic material itself, and mechanisms could be discussed directly. Similarly, the crying need at the moment is for some knowledge of the level of brain organisation that is critically altered by new information, not necessarily the exact locus but the kind of change that stores the information. This known, a rational assay could be designed and then one could set about finding how environmental effects produce it and how subsidiary reactions modulated it.

There are two ways of searching for this proposed level of change. It is possible that pharmacological research on animal behaviour can one day come up with a chemical agent that is of enormous power and quantitative predictability in behavioural terms and the pharmacology of which is unitary and unequivocal such that there is only one conceivable mode of action. Such a discovery would immediately limit the choice of mechanisms and set off a new wave of well-founded experiments to find out how the key mechanism is incorporated into the many aspects of behaviour that use memory.

The other strategy is to set the whole experiment in neurophysiological terms and, by means of a preparation that shows use-dependent changes, investigate the mechanism directly. This approach of using simple defined systems is relatively meagrely represented in this volume, but the results that Kandel (*this volume*) presented on the mechanisms of habituation of gill withdrawal in *Aplysia* were some of the most illuminating. The habituation is shown to occur at the synapse between sensory and motoneurones and to involve a reduction in transmitter output to the extent that many sensory synapses become completely silent. The ineffective synapses may be re-awakened most crudely by electrical stimulation of the head, but there is good pharmacological evidence that this occurs via the release of serotonin, which activates presynaptic cyclic AMP. This is work of immense promise in that hypotheses for experiments can be very specific and that techniques are available to investigate many of the aspects of synaptic transmission involved. Whether this mechanism of synaptic plasticity is of wide applicability and how it has access to a process of more permanent change remain to be seen. Given the uniformity of the fundamentals of neurophysiology from sea hares to man it seems likely that one process could be used in many different ways to build up various adaptive behaviours. This work also suggests that the nature of the behavioural reflex is coded by genetically determined connections between neurones and that the use-dependent process is the efficacy of synaptic transmission and particularly the process of transmitter mobilisation, which, although not by any means understood, is well described at such accessible synapses as neuromuscular junctions.

Although simple adaptive behaviour can be studied in neurophysiological terms, some may feel that it is far from learning in the human sense. Since the phenomena lack the rapidity of action, durability, enormous information capacity, and time and context dependence that characterise memory of higher animals, they may be good physiology but not relevant. This criticism may also be applied to the biochemical studies summarised by Rose (*this volume*). He has chosen to ignore the behavioural responses produced in his animals and to confine himself to biochemistry. The effects are produced by raising rats in the dark, bringing them abruptly into the light, and following biochemical changes in the visual as compared to the motor areas of the brain. His methods are sensitive enough to reveal both long-term and transient alterations in biochemical measures of neuronal function. One of the most interesting concerns the awakening of a cholinergic system in the forebrain that includes a very large but transient increase in binding to muscarinic receptors. This is innovative and delicate biochemistry, but the question whether learning as opposed to simple stimulation underlies the changes is a matter for discussion rather than experiment. Other collaborative work by Rose on imprinting in chickens, to which he refers in his chapter, comes closer to direct correlations of biochemical changes with the development of behavioural change. Nevertheless, such correlations with experience or learning exist in an amorphous world with no hypothetical framework to indicate where, in a supposedly causal chain of events, the various experimental facts should fit. It is the same problem that occurs with the use of exogenous inhibitors or enhancers of learned behaviour. How can one make sense of effects when the mechanisms of the steps from behaviour to biochemistry and back to behaviour are not understood in principle?

In the end I believe a unifying hypothesis must grow out of interdisciplinary research of the kind that many contributors to the volume have attempted. It seems clear, however, that if one is trying to correlate biochemical, physiological, and behavioural events the results cannot be better than the weakest techniques allow. It is essential that the professionalism be equally distributed and behavioural nuances be no less heeded than the pharmacological. It must be very rare to find the necessary skills in one person, so this kind of research seems bound to be carried out by groups, where consensus of purpose is combined with genuine respect for the different points of view that must be accommodated. This is no more than a reaffirmation of the principles that must have motivated David Krech (5) when he began his interdisciplinary work in Berkeley years ago. The lack of spectacular progress since then should not be a cause for pessimism even if we do allow a little disappointment. The techniques applicable to all the brain sciences have become notably enriched in the last few years, and their combination plus a little luck and inspiration show the greatest promise of revealing a unifying framework, however rickety to begin with. In adopting this strategy, it seems essential to strive for a comprehensive theory and not be satisfied with mere correlations. The literature on such matters is now extremely large although not of uniform credibility. The very many biochemical correlations with behaviour and modulations of learning that do stand up to critical analysis must all have a place.

To be simplistic, dogmatic, or chauvinistic is incompatible with success along these lines. I suspect that when the biochemistry of learning is mapped out it will be about as complex as that of the metabolic pathways of carbohydrate metabolism. Perhaps we have almost as great a quantity of information on learning already scattered through the literature, and all we lack is knowledge of the equivalent of the tricarboxylic acid cycle.

REFERENCES

1. Adrian, E. D. (1928): *The Basis of Sensation: The Action of the Sense Organs.* Christophers, London.
2. Hambley, J. W. (1978): *To be published.*
3. Miller, L. H., Sandeman, C. A., and Kastin, A. J. (editors) (1977): *Neuropeptide Influences on the Brain and Behavior.* (*Advances in Biochemical Psychopharmacology, Vol. 17.*) Raven Press, New York.
4. Monod, J. (1966): From enzymatic adaptation to allosteric transitions. *Science,* 154:475–483.
5. Petrinovich, L., and McGaugh, J. L. (editors) (1976): *Knowing, Thinking and Believing. Festschrift for Professor David Krech.* Plenum Press, New York.

Author Index

---

*Numbers in parentheses before page of citation are reference numbers; italicized numbers represent the page on which the reference information appears.

† Unpublished material.

Subject Index